PUERTO RICAN
WOMEN'S
HISTORY

Perspectives on Latin America and the Caribbean

PUERTO RICAN WOMEN'S HISTORY

New Perspectives

EDITORS

Félix V. Matos Rodríguez
and Linda C. Delgado

M.E. Sharpe
Armonk, New York
London, England

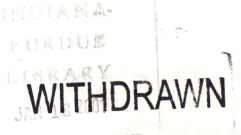
Library of Congress Cataloging-in-Publication Data

Puerto Rican women's history: new perspectives / Félix V. Matos Rodríguez
and Linda C. Delgado [editors].
p. cm.—(Perspectives on Latin America and the Caribbean)
Includes bibliographical references (p.   ) and index.
ISBN 0-7656-0245-8 (c: alk. paper)—ISBN 0–7656–0246–6 (pbk.: alk. paper)
1. Women—Puerto Rico—History. 2. Women—Employment—Puerto Rico—History.
3. Working class women—Puerto Rico—Social conditions.
4. Women in politics—Puerto Rico—History.
I. Matos Rodríguez, Félix V., 1962– . II. Delgado, Linda C., 1947– . III. Series.
HQ1522.P84   1998
305.4′097295—dc21   98-10750
CIP

Printed in the United States of America

The paper used in this publication meets the minimum requirements of
American National Standard for Information Sciences—
Permanence of Paper for Printed Library Materials,
ANSI Z 39.48-1984.

BM (c)   10   9   8   7   6   5   4   3   2   1
BM (p)   10   9   8   7   6   5   4   3   2   1

To the five generations of Puertorriqueñas in my life: Julia, Selina, Bev, my beautiful Danielle, and granddaughter Brittany.
Linda C. Delgado

To Liliana Arabia, because I should have done this some fifteen years ago.
Félix V. Matos Rodríguez

Contents

Acknowledgments

Contrary to all warnings from colleagues and friends about the difficulty of preparing an anthology, producing this one has been a most enjoyable experience. Both editors want to begin by thanking our distinguished contributors for believing in this project and for being an extremely creative, punctual, and patient group. Working with all of you has been a great experience—and we hope you can say as much about having to work with us! Several colleagues provided important support that we would like to acknowledge here: Luz del Alba Acevedo, Lynn Stephen, William Rodriguez, Eileen Findlay, and Nelly Cruz. The editors also want to thank our Northeastern University "familia"—the folks at the Latin American Student Organization (LASO), the History Department, the Latino, Latin American, and Caribbean Studies Program, and the Latino/a Student Cultural Center—for their help and crucial encouragement. The staff at M.E. Sharpe, particularly our editor Stephen Dalphin and his assistant Esther Clark, have been supportive, understanding, and extremely committed to this project. *Gracias.* Finally, a special word of thanks to two individuals who saved our lives on more than one occasion: Melissa Ocasio and Professor Amilcar Barreto. Without their help, computer assistance, and patience this book would have never—literally—been finished.

Linda wishes to thank the people who have made the difference in her professional life, people who have supported and assisted her along the way: Professor Carol Berkin is a doctoral student's best friend and a historian in the truest sense. Professor Jesse Vázquez, friend, mentor, and colleague, has held my hand via e-mail at 3:00 A.M many, many, many times; and Virginia Sanchez Korrol, whom I met when I began this journey. She has directed me to the brightest lights of academia and helped to steer me away from its pitfalls. Professor David Krikun taught me what a historian is and unselfishly shared his knowledge, time, books, and every article that could ever matter to my work. Thanks to my husband Doug, my best reader and critic, and to the other important men in my life, Neal Jr., Chris, and Mikey—whom I seldom see because I am buried in my world of books and history—thanks for always being there, and for your love. To *abuela* and *la familia,* thanks for not getting too angry when I do not call. To my mother, because it was your endless nights of doing piecework for Irving Block that paid for the education that guided and shaped my life and brought me to this point. To the best co-author, who is a colleague, a confidante, and, most of all, a friend . . . thank you, Felo. It is with the knowledge, understanding, support, encouragement, and honest caring shared with me by these and many others that I have completed this venture.

Felo wants to thank some of the people who provided special support for this project: Pedro San Miguel, Luis Falcón, Jorge Duany, Emilio Kourí, Brodie Fisher, Ruth Glasser, Jorge Arteta, José Flores, Victor Pérez, Odile Carro, Andrés Torres, Edwin Meléndez, Emilio Pantojas García, and Ricardo and Dora Mendes. To Linda Delgado, thanks so much for taking on yet another collaborative venture. I also want to thank my family for all the *cariño,* long-distance support, and perennial sense of humor. Finally, a special *gracias* to Liliana Arabia, impatient and loving companion, to whom this book is co-dedicated for all the obvious reasons.

PUERTO RICAN
WOMEN'S
HISTORY

Introduction

The essays collected in this anthology reflect some of the new trends in historical writing regarding Puerto Rican women on the Island and in the United States. After pioneering breakthroughs in the 1970s and 1980s, it has been in the current decade that the field of Puerto Rican women's history proper has come of age. The essays collected here show not only the ongoing interest in this field but also new areas of scholarly attention and "older" ones that are being revisited.

In the 1970s Puerto Rican historians began to wonder how the stories that made up different aspects of the Island's history would change if they were told from the perspective of women. More and more, the history of the Puerto Rican people includes the perspective of women. This has led to a revisiting and re-evaluation of many of the Island's traditional historical narratives, from the nature of Taino society in pre-Columbian times to the structure and dynamics of the labor migration into the United States in the twentieth century. More and more, too, gender and cultural studies have provoked the question of whether such a thing as a women's perspective exists, and whether it can be easily identified.[1]

This anthology does not pretend to cover all areas or to include all the colleagues who are working in the field of Puerto Rican women's history. We wanted to include work that exemplified new research being done on neglected topics, such as prostitution and urban slavery, and in already established ones, such as the women's suffrage movement and the participation of women in the cigar-making industry. The lack of attention to certain areas and the geographical imbalance among the essays reflect more the nature of the field itself than the editors' interests and professional networks. With only one exception, all the contributors are historians. The editors also decided to keep the focus of the anthology in history, not because no excellent scholarly work is being currently produced in other fields such as anthropology, cultural studies, literature, psychology, and sociology, but in order to highlight the scattered historical work being produced in the United States and on the Island. It is the hope of all the contributors that the anthology will serve as a point of departure for further historical and interdisciplinary work in the fields of women's and gender studies.

The anthology opens with two historiographical essays by Félix V. Matos Rodríguez and Altagracia Ortiz. Matos Rodríguez's piece discusses the development of Puerto Rican women's history in the last three decades. It provides a brief account of the main contributions to the field, from its origins under the shadows of the *nueva historia* on the Island and Puerto Rican studies in the United States, to the recent surge in historical monographs in the 1990s. The essay argues that although much has been accomplished in terms of including women as protagonists in Puerto Rico's history, much remains to be done, particularly in terms of empirical research. Matos Rodríguez's historiographical essay also serves to contextualize the essays included in this anthology. Ortiz's essay, although more thematically focused, presents a chronological survey of the approaches used in various academic disciplines—anthropology, sociology, economics, and history—to discuss twentieth-century Puerto Rican women workers. She uses the transformations in Puerto Rico's colonial economy to show the historical development of scholarly approaches to Puerto Rican women as workers. Drawing from the literature in both Puerto Rico and the United States, Ortiz documents the interconnected nature of capitalism, colonialism, and migration and the effects of these forces upon women.

There has been little research about the lives of women or about the development of gender subjectivities in Puerto Rico between the fifteenth and nineteenth centuries. In Chapter 3, Félix V. Matos Rodríguez illustrates the role that urban slavery, particularly female domestic workers, played in the debates regarding the abolition of slavery during the second half of the nineteenth century. He shows the importance of female domestics in the urban economy of San Juan. Furthermore, the essay documents how both sides of the abolitionist debate manipulated the images of urban domestic slaves in pursuing their agendas. Finally, the essay concludes by arguing that many of the beneficent institutions created in San Juan during the second half of the nineteenth century were, in part, attempts by the elite to guarantee abundant, cheap, and docile domestic laborers at a time when the end of slavery seemed near.

Another neglected aspect of women's history in Puerto Rico has been the regulation and prosecution of prostitution. The chapter by José Flores Ramos attempts to fill a historiographical void in the literature by documenting how Puerto Rico's colonial status influenced the regulation of prostitution in San Juan during the early decades of the twentieth century.[2] He illustrates how U.S. officials continued the legacy of Spanish colonialism and tolerated prostitution in the city until the outbreak of World War I. This war accentuated Puerto Rico's role as a military garrison and thus moved colonial authorities to crack down on prostitution, alluding to medical, health, and moral issues. Although some work-ing-class sectors resisted some of the most punitive aspects of the new anti-pros-titution policies, Flores Ramos shows how other sectors, like the Protestant churches, took advantage of the opportunity to advance what they considered as an Americanization agenda.

Often, the history of those Puerto Ricans who have migrated to the United States is treated as separate from the core of Puerto Rican history books or courses. This trend has been fought particularly by Puerto Rican women's stud-ies scholars, who have attempted in their writings and in their professional en-deavors to look at the history of the Puerto Rican diaspora as an integral part of the Island's historical process. This anthology follows in that tradition as the essays by Linda Delgado, Altagracia Ortiz, and Carmen Whalen show.

Whalen's chapter calls for the inclusion of the varied types of work per-formed by women in the concept of labor migration often used to explain the Puerto Rican exodus to the United States. Using oral histories from women in Philadelphia, she explores the competing narratives of women's work as under-stood by the women migrants themselves, Puerto Rican governmental authori-ties, and U.S. work and welfare agencies. She shows, for example, how what is popularly conceived of as "community work" or volunteerism was included by the Puerto Rican women migrants in their broad definitions of work or labor. Whalen asserts that, contrary to the common wisdom around Puerto Rican mi-gration, women did not come to the United States to follow their husbands and boyfriends, but to work.

Delgado's essay is another example of how the Puerto Rican migratory expe-rience changes if analyzed through the prism of gender. Her work on Rufa Concepción Fernández, nicknamed Concha by her friends, is taken from her doctoral dissertation research. Concha married Jesús Colón, a well-known Puerto Rican community activist. Delgado's chapter analyzes the implications that come from considering other types of sources in doing research about Puerto Rican women in the United States. These women leave behind stories, letters, poems, and dreams—not mountains of legal papers—from which researchers must piece together their stories about their role in the migration experience. Concha was the link that kept Colón grounded in the values of his homeland while he navigated through the barriers of Jim Crow America and fought to create a space for the Puerto Rican worker. Delgado illustrates how the personal letters between Concha and Jesús Colón reflect the concepts of transmigration and transnationalism as proposed by Nina Glick Schiller, Linda Basch, and Cristina Blanc-Szanton.[3]

The way in which gender relations shaped and were shaped by socioeconomic conditions in Puerto Rico is explored in Chapter 5 by Juan Baldrich. Baldrich documents the consequences of the incorporation of women into the cigar-mak-ing industry on the Island after the U.S. invasion. The industry, according to Baldrich, was transformed as the craft of cigar-making was decomposed by mechanization and by the feminization of the industry. His essay demonstrates how although sexual segregation of work remained a constant during the first three decades of the twentieth century, wage differentials were not permanent. As cigar-making became more mechanized, women began to receive higher salaries than male artisans who still produced cigars in the traditional way.

The political situation in Puerto Rico during the first half of the twentieth century is the subject of several essays in this collection. Previous historical references to women and politics have tended to overemphasize the exceptional: the suffragist campaign; the first woman mayor, legislator, or senator; special government units dealing with women's problems. The essays by María Barceló Miller, Gladys Jiménez-Muñoz, Félix Muñiz-Mas, and Mary Frances Gallart show how events associated exclusively with women's issues are fundamentally linked to the larger political and economic processes and structures in Puerto Rico. These essays demonstrate how a gendered perspective of Puerto Rico's political history can bring new and fresh perspectives to topics—such as labor union politics; the industrialization and modernization ideology of the Partido Popular Democrático (PPD); and the relationship between the Creole elite, political party leaders, and colonial administrators, for example—that have drawn considerable scholarly attention in the past.

The essays by Barceló Miller and Jiménez-Muñoz do more than just provide new insights into the campaigns of early-twentieth-century Puerto Rican women to obtain the right to vote. First, they show the political and discursive linkages of the suffragist movement with other early-twentieth-century campaigns such as the drive for U.S. citizenship, higher levels of local political autonomy, the temperance movement, and the "Americanization" campaign promoted by colonial officials and groups such as the Protestant churches in Puerto Rico. Second, the essays document the links that several women's groups in Puerto Rico had with U.S. and international organizations such as the Women's National Party and the International League of Women Voters. Finally, the works by Barceló Miller and Jiménez-Muñoz show that the different political parties in the 1920s and 1930s were concerned about the power of female voters and the potential impact that a massive mobilization of women would have in what was a very volatile and competitive political arena.

Within the local scholarship of the suffragists and of women's movements, the contributions by Barceló Miller and Jiménez-Muñoz open new paths to understanding these movements. Jiménez-Muñoz places her emphasis on the ambivalent language and images employed during the debate on granting literate, and subsequently all, women the right to vote. Her essay shows the willingness of U.S. officials and genteel Creoles to create a sense of otherness based on race, class, and gender. This otherness was embodied in two figures: prostitutes and working-class women of allegedly loose morals. These two figures were used by those opposed to granting women the right to vote.

Barceló Miller's essay underscores the fundamental class divisions that marked the suffragist movement in Puerto Rico and argues against previous interpretations, which had depicted working-class feminists as the vanguard of the suffragist movement.[4] Elite suffragists used their class and political connections to obtain voting rights for literate women only in 1929. Barceló Miller shows how the struggle to vote was just one among the many mechanisms working-class women considered in their fight against oppression. These working-class feminists also manipulated the "cult of domesticity"—a principal weapon in the ideological and rhetorical arsenal of the bourgeois feminists and suffragists—to advance their claims for better wages and working conditions that would ultimately advance the economic well-being of their entire families.

The traditional wisdom about the marginal importance of women in the creation and development of the PPD and its colonial-industrial-nationalistic ideology is challenged by the essays of Muñiz-Mas and Gallart. Muñiz-Mas gives historical depth to many recent sociological, anthropological, and political studies regarding the connection between Puerto Rican women and the PPD's industrialization campaign.[5] He pursues the question of how the PPD and the colonial state helped to construct gendered subjectivities in Puerto Rico between the 1940s and 1950s. The PPD's reforms, according to Muñiz-Mas, were based on and reinforced gender divisions in Puerto Rican society that identified women as mothers and wives, even when growing numbers of women were participating in light manufacture, garment, or domestic work. He uses the records from the Women's Bureau, formed by the Labor Department in 1945, to document the fact that the PPD's modernization agenda was gender-biased. Muñiz-Mas also comments on the work of some of the female social workers attached to the Women's Bureau. This is one of the earlier instances in the historical literature to the work performed by these new female professionals.

Gallart's essay is a significant contribution to the history of internal democracy among Puerto Rico's political parties. By telling the story of how a group of women from the town of Guayama played a pivotal role in forcing a reluctant PPD to adopt and adhere to internal primaries, Gallart shows how women's incursion into the political realm was not a self-serving one focused exclusively on advancing women's issues. The approval of a primary law in 1956 by the local colonial legislature was an important step toward democratizing the entire political system in Puerto Rico. Obviously, Obdulia Velázquez de Lorenzo and her followers were interested in making sure that she would be re-elected as mayor of Guayama, and that was only part of the motivation behind their struggle in favor of a primary law. Also, party primaries were seen by these women as a way of advancing women's political gains as any kind of democratizing effort would weaken the tight control that party leaders—almost all exclusively male—had over the political process and the naming of candidates for elected and appointed public office.

History, in Puerto Rico and elsewhere, is undergoing a moment of profound epistemological and theoretical introspection. Women's history and gender studies have been an important component in the transformation of the discipline of history over the last three decades and will undoubtedly continue to play a fundamental role in shaping the field in years to come.

Notes

1. See, for a general perspective, Joan W. Scott, *Gender and the Politics of History* (New York: Columbia University Press, 1988), 15–92. For a localized discussion see Nydza Correa de Jesús et al., "Las mujeres son, son, son. . . . Implosión y recomposición de la categoría," in Heidi Figueroa-Sarriera et al., eds., *Más allá de la bella (in)diferencia: Revisión post-feminista y otras escrituras posibles* (San Juan: Publicaciones Puertorriqueñas, 1994), 33–50.

2. For an analysis of the prosecution of prostitutes in Ponce, see Eileen Findlay's "Domination, Decency and Desire: The Politics of Sexuality in Ponce, Puerto Rico, 1870–1920" (Ph.D. diss., University of Wisconsin–Madison, 1995), 168–287, 421–507.

3. Nina Glick Schiller, Linda Basch, and Cristina Blanc-Szanton, "Transnationalism: A New Analytic Framework for Understanding Migration," in *The Annals of the New York Academy of Sciences* 645 (1972): 1–24.

4. See, for example, Yamila Azize Vargas's "The Roots of Puerto Rican Feminism: The Struggle for Universal Suffrage," *Radical America* 23, no. 1 (1989): 71–79.

5. See the essays by Luz del Alba Acevedo and María del Carmen Baerga in Baerga, ed., *Génro y trabajo: La industria de la aguja en Puerto Rico y el Caribe Hispánico* (Río Piedras: Editorial de la Universidad de Puerto Rico, 1993); Lydia Milagros González García, *Una puntada en el tiempo: La industria de la aguja en Puerto Rico (1900–1920)* (Río Piedras and Santo Domingo: CEREP and CIPAF, 1990); Carmen A. Pérez Herranz, "The Impact of a Development Program on Working Women in the Garment Industry: A Study of Women and Production in Puerto Rico" (Ph.D. diss., Rutgers University, 1990); and Palmira N. Ríos González, "Women and Industrialization in Puerto Rico: Gender Division of Labor and the Demand for Female Labor in the Manufacturing Sector, 1950–1980" (Ph.D. diss., Yale University, 1990).

1

Women's History in Puerto Rican Historiography: The Last Thirty Years

Félix V. Matos Rodríguez

In 1972, journalist Federico Ribes Tovar acknowledged in his introduction to *La mujer puertorriqueña*—one of the first books solely dedicated to providing a historical account of the contributions and experiences of Puerto Rican women—that "history, in general, tells us little or nothing regarding women."[1] Twenty-five years later, historians can only claim a mixed record in their attempts to learn more about the history of Puerto Rican women. In some areas, like the role women played in early-twentieth-century labor organizations or the suffragist movement, there has been significant and important new research and findings. Unfortunately, however, we do not know much more about women's history in Puerto Rico today than we did twenty-five years ago.

The purpose of this essay is to provide a historiographical review of the women's history literature in Puerto Rico and in Puerto Rican communities in the United States since 1970. While it is undeniable that more attention has been given in scholarly circles to the historical roles women have played in Puerto Rico, there have been few attempts to review this literature in a comprehensive way.[2] As new related research areas emerge, such as the history of sexuality or lesbian studies, for example, it is important to see how the historical writing about women in Puerto Rico has evolved, what have been its most significant contributions and its most salient disappointments, and what are the new challenges and areas of inquiry for future research.

As academic disciplines go, history in Puerto Rico lags significantly behind most social sciences and humanities in the attention given to women's issues. The problem seems endemic to the discipline in the Caribbean, the United States, and Europe as well.[3] This might be related to the women's studies interest in solving public policy problems—discrimination, unequal pay, or domestic violence, for example—and the need to turn to the social sciences for answers. It is precisely because of this social science emphasis that more historically grounded work is needed regarding Puerto Rican women. Most social science or literary studies related to women have been done with little or no historical context. Many times women's roles have been ahistorically analyzed, making for very poor scholarship. Still, there seems to be increasing interest in studying woman-related topics among Puerto Rican historians in the last decade.

Although there is substantial controversy about what constitutes the field or the discipline of women's studies, few would argue that one of its most important defining elements is its interdisciplinary nature.[4] If some of the earlier tasks of women's studies were to "fill in the gaps" of knowledge about women, to identify and correct male biases in the epistemological construction of academic disciplines, and to redress power relations in the definition of knowledge and practice, it was logical that the canonical boundaries of disciplinary studies needed to be crossed. Still, while recognizing that a purely discipline-based perspective might not do justice to the richness of the field, I will concentrate this essay almost exclusively on works published by historians or on works that are historically oriented. I believe that this narrower focus will facilitate tracing the development of historical writing about Puerto Rican women and pointing to new directions for future research. Since this is a first attempt at providing an overview of the historical literature about Puerto Rican women, I have decided to use a chronological format on this essay. I am aware that several other approaches, such as a thematic one, could have been employed also. Yet, since I am trying to provide the most comprehensive coverage possible, I have decided to keep the range as inclusive as possible. I hope that more focused thematic studies follow this essay.

Women and Historical Writing: 1900–1960s

Until the early 1960s, there was no such thing as women's studies or women's history in Puerto Rico. Prior to that decade historians and other intellectuals had included women in their narratives mostly to address what were considered "feminine" topics, such as family, fashion, domesticity, and religion. Sporadically, several books had appeared dealing with woman-related issues, such as Gabriel Ferrer's *La mujer en Puerto Rico: Sus necesidades presentes y los medios más fáciles y adecuados para mejorar su porvenir* (1881), or biographies of notable women such as Angela Negrón Muñoz's *Mujeres de Puerto Rico: Desde el primer siglo de colonización hasta el primer tercio del siglo XX* (1935).[5] Most of these books, however, were not part of a systematic inquiry into the history of women in Puerto Rico. María F. Barceló Miller has done a succinct analysis of the treatment given to women by Puerto Rican historiographical schools prior to the 1960s.[6] She has characterized the historical writing about women generated in the early decades of the twentieth century as paternalistic and elitist. Women played a secondary and marginal role in the Island's past, usually as shadows of men, who were the real protagonists of history. Barceló Miller also shows that the dominant historical vision emerging after the 1930s—particularly that of leading authors such as Tomás Blanco and Antonio S. Pedreira—was clearly anti-feminist.[7] The gains of the early-twentieth-century feminists and suffragists alarmed patriarchal writers such as Blanco and Pedreira.

It is important to remember that although authors such as Salvador Brau, Blanco, and Pedreira represented the boundaries of dominant historical and humanistic disquisition in the first four decades of the twentieth century, there were other contesting voices in the historiographical discourse. One such voice, for instance, was writer, feminist, and labor leader Luisa Capetillo. Her writings advocating women's and workers' rights in Puerto Rico have been recently described by literary critic Julio Ramos as a "hybrid discourse."[8] The hybrid nature of Capetillo's writing—a combination of academic and plebeian oral discourses written in various literary genres such as letters, essays, autobiography, and poetry—was a challenge to more nationalistic, essentialist, and exclusivist discourses engaged in by the majority of Puerto Rican writers in the early decades of the twentieth century. Capetillo's writings, according to Ramos, were an attempt to open an alternative space, one with fresh representational strategies and new social agents, including among them, of course, women. Unfortunately, the influence of Capetillo and other writers like her did not make a substantial mark on the dominant writers of the first half of the twentieth century, and their historiographical contributions have only recently begun to be reassessed by contemporary historians.

The so-called "Generación del '40"—responsible for most of the historical writing produced in the 1950s and 60s—neglected women as historical subjects worthy of research and attention. It was this generation, with scholars such as Arturo Morales Carrión, Aída Caro Costas, Isabel Gutiérrez del Arroyo, and Luis Díaz Soler, among others, that provided Puerto Rico with its first cohort of professional historians. Paralleling developments occurring at the Institute for Puerto Rican Culture and other cultural and intellectual institutions, this generation of historians was responsible for shaping, organizing, and constructing much of the historical infrastructure—archives, journals, documentary and bibliographic collections, and research centers—which exists in the Island today. It is with and against this infrastructure—the legacy of a delayed positivist heritage and of institutionalizing cultural nationalism—that many of the historians researching women's issues have had to work with since the 1970s.

The historians of the Generación del '40 focused much of their research on institutions, political parties, diplomacy, legal issues, and patriotic figures.[9]

Given these research interests, it is not surprising that women and marginalized groups did not stand much of a chance of being treated as worthy or interesting historical agents unless, of course, they proved to be extraordinary in some way. As part of the ideological backbone of the ruling Partido Popular Democrático (PPD), many of the historians of the Generación del '40 emphasized the nineteenth-century liberal ideology that generated a short-lived autonomous political relationship with Spain months prior to the United States' invasion in 1898. For these scholars, particularly Morales Carrión, there was a historical link between those nineteenth-century liberals and the current leadership—himself included—of the pro-Commonwealth-status PPD. Yet even historians committed to Puerto Rico's political independence shared a theoretical and methodological vision, which privileged institutional, political, and patriotic history.

For the historians of the Generación del '40, women did not represent a coherent group for analysis or research. One finds scant references to women in their works, and these references are usually present in one of two forms: either in chapters or sections dealing with local customs, dress, religiosity, or marriage, or in reference to extraordinary women or pioneers, such as the early-nineteenth-century pro-independence activist María Barbudo, or the poetess Lola Rodríguez de Tió. Due to their rigid adherence to documentary materials, these historians reproduced what are now some of the best-known clichés regarding pre-twentieth-century women, such as the great skill of women horse riders and the amusing portrayal of women smoking cigars.[10] In essence, this generation of historians, ground-breakers and pioneers in many aspects of historical inquiry and endeavor, passed on a legacy of depicting Puerto Rican women as either passive, caricaturesque, or exceptional.

Women and the *Nueva Historia*

Local and international developments in the 1960s and 1970s had transformative effects in Puerto Rican historiography. On the Island, the "new historians" altered the way history was written, analyzed and studied. In the United States, particularly in New York City, the field of Puerto Rican Studies was born out of the struggles of students and community activists tired of being marginalized by U.S. educational institutions.[11] Several institutions—such as the Center for Puerto Rican Studies in New York City and the Centro de Estudios de la Realidad Puertorriqueña (Center for Studies of the Puerto Rican Reality, CEREP) in Río Piedras—and individuals—César Andreu Iglesias, Frank Bonilla, and Ángel Quintero Rivera, for example—played key roles creating links between the new historians and the practitioners of Puerto Rican Studies. However, even when there was some collaboration and cross-influencing between scholars and institutions in the United States and on the Island, closer institutional connections and dissemination of research findings had to wait until the 1980s.

The origins and agendas of the *nueva historia* have been the subject of much scrutiny lately.[12] The historical work produced between the late 1960s and the early 1980s, which marked the peak of productivity and influence of the new history, saw a fundamental shift in methodology, theoretical approaches, and thematic concerns. The paradigms that had guided the works of the Generación del '40 were rejected by the new generation of historians. In general, the new historians were interested in documenting the life of oppressed and marginalized people in Puerto Rico, such as peasants, slaves, and workers. To achieve this, the *nueva historia* dug into new and often untapped primary sources, such as notary and trial records, tax data, and hacienda records. New historians also moved away from relying on the humanities as a source for theoretical and methodological insights and looked for models in the social sciences. Furthermore, for most new historians economics and material conditions became central explanatory phenomena. In many ways, Puerto Rican scholars were responding to and engaging the changing political and scholarly currents emerging from the United States, Europe, Latin America, and Africa. Finally, the *nueva historia* wanted to reach audiences beyond the scholarly community and, as a result, was concerned with disseminating the results of historical research in the broadest possible way.

Women were among the neglected and marginalized groups that the new historians were supposed to incorporate into the mainstream. Yet for most of the better-known figures of the *nueva historia* movement, such as Gervasio García, Fernando Picó, Ángel Quintero Rivera, Blanca Silvestrini, and Guillermo Baralt, women were not a central concern, although they did include important sections in their respective studies regarding women cigar-workers, mothers and daughters of *jornaleros,* and rebellious female slaves, among others.[13] Some of these authors, like Picó and Silvestrini, published essays focusing exclusively on women's history.[14] Although some authors have been critical of the lack of attention that many new historians paid to women's history, it is important to acknowledge the extremely influential task performed by many of the new historians as teachers and mentors of younger scholars who later did groundbreaking work in women's history. Given the difficult odds, lack of resources, and often disheartening working conditions faced by Puerto Rican scholars both on the Island and in the United States, publishing is not always easy. Therefore, in pursuing any kind of historiographical study about Puerto Rico it is crucial to accentuate the importance of teaching and mentoring in shaping emerging methodological and thematic currents.

Most of the works that specifically addressed women's history topics in the 1970s tended to be short essays. Many essays were the result of work in progress, which latter evolved into full-length monographs. Others were the result of conferences, usually sponsored by CEREP, different university-affiliated programs, or a government agency such as the Comisión para el Mejoramiento de los Derechos de la Mujer (Commission for the Improvement of Women's Rights). The lectures given in 1975 by anthropologist Jalil Sued-Badillo, for example, regarding women in Taino society—as part of a CEREP-sponsored Women's History Week series—later formed the basis for his book *La mujer indigena y su sociedad.*[15]

Some of the most influential essays were the ones by Marcia Rivera Quintero, Isabel Picó, Blanca Silvestrini, Edna Acosta-Belén, and Norma Valle Ferrer, incorporated into the anthology *The Puerto Rican Woman* (1979). This anthology—a slightly modified version of which was immediately published in Spanish—became one of the standard scholarly references in the field of Puerto Rican women's studies in the 1980s. Of the eleven essays included in the first edition, the three by Rivera Quintero, Isabel Picó, and Valle Ferrer were clearly of a historical nature, even when none of the authors was a historian.[16] Like the field of women's studies, the anthology was interdisciplinary in its composition, although the importance given to historical questions was to be expected since an important goal of the anthology was "to present primary source material that would provide an overview of the Puerto Rican woman within the various historical, socioeconomic, and cultural processes that have taken place in Puerto Rican society."[17] The essays collected in the anthology provided not only an overview of the contributions and the situation of women in several areas of Puerto Rican society, but also indicated the main thematic and historiographical trends in the young field of women's studies in the late 1970s.

Rivera Quintero's essay deals with the role women played in the transition from a precapitalist into a capitalist mode of production in the early twentieth century. The debate regarding identifying Puerto Rico's dominant mode of production—particularly whether the nineteenth century was precapitalist, feudal, or something else—was a pressing one for historians and social scientists in the 1970s.[18] Rivera Quintero is critical of that debate because it ignored the significant participation of women in the labor force and because it neglected the unequal and sexist way in which thousands of women were incorporated into the labor force in the early decades of the twentieth century. The final section of her essay explores the structural trends in labor force participation and occupational and wage differentials by sex since the 1930s. To explain the ongoing discrimination, labor segregation by sex, and low rates of participation in some sectors of the economy, Rivera Quintero looked at the roots of this problem in the early decades of the twentieth century.

The anthology's essay by Isabel Picó is also concerned with discovering the historical roots of women's inequality, particularly in the political realm. Picó explains the different kinds of jobs available to women between 1900 and 1930 and documents the class divisions of the early suffragist movements in Puerto Rico. For Picó, "the seed bed of the suffrage movement that developed in Puerto Rico was the increase in respectable jobs open to women of the upper and middle classes."[19] It was this class difference, Picó believes, that prompted upper-class feminists to dismiss female working-class concerns, and ultimately made gaining the right for literate women to vote in 1932 an ineffective vehicle to transform sexual inequities in Puerto Rico. This failure, according to the author, was ultimately responsible for the isolation of the feminist movement after the 1930s.

The theme of the origins and development of women's and feminist movements in Puerto Rico is further explored in Valle Ferrer's essay. The author argues that feminist organizations in Puerto Rico, as in other parts of the world, were a result of the industrial revolution—in Puerto Rico's case, of the industrialization phase that started in the 1940s–50s—which forced women out of their homes and into the public waged-labor force.[20] Valle Ferrer then proceeds to trace the genealogy of the both proletarian and petit-bourgeois (suffragist) feminisms from the mid-nineteenth century until the 1970s. The essay concludes with a critique of socialist or left-oriented parties that relegate the emancipation of women to a secondary position in their efforts to transform Puerto Rican society.

Taken together, the essays by Valle Ferrer, Rivera Quintero, and Isabel Picó represent an attempt to rescue the history of women—working-class women foremost—in the first three decades of the twentieth century. This historical exercise was placed at the service of strategizing on how to transform the reality of discrimination and oppression faced by Puerto Rican women in the 1970s. The work of these authors, plus that of Silvestrini and Acosta Belén (added to the anthology's second edition in 1986), was very influential in the subsequent scholarship and became a key departure point for those writing about women's history in the late 1970s and early 1980s.

Another important monograph published in the late 1970s was Yamila Azize's *La mujer en la lucha* (1979). The book documents the first three decades of feminist struggles in the twentieth century, with particular emphasis on the condition of women workers. Azize's work follows the earlier lead of scholars like Rivera Quintero, Silvestrini, Valle Ferrer, and Isabel Picó, who wrote about turn-of-the-century working-class women, the growth and development of the feminist movement, the suffragist struggle, and exceptional leaders such as Luisa Capetillo. Although Azize's work rides the 1970s wave of growing interest in women's history, she cautions that her work is a reaction against copying foreign models of feminism and against applying facile solutions to the problems affecting Puerto Rican women without any kind of historical context.[21] Azize sees her research as a tool to help contemporary feminists strategize about how to strive for a more egalitarian and just Puerto Rico.

Azize claims there were two main feminist strands in early-twentieth-century Puerto Rico: workers' feminism and suffragist feminism. Both emerged as responses to the incorporation of women into the Island's workforce, particularly as cigar-workers, garment industry workers, or domestics. For Azize, working-class feminists supported a broader and more emancipatory agenda of women's rights, as opposed to suffragist feminists, whose goals were more narrowly centered on obtaining the right to vote.[22] Azize also believes that working-class feminists were more successful in changing sexist attitudes among their male peers given the latter's support for "free love" and usage of terms like *compañera* and *camarada*. Suffragist feminists faced bitter opposition from their male counterparts, particularly those in politics, who opposed giving women voting rights.[23] Although more recent studies of the suffragist movement and the participation of women in the needlework industry have nuanced and contradicted some of the polarities established by Azize in her work, her book was an important contribution to the study of early-twentieth-century feminism and working-class women.

There were also a few short biographies of exceptional women written in the 1970s. Norma Valle Ferrer prepared her biography of Luisa Capetillo in mimeograph form in the mid-1970s. Later, her book *Luisa Capetillo: Historia de una mujer proscrita* was published in 1990.[24] Another woman who attracted biographical attention was San Juan's charismatic mayor, Felisa Rincón de Gautier, affectionately known as Doña Fela. A biography for young readers published in 1972 tells the story of Doña Fela's rise in political life, her open-house policy as mayor of San Juan, and her love for the city's children.[25] Doña Fela's politics are described as being based on a life-long commitment to fight poverty and to improve the situation of women in Puerto Rico. On the opposite side of the political spectrum was Lolita Lebrón, famous for being one of the members of the Nationalist Party who attacked the U.S. House of Representatives in 1954. Lebrón is the subject of a short biography by journalist Federico Ribes Tovar in which she is heralded as a martyr of the Puerto Rican independence movement and shown as an example of a courageous and politically commited woman.[26]

It is not surprising that some of the first essays and monographs about women's history in Puerto Rico emphasized issues such as early-twentieth-century working-class and political history. This was a logical outcome of the dynamism in areas of research in vogue among the new historians and the members of discussion–research groups such as CEREP. It was also connected to the activism and political work of many authors who considered their scholarship a concrete way to provide background and strategic insights into the public policy and political issues facing women in the 1970s. As women's political, governmental, legal, and labor organizations developed in the 1960s and 1970s there was a need to historically contextualize their struggles and to provide a sense of connection with early-twentieth-century feminist organizations.

The colonial relationship between Puerto Rico and the United States also generated its share of influence on the research topics regarding women's history. Many articles and monographs were destined to show the impact of U.S. colonial policies on Puerto Rican women. Perhaps the best examples of this literature are the studies focusing on the birth control experimentation and sterilization of Puerto Rican women that took place from the 1950s to the 1970s.[27] Most of this literature demonstrates how Puerto Rico served as a birth control laboratory for U.S. agencies, companies, and scholars due to the lack of sovereignty the colonial status provided. In this context, Puerto Rican women were doubly victimized as a result of their status as colonial subjects and as women.

Another important factor in the development of women's history as a field in Puerto Rico has been the influence of U.S. women's studies research and historiography. Obviously, the works regarding Puerto Rican women in the United States have been shaped by the historiographical tendencies in U.S. social, ethnic, and women's history. Yet, the Island's research agenda has also experienced this influence, as the emphasis on the study of women's suffrage indicates. The struggle to secure the right to vote is a major theme in U.S. women's history, and Puerto Rican historians have engaged that literature for comparative perspectives and methodological insights.[28] As the field of women's studies in Puerto Rico has developed, comparative and methodological perspectives have also been drawn from European and Latin American scholars.

Women's History and Puerto Rican Studies

The origins of a Puerto Rican Studies field date to the struggles of the 1960s and 1970s by the Puerto Rican community, particularly in New York City, to achieve broader gains in civil, political, economic, and educational rights. Coinciding with those efforts was the need to critique and reformulate a tradition of social science research about the Puerto Rican communities in the United States, which had previously been done mostly by outsiders and had often accentuated the most negative aspects of the communities. Many Puerto Rican academics, particularly second-generation ones born in the United States, began to research the experiences of their own community. Some were doing it from the context of the recently created Puerto Rican Studies departments or programs. These programs "rejected traditional approaches to learning about Puerto Ricans and defined new sources of learning that stemmed from within the Puerto Rican experience."[29] Finally, there was a commitment among Puerto Rican Studies teachers, students, and scholars to apply academic knowledge to solving the pressing social problems affecting Puerto Ricans, and the view that academic research needed to be validated by its connection to the needs of the community at large. As such, Puerto Rican Studies shared with the new historians a desire to go beyond academia, not just in the dissemination of research, but also in developing a problem-oriented methodology.

The scholarship about Puerto Ricans in the United States tended to accentuate the negative aspects of their migration. Many U.S. social scientists, particularly those working out of urban environments, also tended to blame Puerto Ricans for many urban problems such as poverty, welfare dependency, gentrification, and drugs. Oscar Lewis's depiction of Puerto Rican families as quintessential representatives of the culture of poverty, and reports like the one by Nathan Glazer and Daniel Patrick Moynihan, which argued that Puerto Ricans had no social or cultural institutions of any value in their communities, dominated the literature.[30]

Puerto Rican Studies rejected these paradigms and began to search for more nuanced and less biased accounts of the Puerto Rican migrant experience in the United States, particularly New York City.

Scholars from different disciplines were part of the early Puerto Rican Studies movement. It shares, along with women's studies, for example, a strong interdisciplinary perspective. A few historians, such as Olga Jiménez Wagenheim and Virginia Sánchez Korrol, played very active and important roles in this movement. History, as a way of empowering the Puerto Rican community, was a central element in the Puerto Rican Studies movement, particularly as it became institutionalized in curricula on U.S. college campuses. One of the first conferences organized by the Center for Puerto Rican Studies after its inauguration in 1972 was a "Conference on Puerto Rican Historiography" in 1974, accompanied by the creation of a permanent History Task Force at the Center.[31]

In the field of Puerto Rican Studies, the attempt to incorporate women as a central category of analysis and interest was initially more successful than in the *nueva historia*. While many of the discussion groups, departments, symposiums, and other academic institutions were clearly dominated by male scholars, women such as Rosa Estades, Clara Rodríguez, and Virginia Sánchez Korrol, among others, made an early mark in the field of Puerto Rican Studies. Another important development in advancing historical interest and research about the Puerto Rican community in New York was the publication of Bernardo Vega's memoirs in 1977.[32] Vega, a cigar-maker and working-class leader, migrated to New York City from Cayey in 1916 and wrote an important chronicle of the life of the early-twentieth-century Puerto Rican community in the city. Although its main focus was not the experience of women, Vega's memoir did include commentaries and references to women's experiences in New York, particularly those of important women leaders such as Luisa Capetillo and Julia de Burgos. More than anything else, the publication of Vega's memoir provided impetus for further historical research about the early Puerto Rican communities in the United States.

The important anthology, *Historical Perspectives on Puerto Rican Survival in the U.S.* (1980), includes two essays dedicated exclusively to women's issues. This anthology, born out of a 1975 conference, collects most of the early works or works-in-progress of a young generation of scholars who had fought for the creation of an academic space for Puerto Rican researchers in the United States. One of the essays on the anthology, written by Sánchez Korrol, explores the historical experiences of Puerto Rican women in pre–WWII New York City.[33] Sánchez Korrol shows how women played an important role in gathering vital social and economic information in the emerging *colonias,* participating in volunteer, social, and religious organizations, and taking care of children and lodgers. Puerto Rican women were not only busy as housewives, but many also worked as cigar-makers, garment industry employees, domestics, or agricultural fieldworkers. Sánchez Korrol's methodology—which she pursued in her study of the Puerto Rican community between 1900 and 1942—combined quantitative census data analysis with interviews and oral history. Not only was Sánchez Korrol's work pioneering in tracing the historical roots of the Puerto Rican communities prior to the "big migration" (1946–1964) and showing the important roles played by women in the building of those communities, but she also opened the path for the inclusion of oral history within the field of Puerto Rican Studies. Oral history would become an important tool in the research of Puerto Rican women's history in the United States in the 1980s and 1990s.

Most of the other research on Puerto Rican women in the United States produced by scholars in the 1970s was related to the social sciences or to public policy. In many of these essays, the authors included brief historical sections to provide some background for the discussion of the central issue, be that double discrimination, labor force participation, the psychological legacy of machismo, or household structures. The authors writing about Puerto Rican women in the United States were Lourdes Miranda King, Alice Colón, Clara Rodríguez, and Rosemary Santana Cooney, among others.[34]

Women's History in the 1980s and 1990s: Consolidation and Challenges

In the 1980s and 1990s the field of Puerto Rican women's studies became institutionalized in academic, political, and publishing circles. Academia and publishing lingered behind the political institutionalization of women's units in political parties and associations, and the creation of independent women's entities that occurred in the 1970s.[35] In the 1980s, for instance, many of the most active and influential university programs specifically oriented to researching and publishing women's issues, such as the Centro Coordinador de Estudios, Recursos, y Servicios a la Mujer (Coordinating Center of Studies, Resources, and Services for Women, CERES) at the University of Puerto Rico–Río Piedras campus and the Proyecto de Estudios de la Mujer (Women's Studies Project) at the UPR–Cayey campus, were created. Also, many of the leading scholarly journals dedicated thematic issues to the scholarship on women's studies—usually gathering scattered previously published materials—in which several historical essays were published. Examples of this trend are *Homines*, "Mujeres Puertorriqueñas, Protagonistas en el Caribe" (1987), and the Center for Puerto Rican Studies, *Centro Bulletin*, "Puerto Rican Women as Workers and Writers" (1989).[36]

Part of the continuing institutionalization of the field of women's studies has been the exchange programs that have been created by scholars in both Puerto Rico and the United States. The most successful example of these exchanges is the "Encuentros" (literally, encounters) that have been held since 1989 between researchers in the University of Puerto Rico and the City University of New York (CUNY) system. These have been multidisciplinary exchanges in which scholars have shared their research agendas and debated methodological, disciplinary, and theoretical issues. Besides their evident value as mechanisms of debate, exchange, criticism, and networking, the encounters have produced several important publications, such as an interdisciplinary volume on Puerto Rican women based mostly on papers presented at the first meeting and the publication of the proceedings of the third "Encuentro."[37]

The 1980s and 1990s have also fulfilled some of the promises of both Puerto Rican Studies and the *nueva historia,* particularly as they related to the study of women. Some of the earlier 1970s research, which was mostly published and disseminated in essay form, developed into full-length monographic studies. New avenues of research were also beginning to be explored and found their way into regular journals or into anthologies such as Yamila Azize's *La mujer en Puerto Rico: Ensayos de investigación* (1987).

Although the 1980s saw the publication of several important anthologies and the institutionalization of many academic programs and courses, historical writing about Puerto Rican women on the Island suffered. Not a single book-length study regarding women and history was published in Puerto Rico in the 1980s. This could be perplexing given the consolidation of the programs and centers mentioned above. Yet, given the interdisciplinary nature of women's studies, most of these centers were not staffed by historians. Also, since many of the centers focused on public policy issues, historical expertise was not valued as much as quantitative or statistical analysis. Another reason for the lack of book-length monographs on women's history in the 1980s could have been the long hours and hard work involved in both archival and oral history research.

There were some advances in the field of demographic history, however, as several authors produced essays using data from nineteenth-century parish records or the 1910 manuscript censuses. Rosa Santiago Marazzi published an article about the migration of Spanish women during the conquest and colonization phase in Puerto Rico.[38] This article discusses the demographic trends of Spanish female migration from the sixteenth through the early nineteenth century and the legislation enforced by the colonial authorities regarding the migration of Spanish women to Puerto Rico. Carlos Rodríguez-Villanueva and Gregorio Villegas wrote important master's theses analyzing the eighteenth- and nineteenth-century demographic behavior of the city of Guaynabo, today a suburb of San Juan.[39] These authors produced some of the few attempts at analyzing issues such as common-law marriages, concubinage, age at first marriage, and other demographic facts about nineteenth-century municipal life. María F. Barceló Miller, moving away from strictly demographic work, searched church records to document how the Catholic leadership shifted its views regarding the spiritual and moral worth of Puerto Rican women. She documented how women moved from being perceived by church officials in the eighteenth century as dangerous, corrosive, and sinful elements in society, particularly because of their influence over men, to being virtuous and innocent by the mid-nineteenth century.[40] Barceló Miller shows how the Catholic hierarchy tried to use women to gain back influence in the increasingly secular society of the late nineteenth century.

Fernando Picó published several articles regarding the living conditions of families in coffee-producing regions and the life of female tobacco-industry workers in Utuado based on 1910 census data.[41] Also using the 1910 census data, Arlene J. Díaz Caballero produced a detailed demographic profile of working women in the Santurce barrio.[42] By the end of the 1980s several projects were launched that culminated in books and dissertations completed in the early 1990s.

The 1990s saw a surge of historical doctoral dissertations, which are slowly evolving into book form as the decade ends. Among these are two of the first three dissertations of the recently created doctoral program in history at the University of Puerto Rico–Río Piedras completed by Mary Frances Gallart and María F. Barceló Miller. Gallart's study of one of the first woman mayors in Puerto Rico, elected in the town of Guayama in 1952, marks an important development in the analysis of female politicians and gender politics at the municipal or local level.[43] Although most political historians point to Doña Fela as the only female leader in the PPD throughout the 1950s and 1960s, Gallart's study on Obdulia Velázquez de Lorenzo and the women who helped her to become Guayama's mayor dispels this notion. Gallart's research is important because it shows that women's political struggles did not end with the suffragist victory in 1932 and that women had to fight very hard for their space in party politics. Furthermore, by documenting the role that Velázquez played in having the first primary law approved in Puerto Rico, Gallart shows the connection between women's struggles for inclusion in politics and other democratizing efforts pursued by women that would benefit Puerto Rico's overall political life.

María F. Barceló Miller's dissertation on the growth and evolution of the suffragist movement in Puerto Rico in the 1920s–30s is an excellent study of the interplay of class and gender in the development of women's political associations.[44] In her work, Barceló Miller counters previous interpretations of the suffragist movement in which working-class suffragists are seen as the leading actors of the movement, and argues that elite women were the vanguard of the movement. She also sets out to nuance the dichotomies developed by Azize and others regarding the radicalism of working-class feminists and suffragists in early-twentieth-century Puerto Rico. Proletarian feminists, argues Barceló Miller, also employed the cult of domesticity to advance their claims, not as a rhetorical strategy—as the elite feminists did—but as a response to the poverty and misery faced by them and their children.[45] Finally, Barceló Miller demonstrates the importance of understanding suffragists as part of a social movement that played an important political and intellectual role in the Island's political life of the 1920s and 1930s, a formative period for Puerto Rico's modern political landscape.

Barceló Miller's study is complemented by the work of Gladys Jiménez-Muñoz, who focuses on the racial dimension of the suffragist debate and argues for incorporating a racial perspective into the study of the Island's suffragist movement.[46] Jiménez-Muñoz also shows the rhetorical connections between the debate to grant Puerto Rican women the right to vote and the 1898–1917 debate on the merits of granting Puerto Rican "natives" U.S. citizenship. In both cases, those in power—the colonial government and certain sectors of the elite, depending on the case—designated women and natives as having deficient identities. If Barceló Miller is interested in highlighting the role of elite feminists in the suffrage movement, Jiménez-Muñoz is more interested in the ideological representations and narratives defining the debate. She wants to emphasize "the objective positions and social effects of these narratives by showing how the terms of the debate were actually more complicated than its participants—and current historiography—thought or intended."[47] Works by both Barceló Miller and Jiménez-Muñoz show the ongoing interest in the topic of the women's suffrage movement in Puerto Rico. They also indicated a growing sophistication, as the early and binary oppositions between proletarian suffragists and bourgeois suffragists have been nuanced and the complexity of other elements of analysis, such as race, has been added to the mix.

Other 1990s dissertations have explored different topics, paying more attention to the situation of women in the nineteenth century. It is ironic that given the emphasis new historians and historians after them placed on the nineteenth century, so little has been written about Puerto Rican women prior to the twentieth century.[48] Contrary to the interest in women and slavery that has yielded so many solid historical monographs in the Caribbean and the United States, there have been just a few essays on this topic in Puerto Rico.[49] Mariano Negrón Portillo and Raúl Mayo Santana have illuminated several aspects of the lives of domestic and urban female slaves in San Juan in their recent study of urban slavery in that city.[50] Their research and my own on the economic roles played by women in San Juan has begun to provide a sense of the importance of domestic and urban slavery in Puerto Rico, given that the slavery literature has tended to concentrate on plantation life.[51] Ivonne Acosta Lespier has also published a short article describing the situation of female slaves in Mayagüez based on the 1872 slave registry.[52] This registry, which was prepared to form the basis for the abolition of slavery in 1873, showed that most of the female slaves in Mayagüez were between the ages of 13 and 39 years, single, born in Puerto Rico, and worked in the field in rural areas and as domestics in urban areas. Obviously, any research based solely upon 1872 data will provide a skewed view of slavery in Puerto Rico because the date was close to the end of slavery and past its peak moment. Still, the slave registry provides an interesting window from which to study the transition period between slave labor and free labor that has intrigued so many Caribbean and Puerto Rican scholars in the last two decades.

My own research has focused on how the changes experienced in Puerto Rico as it became an export monoculture economy in the nineteenth century affected women within the urban setting of San Juan.[53] The study examines the roles played by women of different classes, races, and "status" in the city's economy. Women were active participants at all levels in the city's economy. From providing capital for big commercial warehouses, to running small grocery shops, to providing basic household and domestic services, women contributed to San Juan's economic life. My research documents, for example, the important role that women played in the real estate market in San Juan, particularly as a result of Spanish laws that forcibly divided the inheritance among widows and children. The participation of women in both small retail and domestic work presented a key, yet undervalued, element in sustaining the urban economy of San Juan. My study also explores the effects upon women of the decline suffered by the city's economy beginning in the 1840s.

I have also analyzed the emergence of the first documented women's organization in Puerto Rico—the Junta de Damas, founded in 1859. Although the literature on the historical evolution of women's and feminist organizations in Puerto Rico has characterized late-nineteenth-century groups such as the Junta de Damas as proto-feminist and the result of European and U.S. influences on the Island's elite, my research has placed the focus elsewhere.[54] At a time of transition from slave labor to wage labor, women's elite groups such as the Junta de Damas were tied to the growing efforts by urban elites to guarantee access to urban domestic labor.[55] Women's associations were often tied to beneficence efforts, which have their roots in controlling, confining, and rehabilitating potential artisan and domestic workers. The elite women who joined and organized these women's organizations had previous experience in the city's commercial life, and their social and economic ties made them perfect candidates for charitable fund-raising. Women's groups did provide an outlet for urban elite women to participate in more public-type institutions, but their development had less to do with foreign influences and more with responses and adjustments from the upper classes to the economic, social, and racial dislocations brought on by the abolition of slavery.

Another study that enriches our knowledge of women's lives in the nineteenth and twentieth centuries is Eileen Findlay's dissertation on sexuality, power, and politics in Ponce between 1870 and 1920.[56] Findlay sets out to explore the historical changes in the way sexual norms were dictated upon women and the ways in which women struggled for a more independent and autonomous sense of their own sexuality in Ponce in the period moving from the end of slavery to the brink of the depression in Puerto Rico. By studying what traditionally has been considered part of the private realm—sexuality, marriage, and relationships, for example—Findlay shows the important role that controlling sexual norms and practices had for the articulation of the political agenda of many of the new social movements and of both the Spanish and U.S. colonial regimes in the period under study. In the 1890s, prostitutes incarnated all that was evil and undesirable for Spanish colonial officials, liberal members of the local elite attempting to "build a nation" through the moral reformation of women, and bourgeois feminists eager to show the superior values of respectable women as their contribution to the nation-in-the-making. Findlay shows how a similar consensus was not achieved in the 1920s, given the opposition of radical workers, people of color, and feminists, who supported the prostitutes against the harassing demands of U.S. colonial officials and the local politicians.

Findlay's path-breaking work is clearly an important bridge between the historiography of women's history and that of gender studies. Gender is the key element that Findlay applies to her analyses of "decency" and prostitution and to the changing political landscape of turn-of-the-century Puerto Rico. A gendered study of sexuality is also a valuable mechanism in exploring historically contested periods, because, as Findlay argues, "(sexuality) also becomes explicitly politicized at certain historical moments. This seems to be particularly true in times of change and transition."[57] By looking at sexuality, Findlay has been able to challenge some important conceptions of Puerto Rico's history, particularly its political history. One example is her documentation of the attempts of male working-class leaders—whose traditional portrait in the literature has them repudiating bourgeois constructions of female behavior—to impose their own version of female domesticity, which closely resembled the parameters defined by elite liberals about the proper roles for respectable women.[58] Radical working-class leaders—marginalized within their own movements—argued for more emancipatory sexual norms and practices.

It is in the 1990s that one can assess enough critical mass of historical work focused on women and thus properly talk about a field of women's history in Puerto Rico. Ironically, this development coincided with the shift in the field toward gender analysis as the central focus of methodological and theoretical concern. Women's history—or "herstory" as it came to be called—has come to be seen by some as an incomplete way to study the interactive nature of women's lives in the past. The tension between the two approaches is part of an ongoing debate in many other regions, including the Caribbean, as the recent work of Hilary Beckles, Pat Mohammed, and Bridget Brereton show.[59] At the present moment, it is unclear if in Puerto Rico the historical research will move totally in the direction of gender studies.

The History of Puerto Rican Women in the United States: 1980s–1990s

Although some gains have been made in discovering and analyzing the history of Puerto Rican women residing in the United States, there has not been as much historical research on this topic when compared to the production on the Island in the last two decades. This is due, in part, to the shortage of Puerto Ricans getting Ph.D.'s in history in the United States and doing research on the mainland Puerto Rican communities, and to the fact that most mainstream U.S. historians disregard the U.S. Puerto Rican community as a topic of research. Scholars writing about the Puerto Rican diaspora tend to come from sociology, literature, psychology, education, and, anthropology, among other disciplines.[60]

Virginia Sánchez Korrol and, more recently, Altagracia Ortiz have been the most productive and visible historians of Puerto Rican women in the United States in the last two decades. In the early 1980s, Sánchez Korrol continued publishing the results of her late-1970s research making women an important part of her overall history of the Puerto Rican communities in New York City prior to World War II.[61] Sánchez Korrol is also out to disprove the myths propagated by some social scientists such as Oscar Lewis and Daniel Patrick Moynihan regarding the supposed lack of coherent cultural and social institutions in the Puerto Rican community. Women were very active in cultivating the ties that helped to shape the social fabric of immigrant Puerto Rican communities. Although Sánchez Korrol ultimately concludes that for women "migration and work did not produce major changes in their roles within Puerto Rican society," she dedicates a lengthy chapter to the lives of Puerto Rican women.[62] Another author, having reached a similar conclusion, would have probably brushed aside the experiences of these women.

Sánchez Korrol has also documented the lives of Puerto Rican professional women in New York City. She has tried to shown aspects of the "forgotten immigrant" by bringing attention to the contributions made by Puerto Rican nuns, librarians, writers, and bilingual education teachers, among others, to the larger community. These women, often neglected by a literature that has focused on industrial, domestic, or manufacturing workers, have played important leadership roles in the community. Among the important figures analyzed by Sánchez Korrol is Pura Belpré. Belpré was a community activist, writer, and folklorist and the first Puerto Rican librarian in New York City's public library system.[63] Active in numerous cultural and educational initiatives, Belpré exemplifies the educated Puerto Rican female migrant who steered her professional activities to create and nurture ties between Puerto Rico and New York City. Another example of professional women who created cultural and educational linkages between the two shores are the female teachers in the city who led the fight for bilingual education. Sánchez Korrol has studied some of these women, particularly those active in English-as-a-Second-Language (ESL) programs since the 1950s.[64] Many of these women became leaders in the grassroots organizations formed in the late 1960s and early 1970s—such as the People's Board of Education, United Bronx Parents, and ASPIRA—to fight for good public education for Puerto Rican and other Latino/a children. One of the main contributions of Sánchez Korrol's work has been her reliance on oral history as a methodological anchor for her work. Not only has she conducted interviews herself, but Sánchez has drawn upon the materials from Columbia's University Oral History Project, particularly for the interviews with writer Pura Belpré.

Another historian, who was previously a colonial history expert, Altagracia Ortiz has focused her more recent work on Puerto Rican women workers in New York City, particularly those in the garment industry.[65] Many Puerto Rican women entered the home needlework industry in New York City in the 1920s and 30s, as did many of their counterparts on the Island. Ortiz documents the changes in the industry, the increase of women workers after 1945 (replacing European immigrant laborers), and their struggle for membership in the International Ladies' Garment Workers' Union (ILGWU). By the 1960s, the forces of globalization affected the garment industry and thus the livelihood of many Puerto Rican women, a situation that was further complicated by the discrimination they suffered at the hands of ILGWU officials. Many of the women who lost their jobs after the 1960s had little choice but to join the ranks of the unemployed or sub-employed in New York City.

Ortiz has also provided important bibliographic compendiums for the field of Puerto Rican women's history. This is an important area of historical endeavor, particularly for training new generations of scholars and researchers, and it has been dangerously neglected. Ortiz has collected biographical materials regarding leading women in New York's Puerto Rican community, whom she refers to as "pioneers."[66] Finally, Ortiz has attempted to disseminate the results of the exchange programs between female scholars in Puerto Rico and New York in scholarly journals such as the *Journal of Women's Studies*.[67]

A team of scholars at the Center for Puerto Rican Studies has been active in documenting the responses of Puerto Rican women to issues of welfare, poverty, and education. A study by Rina Benmayor, Rosa M. Toruellas, and Ana L. Juarbe has shown the importance of cultural analysis and qualitative research in assessing and formulating public policy decisions about poverty and welfare programs.[68] The authors fight the dominant paradigms that have been applied to study poor Puerto Rican women—one being the "culture of poverty" and the other the "urban underclass" model—and suggest that the women in their study operate under a set of practices which "affirm the right to equal participation in the society through the right to cultural difference."[69] One of their most important methodological tools for this study was oral histories or testimonies from the women attending the literacy classes offered by the Center. Another scholar, Elizabeth Crespo, has also employed oral histories to write about the experiences of Puerto Rican women in New York City.[70] Crespo's research shows that certain topics, such as the often contradictory cultural messages used by Puerto Rican women to survive in the United States, lend themselves to oral history methodology not only because it places the subject at the center of the analysis, but also because it has the potential for capturing the nuances of social life more so than quantitative analysis.

Although their work has not focused on women or on gender issues, the studies by Ruth Glasser and Carmen Whalen contain sections dedicated to these matters. Glasser's *My Music Is My Flag,* for example, analyzes the important role of Victoria Hernández, sister of the famous musician and composer Rafael Hernández, as a music broker, record-shop owner, and financier among Puerto Rican musicians in New York City in the interwar period.[71] Glasser suggests that women might have performed supportive roles for their husbands, brothers, and sons, but not necessarily in the traditional ways often assumed in the literature. Hernández ran an aggressive recording, record shop, musician-contracting business that allowed her more bohemian brother to become a star in the ethnic music business. History, of course, has told us little about Victoria but plenty about Rafael. Carmen Whalen's dissertation, on the other hand, traces the history of the Puerto Rican community in Philadelphia after World War II.[72] Whalan's work, one of the few historical studies of Puerto Rican settlements after the war, contains several sections regarding the job opportunities open to Puerto Rican women. Many women worked as domestics or in agricultural farms in nearby New Jersey and later jumped to Philadelphia in the 1940s. As Philadelphia's sexually segregated postwar labor market provided more opportunities to women than to men, Puerto Rican women came directly from the Island to take advantage of job opportunities, particularly in the garment and food-processing industries.[73]

The 1990s has also been marked by a challenge to the epistemological and theoretical questions that have guided women's history and women's studies. Not only did gender studies acquire strength as a discipline, particularly as a result of the theoretical and methodological insights from authors such as Joan Scott, but also post-structuralist and postmodern concerns began to challenge some of the unitary propositions of "sisterhood." The way in which systems of knowledge about sexual difference are constructed, reproduced, maintained, challenged, and modified is one of the central interests of gender studies. As such, women are only part of the equation, and the construction of concepts of masculinity, for instance, is as important as the construction of concepts of femininity or womanhood. Although there has been collaboration and overlapping between scholars in gender studies and women's studies, there have also been some tensions and disagreements. Many defenders of women's studies are suspicious of the agenda behind gender studies because they fear that the centrality of women will be diluted and the historical oppression experienced by women will be trivialized.[74] For the more theoretically driven scholars of gender studies, gender should become an important category of historical analysis.

Although postmodern methodologies and theoretical insights have made profound and significant inroads in the current social science and literary criticism literature regarding women and/or gender issues, Puerto Rican historians, in general, have been reluctant to incorporate postmodernism into their work. Some important exceptions to this trend are the works by Eileen Findlay, Gladys Jiménez-Muñoz, and Silvia Álvarez Curbelo. Their work follows in the classic pattern of interdisciplinarity—with influences from gender and cultural studies—

that has characterized the field of women's studies since its inception. Findlay and Jiménez-Muñoz show clear signs of influence by the scholarship emerging from subaltern studies with their particular emphasis on new configurations of nationalism and national identity, the development of ambivalent narratives and ideological representations, the interplay between sexuality, racism, and colonialism, and the shifting terrain of contested hegemonies.

Among the historians of Puerto Rican women in the United States there has been little interest in adopting or exploring postmodern methodology or theory. The emphasis on working-class history, in this case of female workers, continues to dominate the field. There has been some overlapping, nevertheless, with the field of cultural studies, a field of great interest and growth among the scholars of the Puerto Rican diaspora.

Where Do We Go from Here?

Even though we might not know much more about the lives of Puerto Rican women today than we did three decades ago, there can be little doubt that the field of women's studies, in its more traditional form or in connection with the developing field of gender studies, has contributed significantly to the historiography of Puerto Rico and of Puerto Ricans in the United States. The work on the struggle for women's suffrage, for example, has injected new insights into the debates on the volatile political situation of the early twentieth century. Research on the roles female migrants played in Puerto Rican communities in New York City has also shattered some commonly held perceptions about the Puerto Rican experience in that city. Still, the historical knowledge base regarding women's lives and experiences in Puerto Rico and in the diaspora remains small. No matter where new theoretical insights from gender studies or postmodernism might take Puerto Rican historiography, it is important to continue paying attention to the historical experiences of women per se, and to continue to expand the knowledge about women in Puerto Rico's history. The momentum gained over the past three decades must continue. Having said this, what are future areas of research or inquiry?

Clearly, more historical work is needed. There is no excuse for the discipline's poor performance in comparison to other disciplines, particularly when there are so many areas in which more historical research and analysis are required. We know little, for instance, about the lives of Puerto Rican women in the Spanish colonial period (sixteenth through nineteenth centuries) or about how constructions of femininity and masculinity were organized, defined, and transformed through that time. Since contraband, for example, played such a vital role in the Island's economy during that period, the roles women played in that economy need to be explored.

Even less is known about women who lived outside the urban enclaves in the sixteenth through nineteenth centuries, as most research focuses on towns and cities such as Arecibo, Ponce, Mayagüez, and San Juan. The recent work by David Stark, for example, regarding the role women played in the family survival strategies of slaves in eighteenth-century Caguas, Cayey, San Germán, and Yauco shows the kind of innovative research that can be done with demographic and parish records.[75] There is also little knowledge about important female institutions of the Spanish colonial period, such as convents, which have provided important perspectives on the lives of women in other Latin American countries.[76] The role of the Carmelite convent in Old San Juan in the social, cultural, and economic life of the colony, for example, awaits historical scrutiny.

For the twentieth century, historians can take advantage of the growing social science literature coming out of women's studies, which has paid considerable attention to issues such as the incorporation of women into the labor force, the effects of industrialization upon women and the role played by women in that industrialization, the role of women in the postindustrial society and their connections to the welfare state, the feminization of poverty, the participation of women's work in development strategies, and the participation and leadership of women in political and community organizations.[77] Many of these social science studies continue to rely on outdated and/or incomplete data regarding the historical experiences of Puerto Rican women. Historians can rely on this body of literature to carve out their own investigations or, even better, to join with other scholars to create truly integrated, interdisciplinary teams that can better decipher complex phenomena and problems.

The list of research topics in the twentieth century is so extensive that I will only point out some of the ones connected the recent trends of Puerto Rico's historiography. For instance, given Puerto Rico's historical military importance—from the Spanish walled garrison mentality to the more contemporary U.S. presence in bases and economic power—the role of women in that militarization and the gendered dimensions of that militarization are in need of serious scholarly attention. How have women responded, participated in, been affected by, and resisted the military roles that Spanish and U.S. colonialism have imposed on Puerto Rico and on Puerto Ricans? What have been the quotidian experiences of women living near military garrisons or bases? In recent years, how has life fared for Puerto Rican women living on military bases? How has the military treated its female employees? These and many additional questions would enhance current scholarly attention given to the importance of militarization in Puerto Rico's history.

There is also need for better historical studies of the struggles faced by marginalized communities in Puerto Rico. One such group, for example, is the women active in the informal economy, who have often been neglected by studies that use more restrictive definitions of the meaning of "work." What is the history of the women who participate in the informal economies in the United States and on the Island? How has their participation helped or affected their survival strategies? Immigrant women are also a group that we know little about. Puerto Rico has received immigrants from many parts of the world, but especially from other parts of the Caribbean. Although sociologists and anthropologists have documented the main trends of current migratory flows of Cuban and Dominican migrants, for example, we know little about the experiences of the women—who comprise a considerable number of the migrants—in these immigrant communities. There are other marginalized communities, such as lesbians, prostitutes, and inmates, for example, which need more historical attention.

Working-class women have received considerable attention from those writing about Puerto Rican women, particularly in the 1970s and 1980s. Less attention has been given to the historical formation of professional women in the United States and on the Island, with the exception perhaps of the research by Sánchez Korrol and an essay by Barceló Miller on female lawyers.[78] What is the history of Puerto Rican lawyers, nurses, teachers, doctors, dentists, engineers, social workers, and other professionals? What has been the historical process of the feminization of some professions, such as nursing, social work, and teaching? The Puerto Rican middle class is an influential one, and more needs to be known about the women of the professional classes.

It is important to continue research in areas where innovative ground-breaking has been accomplished. Clearly, the new studies from Jiménez-Muñoz and Barceló Miller regarding the suffrage movement will generate new thinking regarding the political struggles of feminist groups and the political climate in Puerto Rico after the 1930s. It would be fascinating to examine the similarities and discontinuities with the second-wave feminists of the 1960s and their efforts on behalf of the political empowerment of women. Comparing Puerto Rico's suffrage experience with that of other colonial Caribbean islands might also yield insightful perspectives. Another line of research that needs to continue is the analysis of the relationship between power, sexuality, and politics initiated by Findlay. One initial step would be to see how her findings in Ponce compare with the situation in other areas in Puerto Rico. Furthermore, if Findlay is correct about sexuality getting politicized in conjunctures of crisis, it would be fruitful to explore the struggle over women's sexuality during the political reign of the PPD in the 1950s and 1960s.

Several other research areas could see more integration and growth. One such area is comparative work with other Caribbean societies. Even when some authors have tried to engage the historiographical literature of the Caribbean, this has not been done in a systematic way. Puerto Rico lacks the monographic studies of women and slavery that have been so important in other Caribbean literature. There have not been attempts to explore how several important themes in our women's history—such as the suffrage movement, the impact of industrialization, the effects of colonialism, the experience of women as a result of migration, and others—compare with similar occurrences in neighboring Caribbean countries. In the rest of the Caribbean, for example, there has been a boom in the publication of women's biographies.[79] Unfortunately, this has not been the case in Puerto Rico, even when the genre of biographies and memoirs has blossomed there in the last decade.[80]

The examples provided above have focused mostly, although not entirely, on topics relevant to the Island's experience. The status of the history of Puerto Rican communities in the United States is almost in a state of crisis, given the lack of historians, Puerto Rican or not, engaged in this kind of work. As a result, the history of Boricua women in the diaspora has also suffered. Although more work regarding the situation of women in New York City is required, one area that requires immediate attention is research about the lives and the experiences of Puerto Rican women in other U.S. cities, such as Chicago, Philadelphia, Hartford, Newark, Orlando, and Boston, and in rural agricultural communities in Ohio, New Jersey, Michigan, Pennsylvania, and Connecticut, for example.

One potential area of research involves the roles played by Puerto Rican women in defining their cultural and ethnic identity in the United States. This is one topic where the field of Puerto Rican Studies could benefit from the work of the Chicano/a and African-American communities. In the case of other Latin American–origin communities in the United States, scholars are debating the emergence of Hispanic and Latino identities in general terms, and of Mexican, and Chicano identities in particular.[81] A recent study by George Sánchez documenting the evolution of Mexican-American identity in Los Angeles during the first four decades of the twentieth century could serve as a model.[82] Sánchez's book demonstrates, for example, the way in which Mexican-American women participated in this evolution and how, at times, they were specifically targeted by state officials in overt Americanization campaigns. Similar historical studies about the evolution of Puerto Rican identity in the United States, with regional variations, and the participation of women in that process would be of great scholarly value. In general terms, a more intense dialogue with the historical literature of other communities of color in the United States, particular those of the Mexican-Americans and the Cubans, would yield some valuable insights.

The role of women in politics, and the ways in which women define, understand, and manipulate politics, requires more historical research. Puerto Rican women have been crucial mobilizing forces in partisan and communitarian events in Boston, New York, and other cities.[83] How has that mobilizing role changed through time? If, for example, Carol Hardy-Fanta's research about Latina women in Boston applies to Puerto Rican women in other towns and cities, for instance, how did this gendered vision of politics and *lo político* develop historically? What historical events, if any, in each particular community help to explain gendered notions of politics and political participation?

These are just a few of the many possibilities for a future research agenda for Puerto Rican women's history. With such a broad potential agenda, I hope that this essay encourages current and future historians to incorporate the history of Puerto

Rican women into their research, and thus helps to enrich and transform the historiography of Puerto Rico and of its diaspora communities in the United States and elsewhere.

Notes

The author wishes to thank Ruth Glasser and Emilio Kourí for their feedback, close reading, and suggestions. The author is, of course, solely responsible for the article's contents.

1. Federico Ribes Tovar, *La mujer puertorriqueña: Su vida y evolución a través de la historia* (New York: Plus Ultra, 1972), 12.

2. See the following historiographical essays: María F. Barceló Miller, "La mujer en la literatura histórica puertorriqueña de Brau a la Generación del 40," *Revista del Instituto de Cultura Puertorriqueña* 97 (1987): 12–18; Olga Jiménez de Wagenheim, "The Puerto Rican Woman in the 19th Century: An Agenda for Research," *Revista/Review Interamerica* 11, no. 2 (1981): 196–203; Blanca G. Silvestrini, *Women and Resistance: Herstory in Contemporary Caribbean History: The 1989 Elsa Goveia Memorial Lecture* (Mona, Jamaica: Department of History, University of the West Indies, 1989); and Gladys Jiménez-Muñoz, "Rethinking the History of Puerto Rican Women's Suffrage," *Centro* 7, no. 1 (1995): 96–106. Although not a historiographical essay, also see Edna Acosta-Belén, "Puerto Rican Women in Culture, History and Society," in Edna Acosta-Belén, ed., *The Puerto Rican Woman: Perspectives on Culture, History and Society* (New York: Praeger, 2d edition, 1986), 1–29.

3. For a similar unflattering appraisal of the situation in the United States, see Ellen Carol Dubois et al., *Feminist Scholarship: Kindling in the Groves of Academe* (Urbana: University of Illinois Press, 1985), 163–70. Regarding the Caribbean, see Silvestrini, *Women and Resistance,* 3–4.

4. As examples of the debates regarding the definition of women's studies see, among others, Joan W. Scott, *Gender and the Politics of History* (New York: Columbia University Press, 1988), 1–50; and Diane Richardson and Victoria Robinson, eds., *Thinking Feminist: Key Concepts in Women's Studies* (New York: The Guilford Press, 1993).

5. Gabriel Ferrer, *La mujer en Puerto Rico: Sus necesidades presentes y los medios más fáciles y adecuados para mejorar su porvenir* (San Juan: Imprenta El Agente, 1881); and Ángela Negrón Muñoz, *Mujeres de Puerto Rico: Desde el primer siglo de colonización hasta el primer tercio del siglo XX* (San Juan: Imprenta Venezuela, 1935).

6. Barceló Miller, "La mujer en la literatura."

7. Ibid., 14.

8. Julio Ramos, ed., *Amor y anarquía: Los escritos de Luisa Capetillo* (Río Piedras: Ediciones Huracán, 1992).

9. For a historiographical assessment of their thematic repertoire, see María de los Ángeles Castro, "De Salvador Brau hasta la 'novísima' historia: Un replanteamiento y una crítica," *Op. Cit.* 4 (1988–89): 22–32.

10. Arturo Morales Carrión passed on these clichés from the travel literature in a book for a high school audience. See his *Historia del pueblo de Puerto Rico: Desde sus orígenes hasta el siglo XVIII* (San Juan: Editorial Cordillera, 5th edition, 1983), 251, 261. Kenneth Kipple has also alluded to the reference to women smokers as one of the clichés of the nineteenth-century travel literature in Cuba. See his *Blacks in Colonial Cuba, 1774–1899* (Gainesville: University of Florida, 1976), 13.

11. For the development of the field of Puerto Rican studies see Clara Rodríguez and

Virginia Sánchez Korrol, eds., *Historical Perspectives on Puerto Rican Survival in the United States* (Princeton: Marcus Wiener, 3d edition, 1996), vii–10.

12. For critiques of the "new history," see James Dietz, "Puerto Rico's New History," *Latin American Research Review* 19, no. 1 (1984): 210–22; Mariano Negrón Portillo and Raúl Mayo Santana, "Trabajo, producción y conflictos en el siglo XIX: Una revisión crítica de las nuevas investigaciones históricas en Puerto Rico," *Revista de Ciencias Sociales* 24, nos. 3–4 (1985): 469–96; Blanca G. Silvestrini, "Perspectivas de lo estudios históricos en Puerto Rico en la década de los setenta," *Cuadernos de la Facultad de Humanidades* 10 (1983): 25–54; Castro, "De Salvador Brau," 9–56; Gervasio L. García, *Historia crítica, historia sin coartadas: Algunos problemas de la historia de Puerto Rico* (Río Piedras: Ediciones Huracán, 1983); Arcadio Díaz-Quiñones, *La memoria rota* (Río Piedras: Ediciones Huracán, 1993); and Arturo Torrecilla, *El aspector posmoderno: Ecología, neoproletariado, intelligentsia* (San Juan: Publicaciones Puertorriqueñas, 1995), 83–148.

13. Some references to women in the works of the new historians include: Fernando Picó, *Libertad y servidumbre en el Puerto Rico del siglo XIX* (Río Piedras: Ediciones Huracán, 2nd edition, 1982), 107–10, 138, 170–73; Guillermo Baralt, *Esclavos rebeldes: Conspiraciones, y sublevaciones de esclavos en Puerto Rico (1795–1873)* (Río Piedras; Ediciones Huracán, 1982), 79, 158; and A.G. Quintero Rivera, "Socialist and Cigarmaker: Artisans' Proletarianization in the Makings of the Puerto Rican Working Class," *Latin American Perspectives* 10, nos. 2–3 (Spring–Summer 1983): 24–26.

14. Fernando Picó, "Las trabajadoras del tabaco en Utuado, Puerto Rico, según el censo de 1910," *Homines* 9, nos. 1–2 (1985): 269–82; and Blanca Silvestrini, "Women as Workers: The Experience of the Puerto Rican Woman in the 1930s," in Edna Acosta-Belén, ed., *The Puerto Rican Woman: Perspectives on Culture, History and Society* (New York: Praeger, 2d edition, 1986), 59–74; and Silvestrini, *Women and Resistance.*

15. See the preface to Jalil Sued-Badillo's *La mujer indígena y su sociedad* (Río Piedras: Editorial Cultural, 1979).

16. In the book's second edition (1986), of eleven essays six are of a historical nature and two historians, Blanca Silvestrini and Virginia Sánchez Korrol, were added to the list of contributors.

17. Edna Acosta-Belén, ed., *The Puerto Rican Woman* (New York: Praeger, 1st edition, 1979), vi.

18. For a review of Puerto Rico's version of the mode of production debate, see Gervasio Garcia's, *Historia crítica,* 51–52, 100–02.

19. Picó, "The History of Women's Struggle for Equality in Puerto Rico," in Acosta-Belén, *The Puerto Rican Woman* (1st edition), 33. This essay was published previously in 1976 in June Nash and Helen Safa, eds., *Sex and Class in Latin America* (New York: Praeger, 1976), 202–13.

20. Norma Valle Ferrer, "Feminism and Its Influence on Women's Organizations in Puerto Rico," in Acosta-Belén, *The Puerto Rican Woman* (1st edition), 38.

21. Yamila Azize, *La mujer en la lucha* (Río Piedras: Editorial Cultural, 1985), 8–9, 12–14, 166.

22. Ibid., 164–65.

23. Ibid., 165.

24. Norma Valle Ferrer, *Luisa Capetillo: Historia de una mujer proscrita* (Río Piedras: Editorial Cultural, 1990).

25. Ruth Gruber, *Felisa Rincón de Gautier: The Mayor of San Juan* (New York: Thomas Y. Crowell, 1972).

26. Federico Ribes Tovar, *Lolita Lebrón, la prisionera* (New York: Plus Ultra, 1972).

27. Most of the published work regarding the subject of sterilization was not done by

historians, but by demographers, sociologists, and anthropologists. See, for example, José Vázquez Calzada, "Female Sterilization in Puerto Rico," *Revista de Ciencias Sociales* 17, no. 3 (1973): 281–308; Carmen Guzmán, "La política de control poblacional y la mujer puertorriqueña," *Puerto Rican Journal of Human Rights* 2, no. 1 (1978): 78–84; and Harriet Presser, *Sterilization and Fertility Decline in Puerto Rico* (Los Angeles: Institute of International Studies, UCLA, 1973).

28. See, for example, Alice Colón et al., *Participación de la mujer en la historia de Puerto Rico (las primeras décadas del siglo veinte)* (Río Piedras: Centro de Investigaciones Sociales, Universidad de Puerto Rico–Río Piedras, 1986), 31–53; Yamila Azize, "The Roots of Puerto Rican Feminism: The Struggle for Universal Suffrage," *Radical America* 23, no. 1 (January–February 1989): 71–80; María F. Barceló Miller, "Voto, colonialismo y clase: La lucha por el sufragio femenino en Puerto Rico, 1896–1935" (Ph.D. diss., University of Puerto Rico–Río Piedras, 1993), recently published as *La lucha por el sufragio femenino en Puerto Rico, 1896–1935* (Río Piedras: Ediciones Huracán y Centro de Investigaciones Sociales, 1997); and Gladys M. Jiménez-Muñoz, " 'A Storm Dressed in Skirts': Ambivalence in the Debate on Women's Suffrage in Puerto Rico, 1927–29" (Ph.D. diss., State University of New York–Binghamton, 1994).

29. Rodríguez and Sánchez Korrol, eds., *Historical Perspectives,* xiv. For a comprehensive review of the origins and development of Puerto Rican Studies in the United States, see María Sánchez and Antonio Stevens Arroyo, eds., *Toward a Renaissance of Puerto Rican Studies: Ethnic and Area Studies in University Education* (Boulder, CO: Atlantic Research and Publications, 1987).

30. See Oscar Lewis, *La Vida: A Puerto Rican Family in the Culture of Poverty—San Juan and New York* (New York: Random House, 1966), and Nathan Glazer and Daniel Patrick Moynihan, *Beyond the Melting Pot* (Cambridge: MIT Press, 1970).

31. Center for Puerto Rican Studies, *Labor Migration under Capitalism: The Puerto Rican Experience* (New York: Monthly Review Press, 1979), 10.

32. César Andreu Iglesias, ed., *Memorias de Bernardo Vega* (Río Piedras: Ediciones Huracán, 1977).

33. Virginia Sánchez Korrol, "Survival of Puerto Rican Women in New York Before World War II," in Rodríguez and Sánchez Korrol, eds., *Historical Perspectives,* 57–67. Some of the material for that essay appeared in "On the Other Side of the Ocean: The Work Experiences of Early Puerto Rican Migrant Women," *Caribbean Review* 8, no. 1 (1979): 22–28.

34. See the relevant essays in Rodríguez and Sánchez Korrol, eds., *Historical Perspectives.* Also, Lourdes Miranda King, "Puertorriqueñas in the United States: The Impact of Double Discrimination," in Acosta-Belén, *The Puerto Rican Woman* (1979 edition), 124–33.

35. Marie Ramos Rosado, "El impacto filosófico del feminismo en las mujeres puertorriqueñas negras," *Onda apretada,* no. 1 (July–December 1996): 59.

36. *Homines* 10, no. 4 (February 1987); *Centro Bulletin* 2, no. 7 (Winter 1989–90).

37. Altagracia Ortiz, ed., *Puerto Rican Women and Work: Bridges in Transnational Labor* (Philadelphia: Temple University Press, 1996); and Alice Colón, ed., *Gender and Puerto Rican Women* (Río Piedras: Center for Social Research, University of Puerto Rico, 1994).

38. Rosa Santiago Marazzi, "La inmigración de mujeres españolas a Puerto Rico en el periodo colonial español," *Homines* 8, no. 1 (1984): 291–302.

39. Carlos Rodríguez Villanueva, "Guaynabo en 1860," *Anales de Investigación Históricos* 8, nos. 1–2 (1981): 127–62; and Gregorio Villegas, "Fluctuaciones de la población en Guaynabo en el periodo 1780–1830," *Anales de Investigación Históricos* 8, nos. 1–2 (1981): 90–126.

40. María F. Barceló Miller, "De la polilla a la virtud: Visión sobre la mujer de la Iglesia jerárquica de Puerto Rico," in Yamila Azize, ed. *La mujer en Puerto Rico: Ensayos de Investigación* (Río Piedras: Ediciones Huracán, 1987), 49–88.

41. See Fernando Picó, "Mitos y realidades en la historia de la familia puertorriqueña en la zona cafetalera en el siglo 19," *Homines* 7, nos. 1–2 (1983): 223–26; and F. Picó, "Las trabajadoras del tabaco," 269–82.

42. See Arlene J. Díaz Caballero, "Las trabajadoras asalariadas en Santurce, 1910," *Anales de Investigación Históricos* New Series 1 (1988): 1–119.

43. Mary F. Gallart, "Mujeres, aguja y política en el siglo 20 en Puerto Rico: Obdulia Velázquez de Lorenzo, alcaldesa de Guayama, 1952–56" (Ph.D. diss., University of Puerto Rico–Río Piedras, 1992).

44. Barceló Miller, "Voto, colonialismo y clase."

45. Ibid., xxxiii–xxxiv.

46. Jiménez-Muñoz, "'A Storm Dressed in Skirts.'"

47. Ibid., 434.

48. Most of the thematic agenda proposed by Jiménez de Wagenheim in her 1981 article regarding future research on nineteenth-century women has gone unanswered. See her "The Puerto Rican Woman in the 19th Century," 196–203.

49. See, as examples, Rhoda Reddock, "Women and Slavery in the Caribbean: A Feminist Perspective," *Latin American Perspectives* 12, no. 1 (1985): 63–80; and Hilary Beckles, "Sex and Gender in the Historiography of Caribbean Slavery," in Verene Shepherd et al., eds., *Engendering Caribbean History* (Kingston: Ian Randle, 1995), 125–40.

50. Mariano Negrón Portillo and Raúl Mayo Santana, *La esclavitud urbana en San Juan* (Río Piedras: Ediciones Huracán, 1992).

51. See my "Economy, Society and Urban Life: Women in Nineteenth Century San Juan, Puerto Rico (1820–1870)" (Ph.D. diss., Columbia University, 1994); and also, Ivette Pérez Vega, "Juana María Escobales, Liberta 'Liberada,'" *Homines* 11, nos. 1–2 (1988): 397–402.

52. See Ivonne Acosta Lespier, "Las esclavas de Mayagüez, 1872," *Cupey* 10, nos. 1–2 (1993): 106–18.

53. See my "Economy, Society and Urban Life: Women in Nineteenth Century San Juan, Puerto Rico (1820–1870)" (Ph.D. diss. Columbia University, 1994).

54. See, for example, Norma Valle Ferrer, "Primeros fermentos de lucha feminina en Puerto Rico," *Revista del Instituto de Cultura Puertorriqueña* 84 (1979): 15–19.

55. Matos Rodríguez, "Economy, Society," 264–308.

56. Eileen Findlay, "Domination, Decency and Desire: The Politics of Sexuality in Ponce, Puerto Rico 1870–1920" (Ph.D. diss., University of Wisconsin–Madison, 1995).

57. Findlay, "Domination, Decency and Desire," 14.

58. For examples of the characterization of working-class leaders as supportive of feminist ideals, see Azize, *La mujer en la lucha,* 69–78; and Quintero Rivera, "Socialist and Cigarmaker," 25–26.

59. Beckles, "Sex and Gender"; Bridget Brereton, "General Problems and Issues in Studying the History of Women," in Patricia Mohammed and Catherine Shepherd, eds., *Gender in Caribbean Development* (Mona, Jamaica: Women and Development Studies Project, University of the West Indies, 1988), 125–43; and Patricia Mohammed, "The Negotiation of Gender Relations among Indian Men and Women in Post-Indenture Trinidad Society, 1917–47," in Shepherd et al., eds., *Engendering Caribbean History,* 20–47.

60. Ruth Glasser, "En Casa en Connecticut: Towards a Historiography of Puerto Ricans Outside of New York," *Centro* 7, no. 1 (1995): 53.

61. Virginia Sánchez Korrol, *From Colonia to Community: The History of Puerto Ricans in New York City* (Berkeley: University of California Press, 1983 [1996, 2d edition]).

62. Ibid., 2d edition, 114.

63. Virginia Sánchez Korrol, "The Forgotten Migrant: Educated Puerto Rican Women in New York City, 1920–1940," in Acosta Belén, *The Puerto Rican Woman* (2d edition), 173–74.

64. Virginia Sánchez Korrol, "Toward Bilingual Education: Puerto Rican Women Teachers in New York City Schools, 1947–1967." In Altagracia Ortiz, ed., *Puerto Rican Women and Work: Bridges in International Labor* (Philadelphia: Temple University Press, 1996), 82–104.

65. Altagracia Ortiz, "'En la aguja y el pedal eché la hiel': Puerto Rican Women in the Garment Industry of New York City, 1920–1980," in Ortiz, *Puerto Rican Women and Work*, 55–81.

66. Altagracia Ortiz, "The Lives of Pioneras: Bibliographic and Research Sources on Puerto Rican Women in the U.S.," *Bulletin Centro de Estudios Puertorriqueños* 2, no. 7 (Winter 1989–90): 40–47.

67. Altagracia Ortiz, "Women's Studies Conference in Puerto Rico," *Journal of Women's Studies* 1, no. 2 (Fall 1989): 179–81.

68. See their *Responses to Poverty among Puerto Rican Women; Identity, Community and Cultural Citizenship* (New York: Centro de Estudios Puertorriqueños, 1992).

69. Ibid., 3. This practice is defined by the authors as cultural citizenship.

70. Elizabeth Crespo, "Puerto Rican Women: Migration and Changes in Gender Roles," in Rina Benmayor and Andor Skotnes, eds., *Migration and Identity* (Oxford: Oxford University Press, 1994), 137–50.

71. Ruth Glasser, *My Music Is My Flag: Puerto Rican Musicians and Their New York Communities: 1917–1940* (Berkeley: University of California Press, 1995), 106–10, 144–49.

72. Carmen Whalen, "Puerto Rican Migration to Philadelphia, PA, 1945–1970: A Historical Perspective on a Migrant Group" (Ph.D. diss., Rutgers University, 1994).

73. Ibid., 263–66, 314–25.

74. Victoria Robinson, "Introducing Women's Studies," in Diane Richardson and Victoria Robinson, eds., *Thinking Feminist: Key Concepts in Women's Studies* (New York: Guilford Press, 1993), 23–24.

75. David Stark, "Discovering the Invisible Puerto Rican Slave Family: Demographic Evidence from the Eighteenth Century," *Journal of Family History* 21, no. 4 (October · 1996): 395–418.

76. See, for example, Asunción Lavrin's, "Female Religious," in Louisa Hoberman and Susan Socolow, eds., *Cities and Society in Colonial Latin America* (Albuquerque: University of New Mexico Press, 1986), 165–95.

77. Some examples of this literature include Heidi Figueroa-Sarriera et al., eds., *Más allá de la bella (in)diferencia: Revisión post-feminista y otras escrituras posibles* (San Juan: Publicaciones Puertorriqueñas, 1994); María del Carmen Baerga, ed., *Género y trabajo: La industria de la aguja en Puerto Rico y el Caribe hispánico* (Río Piedras: Editorial de la Universidad de Puerto Rico, 1993); Lydia M. Gónzalez García, *Una puntada en el tiempo: La industria de la aguja en Puerto Rico (1900–1929)* (San Juan: CEREP, 1990); Cynthia T. García Coll and María de Lourdes Mattei, eds., *The Psychosocial Development of Puerto Rican Women* (New York: Praeger, 1989); Margarita Ostalaza Bey, *Política sexual en Puerto Rico* (Río Piedras: Ediciones Huracán, 1989); and Margarita Fernández Olmos, *Sobre la literatura puertorriqueña de aqui y de allá: Aproximaciones feministas* (Santo Domingo: Editora Alfa y Omega, 1989).

78. María F. Barceló Miller, "Estrenando togas: La profesionalización de la mujer en Puerto Rico, 1900–1930," *Revista del Instituto de Cultura* 99 (1992): 58–70.

79. Among some of the recent biographies of notable women in the Caribbean are Francis W. Blackman, *Dame Nita: Caribbean Woman, World Citizen* (Kingston: Ian

Randle, 1995); Janet Higbie, *Eugenia: The Caribbean's Iron Lady* (London: Macmillan, 1993); and Lizabeth Paravisini-Gebert, *Phyllis Shand Allfrey: A Caribbean Life* (New Brunswick, NJ: Rutgers University Press, 1996).

80. There has been a recent surge in memoirs in Puerto Rico, but only a few about women—Nilita Vientós Gastón and Rosario Ferré, among them—have been published. A rare autobiography of a *jíbara* was also recently published, Carmen Luisa Justiniano, *Con valor y a como dé lugar: Memorias de un jíbara puertorriqueña* (Río Piedras: Editorial de la Universidad de Puerto Rico, 1994).

81. This literature is becoming quite vast. See, as examples, Félix Padilla, *Latino Ethnic Consciousness: The Case of Mexican-Americans and Puerto Ricans in Chicago* (Notre Dame, IN: University of Notre Dame Press, 1987); and Virginia Sánchez Korrol, "Latinismo among Early Puerto Rican Migrants in New York City: A Socio-Economic Interpretation," in Edna Acosta-Belén and Barbara R. Sjostrom, eds., *The Hispanic Experience in the United States* (New York: Prager 1986), 170–79.

82. George Sánchez, *Becoming Mexican American: Ethnicity, Culture and Identity in Chicano Los Angeles, 1900–1945* (New York: Oxford University Press, 1993).

83. Carol Hardy-Fanta, *Latina Politics, Latino Politics* (Philadelphia: Temple University Press, 1992).

2

Puerto Rican Women Workers in the Twentieth Century: A Historical Appraisal of the Literature

Altagracia Ortiz

Introduction

The labor of women has been tied to the economic development of Puerto Rico and to developments within the capitalist system both on the island and in the United States mainland since the early 1900s. Yet we still lack a general histori-cal analysis that recognizes the contributions of Puerto Rican women workers (Puertorriqueñas) to economic developments in Puerto Rico or to the evolution of U.S. capitalism in the twentieth century. One major reason for this historio-graphic problem is the limited number of monographs dealing with women's experiences in particular industries or during specific periods. In the last two decades, however, scholars from different disciplines, both on the island and the states, have begun to document the lives of wage-earning Puertorriqueñas in the twentieth century. An appraisal of this literature now enables us to historically establish the connections between women's work and economic transformations in Puerto Rico, clarify the role of Puerto Rican women workers in the constant reconfigurations of the capitalist system in the mainland, evaluate the effects of capitalism on Puerto Rican women workers' lives, and appreciate more pro-foundly the responses of women to capitalist structures and processes on the island and the mainland.[1]

A historical exploration of the literature on women workers in Puerto Rico and of Puertorriqueñas in the states can also serve as the basis for a comparative analysis of women's work in two different political and economic contexts. In Puerto Rico between 1900 and 1952, women's wage work evolved within the confines of U.S. congressional policies enacted for the colony of Puerto Rico and in response to the economic interests of U.S. entrepreneurs who made the island their own private domain. Thus, Puerto Rican women were incorporated into the island's labor market as *colonial subjects* of the United States, and into industries—mainly tobacco and needlework—that were an extension of mainland businesses. Since 1952, even though the island was granted a new political status (El Estado Libre Asociado, or Commonwealth of Puerto Rico), the Puerto Rican government and labor market (and other aspects of its economy) have been so tightly controlled by U.S. legislation and business interests that Puerto Rican women's work has continued to evolve within a political and economic framework that some still classify as "colonialist."[2] Meanwhile, the transformations that Puerto Rico has experienced as a territory of the United States in this century have led to a series of migration cycles that encouraged a large number of women workers to look for work in the states. Here, on the mainland, migrant women from Puerto Rico presumably had the blessings of *full* American citizenship; but, the testimonies of many migrant women leave a record of racial and gender discrimination and exploitation that often mirrors that of other women of color in the United States.

A comparative analysis of the literature on Puertorriqueñas working on the island and the mainland also helps break the dichotomy that in traditional scholarship has fragmented the lives of Puertorriqueños into two seemingly separate realities—that is, the *island experience* and the *mainland experience*—and attempts to present a more unified and comprehensive vision of the history of Puerto Ricans in the twentieth century. The need for this kind of an approach in historical analyses was first noted by Manuel Maldonado Denis in *Puerto Rico y Estados Unidos: Emigración y colonialismo: Un análisis socio-histórico de la emigración puertorriqueña* (1979) when he suggested that scholars take into consideration the entire Puerto Rican community, including *emigrantes* (migrants), in their investigations.[3] This unified approach was essential to an understanding of the Puerto Rican people because, he pointed out,

> the Puerto Rican working class is in fact the object of a double oppression that has no geographic escape. This exploitation goes on both in Puerto Rico and in the metropolis, like the two faces of the same social reality. In Puerto Rico under a system whose necessary consequences are unemployment, marginalization and emigration; and in the United States, under a capitalist society where racism assigns the Puerto Rican workers to the "bottom of the social ladder."[4]

Thus, this essay expects to create a historical framework that not only presents a more holistic view of the work experiences of Puerto Rican women, but invites a comparative reflection on the lives of workers whose histories have been intrinsically connected to developments within the United States capitalist system both in Puerto Rico and in the mainland United States since 1900.

The Literature on Women Workers under Early Colonialism

In Puerto Rico, several studies have noted that the 1898 United States takeover of the island resulted in the expansion of colonial economic interests that incorporated large numbers of women into the insular paid labor force.[5] Some studies indicate, however, that long before American capitalism began to transform Puerto Rico's economy, Puertorriqueñas were already involved in the production and service sectors of the island as a colony of Spain.[6] The works of Luis Díaz Soler and Guillermo Baralt, for example, point out that until the abolition of slavery in 1872, as in other slave societies, enslaved black women were found among field workers, planting and harvesting coffee, sugar, and other products, and as household servants, cooking, caring for children, sewing, washing and ironing clothes, and cleaning the master's or mistress's house.[7] Before and after 1872, as Olga Wagenheim and others note, free black women, as well as other white and racially mixed *jornaleras* (wage-workers), earned their livelihood by also doing domestic service, selling home-prepared foods and candies, or working in the fields for agricultural *hacendados*.[8] Some sources note that women continued to work as farm hands in plantation agriculture (e.g., on coffee plantations) well until the end of the nineteenth century. But analyses of the first United States employment survey (derived from the 1899 census of Puerto Rico) by Marcia Rivera and Yamila Azize indicate that at the dawn of U.S. colonial capitalist economy in Puerto Rico, women were concentrated in jobs that were simply an extension of their female roles in the home: there were some 18,453 domestics; 16,855 laundresses; and 5,785 seamstresses.[9] There were few *talleres* (workshops or factories) on the island at this time, and so the census of 1899 records only sixty operators, and these were found exclusively in the tobacco industry. The census did record the presence of women in the teaching (563), nursing (64), and sales (25) occupations, and in the straw-hat-making industry (387); but no women were recorded among office, needle, garment, and public service workers. Yet, by 1930 women were more than visible in these new expanding job categories: there were 2,500 office workers; 3,635 needleworkers; 6,383 garment workers. Additionally, there were now some 9,290 tobacco factory operators; 4,254 teachers; 34,345 seamstress; 921 nurses; 828 sales "girls"; and 691 straw-hat makers.[10] In contrast, by the same year the majority of the male labor force had been channeled into the sugar cane production that came to dominate the island's economy in the first three decades of United States rule in Puerto Rico.[11] The literature on Puerto Rican women's work during this period clearly points out that the incorporation of women into Puerto Rico's colonial labor force created a sex-segregated labor market that saw the rise of "female occupations," many of which were directly related to the needs of United States colonial capitalism on the island, and many of which have historically exploited women's work in the twentieth century.

The literature on Puerto Rican women workers during this early period indicates that the two U.S. industries that most starkly illustrate the gendered divisions, segregation, and deplorable employment conditions affecting women workers in Puerto Rico at the time were tobacco and needlework. In the tobacco industry, as the work of Amilcar Tirado Avilés so poignantly illustrates, thousands of women worked excruciatingly long hours, for extremely low wages, under dangerous health conditions as leaf-strippers, sorters, and packers, while men usually were employed in the more skilled trade of cigar-making, consequently earning higher wages.[12] On the other hand, the historical analyses of Fernando Picó discovered that many of the women who first entered the tobacco industry were young, unmarried, and daughters still living at home, and perhaps because of this, they brazenly challenged the oppression they experienced in this industry by demanding that the male-led Unión de Tabaqueros (Tobacco Workers' Union) organize and represent them, and by participating in strikes and other work actions against the American tobacco companies that exploited their labor.[13] One of their most vocal supporters was the energetic, socialist-feminist Luisa Capetillo, a *lectora* (reader) in cigar-making factories in Puerto Rico and the United States, who fought for their rights not only as workers but as women. As the biographical studies by Norma Valle Ferrer demonstrate, from 1905 until her death in 1922, Capetillo mobilized women workers in Puerto Rico, Tampa (Florida), and New York City, demanding their equal economic, legal, and political integration into society.[14] By 1919 Capetillo and tobacco activists had won a minimum-wage law from the island's legislators, but the gains expected under this law were soon nullified by precipitous declines in the cigar-making industry caused by cigarette competition from the North American south in the following decade. During the early 1920s, however, some women continued to work as leaf processors for the export trade, yet hundreds of others lost their jobs. Increasingly, as the decade enfolded, Puertorriqueñas looking for work emigrated to the United States or sought work in the needle trades, an industry equally notorious for its exploitation of women.

In their research, Lydia Milagros González and Luisa Hernández Angueira have discovered that this exploitation began almost immediately after the United States occupation and involved the collaboration of national entrepreneurs.[15] Working together with foreign investors, native entrepreneurs, or *comisionistas* (contractors) as they were known in Puerto Rico, transformed this simple island-industry into one of the United States' major colonial enterprises after World War I. González writes that as early as 1905, for example, Brígida Román and María Luisa Arcely, two of the best-known *comisionistas,* began selling home-made workers' *calados* (finely embroidered and laced linens) and crochet pieces to the stewardesses and passengers of the United States–owned Puerto Rico

Steamship Company vessels that stopped at the ports of San Juan and Mayagüez. Soon, they were joined by North American white women, who saw in the export needle-trade an acceptable business for their gender, and by religious humanitarians and public school educators, desirous of teaching needle skills to destitute women in order to prevent "immorality" and idleness among the poor. By the 1920s these various interests had succeeded in influencing the colonial Department of Public Instruction in San Juan to implement a needlework curriculum that trained female pupils in the few public schools scattered across the island. Thus, when the needle-trade between Europe and the United States was interrupted by World War I commercial blockades, Puerto Rican and North American intermediaries were ready to deliver a highly skilled needlework labor force to larger mainland entrepreneurs who greatly expanded the export trade in the next decade.[16]

As the demands of a more aggressive needle-trade market increased in the 1920s, native entrepreneurial shops sprang up in urban centers (e.g., Mayagüez, San Juan, Ponce), easily drawing for their labor force upon the growing number of unemployed urban tobacco workers and rural women migrating from the nearby countryside—including those who had lost their jobs due to decreases in tobacco agricultural production. A few of these shops came to employ a sizable population (four had about one thousand workers); most were just small producers, averaging about two hundred to three hundred workers. But, as the island's economy worsened in the late 1920s and 1930s, shop owners increasingly acted as intermediaries for the fast-growing home needlework trades. According to González, by 1935 there were an estimated 49,714 women working at home. However, she believes this figure, taken from the 1935 census, is much too conservative in light of the fact that almost all home needleworkers had relatives or other women helping them in the production of garments. If we add one assistant to each of the workers recorded by the census, she argues, we arrive at close to 100,000 workers who were employed by the needlework industry at the height of the Great Depression in Puerto Rico. Increases in the number of workers raised production between 1935 and 1939 to almost $14.7 million, the highest level of production in the history of the industry in Puerto Rico.[17]

These were the years of greatest exploitation of women needleworkers on the island, too. The 1933 investigation of conditions in the industry by Caroline Manning showed that *comisionistas* often tricked women out of their meager wages by charging exorbitant commissions, sometimes as high as 50 percent of their earnings; others paid workers in kind (e.g., shoes, groceries).[18] Consequently, home needleworkers' wages never rose above survival levels since most women earned only a penny or two an hour (about a dollar a day). Yet, needleworkers in Puerto Rico continued to slave over their bundles of garments throughout the 1930s, using just a needle and thread or a tiny sewing machine, in dingy *bohíos* (shacks) to support their families. In spite of the centrality of labor to the Puerto Rican economy and to the survival of their families during this period of economic crisis, María del Carmen Baerga found that women saw their wages only as "something extra," as a *complement to the supposed primary income of the male head of household.*[19]

Baerga adds:

> What they did not see, though, was that ... their skills as needleworkers represented a great source of accumulation for the North American companies, which paid one and two cents per hour for the production of commodities later sold as luxury ones and that ... they were subsidizing capital in a double way. On the one hand, while being the ones responsible for the domestic tasks within the household, they performed an amount of unpaid labor necessary for [male] workers to come back every morning ready to work. Further, while contributing with a 'little extra' cash to the household, they not only sustained low wages in other industries [i.e., sugar] but actually assumed the responsibility for the reproduction of the male workers during periods of unemployment and underemployment.[20]

Because needlework was so essential for the survival of the Puerto Rican household during this period, women hesitated to engage in labor struggles that might jeopardize the existence of this industry on the island. Nevertheless, Blanca Silvestrini records the organization of some 3,000 home workers into nine unions by the Federación Libre de Trajadores in 1934.[21] She also notes the presence of unemployed needleworkers in a major strike that took place in Mayagüez in November of the same year when the National Recovery Act (NRA) was applied to Puerto Rico. The NRA, a New Deal government measure passed in 1933 to stabilize the mainland economy, contained some 120 codes that regulated or eliminated many paid homework activities in the United States. The law was applied to Puerto Rico in July 1934 because of mainland clothing manufacturers' fears concerning the great differentials in wages and production processes that existed between the North American and island needle-trades. Regulating the needlework industry in Puerto Rico, therefore, became essential for the survival of certain sectors of the manufactured clothes industry in the states; but, for Puerto Rico, stringent regulation or complete elimination of the needle-trades, especially homework, at this time would have spelled disaster. Thus, Puerto Rican needleworkers demanded that both shop and home needlework be continued, but that the industry be regulated in order to guarantee the workers better work conditions and higher wages. In her study of the application of the NRA in Puerto Rico, Eileen Boris illustrates how, despite differences regarding gender roles and women's right to work, needleworkers established a coalition consisting of local officials, shop workers, and owners, some union leaders, and homeworkers, which succeeded in getting the federal government to create a special code for Puerto Rico.[22] The code called for a minimum wage of five dollars for shop workers; three dollars for home needleworkers; registration of *comisionistas* to safeguard against abuses; the determination of fair piece-rates by commissions; the abolition of some needlecraft processes (e.g., cutting, stamping, and washing); and an investigation of the possibility of establishing communal needlework centers in the future. Thus, the special NRA code for Puerto Rico enabled the needlework industry to continue to operate on the island, but, as Boris notes, this code did not succeed in eliminating abuses in the trade. After 1945 the needlework industry entered an accelerated period of decline, and has almost disappeared as a result of the introduction of modern clothing factories since the 1950s.[23]

The Literature on Women Migrant Workers

Accompanying the integration of women into the U.S. colonial economy in Puerto Rico during the first three decades of the twentieth century was the beginning of a labor migration process that likewise resulted in the incorporation of Puerto Rican migrant women into important sectors of the mainland economy. During these early years Puertorriqueñas mainly emigrated to New York City and, as in Puerto Rico, they soon became a source of cheap labor for the city's needle and garment trades. In the 1930s, Lawrence Chenault observed that Puerto Rican women were mostly found in the home needlework industries, which at this time included—in addition to piecework in blouses, handkerchiefs, and undergarments and the embroidery and crocheting of linens and garments— the decoration of lamps and flower-making.[24] Although home-needlework wages were slightly higher in New York than on the island, conditions in the industry were no different: migrant Puerto Rican women spent long hours after their house chores were done, finishing hundreds of garments for a few dollars a week in order to make ends meet. By the late 1940s, however, the International Ladies' Garment Workers' Union (ILGWU) campaigns against homework and the brief post–World War II expansion of the clothing trades had begun to harness the labor of migrating Puertorriqueñas into garment factories throughout the entire city. In my historical investigations I have explored the experiences of Puerto Rican women in these garment shops. At first glance, their experiences appear to duplicate the histories of past women workers in the industry.[25] Indeed, like earlier European immigrant women, Puerto Rican women experienced gender-segregated workplaces, low wages, deskilled jobs, and limited opportunities for advancement either in the trades or in their major labor organization, the ILGWU. And with African American women and other Hispanics in the trades, Puertorriqueñas shared a history of discrimination, not only because of their race but also because of their ethnicity.[26] In the case of Puerto Rican women, however, this gender and ethnic discrimination was compounded by increasing market and production changes that profoundly affected their lives, as the industry entered a period of modernization and globalization after the 1950s.

I therefore place the history of Puerto Rican garment workers in New York City within the context of an industry already rigidly stratified by gender, ethnicity, and race. But it is also important to place Puerto Rican women's work within the capital and labor market transformations that have affected the labor force participation of migrant Puertorriqueñas in this industry.[27] By the time migrant women from the island entered the city's garment industry in the 1920s, the gender divisions in the industry had been clearly established. With the expansion of the industry in the early 1900s, Jewish and Italian immigrant women, who constituted the bulk of the female labor force during these early years, had been assigned to do "women's work" in the trades. In the better coat and suit industries, this meant they usually only hemmed and sewed on buttons by hand; in the trades that were experiencing standardization (or piecework), such as the production of cheaper women's dresses and suits, children's wear, and underwear, women were the sewing-machine operators, cleaners, and packers, while men performed the designing, cutting, tailoring, and retailing operations. From 1920 to 1960, the most active years of Puerto Rican women's labor force participation in the garment trades, immigrant white women usually held the "women's jobs" in the better-paid shops. However, declines in white women's labor due to immigration restrictions imposed by World War I and the National Origins Act of 1924 opened up the medium- and lower-priced shops to Puertorriqueñas after 1920. By 1950 they were the essential labor force in the dress and skirt industries (the most standardized items of production in the city's shops), but were also present in blouse, children's wear, and underwear manufacturing.

Although Puerto Rican women encountered white-worker hostility in many of the shops, it was in the locals of the ILGWU, the largest of the clothing workers' organizations, that Puertorriqueñas came to feel the full impact of ethnic discrimination in the garment industry. In the 1930s and 1940s they had to wage a struggle with white union members for admission into Dressmakers' Local 22 and other low-wage locals, and in succeeding decades they never made it into the more prestigious locals—namely Cutters' Local 10 (still a male domain), the Italian Dressmakers' Local 89, or the Italian Cloakmakers' Local 48. When they joined other Hispanic workers in petitions to organize their own local, they were hastily dismissed by ILGWU leaders with the excuse that the creation of other-language locals would further splinter the union. Yet, the Italian locals were permitted to function uninterrupted, even after the number of Italian women had dwindled in the trades and, perhaps more surprisingly, after ethnic locals were declared illegal by the state in 1948. In the meantime, the top leadership of the ILGWU, in the hands of Jewish male workers (whose numbers also had declined considerably since they helped organize the union in 1900), controlled: all appointments to vacancies in the locals; an election process that denied nonincumbents equal access to workers in the shops and union newspapers; the distribution of union funds; and all decisions regarding contracts. This consistently patriarchal and undemocratic climate made it impossible for Puertorriqueñas, who constituted the bulk of the ILGWU membership after WW II, to confront the industrywide problems—especially those caused by technological and clothing style changes, foreign competition, and relocation of businesses to lower-wage areas—that eventually contributed to the decline of significant sectors (and hence their employment) in this industry in New York City in later decades.

Even though the literature on other Puerto Rican migrant women workers in New York City (or the United States for that matter) in the twentieth century is scanty, a few sources do cite the presence of Puertorriqueñas in the city's tobacco, confectionery, and meat-packing industries, as well as in domestic, laundry, and clerical services.[28] Recent studies have also located Puerto Rican migrant women among the city's professionals during these early years.[29] Two women stand out in these works: Pura Belpré, a librarian and author, and Carmela Zapata Marrero, a religious community organizer. Belpré, the subject of brief biographical studies by Lillian López and Virginia Sánchez Korrol, was a college-educated migrant who trained in library sciences in New York City and soon found employment in the city's public library system in 1924.[30] In succeeding decades she went on to recount Puerto Rican folktales in delightful children's books. The life of Marrero Zapata, or Sister Carmelita, as she is known in the Puerto Rican community, has also been explored by several scholars.[31] She was the first nun assigned by the Church to work among Hispanics in New York City. From 1923 to the early 1970s when she retired, Sister Carmelita developed and administered dozens of social and educational programs that enriched the lives of Puerto Rican children and adults.

Through their work in factories, their neighborhoods, and other places in the city, these and other early "pioneer" women contributed to the emergence of a Puerto Rican community that became a new home to thousands of Puertorriqueños who emigrated after World War II.[32] Most of these "newcomers" were blue-collar workers in search of better employment opportunities made possible by the postwar expansion of certain sectors of the United States economy (such as the garment industry in New York City, as noted above). Although an exact number of post-1945 Puerto Rican migrants to the states has been difficult to calculate, Adalberto López and James Petras estimate that

> between 1940 and 1950 an average of 18,700 Puerto Ricans migrated to the United States annually. In the decade of the 1950s the average rose to 41,200 per year, and in the 1960s it declined to an average of about 14,500 annually. In 1953 alone, when the migration reached its peak, about 69,000 Puerto Ricans left the island to settle in the United States mainland.[33]

Similarly, there are also no complete accounts of the number of children that came with these migrants, but by 1948 the Committee on Puerto Ricans in New York City of the Welfare Council of New York instructed the city's Department of Education to keep counts of the number of Puerto Rican children in its various school districts. In January of 1948: "There were 24,350 Puerto Rican children in the public schools of the five boroughs and about 5,000 in the parochial schools."[34] Because many of these children knew no English—the only language of instruction on the mainland at the time—in 1949 the New York City Board of Education created the position of a Spanish-speaking Substitute Auxiliary Teacher (SAT) to help integrate the new pupils into the city's school system.

Virginia Sánchez Korrol's investigations of the activities of SATs who taught in New York City between 1947 and 1967 indicate that although they were originally hired to teach English to Puerto Rican and other Spanish-speaking children in the elementary and intermediate grades, SATs quickly reconceptualized their role as Hispanic educators in the city.[35] First, they challenged the idea that the most effective way of teaching the English language to their pupils was through the "immersion method" (the use of English only in the classroom), maintaining that by using the Spanish and English languages simultaneously, the Puerto Rican migrant child would learn the English language faster and better. With the support of Puerto Rican community leaders and liberal educators throughout the city, SATs eventually developed bilingual and bicultural curriculum materials and implemented teaching pedagogies in their classrooms that Sánchez Korrol believes laid the foundation for bilingual and multicultural education in the United States. SATs also worked very closely with other community leaders on issues of great concern to Hispanics throughout the city. They struggled with the Board of Education for the employment of more Puerto Rican professionals in the school system and sought the licensure of bilingual teachers as "regular" staff members, not just as "substitutes." They contributed to the organizational life of the community by creating the Society of Puerto Rican Auxiliary Teachers, the Puerto Rican Educators' Association, and the SAT chapter of the United Federation of Teachers. Together with parents and other individuals in their school districts, SATs celebrated Hispanic cultural events, disseminated information on crucial topics, such as education and health, and engaged in empowerment struggles to better the lives of Hispanics in the United States. By illustrating the work of SATs in New York City Spanish-speaking *barriadas* (neighborhoods), Sánchez Korrol thus demonstrates the strong presence of working Puertorriqueñas in the construction of their communities in the United States.

Unfortunately, the story of the Puerto Rican SAT in New York City also serves as an example of the integration of educated women into what generally has been classified (both in the United States mainland and in Puerto Rico) as a "woman's profession." Since the 1830s, single women (and in later years married women) were readily granted teaching licenses in the states, but they were poorly paid in comparison to other professions. In Puerto Rico economic and social conditions under Spanish colonial rule denied women similar access to the teaching profession, but they, too, were present in some of the few public and private schools that existed on the island during the nineteenth century.[36] With the extension of the United States educational system to Puerto Rico after 1900, many more women were hired as teachers; by 1920 their numbers had jumped from 563 (as noted earlier) to 2,636.[37] Soon, as Marcia Rivera informs us, they became the majority of the teachers in the island's public school system, predominating most especially in the elementary school grades. Yet, as in the United States, women teachers until recently were paid less than their male counterparts, were not widely considered for supervisory or administrative positions, nor elected to school boards throughout the island.[38] Although most teachers' salaries have remained low in relation to other professionals' salaries—in both Puerto Rico and the United States—the teaching profession has continued to attract Puertorriqueñas. In 1980, in spite of a variety of other occupational opportunities generated by the island's postwar economy and society, over half of all professional women on the island were counted as teachers.[39] In the United States the institutionalization of the position of bilingual teacher in 1960 and the implementation of bilingual, Puerto Rican Studies, and affirmative action programs in the last twenty-five years, also created new openings for Puerto Rican women interested in the field of education.[40]

The Literature on Capitalist Restructuring and Puerto Rican Women

As these few educated Puerto Rican women were moving into the teaching profession in New York City, many blue-collar workers began experiencing the loss of jobs caused by the economic transformation affecting the entire mid-Atlantic region during the 1960s and 1970s. The nature and impact of this transformation was first systematically researched by Rosemary Santana Cooney of Fordham University, who in the late 1970s compared the published census data on women in some fifty-six cities, including mid-Atlantic industrial centers, to seven significant variables (labor market conditions, education, age, family size, marital status, female-headed households, assimilation) applicable to Puerto Rican women in ten of these cities. In her study, published in 1979, Cooney corroborated emerging government reports (e.g., Manpower Report of the President, 1973) indicating a low labor force participation rate—that is, the percentage of workers fourteen years and older in the labor force, for Puerto Rican women, compared to other women throughout the country.[41] However, when examining the labor force participation rates of Puerto Rican women in the previous two decades, Cooney also found that while in 1970 this rate was 29.8 percent (compared to 44.5 percent for African American and 38.9 percent for white women), in 1950 the labor force participation rate for Puerto Rican women had been 38.9 percent, but that by 1960 it had dropped to 36.3 percent. Cooney argues in this pioneer study that Puerto Rican women's declining labor force participation was not only localized to the northeast region of the nation (since in some midwest and West Coast cities the participation of Puertorriqueñas showed an upward trend), but that

> the variable changes that were responsible for a declining Puerto Rican female participation rate in New York [and its environs] were the loss of nondurable

operative [i.e., garment] jobs, the dramatic increase in the number of females
heading families, and a more favorable industry mix for more highly educated
females even after controlling [for] the loss of non-durable operative jobs.[42]

In the next few years, working with a group of dedicated co-researchers,
Cooney continued to explore the relationship between the economic changes in
the mid-Atlantic region and the unique demographic and social characteristics
affecting Puerto Rican women workers in the area.[43] One of these researchers
was Alice Colón-Warren, who in subsequent publications has updated earlier
investigations on the factors that persistently contributed to lower labor force
participation rates among Puerto Rican women between 1970 and 1980 in the
mid-Atlantic states (New York, New Jersey, Pennsylvania).[44] In one of these
studies Colón-Warren notes that by 1980 Puerto Rican women's labor force
participation had increased to 37 percent in the northeast, yet this participation
rate still lagged behind those of African American (52 percent) and white women
(47 percent).[45] Searching for an explanation, Colón-Warren closely correlated
education to labor market conditions in the mid-Atlantic region and found that
Puertorriqueñas have been disproportionally disadvantaged, as members of the
"lower strata of the working class," in the region's educational opportunities,
which she believes ultimately limited their participation in the expanding professional, clerical, and sales occupations in the 1970s. Because white and African
American women were highly concentrated in these occupations during this
period, Puerto Rican women also experienced greater competition in the labor
market. Meanwhile, the loss of jobs in the manufacturing sector did not abate.
Since this sector had been the most important source of employment for Puerto
Rican women in the past, they were, of course, the most affected by its demise:
by 1980, for the first time in United States history, there were fewer Puerto
Rican women employed as operatives than as clericals.

Colón-Warren's work draws our attention to yet another critical research
issue initiated by Cooney—that is, the relationship between Puerto Rican
women's work, family headship, and poverty, one of the most controversial
topics in Puerto Rican women studies in recent years.[46] For Colón-Warren, the
rising rate of poor families headed by women is attributable to two factors:
exclusion of women from gainful employment and lower levels of earnings
when they do obtain employment. She also believes that factors such as English
language skills, presence of children, access to family networks, and home own-
ership may have affected the labor force participation of single women more
than married ones. In a recent analysis, however, Colón-Warren reiterates
Cooney's assessment of labor market conditions for Puerto Rican women subsequent to their employment apogee in 1950, namely that the decline of jobs in the
industrial sector in the mid-Atlantic region placed Puertorriqueñas in a highly
vulnerable economic position.[47] Without adequate educational opportunities and
viable sources of employment, many Puerto Rican women, especially single

heads of household, were forced to turn to public assistance in order to support themselves and their families. Colón-Warren, although critical of the welfare system in general, sees the availability of welfare benefits (and informal economic activities) as a form of "resistance to further deterioration in employment and economic conditions in the Middle-Atlantic Region." Yet, she recognizes that this "resistance" is extremely limited and only has offered Puerto Rican women human survival at a measly poverty level.

The Literature on Women Workers and Operation Bootstrap

Recent transformations in the Puerto Rican economy have led to similar labor and life patterns among women workers on the island. Clearly, since the mid-1970s women workers in Puerto Rico have also been experiencing more job losses, unemployment, and underemployment than before, and increasing difficulty supporting families on the low incomes provided by their wage labor.[48] This is in sharp contrast to the previous two decades when women's employment opportunities, labor force participation (at least in some sectors), and wages had experienced notable increases as a result of the implementation of Fomento, the island's post–World War II economic development program. Conceived in the early 1940s as a strategy for increasing employment opportunities for men, by the 1960s Fomento had succeeded in bringing to Puerto Rico mainly industries heavily dependent on women's labor. Most of these industries came to Puerto Rico in response to various incentives promoted by the island's new Commonwealth government, specifically long-term generous insular tax exemptions, a renovated infrastructure (e.g., electric and water plants, better transportation facilities, more schools, etc.), and the promise of an abundant low-cost labor force. Thus, during this first stage of economic development (1950–65), Manos a la Obra, or Operation Bootstrap (as Fomento is popularly called), succeeded in attracting many United States labor-intensive industries, such as the garment, textile, and leather trades, which provided employment to thousands of women workers on the island.[49]

Although in the 1960s and throughout the 1970s Fomento attempted to shift Puerto Rico's economy to more capital-intensive, high-technology enterprises (i.e., petrochemicals, pharmaceuticals, electronics, electrical equipment and appliances) with hopes of generating more jobs for men, the bulk of the major industries that were created or expanded during this period predominantly hired women workers also. More significantly, until the early 1970s the garment industry continued to be an important source of wage work for women on the island. As Puerto Rican workers' demands for higher wages increased in the 1980s, however, many of these enterprises, notably garment businesses, began reducing operations in Puerto Rico and relocating to other lower-wage areas in Latin America and Asia.[50]

A historical assessment of the impact of these economic changes on Puerto

Rican women's lives has yet to be done, but a number of social science studies have paved the way for a greater understanding of the relationship of women's work to the island's industrialization process and of the effects of Operation Bootstrap on women workers in recent years.[51] For example, the anthropological analyses of a 1980 survey of 157 garment workers in the western part of Puerto Rico, designed by Helen Icken Safa and conducted by her graduate research assistant, Carmen Pérez-Herranz, have provided important information on the impact of economic development on women factory workers.[52] In her interpretation of this survey, Safa notes that employers in Puerto Rico preferred hiring young women workers (20–24-year-olds) for their production jobs, but worsening conditions in the garment industry (and the availability of clerical jobs for younger women) in the early 1980s resulted in the employment of a much older (30 and over) work force in some plants. Many of these older women had little formal education, yet when it came to workers' rights in the factory they tended to be more assertive than younger women, most of whom had high school degrees. This obviously was one of the reasons why employers sought younger women. Safa also points out that, unlike workers in the "global factory" of multinational corporations, many garment workers in Puerto Rico tended to be married with children. Another unique pattern among Puerto Rican garment workers was the presence of an increasing number of women heads-of-household. In general, whether single or married, most of these women were part of large households and/or kinship networks that served as support systems or problem-solving mechanisms in the factories, at home, or in the community. In the factories and union locals, just like Puertorriqueñas in the garment industry in New York City, garment workers in Mayagüez encountered the problems of low wages, occupational segregation, paternalistic attitudes from management, and plant closings, while at home they were beleaguered by the burdens inherent in women's "double-shift" and head-of-household status (e.g., incomes too low to support families adequately). Although Safa noticed an increased awareness of these work and gender issues among women in Puerto Rico, she concludes women "remain quite apathetic in their responses to these problems."[53]

In her study of women garment workers in the southwestern part of Puerto Rico, Carmen A. Pérez-Herranz generally corroborates Safa's findings, but her detailed accounts of these worker's lives generates an image of women actively and earnestly seeking solutions to their wage-work and household problems.[54] To cope with the more stressful demands of their garment jobs, women brought to the factory their kin and other affinal relations. This meant that mothers, daughters, sisters, cousins, and *comadres* (one of whom is godmother to the other's child) were co-workers, ready to give support whenever it was needed. On occasion, an attempt was made to incorporate management into the *compadrazgo* (godparenting) system. Even though, as Pérez-Herranz points out, the introduction of these personal relations into the modern factory is reminiscent of the " *peón–patrón*" relationship of the hacienda system, she adds that the presence of relatives and friends in their workplaces gave women, especially older women, a great sense of security and empowerment. Because they saw the ILGWU as a "company union" (since, in fact, the union had been invited by the company to organize them), women rarely brought their grievances to their union representatives, and—either individually or through their kin relations—resolved conflicts by themselves. Pérez-Herranz believes that women did not resort to more organized and confrontational tactics because they considered these "too aggressive" or "manly," and because, for the most part, their "subtle strategies" gave them the results they expected. In their "private worlds" women also employed a variety of strategies to carry out their family, household, and community responsibilities: women efficiently routinized their work schedules; enlisted the aid of relatives and friends; and sought husbands or mates to help out with some of the chores. At home, women workers also expected greater participation in decision making and information sharing.

The Literature on Women's Recent Labor Struggles

Other investigations on the strategies Puerto Rican women have adopted or developed to confront problems in and out of the labor force indicate that Puertorriqueñas have explored a variety of alternatives for resolving issues that have critically affected them as wage and/or household workers. These studies document the experiences of Puerto Rican women with different modes of resistance and action that have empowered them to challenge restrictive gender and work ideologies in more recent times, either on the island or the mainland. One study by Marya Muñoz Vázquez deals with a group of women workers in the Guanajibo-Castillo Industrial Park in Mayagüez who between 1983 and 1989 helped organize El Comité Pro-Rescate de Nuestra Salud (CPRNS) (Committee to Rescue Our Health) with the aim of forcing employers to establish a safer work environment and grant them indemnity for damages to their health, after toxic gas emissions repeatedly contaminated their workplace.[55] In a study by Rosa M. Torruellas, Rina Benmayor, and Ana Juarbe, we see an articulation of poor Puerto Rican migrant women's claims in the late 1980s to public funds and services to help raise their families—a responsibility they viewed as significant "work," as well as a cultural right.[56] The last work I wish to refer to here is by Geraldine J. Casey, who evaluates the efforts—including the use of an organized trade union and a professional association—of clerical and secretarial workers on the island to combat the problems they have encountered in their offices in the last few years.[57] Although these various strategies have not generated all of the results Puerto Rican women have expected, nevertheless, they stand as examples of courageous attempts on the part of the Puerto Rican working class to overcome the oppressive socioeconomic conditions that today are threatening its continued existence.

One of the most crucial battles in the Puerto Rican working-class struggle for survival has pitted women workers in the Guanajibo-Castillo Industrial Park of

Mayagüez against U.S. transnational corporations operating in the complex over the issues of occupational safety and environmental health. The battle began in 1980 when residents living near the industrial site complained to governmental authorities of a stench given off by the liquids and gases from the park. In the next few years several large gas emissions occurred, and after each incident, workers in the complex (as well as their neighbors) experienced a variety of symptoms, such as headaches, dizziness, vomiting, and diarrhea. Convinced that there was a correlation between their illness and the toxic gas discharges in the industrial park, workers demanded that the companies in the complex and governmental agencies conduct an investigation of the origins and effects of the emissions. Their pleas were ignored. In the fall of 1983, workers—mainly women from the garment factories in the site—and residents in the nearby *barrios* organized themselves into CPRNS and began to push for a quick resolution to the environmental problems in the Guanajibo-Castillo area. From its inception the group functioned as a collective, and routinely invited labor organizers, doctors and other scientists, and lawyers to advise them in planning strategies. Muñoz Vázquez was one of the psychologists who participated in the collective from 1986 to 1988. In her study of this collective, Muñoz Vázquez evaluates the origins, decision-making process, and impact of CPRNS on women's health struggles in Puerto Rico during the two years she worked with the organization. Muñoz Vázquez believes that in establishing a collective decision-making process in CPRNS, committee organizers, such as Cielo Martín and Santos Feliciano, made it possible for women to participate more actively in the organization's proceedings and activities. Thus, CPRNS encouraged women to counteract doctors' misdiagnoses of their symptoms (i.e., that their illnesses were due to "hysteria" about possible emissions in the future, problems with husbands, menopause, etc.); insist on on-site investigations of their physical conditions and work environments; and bring suit against the companies suspected of the contamination. Although CPRNS did not succeed in obtaining indemnity for the workers, Muñoz Vázquez urges us to appreciate the fact that as a result of CPRNS's efforts, governmental agencies (e.g., the Department of Health) conducted several studies that led to production changes inside the Guanajibo-Castillo Park. And on a broader scale, as Muñoz Vázquez's study illustrates so well, CPRNS also signifies women's capacity for developing effective grassroots leadership and collective political action in the modern-day Puerto Rican workplace.

Another arena of contestation in the contemporary survival struggles of the Puerto Rican working class is the use of public assistance programs (i.e., welfare, food stamps, medicare) by Puertorriqueñas on the mainland. On the side of critics of the welfare state, Linda Chávez (a Mexican American Republican "trouble-shooter") has argued that welfare has created a perennial dependency on the state among Puerto Rican women heads-of-household—a life pattern that she believes has undermined "patrimony," family support systems, and the "responsibilities of autonomous adults" within the Puerto Rican community. Discounting the egregious effects of deteriorating socioeconomic conditions in the north-east (where the bulk of the Puerto Rican population has resided) since the 1970s and of racial/ethnic discrimination (which may account for women's participation in welfare programs), Chávez has implied that Puerto Rican women are on public assistance because they have a "surprisingly strong family attachment," a "propensity" to have children out of wedlock, a desire to care for school-age children themselves, and lack a "strong work ethic."[58] The study by Torruellas, Benmayor, and Juarbe, based on the detailed life histories of thirteen migrant Puertorriqueñas on public assistance in New York City in the late 1980s, conveys a very different interpretation of the connections between Puerto Rican women and the welfare state. As other analyses of welfare recipients have shown, Torruellas, Benmayor, and Juarbe demonstrate that, far from lacking a work ethic, the Puertorriqueñas they studied considered work an integral part of their lives. As child-laborers many of them had helped support siblings by doing "women's work"—babysitting, home needlework, and so forth. Too, in the decision to migrate, women had envisioned doing wage-work to better their poor economic status. Once in the states, almost all of them had worked at different jobs until, as Torruellas, Benmayor, Juarbe argue, declining economic conditions in the mid-Atlantic region in the 1980s—combined with a lack of formal education, training, or skilled-occupational experiences—caused some of them to lose their jobs and eventually permanently withdraw from the labor force. Other women found themselves with unemployed or disabled husbands, became widows, or separated from mates, resulting in head-of-householdships. These women, therefore, turned to welfare for a variety of reasons, and only after exhausting other income-generating possibilities. Even then, they did not become passive "dependents" of the state, for by 1986 all of them were enrolled in *El Barrio* Literacy Education Program, a project initiated for the Puerto Rican community in East Harlem by the Language Policy Task Force of the Centro de Estudios Puertorriqueños (CEP) (Puerto Rican Studies Center) of Hunter College of the City University of New York.

Working closely with a group of CEP staff members, which included Torruellas (director of the program), Benmayor, and Juarbe, these welfare recipients in the next five years were to transform the CEP's literacy program into an adult-learners' collective that encouraged them to further explore important issues affecting their lives. One of these issues was compliance with the Family Security Act of 1988, requiring welfare mothers of children one year of age and older to participate in educational or work programs that would presumably help them become economically self-sufficient. As a result of this act, Puertorriqueñas in the CEP literacy collective were assigned to such menial, low-wage, part-time jobs (such as cleaning abandoned lots) that they concluded that the government was not interested in bettering their lives, but in humiliating them because they were poor mothers. The indignation that explodes in Torruellas, Benmayor, and Juarbe's account of these women's "workfare" experiences takes on greater meaning as these women's gender and work expectations are placed into perspective. Because, as Puertorriqueñas, they had been socialized into a culture that values motherhood and recognizes family and household responsibilities as "work," these women grew up believing that being mothers was their most significant social responsibility as "autonomous adults." Now on the mainland, they argue that, as migrants from a U.S. territory, and thus American citizens, they are entitled to exercise their "cultural citizenship rights" to motherhood—even if they are on public assistance. Unfortunately, welfare claims based on the cultural rights of motherhood have long been under attack by feminist critics, who see the origins and evolution of the modern welfare state as a product of "maternalist politics" that have failed to address women's independence from state patriarchy and their rights as workers in the twentieth century.

In her study on *oficinistas,* or clerical workers, in Puerto Rico, Geraldine Casey examines how gender and class mediated the lives of women working in offices at the Río Piedras campus of the University of Puerto Rico (UPR) in the early 1990s, and how these *oficinistas* responded to the challenges that these issues have posed for women workers on the island. Casey discovered that traditional gender assumptions regarding women's performance, attire, and speech still permeate the office environment at UPR. Thus, women workers are perceived as sexy, "fluffy-headed females," who must render personal services to management, and dress and speak "appropriately" in the office. This usually means women are not seen as capable of acquiring the ever-changing computerized technology of clerical work, often are asked to take care of male bosses' private needs (e.g., buying gifts for wives), must wear "fashionable" clothes, and must not use "slang" terms, such as "Ay bendito, m'hija," in the office. *Oficinistas* themselves maintain popular gender images in their workplaces by celebrating—through parties and gift-giving—"women's holidays," especially Mother's Day and St. Valentine's Day, which incidentally were both imported from the United States. Casey found that class manifestations were not as visible as the gender issues between workers and management at UPR, but that—as part of the working class on the island and more specifically as workers in the public sector—clerical workers are daily being affected by changing work conditions. In recent years, for example, cutbacks in federally funded programs, technological innovations, and "scientific" office management have led to reduced training programs, underemployment, and unemployment.

How have Puerto Rican women clerical workers coped with or resolved these problems? The 167 women interviewed by Casey between 1990 and 1992 provided multiple, and sometimes opposing, responses to this question. While some *oficinistas* simply have accepted existing work and labor market conditions, others—either as individuals or as members of Professional Secretaries International (PSI) and/or La Hermandad de Empleados Exentos No Docentes (HEEND) (Brotherhood of Exempt, Non-Teaching Employees), an office workers' association and trade union, respectively, are determined at least to create a workplace that is more receptive to women's gender issues and concerns. Some women have begun to substitute celebrations of their art and poetic work or their labor struggles for the commemoration of women's traditional roles. To counter the image that women are incapable of dominating the new technology, and also because they need to maintain a competitive edge in an already flooded labor market, *oficinistas* at UPR attend workshops to update their secretarial and computer skills. Additionally, they have participated in or organized collective groups to learn to cope with stress, develop a sense of self-esteem, and deal with health and safety issues. But they have not been able to halt deteriorating work conditions, especially the low salaries, and, thus, employed clerical workers often engage in "moonlighting" activities (e.g., selling clothes, jewelry, cosmetics, foods) to supplement their salaries or help support unemployed family members.[59] Casey notes that the problems of underemployment and unemployment have led to an exodus of women clerical workers to the United States.

Conclusion

This appraisal of the literature on working Puertorriqueñas has helped to uncover the most significant historical themes in the lives of women who have worked under extremely adverse conditions in different time periods, geographic regions, and workplaces either in Puerto Rico or the U.S. mainland. Most of this literature has focused on the work and labor struggles of women in the needlework and garment industries, thus reflecting the importance of Puerto Rican women's work in these industries and the significance of these industries to the survival of Puertorriqueñas as well. Scholars also have expressed interest in Puerto Rican teachers and, more recently, women in the medical professions, which like clerical and other administrative positions have harnessed the labor of educated and middle-class Puertorriqueñas since the early 1900s.[60] Although the literature on Puerto Rican women workers presently gives us a better understanding of the relationship between the work and labor struggles of Puerto Rican women and the exigencies of U.S. industrial capitalism both in Puerto Rico and in the states in the last one hundred years, further research is needed in a number of areas in order for us to completely reconstruct the history of Puerto Rican women workers. Included among these should be investigations on the changing gender images that have permitted women (whose lives generally have been circumscribed by traditional cultural values) to participate in the wage-labor force; the effects of birth control programs on women's productive labor; women's relationships to the informal economy; the impact of job production and stress on women; women's double-shift; and the continuing gender discrimination women still experience. More individual scholarly monographs in these and other areas of research will not only provide a more solid framework for future historical analyses of Puerto Rican women's work experiences, but give us a fuller appreciation of the present contributions that women workers make to our daily lives.

Notes

1. This is a revised version of the introductory chapter to my book, *Puerto Rican Women and Work: Bridges in Transnational Labor* (Philadelphia: Temple University Press, 1996), 1–32.

2. See, for example, Edna Acosta-Belén, ed., *The Puerto Rican Woman: Perspectives in Culture, History, and Society* (New York: Praeger, 1986); Adalberto López and James Petras, eds., *Puerto Rico and Puerto Ricans: Studies in History and Society* (New York: John Wiley and Sons, 1974).

3. Manuel Maldonado Denis, *Puerto Rico y Estados Unidos: Emigración y colonialismo; Un análisis socio-histórico de la emigración puertorriqueña* (Mexico: Siglo Ventiuno, 1976), 27–46.

4. Citations are from the English-language edition: Manuel Maldonado Denis, *The Emigration Dialectic: Puerto Rico and the U.S.A.* (New York: International, 1980), 29.

5. Among these are included: Juan S. Marcano, "Páginas Rojas: Unidos venceremos," in *Lucha Obrera: Antología de grandes documentos en la historia obrera puertorriqueña*, ed. Angel Quintero Rivera (Río Piedras: Centro de Estudios de la Realidad Puertorriqueña, 1971), 66–67; Yamila Azize, *La mujer en la lucha* (Río Piedras: Editorial Cultural, 1985), 40–60; Marcia Rivera, "The Development of Capitalism in Puerto Rico and the Incorporation of Women into the Labor Force," in Acosta-Belén, *The Puerto Rican Woman*, 30–45.

6. See for example, Marcia Rivera, "The Development of Capitalism in Puerto Rico," in Acosta-Belén," *The Puerto Rican Woman*, 32–33.

7. Luis Díaz Soler, *Historia de la esclavitud negra en Puerto Rico* (1953) (Río Piedras: Editorial Universitaria, 1970), 155; Guillermo Baralt, et al., *El machete de Ogún: Las luchas de esclavos (siglo 19)* (Río Piedras: Centro de Estudios de la Realidad Puertorriqueña, 1989), 25. See also James Dietz, *Historia económica de Puerto Rico* (Río Piedras: Editorial Huracán, 1989), 39.

8. Olga Jiménez de Wagenheim, "Mujer y sociedad en el siglo XIX," *Boletín del Centro de Estudios Puertorriqueños* 2, no. 7 (Winter 1989–90): 12–21; Dietz, *Historia económica de Puerto Rico,* 52; Baralt, et al., *El machete de Ogún,* 108.

9. Rivera, "The Development of Capitalism in Puerto Rico," 35; Azize, *La mujer en la lucha,* 41, 58.

10. Rivera, "The Development of Capitalism in Puerto Rico," 35.

11. Victor S. Clark, et al., *Porto Rico and Its Problems* (Washington, DC: Brookings Institution, 1930, New York: Arno Press, 1975), 13–14.

12. Amilcar Tirado Avilés, "Notas sobre el desarrollo de la industria del tabaco en Puerto Rico y su impacto en la mujer, 1898–1920," *Boletín del Centro de Estudios Puertorriqueños* 2, no. 7 (Winter 1989–90): 23–27.

13. Fernando Picó, "Las trabajadoras del tabaco de Utuado, Puerto Rico, según el censo de 1910," *Homines* 10, no. 2 (1986–87): 178–79.

14. Norma Valle Ferrer, *Luisa Capetillo: Historia de una mujer proscrita* (Río Piedras: Editorial Cultural, 1990): 59–133; Norma Valle, "Luisa Capetillo (1879–1922), una hereja en la sociedad puertorriqueña," *Caribe* 4–5, no. 5–6 (1983–84): 3–33; Norma Valle Ferrer, *Luisa Capetillo* (San Juan, PR, 1975).

15. Lydia Milagros González, *Una puntada en el tiempo: La industria de la aguja en Puerto Rico (1900–1929)* (Santo Domingo, D.R.: Editora Taller, 1990), 4–6, 18, 64, 72, 76–77; Luisa Hernández Angueira, "El trabajo femenino de la aguja en Puerto Rico, 1914–1940," in *Género y trabajo: La industria de la aguja en Puerto Rico y el Caribe Hispánico,* ed. Mariá del Carmen Baerga (San Juan: Editorial de la Universidad de Puerto Rico, 1933), 86–87.

16. González, *Una puntada en el tiempo,* 11–12, 18–21, 34–35.

17. Lidia Milagros Gonzalez, "La industria de la aguja en Puerto Rico y sus origenes en los Estados Unidos," in Baerga, *Género y trabajo,* 74.

18. Caroline Manning, "The Employment of Women in Puerto Rico, United States Department of Labor," Women's Bureau, *Bulletin of the Women's Bureau* 118 (Washington, DC: Government Printing Office, 1934), 11–13.

19. Mariá del Carmen Baerga, "Wages, Consumption and Survival: Working-Class Households in Puerto Rico in the 1930s," in *Households and the World Economy,* ed. Joan Smith, et al. (Beverly Hills: Sage, 1984), 248.

20. Ibid.

21. Blanca Silvestrini, "Women as Workers: The Experience of the Puerto Rican Women in the 1930s," in Acosta-Belén, *The Puerto Rican Woman,* 68–69.

22. Eileen Boris, "Needlewomen under the New Deal in Puerto Rico, 1920–1945," in *Puerto Rican Women and Work: Bridges in Transnational Labor,* ed. Altagracia Ortiz (Philadelphia: Temple University Press, 1996), 33–54. See also, Eileen Boris, *Home to Work: Motherhood and the Politics of Industrial Homework in the United States* (New York: Cambridge University Press, 1994), 231–39.

23. According to a 1984 study of the Needle Trades Association, homework was still in existence in Puerto Rico at the time. (Alice Colón, "La participación laboral de las mujeres en Puerto Rico: Empleo o sub-utilización," *Pensamiento Crítico* 8, no. 44 (May–June 1985): 87.

24. Lawrence R. Chenault, *The Puerto Rican Migrant in New York City* (New York: Russell and Russell, 1970), 76.

25. Altagracia Ortiz, "Puerto Ricans in the Garment Industry of New York City, 1920–1960," in *Labor Divided: Race and Ethnicity in United States Labor Struggles, 1835–1960,* eds. Robert Asher and Charles Stephenson (Albany: SUNY Press, 1990), 105–25.

26. Altagracia Ortiz, "En la aguja y el pedal eché la hiel: Puerto Rican Women in the Garment Industry of New York City, 1920–1980," in Ortiz, *Puerto Rican Women and Work,* 55–81.

27. Altagracia Ortiz, "The Labor Struggles of Puerto Rican Women in the Garment Industry of New York City, 1920–1960," *Cimarrón* 1, no. 3 (Spring 1988): 39–59. Colón, "La participación laboral de las mujeres en Puerto Rico," 87.

28. For example, Chenault, *The Puerto Rican Migrant,* 62, 70, 73, 74; Virginia Sánchez Korrol, "On the Other Side of the Ocean: The Work Experiences of Early Puerto Rican Migrant Women," *Caribbean Review* (January 1979): 26–27.

29. For example, Ruth Glasser, " 'Que Vivío Tiene la Gente Aquí en Nueva York': Music and Community in Puerto Rican New York, 1915–1940" (Ph.D. diss., Yale University, 1991), 37–38, 177–82, 302–10, 332–38; Virginia Sánchez Korrol, "The Forgotten Migrant: Educated Puerto Rican Women in New York City, 1920–1940," in Acosta-Belén, *The Puerto Rican Woman,* 170–79.

30. Columbia University, Oral History Project, interviews with Pura Belpré by Lillian López, New York City, April 4, 1976; Lillian López and Pura Belpré, "Reminiscences of Two Turned-On Librarians," in *Puerto Rican Perspectives,* ed. Edward Mapp (Metuchen, NJ: Scarecrow Press, 1974), 83–96; Sánchez Korrol, "The Forgotten Migrant," in Acosta-Belén, *The Puerto Rican Woman,* 173–75.

31. See Federico Ribes Tovar, *La mujer puertorriqueña: Su vida y evolución a través de la historia* (New York: Plus Ultra, 1972), 231–33; Virginia Sánchez Korrol, "In Search of Unconventional Women in Religious Vocations before Mid-Century," *Oral History Review* 16, no. 2 (Fall 1988): 50–55.

32. For more information on early Puerto Rican migrant women, see Altagracia Ortiz, "The Lives of Pioneras: Bibliographic and Research Sources on Puerto Rican Women in the United States," *Boletín del Centro de Estudios Puertorriqueños* 2, no. 7 (Winter 1989–90): 41–47.

33. López and Petras, *Puerto Rico and Puerto Ricans,* 318–19.

34. Committee on Puerto Ricans in New York City of the Welfare Council of New York City, *Report of the Committee on Puerto Ricans in New York City* (New York: Welfare Council, 1948), 6.

35. Virginia Sánchez Korrol, "Toward Bilingual Education: Puerto Rican Women Teachers in New York City Schools, 1947–1967," in Ortiz, *Puerto Rican Women and Work,* 82–104.

36. Juan José Osuna, *A History of Education in Puerto Rico* (Río Piedras: Editorial de la Universidad de Puerto Rico, 1949), 43, 88; Marcia Rivera, "El proceso educativo en Puerto Rico y la reproducción de la subordinación femenina," in *La mujer en Puerto Rico: Enseyos de investigación,* ed. Yamila Azize (Río Piedras: Ediciones Huracén, 1987), 121.

37. Azize, *La mujer en la lucha,* 44.

38. Marcia Rivera, "El proceso educativo en Puerto Rico," in Azize, *La mujer en Puerto Rico,* 117–18, 132; Azize, *La mujer en la lucha,* 46.

39. Luz del Alba Acevedo, "Industrialization and Employment: Changes in the Patterns of Women's Work in Puerto Rico," *World Development* 18, no. 2 (1990): 242–43.

40. Works on Puerto Rican teachers in the United States are few, but two interesting unpublished studies correlating Puerto Rican women to high job satisfaction in the profession are: Patricia Cintrón de Crespo, "Puerto Rican Women Teachers in New York: Self-Perception and Work Adjustment as Perceived by Themselves and by Others," (Ph.D. diss., Columbia University, 1965); and Elizabeth Iglesias, "Human Islands of Success: Professional Puerto Rican Women in Higher Education," (Ph.D. diss., Pennsylvania State University, 1988).

41. Rosemary Santana Cooney, "Intercity Variations in Puerto Rican Female Participation," *Journal of Human Resources* 14, no. 2 (Spring 1979): 222–35.

42. Ibid., 231.

43. Rosemary Santana Cooney and Alice E. Colón-Warren, "Declining Female Participation among Puerto Rican New Yorkers: A Comparison with Native White Non-Spanish New Yorkers," *Ethnicity* 6 (1979): 281–97; Rosemary Santana Cooney and Kyonghee Min, "Demographic Characteristics Affecting Living Arrangements among Young Currently Unmarried Puerto Rican, Non-Spanish Black, and Non-Spanish White Mothers," *Ethnicity* 8, no. 2 (1981): 107–20; Rosemary Santana Cooney and Vilma Ortiz, "Nativity, National Origin, and Hispanic Female Participation in the Labor Force," *Social Science Quarterly* 64, no. 3 (September 1983): 510–23.

44. See, for example, Rosemary Santana Cooney and Alice Colón, "Work and Family: The Recent Struggles of Puerto Rican Females," in *The Puerto Rican Struggle: Essays on Survival in the U.S.A.,* ed. Clara Rodriguez, Virginia Sánchez Korrol, and José Oscar Alers (New York: Puerto Rican Migration Research Consortium, 1980), 58–73.

45. Alice Colón-Warren, "The Impact of Job Losses on Puerto Rican Women in the Middle Atlantic Region, 1970–1980," in Ortiz, *Puerto Rican Women and Work,* 116.

46. Christine E. Bose, "Puerto Rican Women in the United States: An Overview," in Acosta-Belén, *The Puerto Rican Woman,* 158–62.

47. Colón-Warren, "The Impact of Job Losses on Puerto Rican Women," 114–29.

48. Isabel Picó Vidal, "La mujer puertorriqueña y la recessión económica," *Avance* 2, no. 145 (May 1–15, 1975): 5–8; Colón, "La participación laboral de las mujeres en Puerto Rico," 28; Acevedo, "Industrialization and Employment," 250; Havidán Rodríguez, "Household Composition, Employment Patterns and Economic Well-Being in the United States and Puerto Rico, 1970–1980." (Ph.D. diss., University of Wisconsin-Madison, 1991), 280.

49. For accounts of the integration of women into these industries, see Luz del Alba Acevedo, "Género, trabajo asalariado y desarrollo industrial en Puerto Rico: La división sexual del trabajo en la manufactura," in Baerga, *Género y trabajo,* 161–212; Palmira Ríos, "Export-Oriented Industrialization and the Demand for Female Labor: Puerto Rican Women in the Manufacturing Sector, 1952–1980," in *Colonial Dilemma: Critical Perspectives on Contemporary Puerto Rico,* ed. Edwin Meléndez and Edgardo Meléndez (Boston: South End Press, 1933), 89–101.

50. Helen Icken Safa, "Female Employment and the Social Reproduction of the Puerto Rican Working Class," in Acosta-Belén, *The Puerto Rican Woman,* 90.

51. In addition to the works of Acevedo and Ríos, see Isabel Picó de Hernández, "Estudio sobre el empleo de la mujer en Puerto Rico," *Revista de Ciencias Sociales* 19, no. 2 (June 1975): 141–64; Helen Icken Safa, "Class Consciousness among Working-Class Women in Latin America: Puerto Rico," in *Sex and Class in Latin America: Women's Perspectives on Politics, Economics, and the Family in the Third World,* ed. June Nash and Helen Icken Safa (South Hadley, MA: Bergin, 1980), 69–85. See also, Helen Icken Safa, "Women and Industrialization in the Caribbean," in *Women, Employment and the Family in the International Division of Labor,* ed. Sharon Stichter and Jane Parpart (New York: Macmillan, 1990), 72–97.

52. Safa, "Female Employment," in Acosta-Belén, *The Puerto Rican Woman,* 94–98.

53. Helen Icken Safa, *The Myth of the Male Breadwinner: Women and Industrialization in the Caribbean* (Boulder, CO: Westview Press, 1995), 95.

54. Carmen Pérez-Herranz, "Our Two Full-Time Jobs: Women Garment Workers Balance Factory and Domestic Demands in Puerto Rico," in Ortiz, *Puerto Rican Women and Work,* 139–60.

55. Marya Muñoz Vázquez, "Gender and Politics: Grassroots Leadership among Puerto Rican Women in a Health Struggle," in Ortiz, *Puerto Rican Women and Work,* 161–83. See also, Marya Muñoz Vázquez, "La salud ocupacional y ambiental: Reto organizativo para el femenismo," *Pensamiento Crítico* 11, no. 58 (March–April 1988): 6.

56. Rosa M. Torruellas, Rina Benmayor, and Ana Juarbe, "Negotiating Gender, Work, and Welfare: Familia as Productive Labor among Puerto Rican Women in New York City," in Ortiz, *Puerto Rican Women and Work,* 184–208. See also Rosa Torruellas, et al., "Affirming Cultural Citizenship in the Puerto Rican Community: Critical Literacy and the *El Barrio* Popular Education Program," in *Literacy as Praxis: Culture, Language and Pedagogy,* ed. Catherine E. Walsh (Norwood, NJ: Ablex, 1991), 183–219.

57. Geraldine J. Casey, "New Tappings on the Keys: Changes in Work and Gender Roles for Women Clerical Workers in Puerto Rico," in Ortiz, *Puerto Rican Women and Work,* 209–233.

58. Linda Chávez, *Out of the Barrio: Toward a New Politics of Hispanic Assimilation* (New York: Basic Books, 1991), 145, 159.

59. For further information on women and the informal economy, see Janice Petrovich and Sandra Laureano, "Towards an Analysis of Puerto Rican Women and the Informal Economy," *Homines* 10, no. 2 (1986–87): 70–80.

60. See, for example, Yamila Azize Vargas and Luis Alberto Avilés, "Los hechos

desconocidos: Participación de la mujer en las profesiones de salud en Puerto Rico (1898–1930)," *Puerto Rico Health Sciences Journal* 9, no. 1 (April 1990): 9–16; Annette B. Ramírez de Arellano, "Medicina de 'cuello rosado': Implicaciones de la feminización de la profesión," *Puerto Rico Health Sciences Journal* 9, no. 1 (April 1990): 21–24.

3

"¿Quién trabajará?": Domestic Workers, Urban Slaves, and the Abolition of Slavery in Puerto Rico

Félix V. Matos Rodríguez

This essay analyzes the role that domestic work and urban slavery played in the process of the abolition of slavery in Puerto Rico. Puerto Rico's historiography has shown the significance that economic, demographic, and social changes among rural slaves played in the demise of slavery. In this essay, on the other hand, I will discuss the importance that colonial authorities and the local urban elites gave to their perceived domestic labor shortage problem in San Juan and other cities. The evidence from continuous specific work regulations, the pro-abolition literature and propaganda, the struggles and frictions with colonial authorities, and the connections with the development of beneficence institutions all indicates that the concern regarding domestic work—although virtually forgotten in Puerto Rican historiography—was far from marginal in the Island's economic, political, and social processes during the second half of the nineteenth century.

Puerto Rico's historians have written extensively on the events leading to the abolition of slavery in 1873.[1] Recently, there has been growing interest in exploring not only the transition from slave labor into so-called "free" labor, but also the processes through which different agents defined complementary and contradictory notions of the concept of "freedom."[2] The exploration of these themes is not an isolated phenomenon in Puerto Rico's historiography but part of a larger dialogue regarding the forces that lead to the eradication of slavery in the

Americas and the behavior and expectations of the different groups involved in the process, including masters, slaves, merchants, and politicians.[3]

My interest in domestic work comes from the need to add new elements to the debates about slavery and its eventual abolition in Puerto Rico. Furthermore, domestic work has begun to be studied more cautiously given the developments in the fields of women's and gender studies.[4] Historically, domestic work in Latin America has been done by women, and nineteenth-century Puerto Rico was no exception to this rule. Recent research has stressed the importance of domestic work to the general economy, particularly in relation to the development of capitalism and urbanization in different regions.[5] In urban enclaves, domestic services, paid or not—such as washing, cooking, ironing, cleaning, and supervising children, ill people, and the elderly—have been key to the growth and development of other sectors of the economy. Although the chores we traditionally associate with domestic work apparently have not changed much over the years—with the exception, perhaps, of technological innovations that have supposedly simplified the work—it is important to recognize that, as with many other sectors of the economy, domestic work has a history. The development and historical evolution of domestic work must be problematized in order to appreciate its contribution to the socioeconomic transformations in Caribbean and Latin American history. This essay is a contribution to re-evaluating the importance of domestic work in Puerto Rico's history.

There was a direct connection between domestic work and urban slavery in nineteenth-century Puerto Rico. If it is true that not all urban women slaves were domestics, it is also true that a majority of urban women slaves performed domestic chores such as being servants, cooks, laundresses, nannies, and maids.[6] Given the lack of interest in domestic work in Puerto Rican and Caribbean historiography, it should not be surprising that urban slavery is also understudied in the region.[7] In most Puerto Rican and Caribbean slavery studies, the emphasis has been on plantation work and sugar processing. In this essay, I will regard domestic work and urban slavery as virtually synonymous, even when aware that not all urban slaves worked as domestics and that in rural plantations the distinctions between domestic and field slaves were often murky.

The selection of San Juan as the focus for this study is based on several important criteria. During the first two-thirds of the nineteenth century, San Juan was the Island's most important political, intellectual, and economic urban center.[8] Throughout the first half of the nineteenth century the importation of slaves increased in Puerto Rico, and also in San Juan. Halfway through the century, the processes that lead to the abolition of slavery started. At the time of abolition, San Juan was the city with the highest number of domestic slaves.[9] This is particularly significant considering that other cities such as Mayagüez and Ponce had far higher total numbers of slaves, both rural and urban. San Juan is, therefore, an appropriate place to analyze the role played by domestics and urban slaves in the abolition process during the second half of the nineteenth century in Puerto Rico.

Table 3.1

Domestic Workers by Race in San Juan: 1846
(Santa Bárbara, Santo Domingo, and San Francisco barrios)

	White	Black	Parda	Mulatto	Totals
Laundresses	19	158	81	101	359
Cooks	2	78	12	8	100
Servants	10	460	115	57	642
Totals	31	696	208	166	1,101

Source: AGPR, Censos San Juan, Barrios Santa Bárbara, Santo Domingo y San Francisco, 1846.

Domestic Work in the Capital

My first inquiry is: Who were domestics and urban slaves in San Juan? We can obtain a description of the characteristics of the women who performed domestic chores in mid-nineteenth-century San Juan through the use of census data and notarial records. Unfortunately, information regarding the lives of domestics is not abundant.[10] Census data, however, allows us to determine the geographic, racial, and marital status distribution of domestics. The only surviving mid-century manuscript census in San Juan is the one taken in 1846.[11] In that census, there is information about three of the four *barrios* (quarters) that composed the walled city: Santa Bárbara, Santo Domingo, and San Francisco. There is also a slave registry for 1872, which has been studied by Negrón Portillo and Mayo Santana.[12] This registry, unfortunately, does not have information regarding free women of color.

Who were San Juan's mid-nineteenth-century domestics and what kinds of jobs did they perform? Table 3.1 shows the number of domestics in the three San Juan quarters included in the 1846 census data.[13] Almost all the individuals listed as domestics in the 1846 census were women. Servants or maids were the most common type of domestics, followed by laundresses. The number of domestics, 1,101, is significant, particularly if we consider that San Juan's total population at that time was around 13,000 inhabitants.[14] Domestics, then, comprised at a minimum 8 percent of San Juan's population in 1846. These numbers, however, must be taken with caution because they could be affected by several factors. One can assume, for example, that many men and women classified as slaves in the census perhaps performed domestic chores in their masters' homes, even if they were not classified with any occupation. Thus, the number of domestics in 1846 was probably higher than the census figures indicate.

Tables 3.1 and 3.2 show the racial composition and the *condición* (free or slave status), respectively, of San Juan's domestics. There was a marked differ-

Table 3.2

Domestic Workers by "Status" in San Juan: 1846 (Santa Bárbara, Santo Domingo, and San Francisco barrios)

	Free	Slave	Totals
Laundresses	265	94	359
Cooks	23	77	100
Servants	67	575	642
Totals	355	746	1,101

Source: AGPR, Censos San Juan, Barrios Santa Bárbara, Santo Domingo y San Francisco, 1846.

ence among domestics in the city: the majority of the laundresses were free women (73 percent), while the majority of the servants or maids (90 percent) and the cooks (77 percent) were slave women. In 1846, slaves comprised about 20 percent of San Juan's total population.[15] Given the data provided above, it should not be unexpected to find that a high percentage of the cooks (78 percent) and the maids (72 percent) in San Juan were black. Among domestics, only laundresses had a less polarized racial breakdown: 49 percent of them were black, 23 percent were *pardas*, and 28 percent were mulattos.[16] Irrespective of the racial differences found among the laundresses and other domestics, it is clear that a majority of San Juan's domestics were black or colored (97 percent) and that a high percentage of them were slaves (68 percent).

The 1846 census also allows us to explore other characteristics of San Juan's domestics. The census data show that most domestics were between 10 and 44 years of age.[17] Servants or maids tended to be younger than cooks and laundresses. Table 3.3 shows the marital status of San Juan's domestics. The great majority of the city's domestics were single (93 percent). Almost all the servants were single (99 percent). These servants usually lived in the residence of their master or employer. Most of the cooks were also single (91 percent). Finally, among the laundresses, four out of five were single. In the case of laundresses, even though most were single, there was a high percentage of heads of household.[18] Thirty-eight percent of the laundresses and 13 percent of the cooks were heads of household. These figures contrast with those of the servants, given that not one servant was a head of household in 1846. The percentage of heads of household among laundresses points to a high number of single mothers among them.

The 1872 data from San Juan's slave registry confirms some of the trends identified in the 1846 data, even when the 1872 data do not include free domestics. In 1872, a majority of the domestic slaves in San Juan were women between 10 and 40 years of age.[19] Although by 1872 the total number of slaves in the city

Table 3.3

Domestics Workers by Marital Status in San Juan: 1846.
(Santa Bárbara, Santo Domingo, and San Francisco barrios)

	Married	Single	Widows	Totals
Laundresses	30	291	39	360
Cooks	5	94	4	103
Servants	4	657	1	662
Ironer	—	1	—	1
Totals	39	1,043	44	1,126

Source: AGPR, Censos San Juan, Barrios Santa Bárbara, Santo Domingo y San Francisco, 1846.

had decreased compared to the mid-century numbers, it seems that the characteristics of domestic slaves had not changed much.

The work done by domestics was quite arduous. In the case of laundresses, for example, their work required much physical strength. Laundresses could be employees or slaves working full-time in a single residence, military barrack, or monastery, or they could sell their services to multiple clients. In the latter case, laundresses probably collected clothes from their clients and took them to wash in their own homes or to one of the public water fountains in the city. Among these itinerant laundresses one could find slaves who, although mostly responsible for washing and folding their masters' family clothes, also rented their services—or were rented out by their masters—to other families.[20] This system of slave rentals was pretty frequent in the city, to the extent that it drew heavy criticism, censure, and requests for its eradication from the both the *Cabildo* (city council) and the central government.[21]

Washing clothes was not a simple task in a city lacking easy access to fresh water. In other Puerto Rican towns or cities, women took their wash to the nearest river, usually located at the outskirts of the town or city. San Juan had no such nearby rivers. San Juan's residents depended on three water fountains and several wells to supply them with water. The fountain with the highest volume and best quality of water was located in the Condado area near the San Antonio bridge—a considerable walk from the city's walls.[22] Another well was located in the Puntilla area, but the water quality there was poor and city residents stopped using it during the mid-nineteenth century. The Miraflores islet, located even farther away than the Condado fountain, had water of excellent quality. The city also had three intramural wells located in the plazas facing the Carmelite and Franciscan convents and the San Justo gate. These wells were opened at the onset of the nineteenth century, but their water supply and volume were unreliable. The intramural wells were closed in the 1860s after repeated complaints from religious leaders regarding the noise, public scandals, and general unruly behavior of the people who used the wells located in front of churches and convents.[23]

Many laundresses took their wash to the Condado fountain or the wells located within the city walls. Other laundresses took water to their homes or used water collected in cisterns. Some had access to the cisterns at the military garrisons or the city's hospital. In all cases, the laundresses' work required carrying a heavy load of either clothes or water for a considerable distance. Laundry work ended with the task of drying the washed clothes so that they could be ironed and returned to their owners. In many cases, the laundresses' children helped collect the soiled clothes and with the drying and ironing processes. The Condado fountain and the other intramural wells were public gathering places for the laundresses and their children.

Very little is known about the work performed by other domestics. Most cooks and servants in San Juan were slaves and lived in the master's residence. These domestics were in proximity to their masters' families, a situation that invited greater intimacy, and at the same time, greater friction with the family. The intimacy, for example, that allowed some slaves to receive their manumission given "good and admirable services" made other domestic slaves the victims of suspicious accusations by their masters, including, for example, poisoning of food.[24] Although domestic chores required many hours of work, San Juan's urban setting and the errands masters often required of their domestics allowed these slaves to spend a considerable amount of time on their own and outside their masters' residences. Some domestic slaves even rented their services to others outside their masters' families.

Slavery remained an active institution in San Juan and the rest of the Island until abolition. During the decade prior to abolition, slaves were still being bought and sold in San Juan.[25] Many of these slaves were later sold to the haciendas in San Juan's periphery as the demand for agricultural slaves remained high and hacienda owners paid higher prices to obtain them. Although the sale of slaves continued in Puerto Rico, statistics show that the slave population decreased in the decade prior to abolition. In San Juan's case, the number of slaves decreased from 1,334 in 1869 to 890 in 1872.[26] The decreasing number of slaves in San Juan was certainly a factor affecting the demand for domestic work in the city.

Domestic Work and Urban Slavery in the Abolitionist Debate

The debates regarding the potential abolition of slavery in Puerto Rico, debates that gathered momentum and intensity in the second half of the nineteenth century, made few references to the situation of domestic slaves. From the perspective of hacendados, merchants, politicians, and intellectuals, the key concerns of the abolition debate were: Will the sugar industry survive? Will we have a cheap and abundant workforce? What will the repercussions of abolition be in the social and political realms? Will masters get compensated for their slaves? What will the diplomatic and international fallout be? How will such a process be handled? Slaves, for their part, also articulated their own visions of what a post-slavery Puerto Rico would be like.

Although the future of domestic and urban slaves was not a central theme in the abolitionist debates, it is important to acknowledge that domestic slaves did figure in the rhetorical strategies of the warring sides of the debate. In the first place, pro-abolition groups used the figures of the total number of domestic slaves to argue that Puerto Rico's agriculture would not be affected by the elimination of slavery. *El Abolicionista,* the propaganda newspaper of the pro-abolition forces, gave the following rationale in Madrid's press:

> Of the 30,000 slaves that exist in the tiny Antille, 25,000 are dedicated to domestic service and their manumission will not affect agricultural production at all. Agriculture right now is done with free laborers, except for the 8,000 slaves that complete the total number of slaves for the entire Puerto Rico.[27]

The manipulation of numbers (not always exact or reliable) and the arbitrary designation of slaves as either agricultural or domestic were some of the ways in which the supporters of abolition presented their argument to minimize fears of a financial and agricultural disaster in Puerto Rico resulting from abolition.

Other pro-abolitionist leaders used the numbers of domestics and the nature of domestic work not to mitigate fears of a potential economic crisis following abolition, but to mitigate fears of a social revolt. For many, their opposition to abolition stemmed not from financial considerations but from social order concerns. The racial hierarchy that slavery provided Puerto Rico could be altered or inverted with the end of slavery, something that worried members of the white elite. Others feared the potentially damaging effects on society of the supposed intellectual and moral inferiority of slaves. To appease those fears, pro-abolitionists used domestic slaves as an example of the docility and obedience that the ruling elite wanted to see perpetuated in a post-abolition Puerto Rico. To this end, the famous Puerto Rican abolitionists Segundo Ruiz Belvis, José Julian Acosta, and Francisco Mariano Quiñones wrote in 1867:

> Of the 41,000 total slaves, the 28,000 employed in mechanical tasks and in domestic service have always seen public authority over the master's authority, respecting both. If this situation keeps the slaves today away from any idea of disturbance, with more reason will it keep it away the day they obtain their freedom.[28]

With explanations such as this, abolitionist leaders tried to dissipate fears of a freedmen's revolt or of any other kind of racial disturbance. The abolitionists manipulated the images associated with domestic slaves—their supposed docility and loyalty toward their masters—to minimize the threats suggested by the anti-abolitionist forces.

One last argument used by the promoters of abolition was to accentuate the lack of employment and work options the domestics would face once slavery disappeared. Abolitionists, again, used domestic slavery to counter the arguments of their antagonists. The pro-slavery forces argued that abolition would create a major havoc in the labor market given that former slaves would seek only well-paid jobs, or they would filter to the countryside to engage in subsistence agriculture.[29] Although abolitionists like Acosta and Ruiz Belvis acknowledged that some alteration in the labor supply was likely once slavery ended, these leaders emphasized the volume of domestics that would probably end up working in the same kind of jobs they had as slaves. Acosta and Ruiz Belvis presented their views in the *Proyecto para la abolición de la esclavitud* (1867):

> Because it has occurred to no one that domestic slaves, most of them women, and those dedicated to mechanical tasks in the towns, will abandon their ordinary tasks when they become free, given that their actual situation is far more benign than that of slaves living in the countryside. The transition from slavery to freedom will be, therefore, less violent.[30]

The abolitionist leaders promoted the image of an orderly and pacific transition after abolition. In the quotation above, abolitionists used the strategy of feminizing domestic slavery by accentuating that the majority of the domestic slaves were women. This feminization attempted to conjure images of docility and submission destined to appease those fearful of the effects of abolition. Pro-abolition leaders utilized the nature of domestic slavery itself, the apparent lack of employment options for the new freedmen and women, and the myth of the domestic slave as a loyal and docile subject in order to promote the eradication of slavery in Puerto Rico.

The Labor "Crisis" and the Struggle to Control the Supply of Domestics in San Juan

Aside from the manipulation in the propaganda in favor of and against the abolition of slavery in Puerto Rico, the colonial authorities and the commercial and agricultural elite had faced what they described as a *crisis de brazos* (labor crisis) since the mid-nineteenth century. Governor López de Baños instituted a registry for wage-laborers *(jornaleros)* in 1838, forcing every landless person age 16 through 60 to register with the municipal vagrancy juntas and list his or her occupation.[31] The so-called labor crisis did not occur because there were not enough workers in Puerto Rico, but because the government and the elite wanted to dictate working conditions and wages on the Island.[32] Social and labor control regulations of those without land continued all through the nineteenth century as profits in the sugar sector dwindled and the possibilities of reproducing a slave labor force decreased. Perhaps the best known of these regulations was the *jornalero* legislation issued by Governor Juan de la Pezuela in 1849. Pezuela's regulations combined all labor control laws approved by previous governors and added a new requirement that forced *jornaleros* to carry a notebook or passbook in which information regarding their labor history was kept. Although labor control mechanisms were applied all through the Island, in San Juan's case repressive and preventive regulations were issued around the reproduction, access, and control of domestic workers.

The apparent shortage of workers affected San Juan in the second half of the nineteenth century. Not only did the abolition of slavery debate cause concerns and re-negotiations, but also the city's elite faced the problem of recruiting domestics in order to keep their privileged lifestyle. The problem was not that there were not enough women ready to work as domestics, but that given demographic and economic changes in San Juan there were fewer women willing to accept the elite's terms of remuneration and working conditions. Among the factors that affected the supply of domestic workers in San Juan were demographic changes (fewer women and fewer people of color), the effects of the cholera epidemic in 1855, the rise in the price of slaves given the end of the slave trade, and the fears rising out of the impending abolition of slavery on the Island.[33]

On the economic side, urban slavery in San Juan—as well as on the rest of the Island—entered a crisis beginning in the second half of the nineteenth century. Rising inflation, ever increasing prices of basic goods, the shortage of domestic slaves, and the difficulty in providing for those slaves directly affected the viability of urban slavery in San Juan. This crisis, similar to the ones that affected several other Caribbean and Latin American urban centers, combined with the changing demographic patterns in San Juan, marked not only the limits of the attempts at regulating domestic work but also the terms of the supply of and demand for domestic work in the capital.[34]

Faced with the difficulty of obtaining domestics, Spanish authorities initiated a campaign of identifying and controlling workers. In 1858, for example, the central government prepared a list of domestics, agricultural workers, and unemployed people in each town.[35] Lists such as this indicated the importance the insular government placed on domestic work—it was, after all, one of the categories of the list—although most official communiqués and contemporary accounts privileged the work of agricultural workers. In 1864, San Juan's Cabildo started another listing of women and men over fourteen years of age who "rent themselves for permanent domestic work in someone else's home, cooking, washing, cleaning and taking care of a home or family or analogous occupations."[36] This municipal listing, created from an Island-wide one, included information regarding all the work contracts issued to domestics. The 1864 regulations required "obedience, fidelity and respect" from the domestics to their employers, a requirement that was not expected to be reciprocated by employers. Violations to the regulations—which included losing your work passbook or not having updated information in the passbook—were only stipulated for the domestic workers. The penalties were: "If you were male you faced six days of correction working in public works in the region at half-pay, and if female a fine of four reales or a day in jail."[37] The only punishment to the employers mentioned in the 1864 regulations was that they were to go to court if they were behind in their payments to the domestic worker. The 1864 regulations were part of ongoing Island-wide efforts throughout the 1860s to reinstate and reinforce some of the coercive labor measures designed in the 1830s and 1840s given the perceived failure to increase the supply of workers.[38] In 1871, the government enacted another set of regulations pertaining to domestic work. Official authorities themselves recognized that these 1871 regulations were not enforced, "perhaps because at that time domestic work was still performed for the most part by slaves."[39]

The impact of the abolition of slavery on the supply of workers in Puerto Rico after 1873, particularly in urban centers, needs to be studied with more care. Nevertheless, it is clear that both Spanish authorities and the local elite were convinced that there was a shortage of domestics in San Juan. The Spanish governor, for example, commented on the negative effects of abolition a few years after it was enacted. He said:

> after the abolition of slavery, [there was] the need to mitigate one of its effects, in the Capital particularly, which was the shortage of domestics, even for the most necessary chores. There were not then, as now, any available replacements.[40]

The governor's commentary referred to a petition to transfer twenty-five inmates from the local jail to perform domestic chores in San Juan due to the difficulty experienced by the elite in finding workers willing to perform domestic services.

In 1876—three years after the abolition of slavery in Puerto Rico—the city regulated domestic work by forcing domestics to carry a passbook, and to register at the local town hall.[41] City authorities justified the new regulations not just because of the so-called shortage of domestics, but also to defend the rights of both workers and employers during contracting. The registry had information regarding the conduct, physical traits, place of birth, marital status, and names of the parents of each domestic.[42] Besides the standard regulations of movement, scheduling, and residency, the 1876 law also attempted to limit the pool of domestics to city residents and thus avoid encouraging immigration into San Juan from other parts of the Island. Domestics not complying with the passbook and the registry were fined three pesos for the first infraction. In the case of a second infraction, the fine increased to six pesos, and the domestic was exiled to her/his city of origin.[43]

It is ironic that city officials complained about a shortage of domestic employees at the same time that they were legislating to ship potential workers out of San Juan. This points to the real purpose behind all the domestic work regulations: to control and manipulate the supply of domestics and dictate the terms of the working conditions of those domestics in the city. Also, the 1876 regulations coincided with the last year of the mandatory contracting of the slaves "liberated" in 1873. Although there are no clear data about the effects of the actual abolition of slavery in San Juan, studies from towns such as Guayama showed a significant increment of former slaves, particularly women, migrating to cities seeking employment as domestics.[44] The 1876 regulations in San Juan were perhaps destined not only to dictate the terms of employment in the city but also to prevent a massive migration of *libertos* (freedmen and women) who might become a safety and economic hazard to the colonial officials and the urban elite.

The different domestic service regulations issued by the colonial government, starting in the 1850s and continuing in various years after slavery was abolished, show similar patterns. First, all regulations were drafted to ameliorate the so-called labor crisis among domestics in San Juan and other parts of Puerto Rico. Second, the regulations copied the mechanisms—registries, passbooks, spatial and geographical restrictions, punitive measures ranging from fines to forced hard labor—employed by insular authorities in the legislation regulating *jornaleros* and other landless people on the Island. Third, the passbooks subordinated workers to the bureaucratic whims and fancies of colonial officials and employers. Given that any improper conduct, from the employers' perspective, had to be recorded in the passbook, domestics were vulnerable to their employers' caprices, in addition to the control the employers had in the areas of contracting and determining wages. Finally, the continuous passing of regulations indicated that even if Puerto Rico's historiography has neglected the importance of domestic work, that was not the case with Spanish authorities and the dominant classes in nineteenth-century Puerto Rico.

Beneficence—Social and Labor Control

Another response by colonial Spanish officials and Puerto Rico's elite to the problem of securing an abundant, cheap, and docile supply of domestics was the proliferation of public and semi-private beneficence institutions in the nineteenth century. The liberal conception of beneficence superseded old notions of charity, which had shaped the way the state, church, and dominant classes had responded to the needs of the poor on the Island.[45] Beneficence institutions became the locale where liberal and modernizing discourses in Puerto Rican society merged with social engineering projects destined to make economic and medically marginal individuals into productive members of society. It was in the *casas de amparo,* the asylums and hospitals, where the elite and the government experimented with their recipes for rehabilitation, vocational instruction, discipline, and job placements in order to, among other objectives, guarantee the reproduction of domestic workers and artisans who could be lost as a result of the abolition of slavery.

The Casa de Beneficencia in San Juan was inaugurated in 1844. From the specific original intent to serve as a "*casa de recogidas, amparo o reclusión*," the Casa was turned into a multi-purpose establishment by the time of its opening.[46] In the Casa, mental patients were committed, slaves and women awaiting trial were "deposited," prostitutes and indigent people were cloistered, and vocational instruction was provided to poor children to turn them into artisans and domestics. On several occasions, the Casa also housed and distributed so-called *emancipados*—slaves illegally shipped into Puerto Rico after the slave trade was abolished—to hacienda owners in need of agricultural or domestic workers.[47] In order to generate its operating revenue, the Casa relied on the profits made by interns who did laundry for the nearby hospitals and military garrisons. This type of arrangement—in which the institution generated its own revenue, women learned domestic service skills that would make them "useful" and productive in the future, and the Spanish bureaucracy's domestic service needs were supplied—was considered ideal by the colonial authorities. It is not surprising, then, to discover multiple petitions by elite city members requesting to house a domestic from the Casa in their residences in the period between 1844 and 1873. Doña Ana María Crosas de Vidal, for example, asked the Cabildo for an orphan girl from the Casa to be employed as a domestic. Crosas de Vidal promised "to take care of and provide for her as if she were one of our own family," and the Cabildo accepted her petition.[48]

The Casa de Beneficencia was not the only institution created in San Juan that combined the rhetoric of beneficence with the training, placement, and control of domestic workers during the decades of the so-called labor shortage prior to abolition. In 1859, for example, a group of ladies in San Juan requested permission to create a beneficence asylum to provide elementary and vocational education to poor children. In 1861, after an intense struggle between San Juan's bishop and the Island's governor regarding who would have jurisdiction over the institution, the Asilo de San Ildefonso opened its doors.[49] The Asilo, administered by a board of elite women and staffed by nuns and volunteers, provided elementary and religious education to poor girls. As in other beneficence institutions established in Puerto Rico at the time—in Ponce, for example, the Asilo de Damas was opened in 1866 and the Asilo Tricoche in 1868—elite women organized institutions that guaranteed a reliable, accessible, and trained supply of domestic workers.[50]

Beneficence in San Juan, like in the rest of Puerto Rico, emerged partly as a response from the colonial authorities and the elite to the labor shortage problems they thought affected the Island starting at mid-century. In San Juan, beneficence establishments were oriented toward recruiting, training, and placing domestic workers. The city's elite women played an important role in creating and administering these institutions, which helped to guarantee their privileged lifestyle and kept them in charge within the public sphere of the domestic staff they supervised in the private sphere of the home. Although much remains to be researched and studied regarding the emergence of beneficence institutions during the second half of the nineteenth century, it is clear that their emergence concurs with the attempts by the dominant class to mitigate the repercussions of the so-called labor crisis on the Island and to prepare themselves for the eventual labor market changes caused by the impending abolition of slavery.

Domestic Workers and Their Conflicts with City Officials

The perception of a lack of domestic workers and their even greater shortage once slavery was abolished was not the only reason why colonial authorities and the elite attempted several labor and social control strategies. Although it is not easy to recover the responses and the activities of nineteenth-century domestics, there is evidence that they fought to improve their working conditions and the remuneration they received for their services. The colonial bureaucracy and the municipal policing authorities had constant clashes with domestics from the mid-nineteenth century on. These clashes were another reason why new mechanisms of labor and social control were tried in San Juan during the second half of the nineteenth century.

Of all the domestic workers in San Juan, it was the laundresses with whom city officials had the most problems and frictions. The reasons for these frictions were many. First, laundresses, for the most part, were black, mulatto, or parda. This, added to their access to visible public spaces (such as water fountains and plazas) and to private spaces (the homes and the bedrooms of their masters or clients), made laundresses highly suspicious in the eyes of city officials. It must be kept in mind that, until the 1850s, San Juan was a demographically black and colored city and that the Creole and Spanish elites were always fearful of a slave and colored revolt.[51] For public safety officials—all of them male—it must also have been uncomfortable and difficult to operate in predominantly female public spaces, such as a water fountain crowded with laundresses and their children.

The fears regarding the behavior of laundresses in San Juan were not merely abstract. At several junctures, city laundresses challenged colonial and police officials. The laundresses at the Hospital de la Caridad, for example, complained and organized work stoppages on several occasions to protest the lack of access to water and the poor working conditions at the hospital.[52] In one of their disputes, the laundresses requested from the Cabildo in 1842 permission to use the water cisterns at the military barracks in Ballajá. A Laundresses' Guild existed in 1876, although there is not much information regarding its activities or membership.[53]

Another incident that shows the repeated frictions between city officials and laundresses occurred in 1857 at Condado's water fountain. The *alcalde* (municipal judge) of Cangrejos—a small suburb outside San Juan—chastised several laundresses at the Condado fountain not only for the noise and bustle they were causing but also for encroaching on private property as they washed and dried their clothes. The *alcalde* argued that his job was

To prevent, as it is expected by the government, all causes of scandal and disorder in the section of the territory to the right of the road leading to San Juan and in the fountain's surroundings, which were being committed by the mentioned laundresses who behaved without any respect to my authority or to the property. Since the laundresses were invading all the land, I asked them to leave the premises given that it was not political nor convenient that they stayed there, particularly when their presence there had led others, not interested in earning a precarious subsistence washing clothes but in creating a scandal and demoralizing the general public and those who traveled near the fountain with their improper and unruly behavior disregarding the provisos of the island's government.[54]

After a heated exchange, the laundresses replied that they did not recognize the *alcalde*'s jurisdiction because the water fountain was located in San Juan and not in Cangrejos. The dispute between the laundresses and the *alcalde* ended up on the governor's desk.

If the clashes with colonial officials did not enhance the laundresses' poor reputations, their status as women who earned a living working in the city's streets did not help them either. Their public persona excluded laundresses from the considerations and respect of men. Laundresses were not protected like other women who did not venture into the streets without an escort and otherwise stayed behind closed doors. The laundresses who worked outside their homes were frequent victims of physical, verbal, and sexual abuse. Not only were they targets of these kinds of abuse, but their condition as public women limited their attempts at vindicating themselves after the abuse was committed. The documentation from the civil courts provides ample evidence of the "presumption of guilt" in cases against women whose work forced them out to the streets escorted only, perhaps, by their children or by fellow domestics, or against women whose work forced them in and out of their clients' homes. Her status as a laundress, for example, was enough for the court to dismiss Juana de Dios González's lawsuit against Pasqual García. González was suing García, a soldier, for "seduction and rape" under the pretension and promise of marriage.[55] González claimed that García visited her house, promised to marry her, and had given her a child; therefore, he had to marry her. In these kinds of cases it was usually enough to know that a man had visited a women's house for the court to rule in favor of the woman, forcing the man either to marry her or to provide her with an adequate dowry. García defended himself by arguing that it was well known that González and her mother were laundresses, and that it was logical to assume that his ins and outs of their house had nothing to do with romance, but with his laundry. The public nature of González's work had cost her her day in court.

Another laundress, Ysabel Avilés, faced a similar fate. She was sued by the soldier Don Julián Gutiérrez for having insulted him publicly. Gutiérrez argued that Avilés, who normally took care of his laundry, had entered his house and told him that "it was enough for him to be a soldier to be indecent, a scoundrel and a thief."[56] Avilés, in her defense, accepted having insulted Gutiérrez, but only after explaining that since he owed her money, she went to his house to collect her payment, only to be publicly insulted by Gutiérrez and violently thrown out of his house into the street. The judge accepted Gutiérrez's version of the story and asked Avilés for a public apology. Avilés did not accept the judge's decision.

Colonial and ecclesiastical authorities both complained about the lack of decorum and order present in San Juan's public plazas. As the nineteenth century advanced, uneasiness grew among the elite regarding the possible abolition of slavery and the potential challenges to the social and economic hierarchy it could unleash. Furthermore, by mid-century, San Juan was beginning to feel the first European influences regarding urban beautification, decoration, and hygiene in open public spaces.[57] This combination of factors lead city officials to approve in the late 1860s the construction of a public washing area to move all the laundresses into Puerta de Tierra, an extramural barrio.[58] In Puerta de Tierra, the laundresses would be sufficiently near the city to be able to provide adequate laundry services and sufficiently far away not to be a public safety, hygiene, and beauty problem. Under the mask of beautification, decoration, and hygiene, Spanish officials and the city elite's hid their fears and insecurities regarding the dislocations and changes that the post-abolition world would bring to San Juan.

Conclusion

The access to and control of domestic work in San Juan played an important role during the 1840–73 period as shown by the multiple regulatory attempts and by the recurring conflicts between domestics and city officials. Although it did not play a leading role, domestic work did figure in the comments and strategies of the two sides in the abolition of slavery debate in Puerto Rico. Even when the Island's historiography has marginalized the study of domestic work in the Island, it is clear that these workers worried many in Puerto Rico during the second half of the nineteenth century.

I have identified three responses to the socioeconomic transformations occurring just prior to the abolition of slavery, particularly as it related to the supply of domestics. The first one was the attempt at increasing the social and spatial control over domestics using lists, registries, and punitive legislation, in response to what the government and the elite saw as a labor shortage. This was not a new pattern in the history of the Spanish colonial government's ongoing struggle to guarantee a cheap, docile, and abundant labor force in Puerto Rico. These attempts trace their ideological roots to the insular laws of the 1840s and the parallel campaigns to eradicate vagrancy and common-law marriage on the Island.[59] Instead of visionary public policy solutions targeted at improving and modernizing the Island's economy, Spanish officials and their allies opted for a tough policing stand to face their perceived labor shortage problems.

The second response was a struggle to control the city's public and private spaces. This struggle had been going on in San Juan, if in a less intense manner, since the beginning of the nineteenth century. The city elites' policies effectively pushed significant numbers of people of color (the majority of them women) out of the city and into the surrounding extramural barrios.[60] The idea of the public washing area in Puerta de Tierra, although it was never constructed, shows the way in which San Juan's upper classes wished to reconfigure the city's social, economic, and racial space. In terms of private spaces, more research is still needed regarding the struggles for control and distance in these spaces. The renegotiations between domestics and their masters or employers that occurred as abolition got nearer and the uncertainty grew regarding the rules that would apply in the post-slavery world await the careful scrutiny of future Puerto Rican historians.

The third response wa; provided through the creation of beneficence institutions. The advocates of beneficence pointed to the intellectual and public policy currents in Europe to rally support for the establishment of beneficence institutions. The ironic twist of this influence is that the elite still needed domestic work to carry out its modernizing agenda. Domestics guaranteed the free time that elite and the new professional classes needed to dedicate themselves to their modernizing social, economic, and cultural projects. Public and semi-private beneficence was a mechanism by which new forms of social control, vigilance, job placement, rehabilitation, and vocational and religious training were experimented with.

A significant part of this essay has focused on analyzing some of the reactions of San Juan's elite to the changes in the mid-nineteenth-century labor market. Unfortunately, I have not been able to document with equal precision the domestics' reactions to the transformations mentioned above. Logically, the mere existence of all the registries and regulations indicates that there was some resistance to doing domestic work under the conditions dictated by the upper classes. Perhaps other sources—diaries, letters, or court testimonies—will allow the exploration of domestic workers' quotidian engagement or distancing from this process. If the experiences of the laundresses are an indicator, one can argue that the Spanish authorities and the elite faced groups of women intent on defining, to the best of their abilities and resources, the terms of their working conditions.

Another element that could shed some light on the development of domestic work in Puerto Rico during the second half of the nineteenth century would be the experience of other Caribbean and Latin American urban centers. In Barbados, for example, Pedro Welch has shown how the experiences with urban slaves in Bridgetown prepared the governmental and commercial elite to consolidate control mechanisms for the period after abolition. Among the mechanisms they instituted were the control and regulation of emigration and the creation of a city police corps to monitor and punish the new freedmen and women.[61] The attempts to regulate post-slavery domestic work in San Juan with mechanisms from the pre-1873 world indicate that in Puerto Rico the colonial authorities also learned from their experiences with the mobility and resistance of urban slaves and *libertos*. It is also likely that the authorities in Puerto Rico were acquainted with the various mechanisms of social and labor control employed in the British and French Caribbean possessions after slavery was abolished in 1833 and 1848 respectively. The experiences in other urban areas of Puerto Rico, such as Ponce, Mayagüez, and Arecibo, could help to corroborate this hypothesis.

San Juan's domestics, many of them urban female slaves, were part of the cast of characters that worried colonial officials, elite members, and those debating the wisdom of abolition. This essay has attempted to highlight the importance of domestic service to the urban economy of San Juan at a time of transition from slave labor to so-called "free" labor. I have also analyzed how domestic service was linked to other developments in San Juan such as the institutionalization of public and semi-private beneficence establishments. Many questions emerge from the evidence presented here regarding San Juan, and they merit further study. What can be learned from the evidence of other urban centers in Puerto Rico? How do they compare with San Juan's experiences? Why have domestic labor and urban slavery attracted so little attention in Puerto Rican historiography? How can the history of abolition and slavery in Puerto Rico begin to be rewritten considering the experiences of urban centers? I hope that this study stimulates further historical research regarding domestic work and its connections with the significant socioeconomic transformations of Puerto Rico, such as the abolition of slavery.

Notes

Abbreviations

AGPR	Archivo General de Puerto Rico
AHD	Archivo Histórico Diocesano
AHN	Archivo Histórico Nacional
C	Caja
CP	Fondo Colecciones Particulares
E	Expediente
f	folio
FAT	Fondo Audiencia Territorial
FGEPR	Fondo Gobernadores Españoles
FMSJ Fondo	Municipal San Juan
FOP	Fondo Obras Públicas
FPN	Fondo Protocolos Notariales
L	Legajo
P	Pieza/Parte
S	Serie
Se	Sección
v	vuelto

This article was originally published as "'¿Quien Trabajará?' Trabajo doméstico, esclavitud urbana y abolición en San Juan en el siglo XIX", in the journal *Revista de Ciencias Sociales*, and is translated with their permission.

The author wishes to thanks Emilio Kourí, Luis Figueroa, Eileen Findlay, Jorge Duany, Pedro San Miguel, and Joan Krizack for their helpful commentaries and suggestions.

1. See, among others, Centro de Investigaciones Históricas, *El proceso abolicionista en Puerto Rico: Documentos para su estudio,* 2 vols. (San Juan: Instituto de Cultura Puertorriqueña, 1974–78); José Curet, "About Slavery and the Order of Things: Puerto Rico, 1845–1873," in *Between Slavery and Free Labor: The Spanish Speaking Caribbean in the Nineteenth Century,* ed. Manuel Moreno Fraginals, Frank Moya Pons, and Stanley L. Engerman (Baltimore: Johns Hopkins University Press, 1985), 117–40; Luis M. Díaz Soler, *Historia de la esclavitud en Puerto Rico,* 3d ed. (Río Piedras: Editorial Universitaria, 1981); Arturo Morales Carrión, *Auge y decadencia de la trata negrera en Puerto Rico (1820–1860)* (San Juan: Centro de Estudios Avanzados de Puerto Rico y el Caribe & Instituto de Cultura Puertorriqueña, 1978); Benjamín Nistal-Moret, "Problems in the Social Structure of Slavery in Puerto Rico During the Process of Abolition, 1872," in Moreno Fraginals, Moya Pons, and Engerman, *Between Slavery and Free Labor,* 141–57; and Andrés Ramos Mattei, *La hacienda azucarera: Su crecimiento y crisis en Puerto Rico (siglo xix)* (San Juan: Centro de Estudios de la Realidad Puertorriqueña [CEREP], 1981).

2. See Curet, "About Slavery"; Andrés Ramos Mattei, ed. *Azucar y esclavitud* (Río Piedras: Editorial Universitaria, 1982); and Luis Figueroa, "Facing Freedom: The Transition from Slavery to Free Labor in Guayama, Puerto Rico, 1860–1898," (Ph.D. diss., University of Wisconsin–Madison, 1991).

3. This literature is quite extensive. See, among others, Robin Blackburn, *The Overthrow of Colonial Slavery, 1776–1848* (London: Verso Books, 1988); Arthur F. Corwin, *Spain and the Abolition of Slavery in Cuba, 1817–1886* (Austin: University of Texas Press, 1967); David Brion Davis, *The Problem of Slavery in the Age of Revolution, 1770–1823* (Ithaca: Cornell University Press, 1975); Seymour Drescher, *Capitalism and Slavery: British Mobilization in Comparative Perspective* (New York: Oxford University Press, 1986); William A. Green, *British Slave Emancipation: The Sugar Colonies and the Great Experiment, 1830–1865* (Oxford: Oxford University Press, 1976); Thomas C. Holt, *The Problem of Freedom: Race, Labour and Politics in Jamaica and Britain, 1832–1938* (Baltimore: Johns Hopkins University Press, 1992); Moreno Fraginals, Moya Pons, and Engerman, *Between Slavery and Free Labor;* Rebecca Scott, *Slave Emancipation in Cuba: The Transition to Free Labor, 1860–1899* (Princeton: Princeton University Press, 1985); "Comparing Emancipations: A Review Essay," *Journal of Social History* 20, no. 3 (1987): 565–83; "Exploring the Meaning of Freedom: Postemancipation Societies in Comparative Perspective," *Hispanic American Historical Review* 68, no. 3 (1988): 407–28; Dale W. Tomich, *Slavery in the Circuit of Sugar: Martinique and the World Economy* (Baltimore: Johns Hopkins University Press, 1990); and Pedro L. Welch, "Notes from the Bridgetown Underground: Control and Protest in Post-Emancipation Barbados," paper presented at the 28th Annual Meeting of the Society of Caribbean Historians, Bridgetown, Barbados, April 17, 1996.

4. See, for example, Elsa Chaney and May G. Castro, eds., *Muchachas No More: Household Workers in Latin America and the Caribbean* (Philadelphia: Temple University Press, 1989); Sandra L. Graham, *House and Street: The Domestic World of Servants and Masters in Nineteenth-Century Rio de Janeiro* (Cambridge: Cambridge University Press, 1988); Mary Romero, *Maid in the USA* (New York: Routledge, 1992); and Heidi Tisman, "The Indispensable Services of Sisters: Considering Domestic Service in Latin America and the Caribbean," *Journal of Women's History* 4, no. 1 (1992): 37–59.

5. Tera Hunter, "Household Workers in the Making: Afro-American Women in Atlanta and the New South, 1861 to 1921" (Ph.D. diss., Yale University, 1990); Elizabeth Kuznesof, "A History of Domestic Service in Spanish America, 1492–1980," in Chaney and Castro, *Muchachas No More,* 17–36; and Tisman, "The Indispensable Services."

6. Mariano Negrón Portillo and Raúl Mayo Santana, *La esclavitud urbana en San Juan: Estudio del Registro de Jornaleros de Esclavos de 1872* (Río Piedras: Ediciones Huracán, 1992), 80–81.

7. Rubén Carbonell Fernández, "Las compra-ventas de esclavos en San Juan, 1817–1873" (M.A. thesis, Department of History, University of Puerto Rico–Río Piedras); Félix V. Matos Rodríguez, "Street Vendors, Shop-Owners and Domestics: Some Aspects of Women's Economic Roles in 19th Century San Juan, Puerto Rico," in *Engendering History: Caribbean Women in Historical Perspective,* ed. Verene Shepherd, Bridget Brereton, and Barbara Bailey (Kingston: Ian Randle Publishers, 1995), 176–96; Negrón Portillo and Mayo Santana, *La esclavitud urbana;* and Pedro L. Welch, "The Urban Context of the Slave Plantation System: Bridgetown, Barbados, 1680–1834," (Ph.D. diss., University of the West Indies, 1994).

8. Luis Aponte-Parés, "Casas y Bohíos: Territorial Development and Urban Growth in XIXth Century Puerto Rico" (Ph.D. diss., Columbia University, 1990), 291–99; and Aníbal Sepúlveda Rivera, *San Juan: Historia ilustrada de su desarollo urbano, 1508–1898* (San Juan: Carimar, 1989), 222–24.

9. Centro de Investigaciones Históricas, *El proceso,* 2d vol., 181–82.

10. Aixa Merino Falú, "El Gremio de Lavanderas de Puerta de Tierra, " in *Historias vivas: Historiografía puertorriqueña contemporánea,* ed. Antonio Gaztambide Géigel and Silvia Alvarez Curbelo (San Juan: Asociación Puertorriqueña de Historiadores & Editorial Postdata), 74–79.

11. Félix V. Matos Rodríguez, "Economy, Society and Urban Life: Women in Nineteenth Century San Juan, Puerto Rico (1820–1870)" (Ph.D. diss., Columbia University, 1994), 32; 96–97.

12. Negrón Portillo and Mayo Santana, *La esclavitud urbana,* 9–14.

13. The 1846 census is the first one providing the occupation or employment of women in San Juan. The 1846 data come from three out of the four quarters that made up the city of San Juan then. AGPR, FMSJ, Censos San Juan (Santa Bárbara, Santo Domingo and San Francisco barrios), 1846.

14. Adolfo De Hostos, *Historia de San Juan, cuidad murada* (San Juan: Instituto de Cultura Puertorriqueña, 1983), 21.

15. Matos Rodríguez, "Economy, Society," 105.

16. *Pardo/a* usually refers to light-skinned mulattos.

17. AGPR, FMSJ, Censos San Juan, 1846.

18. I have included as "heads of households" those individuals listed in the 1846 censuses as *jefe* (head) or *inquilino* (tenant). The data come from AGPR, FMSJ, Censos San Juan, 1846.

19. Negrón Portillo and Mayo Santana, *La esclavitud urbana,* 114–17.

20. Ibid., 81–89.

21. Díaz Soler, *Historia,* 158–61.

22. De Hostos, *Historia de San Juan,* 477–79.

23. Sepúlveda Rivera, *San Juan,* 288–90.

24. An example of this type of accusation can be found in the testament of Don Patricio Fogarty. Fogarty accused his *mulata* cook of poisoning his food. AGPR, FPN, San Juan, José María León de Urbina, February 21, 1827, C-442, 84f-85v.

25. Carbonell Fernández, "Las compra-ventas," 29–32.

26. Negrón Portillo and Mayo Santana, *La esclavitud urbana,* 97.

27. Centro de Investigaciones Históricas, *El proceso,* 2d vol., 437. This and all subsequent direct block citations have been translated by the author. The discrepancy in the numbers appears in the original document.

28. Segundo Ruiz Belvis, José J. Acosta, and Francisco M. Quiñones, *Proyecto para la abolición de la esclavitud,* 2d ed. (Río Piedras: Editorial Edil, 1978), 70.

29. Diaz Soler, *Historia,* 278–79.

30. Ruiz Belvis, *Proyecto,* 70–71.

31. Fernando Picó, *Historia general de Puerto Rico,* 2d ed. (Río Piedras: Ediciones Huracán, 1986), 170.

32. Francisco Scarano, "Labor and Society in the Nineteenth Century," in *The Modern Caribbean,* ed. Franklin Knight and Colin Palmer (Chapel Hill: University of North Carolina Press, 1989), 51–84.

33. Matos Rodríguez, "Economy, Society," 88–129.

34. Maria Odila Silva Dias, *Power and Everyday Life: The Lives of Working Women in 19th Century Brazil* (New Brunswick, NJ: Rutgers University Press, 1995).

35. AGPR, FGEPR, Censo y Riqueza, 1858, C-16.

36. AGPR, FMSJ, Actas del Cabildo, C-24, 19 de mayo de 1864, 93f-v.

37. "Reglamento que ha de observarse en la locación del trabajo personal para el servicio doméstico," Chapter 5, Article 6. AGPR, FGEPR, S-Municipios, C-480, June 8, 1964.

38. Gómez Acevedo, *Organización y reglamentación,* 117–23.

39. AGPR, FMSJ, L-24G, E-941, April 3, 1876.

40. AHN, Se-Ultramar, Serie-Gobierno de Puerto Rico, L-5113, E-60, September 5, 1879.

41. De Hostos, *Historia de San Juan,* 81.

42. Article 4, AGPR, FMSJ, L-24G, E-941, April 3, 1876.

43. Article 1, AGPR, FMSJ, L-24G, E-941, April 3, 1876.

44. Figueroa, "Facing Freedom," 359–64.

45. Teresita Martínez Vergne, "The Liberal Concept of Charity: Beneficencia Applied to Puerto Rico, 1821–1868," in *The Middle Period in Latin America: Values and Attitudes in the 17th-19th Centuries,* ed. Mark D. Szuchman (Boulder, CO: Lynne Rienner, 1989), 167–84.

46. Matos Rodríguez, "Economy, Society," 272–73.

47. Teresita Martínez Vergne, "The Allocation of Liberated African Labour Through the Casa de Beneficencia—San Juan, Puerto Rico, 1859–1864," *Slavery and Abolition* 12:3 (1991): 200–216.

48. AGPR, FMSJ, Actas del Cabildo, C-24, December 23, 1864, 216v.

49. Matos Rodríguez, "Economy, Society," 295–97.

50. Ramón Marín, *Las fiestas populares de Ponce,* 1875 reprint (Río Piedras: Editorial de la Universidad de Puerto Rico, 1994), 227–28.

51. Matos Rodríguez, "Economy, Society," 102–07.

52. See, for example, AGPR, FMSJ, Actas del Cabildo, May 4, 1842, 88v, and June 30, 1842, 122f.

53. Merino Falú, "El Gremio de Lavanderas," 74.

54. The *alcalde*'s version is found in AGPR, FOP, Obras Municipales, L-62LL, E-13, C-236, July 14, 1857. Unfortunately, the record does not contain the governor's decision regarding the controversy. It is interesting that the chief naval officer of the Island testified in favor of the laundresses, arguing that the property in question was within his jurisdiction.

55. AGPR, FMSJ, L-73E, (P.I.), E-3, December 22, 1822.

56. AGPR, FMSJ, L-73E, (P.I.), E-12, October 10, 1841.

57. Ángel G. Quintero Rivera, *Patricios y plebeyos. Burgueses, hacendados, artesanos y obreros (Las relaciones de clase en el Puerto Rico de cambio de siglo)* (Río Piedras: Ediciones Huracán, 1988), 23–98; and Sepúlveda Rivera, *San Juan,* 158–91.

58. The public facility was never constructed, although discussion regarding its possible construction lasted into the 1880s. See AGPR, FOP, Obras Municipales, L-62LL, E-15, C-326.

59. Picó, *Historia,* 173–74. Also, Antonia Rivera Rivera, "El problema de la vagancia en el Puerto Rico del siglo XIX," *Exegesis* 5, no. 14 (1992): 12–19.

60. Matos Rodríguez, "Economy, Society," 130–32.

61. Welch, "Notes from the Underground," 20–21.

4

Virgins, Whores, and Martyrs:
Prostitution in the Colony, 1898–1919

José Flores Ramos

Introduction

The findings discussed in this essay are part of a broader investigation about prostitution in San Juan. The investigation was titled "Eugenics, Public Hygiene and Camphor for the Passions: Prostitution in San Juan, Puerto Rico, 1876–1919." It was developed as part of the requirements for the master's degree in history at the University of Puerto Rico. This essay is limited to discussing, primarily, the political game created around prostitution during the first twenty-two years of North American colonialism over Puerto Rico.

The main characters can be divided in two sectors. The first group is composed of the colonial authorities, the submissive and inconsistent municipal authorities of San Juan, and sectors of a Protestant Church in the process of expansion, which supported the Americanization of the Island. The second one, at antipodes to the first, was formed by independent and labor sectors who in 1917 reacted against the arbitrary violations of civil rights. They were encouraged by the first group when they attempted to effect a restraint on prostitution.

In the process that we will now examine, there existed two additional sectors whose common denominator was silence. One of these was the Catholic Church and the other one was the prostitutes themselves. The Church, probably because of prudence or convenience, remained outside the controversies surrounding prostitution.[1] On the other hand, the prostitutes suffered personally, including physically, from the decisions made by the authorities. Because of the marginal character of their class, their voices were lost in the city boroughs, the jail, and the hospital. The Catholic Church, with power to speak, did not speak. The prostitutes shouted, but were not heard. There was yet another reason why prostitutes in Puerto Rico did not get heard.

A bond between the colonial authorities and prostitution was not new for Puerto Rico. In the case of San Juan, such a bond was evident since the beginnings of the conquest under the Spanish regime. As early as 1526, the king of Spain authorized, with ecclesiastic blessing, the establishment of the first house of public women in America. The main justification for the establishment of the brothel was to protect the honesty of married women in the city.[2] A woman's role was understood as being to meet the sexual needs of men. Thus, more than protecting the honesty of married women, the brothel was intended to keep order among the settlers by avoiding confrontations that may have occurred in cases of kidnapping, rape, or infidelity. The brothel was thus presented as an exhaust valve to relieve tensions reflecting population imbalance—where there were more men than women.

There were periods in which Spanish authorities also exercised prohibition against prostitution. In 1824, General de la Torre, maximum civil and military authority on the Island, prohibited the prostitution houses.[3] Although there was an ordinance against prostitution, in the eyes of a pragmatic Felipe IV (in 1623),[4] it seems that it was a non-issue for Puerto Rico.

During the last quarter of the nineteenth century, as was happening in other Western cities, the municipal authorities of San Juan believed that prostitution was a threat to health and good manners. In that situation, the Capital Town Hall, in an ordinary session submitted on April 4, 1876, passed the first ordinance for public women.[5] In this manner, the first steps were taken, at least on paper, to incorporate San Juan into the regulatory wave that proliferated during the second half of the nineteenth century in many European and Hispanic American cities.[6]

The regulatory efforts in 1876 were inconsistent on the part of the state. It was not until the decade of 1890 that the regulations for prostitution were exercised with more consistency in San Juan. These regulations meant, for the prostitute, a loss of her liberty of movement and economic autonomy. However, the municipal government became the great procurer when it imposed fees and fines on part of prostitution's production.[7] Although prostitution was included in the municipal area of Industry and Commerce, this action did not constitute its legitimization. Prostitution was not only prohibited from taking place outside designated areas, prostitutes were also to be segregated when sick. A prostitute was considered a danger to society. Issues of sanity and social control reflected a major concern about scandal. Regulation and hospitalization gave the authorities the repressive arm necessary to deal with both dangers.[8]

Fernando Picó posits that in the last three decades under the Spanish domain, peninsular politics were more influenced by Spain than in any other period. Better traveling facilities, and access to the press and to the correspondence of the travelers strengthened the bonds with Spain.[9] We must consider that the second half of the nineteenth century saw many of the great changes in the social and economic surroundings that combined the bourgeois and modernizing ideas from Europe and North America.[10] Under such conditions, it was more feasible to apply on the Island measures associated with the new times. The "progress" was imposing. The regulation of prostitution was consistent with those aspirations.

Toward the decade of 1890, although Puerto Rico still was predominantly rural, urban life was developing rapidly.[11] In an agricultural exporting economy, generally, subsistence plantations were reduced to give way to harvesting exportable products. Obviously, these actions produced a deficit in local provisions, forcing the country or region to import, thus making the cost of living more expensive. Under those circumstances, the dispossessed moved to urban sites, searching for opportunities. This "recipe" provided ideal conditions for a boom in prostitution—accelerated urban growth together with a large number of dispossessed.

San Juan, an important port and military fortress, offered a great floating population of men who in some cases were single, but in other cases had wives or partners far away. The commercial activity attracted a great deal of traffic to and from the Island, and here were the potential clients for prostitution. The U.S. invasion in 1898 brought to Puerto Rico a series of changes on political and administrative levels. Until June 1900, the Island was under U.S. military rule. However, public administration remained in the hands of *criollo* officers with no power to carry out public policy.[12] With the passage of the Foraker Act in 1900, a civil government was established in Puerto Rico. This act established the United States colonial policy in Puerto Rico. Just as any conqueror, the state thought it necessary to keep the new colony under its protective tutelage. Although the right to elect a House of Delegates was granted to the Puerto Ricans, in practice it was subject to the governor and the Executive Council, both of them appointed by the president of the United States.[13]

The Jones Act of 1917 opened a space for democratic participation. Under this Act, U.S. citizenship was imposed on Puerto Ricans and its government structure was modified. The Executive Council was eliminated and substituted with a Senate to be elected by the population. However, the governor was still named by the U.S. president, and the members of the cabinet confirmed by the Senate of the United States.[14] Behind the democracy and progress speech of the U.S. government during the first thirty years of its domain, what some have called the "imperialism of abandonment" was practiced.[15] Abandonment was expressed, argues Francisco Scarano, in the excessive power of the absentee corporations, the senseless policy of Americanization, and a series of bewildering social problems, such as growing unemployment, poverty, bad health and living conditions, and emigration.[16]

The poor health conditions prevailing on the Island led the United States to make efforts to improve hygiene and health conditions.[17] The treatment given by the state to the issues related to prostitution were influenced by that posture. As a consequence, the process of state intervention into personal daily life increased considerably. However, and in contrast with what happened in the United States, the system of regulations that was based on French models was not abolished until 1917, when the American authorities decided to do so.

Even though the movement to abolish prostitution was widespread in the United States around 1900,[18] it had only the slightest impact in Puerto Rico. Local Protestant churches called for reform but their political impact, at least until 1917, had no effect on the official policy on prostitution. This was an interesting parallel to what happened in India. There, the British authorities remained steadfast in favor of the regimentation system, even after it had long been abolished in Great Britain. Both the Protestant missionaries and the Indian reformers had voiced their desire to abolish the system. However, the political influence of the former was weak in colonial times.[19]

Prostitution Faces the Changing of the Guard

The first twenty-two years of the history of prostitution under the American regime can be divided into two phases. The first phase spans the initial twenty years, when prostitution was barely repressed or regulated. However, the publicity given to this subject and the success of several hygiene campaigns laid the foundation for the repression that would define the second phase.

This second phase was short but intense. The new status of U.S. citizenship opened the way for the entry of thousands of young men into compulsory military service. By 1917, prostitution in Puerto Rico underwent the strongest period of repression in its history. The main objective of this repression was to protect future recruits from venereal diseases. The repression was also an extension of the "American Plan" into the colony. The conflicts that arose as a result of the repression of prostitution brought to the forefront the many political and social tensions that existed within the country.

The First Phase: 1898–1917

Demographically, Puerto Rico was considered an overpopulated colony. It was the urban centers that underwent a marked population boom. In the case of the city of San Juan, it had an increase of 16,728 inhabitants during the period under study. Areas such as Santurce and Puerta de Tierra were also affected by this growth. A large part of these two areas later became poverty belts.[20]

In 1899 the ratio of men to women was 98.2 men for every 100 women. However, at around this same time, 61.7 percent of all inhabitants were single males older than fifteen years of age, including an 8.8 percent segment who were in common-law marriages. This figure was significantly high considering the ratio in the United States at this time was only 39.9 percent.[21] A high single population was also exposed to the influence of a strong military presence, especially in the San Juan area. This became fertile ground for the development of a potential client base for prostitution. It is interesting to note what historian Félix M. Matos identified as the whitening and masculinization of the San Juan population during the 1800s. The population underwent certain changes in the final years of the 1890s.[22] By 1910, the most prevalent racial group in the capital city were blacks, including mulattos. Similar to what happened in the closing years of the eighteenth century and at the beginning of the nineteenth century, the majority of women were black or mulattos. The male population was mainly white, reflecting the strong American military presence as well as many foreign civilian males. Fifty-one percent of the male population was white and 49 percent was black and mulatto. For women, the proportion was 54 percent black and mulatto, and 46 percent white.[23]

It would seem that these demographic changes were related to the poverty in the communities of Santurce and Puerta de Tierra. Poverty, with its black and female profile, became more widespread at the end of the 1800s and accelerated at the beginning of the twentieth century.[24]

Under the new colonial regime, Puerto Rican administrators felt that the deregulating of prostitution was a prevailing issue in the United States. Federico Degetau clearly articulated this in the Town Council minutes and argued then that prostitution in Puerto Rico should not be regulated. A commission was set up to look into the matter and review the law. The commission was made up of Messrs. Federico Degetau, Manuel F. Rossy, Dr. José Celso Barbosa, and Doctor José E. Saldaña.[25] In contrast, these same political figures had just approved the reinstallation of a hospital for prostitutes only, euphemistically calling it Hospital Especial de Mujeres (Women's Special Hospital) in a building called El Picadero (The Chopper). They also included this expense in the fiscal year budget for 1899–1900.[26] Even though there seemed to be clear indication for the preference of deregulating prostitution, this hospital was maintained until 1917.

In August of 1899, the main San Juan precinct contacted the municipal representatives requesting that prostitutes be removed from Luna Street and recommended they be relocated to the La Marina neighborhood. Luna Street was too close to the military garrison at the San Cristóbal fort and this proximity was apparently causing disciplinary problems.[27] When this request was made public, it became evident that the newly created Commission had stopped its operations within two months of having been given its tasks and goals. They had actually never held a meeting, and Doctors Saldaña and Barbosa had resigned from their positions. The municipal government offered no report to the main precinct, but forwarded a copy of the Prostitution Hygiene Rules, dated 1893, and stated that Luna Street was one of the streets designated for prostitution. The response also indicated that until the Commission issued its full report, the municipal government could not assume a stand on the matter.[28]

The long-awaited report was presented in 1900. The Commission examined the Prostitution Hygiene Rules approved under the Spanish administration, especially the sections pertaining to sanitary, judicial, and moral issues. They made use of French and British publications as source references and quoted laws applicable to Puerto Rico. The Commission concluded that regulated prostitution should be abolished in Puerto Rico. They also suggested that all prostitution be ended forcefully if necessary. Following the example of anti-prostitution rhetoric elsewhere in the United States, the Commission issued a call to fight venereal disease.[29] The Commission's recommendations, however, had no immediate impact. In the June 25, 1902, Town Council minutes, an entry for $360 was approved for the expenses of housing prostitution in San Juan.[30] Obviously, the regulation of prostitution in the city continued.

Different social and political groups had the Americanization of Puerto Rico on their agendas. For some, cultural and political assimilation was the main objective. Others saw the incorporation and development of republican and democratic institutions in Puerto Rico as their main goal.[31] Protestant churches belonged to the first group. They believed that the assimilation process would bring moral and spiritual reform to a country that had been under moral "romantic" decay during the last four hundred years.[32]

Similar to what was happening in the United States, the temperance movement took hold on the Island. During the July 16 elections in 1917, in conjunction with the support of various religious groups and the Socialist Party, Puerto Rico ratified a prohibitionist clause before the United States approved its national (eighteenth) amendment on Prohibition.[33] In a report reviewed at a Baptist Churches Congregation held in Cayey on September 13, 1912 (where a committee on temperance was also established), it was mentioned that this movement was very interesting to both Americans and other foreign nations. The Congregation also expressed strong feelings against what they termed to be an apathetic attitude on the subject of temperance in Puerto Rico, calling the Catholic Church a traitor "to the true religion and to pure habits, as it publishes ads for alcoholic spirits in the same pages where it prints the blessings of their popes and the worshipping of their saints."[34]

From its very first year of publication (1912), the periodical *Puerto Rico Evangélic*[35] frequently discussed both alcoholism and prostitution. Its objective was to condemn the lack of morality and the tolerance that characterized the prevailing attitude in Puerto Rico at the time, according to Protestants.[36] They were scandalized by the lackadaisical attitude of local authority figures regarding issues of prostitution. In a messianic vein, the local Protestants named themselves the combatants "against antiquated methods and lame social ideas, byproducts of four centuries of stale Hispanic education."[37] In spite of the increased attacks from religious groups fighting the policy of regimentation of prostitution, during this first phase, particularly between 1905 and 1917, there was a concurrent increase in the application of the European system by the Puerto Rican administrators, including its medical inspections and registration of prostitutes.[38] This suggests that the authority of colonial rule was not interested in abolishing prostitution until it was forced to do so for military reasons at the onset of World War I.

While it is true that colonial rule altered the rules of the game on the Island, Protestant political clout in the United States was different within the colony. One perspective for the study of prostitution at the time can be found by studying the administrative goings-on at the Women's Special Hospital. This hospital was one element of the infrastructure needed to maintain a regulated prostitution framework. It was needed to "house and cure public women who are ill."[39] The hospital became the mechanism for prostitution regulation in San Juan. Once classified as infected, it was of no consequence if a prostitute agreed to be admitted or not.

Even though the hospital was established in 1895, it had an erratic history until December 1905, when it was finally located at number 26 San Sebastián Street under the direction of Doctor Francisco del Valle Atiles.[40] The opening of the hospital in its new surroundings was not free of controversy. Worried about the confusion that its name would cause, Doctor Lugo Viñas, the director of the Women and Children's Hospital, protested to no avail against the name given to a hospital where "women suffering from particular ailments would be assisted and cured." He added that his institution, by contrast, was founded "for the assistance and cure of honest women in need of aid . . . and for the class of women who were able to afford the expenses of being treated at his hospital, for the cure of their ailments."[41] Looking beyond the negative economic conse-quences which could be caused by the confusion in the names, we can see the prejudice against venereal disease patients in Doctor Viñas's statement. It is interesting that Doctor Viñas avoided the use of the term "prostitute." It appears that to him venereal disease itself, and not prostitution, was the determining factor in a woman's honesty.

The founding of the Women's Special Hospital required an initial investment of \$7,727.33.[42] The building was designed so that forty patients could be treated at one time. The staff included a medical director, a practicing student, three nurses, a doorman, a cook, a laundress, and a messenger.[43] In 1906, the hospital's budget was \$5,944, reaching \$6,740 by 1908. However, there was a significant budget cut in 1910, when it was granted only \$3,814. It was closed down tempo-rarily in 1911 when the building was used as a hospital for medical emergencies. Interestingly, this decision was made by the same Doctor Francisco del Valle Atiles, who was the mayor of San Juan at the time[44] he was the director for the hospital.[45] The establishment of a medical emergency hospital was the rationale given for its closing. The Town Council minutes and other related documents that date from that time allow no further view into the matter. However, in 1919 Valle Atiles would clearly manifest that he was against prostitution regulation and that he did not believe prostitution to be a necessary and unavoidable evil.[46] Perhaps he had held these ideas for years, leading him to close down the hospital. The regulation of prostitution fell from grace as a solution for social ills in both the United States and various European countries, such as England, a country that Valle Atiles greatly admired.

In contrast, in a session held by the Municipal Council on March 11, 1912, Robert H. Todd, then mayor of San Juan, and Doctor Valle Atiles agreed to form a Commission to meet with the governor. The objective was to find out if the Insular Health Department would reestablish the Women's Special Hospital. If the state agency would not do it, the Municipal Government would then reestablish it on its own.[47] The Commission managed to meet with the governor and with the director of Insular Health. On March 27, it issued a report to the Municipal Council, informing them that the Central Government accepted no responsibility for the provision of those services. The Commission also stated that they disagreed with the Central Government's position on this because the law of May 9, 1911, organizing the "Insular Health Service" made the Central Government accountable for support of this project.[48]

The governor and the director of Insular Health Department offered, however, some moral support and an unspecified amount in material assistance. The Municipal Government was looking forward to the construction of a new hospital that would cost $40,000, a formidable amount of money. Facing this economic shortage, the Municipal Government was once more forced to use the facilities at San Sebastián Street. In this way, what looked like an ambitious project to begin with ended up being a repair job amounting to no more than $300. On April 14, 1912, and with much fanfare, what was left of the great failed project was inaugurated.[49]

Five years later, based on a U.S. order from the Department of War, prostitutes were moved five miles or more from the grounds of any military installation. The same mayor who had so forcefully tried to establish a system of caring for sick prostitutes had to acquiesce to this new regulation immediately and ordered that no additional women be admitted to the hospital.[50] The hospital now treated women for ailments other than the ones for which it was established originally.[51] Medical Service Corps Lieutenant Herman Goodman reported that between April of 1912 and October of 1917, 1,691 women were admitted to the hospital. Of these women, 515 had been first-time admissions between July of 1913 and July of 1917.[52] These figures point to an obvious venereal disease problem, but the data were "contaminated" with figures of poor sick women referred there by doctors, making it impossible to calculate the real prostitution numbers for San Juan. An example of the impotence of the colonial administrators is present in a letter sent by Mayor Robert H. Todd to the Municipal Council, regarding the suspension of services at the hospital:

> Canceling in an absolute way the admittance of new sick women, the city will have cases of sick women with no protection at all, and with the consequent outcome of spread. Yesterday, a poor young woman came knowing that she

was not of a reproachful life, with a dismissal of Dr. de Juan, accusing the existence of chancres. She was married and her husband is responsible of that painful condition. However, unable to, and not having to order her admission into that hospital, according to the quoted agreement; later on I saw that woman walking through the city streets asking for shelter and being impossible for me to take any possible action to benefit her.[53]

The municipal movement responded to the mayor, claiming that they could see no alternative to the case since the Women's Special Hospital was established precisely to service prostitutes. It appeared that the Municipal Council wanted to close down the hospital and thus made no attempt to keep it open even if only for treatment and control of venereal disease.[54] Later on, the mayor took political advantage of the situation and, "under the aegis of an elevated sense of humanity," established the new Maternity and Children's Hospital at number 26 San Sebastián Street.[55]

A crusade against prostitution, led by the imposing figure of the General Attorney Howard L. Kern, was being promoted as a patriotic duty. Americans had a history of regulation dating back to the nineteenth century. Between 1900 and 1918 this "vice" was attacked quite strongly. American representatives assigned to Puerto Rico rejected the regulatory system. Under the "American Plan,"[56] they were under strict orders to do away with that model; not heeding this order was tantamount to treason.

The Second Phase: "The Porto Rican Experiment, 1917–1919"

The anti-prostitution campaign under the "American Plan" was discussed in prestigious magazines such as *Social Hygiene*. Under the title of "The Porto Rican Experiment," Herman Goodman, the lieutenant of the United States Medical Service Corps, wrote about the effectiveness of the measures taken to eliminate prostitution and venereal disease on the Island. This document is of particular importance since it offers us a view as to the magnitude of the problem, from the perspective of the so-called hygiene "experts."[57] Goodman's discourse was guided by the U.S. notion that it was a nation bringing civilization and moral standards to other countries as reflected in the concept of manifest destiny. Making reference to the writings of Bartolomé de las Casas, Goodman pointed to the fact that syphilis had been a common ailment since the colonization by Spain. He implied that the "amoral" state that prevailed on the Island was geographically and racially determined:

Its people have been little changed by immigration and the population has remained the offspring of the Spanish settler, his black slave, and a mixture of two races in all degrees. Men there are born under the tropical sun, with little of the prejudice of the north, with fewer of the conventions, and only for a score of years under the influence of American institutions.[58]

The high rate of venereal diseases among military troops played an important role in anti-prostitution campaigns. For each one thousand American soldiers, 467.8 were infected within the first six months of the occupation. Approximately one-fourth of the military forces stationed in Puerto Rico eventually contracted venereal diseases. These figures alarmed the military authorities since the contagion rate was 84 per one thousand persons in the United States. To Goodman, this situation paralleled the experience of the British troops stationed in India.[59] The high contagion rate had also been the case for Spanish troops stationed in Puerto Rico toward the end of the nineteenth century. In 1898, for example, 566 out of every one thousand soldiers were infected. The San Juan port was "blacklisted" for visiting warships. In 1903, warships from all nations were barred from using the port facilities of the capital city.[60]

Major Gavin L. Payne, field director for the American Red Cross in Puerto Rico, stated in *Social Hygiene* that with the mobilization of 15,000 Puerto Rican recruits to the Las Casas Camp (located five miles from San Juan) in 1918, the venereal disease problem became an immediate issue. It was generally believed that inhabitants of the countryside and mountain areas were "cleaner" when it came to sexually transmitted diseases. The mobilization of the troops in the capital city was deemed a threat to all young adults, who would be exposed to the prostitution "vice."[61] A Five Mile Ordinance was enacted and the zoning of prostitution was eliminated, at least officially. Brigadier General E.R. Chrisman, commander of the Las Casas Camp, additionally established an order forbidding recruits to visit the city of San Juan.[62] Lieutenant Goodman complained that San Juan lagged behind in all efforts to eliminate this "vice" and that newspapers assumed an antagonistic attitude regarding the measures that had been established. He stated that the closing of San Juan to all military visits except those of an official nature helped to bring about a change in the general attitude.[63]

Some periodicals, however, such as *La Democracia,* far from opposing the military measures, actually supported them. In an article titled "Let's Protect Our Soldiers' Health," this newspaper called attention to the fact that the anti-prostitution campaign "does not seem to have garnered the moral support of the total San Juan population." In a dramatic call to urgency the article narrates:

> One sick woman can cause more deaths in our ranks than 100 German cannons. An infected soldier can transmit his illness to hundreds in one day and it would be the greatest of embarrassments that our recruit figures become decimated by reason of shameful diseases.[64]

These comments can be analyzed from two perspectives—the social and the political. From the social perspective, it is obvious that women were identified as the source of the venereal disease. The destructive potential of the infected female was described as more deadly than war. On the other hand, we can see how the disease itself was described as a shameful predicament. Regarding the political perspective, the article seemed to argue that it would indeed be shameful for the country if its mortality rate were determined by victims of venereal disease.

American citizenship had just been granted through the Jones Act in 1917 and the new Americans felt the need to be equal to their peers up north. Any activity that could be identified as "patriotic" met with the support of public opinion. Both temperance and the prostitution "vice" campaigns fell under this rubric.

Much like in the United States, many civic groups intensely supported the anti-prostitution campaign. Health concerns went further than the military population, since it was known that recruits came from all corners of the Island and this placed the general population in danger of possible contamination.[65] The civilian government had become involved in the anti-prostitution campaign since February of 1917. Approximately 100 arrests had been made. However, on July 22, 1918, Attorney General Howard L. Kern wrote an official memorandum demanding that the judicial branch act more decisively in this matter, and it was then that the persecution of prostitutes reached a dramatic level.

Kern's document, described as "wise and energetic" by the Protestant factions, was directed at judges and prosecutors in Puerto Rico. It expressed the many benefits of doing away with the "Red Light" technique as a measure to protect the health of both military personnel and the general population. Kern added that the prison system could adequately house hundreds of prostitutes in order both to cure them of venereal disease and to teach them an honest endeavor.[66] The writ admonished that more energy was needed for the procurement of evidence and the preparation of cases. All of this would then make the judge's sentencing process easier. Those unable to comply would be "dismissed and substituted by someone more efficient and more patriotic."[67] Kern also called upon municipal governments to issue their own laws against prostitution. The zealous attorney general made clear that the municipal government was hampered by the existing legislation, which limited them to assigning penalties of 15- to 30-day maximums, penalties that would not be sufficient to stop prostitution.[68]

The collaboration of civic and religious forces in this morality campaign was an important element of the strategy to eliminate prostitution. Attorney General Kern stated in his reports to the governor of Puerto Rico that the task being carried out was widely supported by the Women's Christian Temperance Union (WCTU), the American Red Cross, the Rotarians, Four Minute Men, the YMCA, various security associations, and other civic groups.[69] According to historian Mayra Rosario, the WCTU was spearheaded by female members of the Puerto Rican bourgeoisie.[70]

These associations played an important role in the Americanization of Puerto Rico. For them, hygiene and "puritan" morals were part of what the Puerto Rican population needed to learn to become good citizens. As an example, the YMCA invested over $100,000 in the development of craft and recreation activities for recruits. Gameroom entertainment and sports were this group's solution against "vices" within the military camp recruits. The YMCA offered carefully selected movies three nights a week. The movies were screened to entertain and educate. The military camp was presented as a model of hygiene, discipline, and the American way of life for all society.[71]

The anti-prostitution campaign had the full cooperation of the civilian government and carried out the massive arrest of women accused of prostitution. With the repression apparatus going forward and its accompanying social tensions, political and ideological divisions in Puerto Rican society became more evident. If we compare the repression of prostitutes in Puerto Rico with what happened in the United States, we can see that the "Porto Rican Experiment" was stronger than the "American Plan." Historian Ruth Rosen posits that in the United States by the end of World War I, 15,520 infected prostitutes had been imprisoned an average of 70 days in "detention houses" and 365 days in rehabilitation institutions.[72] In Puerto Rico, between February 1917 and June of that same year, 100 women had been convicted of violating the ordinances against prostitution. During the 1918–19 fiscal year, the civilian government processed 1,080 women, finding 983 of them guilty as charged; 149 were found not guilty; and the charges against 48 of them were dropped.[73] Prison terms varied between two months and two years.[74]

The campaign against this "vice" was strongly supported by the evangelist sector in Puerto Rico. The public exhortations against prostitution contained hybrid components of both religious and American patriotic discourse. Thus, the editorial section of the periodical *Puerto Rico Evangélico* wrote congratulatory words for the efforts to repress prostitution, as follows:

> The prostitution cancer in Puerto Rico, just like alcoholism, already demanded the intervention of the surgical knife, not the useless application of compresses and narcotics. And the Attorney has proven to be (like his predecessor, the prohibitionist sector) a good social surgeon. Mr. Howard L Kern has swiftly extracted the disgusting cancer which was rapidly spreading by means of the excesses of libertines and the icy indifference of our authorities.[75]

In spite of this support, the same editorial also criticized the fact that no measures of imprisonment were being established for men who in one way or another participated in the prostitution of women. The *Evangélico* statement expressed both a call for repression of women as well as a view of women as victims of prostitution. Prostitution was presented as a threat to the "sanctity" of female role in society. While understanding that prostitution was promoted by "lecherous men who, by means of influence acquired with money, brute force and cleverness, were responsible for the prostitution of those poor women," the editorial expressed compassion for the prostitute and disdain towards the "creators of her fall."[76] The paper also warned about the ineptitude of the law in combating prostitution. As a religious publication, it prescribed evangelization as an "almighty" remedy against the prostitution "plague."[77] Concerned for the convicted prostitutes who had served their jail terms, the Social Reformist Committee of the Evangelist Union decided to recommend to the Puerto Rico Legislature the establishment of a rehabilitation institution. Some evangelists criticized the imprisonment system. Thus, the promises of the attorney general to rehabilitate instead of imprison the prostitutes were not realized.[78]

Responding to the intense battle in the United States against venereal diseases, religious groups such as the WCTU, provided information campaigns about hygiene and sexual education. The department of education of the WCTU translated and published information in Spanish such as: "The Truth for Adolescents," "Help for Mothers," and "Speaking with the Girls," among others. These were freely distributed among the population. The obligation of the parents to educate their children about sex was reinforced. According to the health authorities, the lack of information was one of the main causes of venereal infection among adolescents.[79] As part of the sexual education efforts, the Social Reform subcommittee of the Puerto Rico Evangelic Union celebrated an activity called "Social Morality Sunday." In this activity the subcommittee distributed 55,000 copies of "Five Reasons in Favor of Personal Chastity," which urged the reader to abstain from sexual degeneration. "It was a way to gain strength, health, happiness, capacity to help others, and for the latter, a way to God."[80]

Those opposed to the repressive government measures found a place for critical and social satire, using El Diluvio, a weekly tongue-in-cheek publication. Using this genre, Pedro Sierra, whose pseudonym was Luis Dalta, attacked Protestant and government "moralists" with his clever pen. Sierra was subjected to several charges of libel during his career and was confined repeatedly to jail because of his "bleeder articles."[81]

Luis Dalta was a militant in the Union Party of Puerto Rico and an advocate of Puerto Rican independence. He and other Unionist leaders joined Rosendo Matienzo Cintrón to create the Independence Party of Puerto Rico.[82] As a journalist, Dalta consistently attacked the hypocrisy of the wealthy classes when it came to social problems. His criticism won him powerful enemies, such as General Attorney Howard Kern.

Protestant groups allied with the attorney general to charge Luis Dalta with libel. His trial was held at the San Juan District Court at the end of September 1918, and was widely covered by the daily press and thus captured much public attention. The writer's defense was led by attorneys J. de J. Tizol and Celestino Iriarte.[83] Interestingly, organized labor was among the sectors supporting Luis Dalta. After the trial, the cigar makers of "La Colectiva" sent a commission to the El Diluvio editorial offices and offered the journalist "moral and material support in the name of one thousand comrades."[84]

For the Protestant sector supporting government repression, Luis Dalta was a true representative of decadence and was accused of being an advocate of the "Red Light." In another article published in Puerto Rico Evangélico he was accused as follows:

> I do not know what unpleasantness occured at del Valle Boulevard but it led to a painful decision by Attorney General Kern. Perhaps it was nothing more than the affection for the warm breezes or, on the other hand, the mysterious song of the ocean waves or the hardened voices of prostitutes. The story goes that he [Kern] could not hide the uneasiness that was produced with the shut down of the sellers of cheap love, the redemption of the slaves of vice and the cleansing of a rotting social life.[85]

For his part, Luis Dalta thought that the Protestants were a group of "Pharisees" working to land him in prison since they were unable to burn him alive. He accused them of disrupting Puerto Rican homes and society. To the alarmist reactions from religious groups he wrote:

> My muse is not the chlorotic lady of the ballrooms, incapable of showing her son one breast for not showing a piece of her flesh. My muse is the impudent Venus that dragged men to the revolution with her kisses, beheaded kings, tilted thrones and pulverized crowned heads. Wild, innocent, aggressive, careless, who does not blush when showing her indiscreet nudity because she is strong and beautiful as a pagan divinity. Therefore, I am more interested in the disputes of impudence . . . than in our legislators' discussions.[86]

Luis Dalta explained that he did not defend prostitution, but that he understood that under the ruling social system it was impossible to "eradicate that cancer." For him, "the richness in few hands and poverty in many" was the main reason for prostitution and many crimes. Socialism was therefore presented as the only alternative for the true change.[87] Dalta wanted to prove through his writings that the legislation imposed by the attorney general was a medieval one and was not in accordance with the democratic principles that ruled the rest of the American nation. He criticized the fact that it was possible for a "criminal, an incestuous person, a parricide" to appeal and to have the right of habeas corpus in the United States, yet those rights were denied to prostitutes.[88] Dalta pointed out in one of his articles that in spite of the campaign against prostitution, he had observed how "veteran meretrixes" walked freely among the crowd without being bothered. This situation evidenced the municipalities' vices, which for the journalist were "more repulsive than that of prostitution."[89] Dalta alluded to the fact that although the authorities were engaged in a repressive campaign, the prostitutes managed to continue their business by buying influence in government.

The campaign against prostitution interdicted the principle of judicial independence. Dalta held that justice in Puerto Rico was being administered through memoranda coming from the attorney general's desk. This situation transformed the judges and prosecutors into puppets of the executive power.

However, not all the judges accepted the impositions of Howard Kern. An example of independent thinking was Judge Geigel, who resigned immediately. This judge's decision was praised in *El Diluvio*.[90] The resignation of Geigel and

Dalta's defense of him illustrated the political dimension that this "moral" campaign gained at that moment. Dalta accused and reacted against the prevalent servile attitude of public officers in Puerto Rico. This servitude, he believed, was a consequence of Puerto Rico's colonial status.

Those sectors opposed to the campaign against prostitution exposed severe injustices. The case of Leonor Crespo was an example. Although this was not the only case where injustice ruled, it was, without doubt, the one that caused the most impact in public opinion. Crespo was arrested at 9:00 P.M. on May 13, 1918, while coming out of the vestibule of the Mayagüez Hotel at Tanca Street with a North American artilleryman named Moll. Trinidad Rosario and Pedro A. Manzano were the policemen who arrested her. Without going through appropriate legal procedures, the young woman was sentenced to thirty days in prison.[91] Journalistic accounts exposed that the arrest was policeman Manzano's form of revenge against Leonor Crespo because she had not responded to his romantic overtures.[92] Crespo was defended on May 21 of that same year by attorney Miguel Guerra Mondragón, who offered his services free of charge. The defendant's main evidence was the virginity of the accused, which was certified by Doctor Carbonel.[93] In Leonor Crespo's case, class and race factors played important roles in the massive public support she received. During the trial, it was revealed that she was a daughter of Añasco's "high society." Añasco pharmacist Pedro T. García de Quevedo stated in *La Correspondencia de Puerto Rico* that Leonor's father was a pharmacist and had been his physiology and chemistry professor and that her mother was a voice and piano professor. At a very young age, Crespo lost her parents and her relatives took her away from her hometown.[94] Letters from different towns in the Puerto Rico, supporting young Leonor Crespo, were received by several newspapers. Public indignation was evident. *El Diluvio* ran a campaign in favor of those who were resentful. Labor groups such as La Colectiva and the cigar-makers of Yauco Cigar Co. expressed their protest against what was perceived as the authorities' abuse.[95]

The case of Leonor Crespo increased social tensions on the island. The "stained" honor of a young woman acquired symbolic prominence for the organized labor class. This was seen in the congratulatory words sent to *La Correspondencia de Puerto Rico* by Marcelina Mejías, an auditor at La Colectiva:

> Keep on, keep on with this type of campaign, for they ennoble and raise to the higher moral level, while they attract the greater confidence of the reasonable country and the greatest appreciation of the working and poor classes of the Island.[96]

For the most part, the more marginal classes were the ones that suffered the weight of this movement of repression. Other women incapable of proving their virginity or counting on public support were imprisoned. Luis Dalta assured a hearing for the stories of the imprisonment of women who were accused of prostitution.[97] The renowned attorney Celestino Iriarte also excelled in the defense of women accused of prostitution. In all the cases he tried, the charges were dismissed. However, the information reported by Luis Dalta regarding the number of cases was at times vague. When describing the acquittal Iriarte won for Georgina Cordova, for example, Dalta limited his remark to writing that with this case, "there are a hundred or so but I don't know."[98] In many cases, the defense's work was facilitated by the lack, or the fragility, of the evidence. Iriarte's work acquired special significance in a moment when many attorneys refused to defend those accused of prostitution for fear of being branded as having committed "treason against the home country."[99]

Many of these cases turned out to be tragedies, such as that of Ramona Rivera. Dalta wrote that despite the evidence, the judge was forced to sentence this woman accused of owning a brothel. As a result of an appeal submitted by Rivera's defense before the Supreme Court, the sentence was revoked. Unfortunately, justice was granted too late for the accused woman who had died two months before in prison, presumably a victim of depression.[100]

This case occurred in the middle of 1919. The Great War had ended and soldier de-mobilization had begun. Persecution, nevertheless, continued. The so-called excesses of the "attorney" led to the issuance of a memorandum at the beginning of 1919 in which he promoted a higher level of zeal against adulterers by designating them as felons.[101] Judicial and social conflicts were detrimental to the political agenda. The influence of U.S. Senator John Worth Kern led to the appointment of his relative Howard L. Kern to the position of Attorney General in Puerto Rico.[102] The 1917 Jones Act gave the United States the authority to designate such appointments in Puerto Rico. Even the appointment for the governorship of Puerto Rico was in the hands of the U.S. president.[103] Despite petitions, the Jones Act was not amended. It allowed people like Howard L. Kern to enjoy and to profit from the colonial status of Puerto Rico.

The campaign against prostitution was a repressive one. The repression was ordered by the U.S. federal government and was an important part of the so-called "American Plan." Howard L. Kern was only a "good soldier," he followed the instructions. On May 26, 1917, the secretary of defense sent a "personal letter" to all the governors of states and territories stating:

> Our responsibility in this matter is not open to question. We can not allow these young men, most of whom will have been drafted to service, to be surrounded by a vicious and demoralizing environment nor can we leave anything undone which will protect them from unhealthy influences and crude forms of temptation. Not only have we an inescapable responsibility in this matter to the families and communities from which these young men are selected, but from the standpoint of our duty and our determination to create an efficient army, we are bound, as a military necessity, to do everything in our

power to promote the health and preserve the vitality of the men in the training camps.[104]

Other high-ranking officers, including the surgeon general, expressed themselves in a similar way.[105] About the campaign against "vice," Major Payne, in his article "The Vice Problem in Porto Rico," stated: "This was a military problem met in a military manner."[106] The priority was to keep the army healthy.

It is important to note how the discussion in Puerto Rico was centered around the local Puerto Rican government's actions, obviating the responsibility of the United States government. The House of Representatives unanimously requested that the U.S. Senate stop the confirmation of Howard L. Kern as attorney general because of his "lack of diplomacy and his incompetence as public officer."[107]

In general terms, since 1900, some important goals had been achieved by improving hygiene and sanitation standards and this was reflected in a lower mortality rate[108] but the rate of prostitution seemed not to have varied much despite the infamous campaign of 1920. On August 2, 1919, *El Mundo* newspaper published an article entitled "Mr. Mayor, hygiene rules." It called attention to the prostitution problem in San Juan and stressed the need for creating a hospital for prostitutes again.[109] Although the budget for that year had already been approved, the mayor submitted the indications published by *El Mundo* to the Municipal Council. According to the new municipal law,[110] each municipality had to create a Department of Health and Welfare. The Council determined that once created, all issues related to the Women's Special Hospital would be submitted to the new department in order to determine how to manage the situation.[111] Less than two years after closing the Women's Special Hospital for "elevated morality reasons," the municipal administrators stated the need for reopening it, displaying support for the so-called moral campaign. This was a campaign influenced by fear and political contrivance.

As we have seen, U.S. colonialism in Puerto Rico did not imply an immediate change in the government policy around the issue of prostitution. On the contrary, the regulation system was applied more consistently allowing, for example, the Women's Special Hospital to achieve its maximum development between 1905 and 1917. The closing of this hospital and the elimination of the regulating system responded to the initiatives of U.S. authorities. The support initially received by the anti-prostitution campaign from large sectors of the Puerto Rican people corresponded in great measure to the will of the recently created U.S. citizens to place themselves at the same level as their continental fellow citizens. However, this situation was not enough to keep up continuous support. The aggressive campaign, started on February 1917, underlined the severe political and social conflicts in which Puerto Rico navigated. The moral campaign against prostitution was as adamant as the campaign against alcohol. Both movements were supported by Protestant reformists and initially they received considerable support from the people. The movements were so similar that, in the end, they failed equally.[112]

Conclusion

The campaign against prostitution was just as artificial a measure as that for the prohibition of alcohol. Both were in response to political pressures and for that reason, they failed in their purposes. The regulation of prostitution was not restored, regardless of support from large political sectors. Although the regulatory system of the nineteenth century was an imitation and an imposition of the colony authorities, the local elite saw it as a benign evil.

In 1938 an attempt was made to legalize prostitution by the submission of Project 716 by the House of Representatives. This project was a more sophisticated version of the regulations that existed in San Juan. The House of Representatives unanimously approved the project, and the Senate approved it by majority. Regardless of this, the governor vetoed the project.[113]

After World War I, the prostitutes in San Juan "rescued" their former working spaces, including the famous Del Valle Boulevard—at least until World War II. They are spaces that, regardless of persecution and criminalization, are always "rescued" by the "cops," and as in any economic activity, only change places when the business is better elsewhere.

Notes

1. We should not be surprised by the silence of the Catholic Church regarding the controversies around the prostitution. During the Middle Ages no effort was made to make it disappear. Prostitution was accepted as a necessary evil. The Thomist conception of evil as an unavoidable essential condition of humanity influenced this acceptance of prostitution as long as it was kept inconspicuous. See Pedro Dufour, *Historia de la prostitución en todos los pueblos del mundo desde la antigüedad más remota hasta nuestros días*. Spanish version by Cecilio Navarro (Barcelona: Juan Pons, 1870) 1: 629–30.

2. "Rectificaciones históricas," in *Boletín Histórico de Puerto Rico*, ed. Cayetano Coll y Toste (San Juan: Tip. Cantero Fernández y Cía., 1914–1927), 349.

3. Ibid., 2: 33.

4. *España, Novísima recopilación de las leyes de España* ... (Madrid: sn, 1805–1807) 4: 419–22.

5. Archivo General de Puerto Rico, Fondos Municipales, Serie San Juan (hereafter cited as AGPR, FM, SJ). "Sanidad: Expediente sobre reglamento de mujeres públicas, 1876."

6. New regulations were approved in the following cities in Spain: Vigo (1867), Gerona (1869), Seville (1870), Cádiz (1870), San Sebastián (1874). Until 1873, in Cuba, the political Governor Pérez de la Riva ordered that there be no increase in the number of prostitutes in Havana. They were enrolled and forced to pay fees and to pay the positions of four women's doctors; see E. Rodríguez Solís, *Historia de la prostitución en España y América* (Madrid: Biblioteca Nueva, 1921), 246–47. In Guatemala, the regulation was approved in 1881; see David McCreery, "This Life of Misery and Shame: Female Prostitution in Guatemala City, 1880–1929," in *Journal of Latin American Studies*, no. 2 (1986): 333–53. In Buenos Aires, a prostitution regulation was approved based on European legislation in 1875; Donna J. Guy, *Sex and Danger in Buenos Aires: Prostitution, Family, and Nation in Argentina* (Lincoln: University of Nebraska Press, 1991), 60.

7. José Flores Ramos, "Eugenesia, higiene pública y alcanfor para las pasiones: La prostitución en San Juan de Puerto Rico, 1876–1919" (M.A. thesis, University of Puerto Rico, 1995).

8. Ibid., 126.

9. Fernando Picó, *Historia general de Puerto Rico*. 5th rev. ed. and augmented (Río Piedras: Ediciones Huracán, 1990), 206.

10. James L. Dietz, *Historia económica de Puerto Rico* (Río Piedras: Ediciones Huracán, 1989), 95.

11. Francisco Scarano, *Puerto Rico: Cinco siglos de historia* (San Juan: McGraw-Hill, 1973), 109.

12. Picó, *Historia general,* 231.

13. Scarano, *Puerto Rico,* 632.

14. Picó, *Historia general,* 244.

15. Scarano, *Puerto Rico,* 624, quoting Gordon K. Lewis, *Puerto Rico: Libertad y poder en el Caribe* (Río Piedras: Edil, 1970).

16. Ibid.

17. Picó, *Historia general,* 236.

18. Ruth Rosen, *The Lost Sisterhood: Prostitution in America 1900–1918* (Baltimore: Johns Hopkins University Press, 1982), 1.

19. Kenneth Ballhatchet, *Race, Sex and Class under the Raj: Imperial Attitudes and Policies and their Critics, 1703–1905* (New York: St. Martin's Press, 1980).

20. U.S. Department of Commerce, Bureau of Census, *Thirteenth Census of the United States Taken in the Year 1910: Statistics for Porto Rico* (Washington, DC: GPO, 1913), 14, 16–17.

21. Department of War, Bureau of the Census of Puerto Rico, *Report of the Census of Puerto Rico* (Washington, DC: GPO, 1900), 68–69.

22. Félix V. Matos Rodríguez, "Economy, Society and Urban Life: Women in Nineteenth Century San Juan, Puerto Rico (1820–1870)," (Ph.D. diss., Columbia University, 1994).

23. Bureau of the Census, 1910, *Statistics for Porto Rico,* 42.

24. Fernando Picó, "El impacto de la invasión norteamericana en la zona cafetalera de Puerto Rico: El caso de Utuado," in *Politics, Society and Culture in the Caribbean,* ed. Blanca Silvestrini (San Juan, 1993), 135. Picó notes that due to the U.S. invasion, the government centralized its services in San Juan. The establishment of the offices in a growing bureaucracy in the Santurce suburbs attracted employees from the central mountain zone.

25. The first three members of the Commission were all autonomist leaders and militants under the Spanish regime. Under U.S. domination all of them favored statehood. Federico Degetau became the first resident commissioner in Washington DC José Celso Barbosa was unquestionably the leader of the statesmen in Puerto Rico during the first part of this century, and Manuel F. Rossy became the leader of the Puerto Rican Republican Party. This party coalesced the most important political forces that favored federated statehood for Puerto Rico. For more information, see Javier Figueroa, "Diccionario histórico-biográfico," in *La gran enciclopedia de Puerto Rico* (Madrid: Ediciones RS, 1976) 14: 101, 29, 315, respectively. See also AGPR, FM, SJ "San Juan, Acta del 1 de junio de 1899," fol. 337v.

26. Ibid., fols. 324–26.

27. AGPR, San Juan "Actas 14 de agosto de 1899," fol. 337v.

28. Ibid.

29. José Colombán Rosario, *La prostitución en Puerto Rico* (Río Piedras: Universidad de Puerto Rico, 1951), 95–116.

30. Archivo Municipal de San Juan (hereafter cited as AMSJ), "Actas Sesión Ordinaria, 25 de junio de 1902," fol. 239.

31. Rafael Bernabe Riefkhol, "Matienzo y la generación del treinta: Una relectura," (unpublished manuscript, 1994).

32. Valentín, Miguel A. "No ahoguemos el grito de protesta," in *Puerto Rico Evangélico* (hereafter cited as *PRE*) 7, no. 8 (October 25, 1918): 5–6.

33. Picó, *Historia general,* 246. For a detailed discussion, refer to Mayra Rosario Urritia, "Hacia un mundo abstemio . . . la prohibición del alcohol en Puerto Rico" (Ph.D. diss., Universidad de Puerto Rico, 1993), 385.

34. The *Puerto Rico Evangélico* was the "official media of the Baptist, Disciples of Christ, Evangélica Unida de Puerto Rico, Methodist, Presbyterian and Lutheran Churches in Puerto Rico." For more information, see Antonio S. Pedreira, *El periodismo en Puerto Rico* (Río Piedras: Editorial Edil, 1969), 519.

35. Ibid.

36. Abelardo M. Díaz, "La temperancia en Puerto Rico," in *PRE* 1, no. 10 (November 25, 1912): 2–3.

37. Eloy Renta, "Testamento y llamamiento," in *PRE* 1, no. 10 (November 25, 1912): 3–5.

38. Enrique G. Cains, "La clase media: Una necesidad social en Puerto Rico," in *PRE* 8, no. 3 (August 10, 1919): 12.

39. AGPR, FM, SJ, "Registro de la búsqueda de un lugar conveniente para alojar a las mujeres de vida pública que están enfermas, 16 de octubre de 1894," file no. 27, 122, no. 48c.

40. AMSJ, "Actas del 21 de diciembre de 1905."

41. AGPR, FM, SJ, "Registro de carta del Dr. Lugo Viñas, solicitando un cambio de nombre para el Hospital Especial de Mujeres, 19 de junio de 1905."

42. AMSJ, "Actas de 1905, 7 de diciembre de 1905," fol. 297.

43. AMSJ, "Actas de 1906, Presupuesto 1906–1907," fol. 134.

44. AMSJ, "Actas 1906–1911," fols., 134, 140–50, 175–6, 214, 195, 71–2, respectively.

45. AMSJ, "Actas del 1905, Sesión ordinaria, 21 de diciembre." For more information on Francisco del Valle Atiles, refer to José Flores Ramos, "Eugenesias," 57–61.

46. F. Valle Atiles, *Un estudio de 168 casos de prostitución: Contribución al examen del problema del comercio carnal en Puerto Rico* (San Juan: Tipografía El Compás, 1919), 4.

47. AGPR, FM, SJ, "Registro designando una Comisión Especial para unirse con el Gobernador de Puerto Rico y tratar con esta autoridad acerca de la necesidad de establecer el Hospital Especial de Mujeres," not catalogued (hereafter nc).

48. Ibid.

49. Ibid.

50. AGPR, FM, SJ, "Registro núm. 174. Disponiendo el cierre del Hospital Especial de Mujeres y la apertura de una maternidad y hospital de niños," nc.

51. Ibid.

52. Goodman, "The Porto Rican Experiment."

53. AGPR, FM, SJ, "Registro núm. 174. Disponiendo el cierre del Hospital . . . ," nc.

54. During World War I, under the order of the United States surgeon general, there commenced a persecution campaign against the prostitutes. The principal goal was to prevent venereal contact among the soldiers. For more information, see Rosen, *Lost Sisterhood.*

55. Ibid.

56. Ibid.

57. Goodman, "The Porto Rican Experiment."

58. Ibid., 185.

59. Ibid.

60. Ibid.

61. Gavin L. Payne, "The Vice Problem in Porto Rico," in *Social Hygiene* 5 (April 1919): 233.

62. Ibid.

63. Goodman, "The Porto Rican Experiment," 189.

64. "Conservemos la salud de nuestros soldados," in *La Democracia* (June 28, 1918): 1.

65. Payne, "The Vice Problem in Porto Rico," 233.

66. "Questiones sociales," in *PRE* 6, no. 4 (August 25, 1918): 12.

67. Ibid.

68. Ibid.

69. *Report of the Governor of Porto Rico to the Secretary of War, 1918* (Washington, DC: GPO, 1918), 567. *Report of the Governor of Porto Rico to the Secretary of War, 1919* (Washington, DC: GPO, 1919), 643.

70. Mayra Rosario Urrutia, "Hacia un mundo abstemio . . . ," 385.

71. Norberto Escabí, "El triángulo rojo en Las Casas," in *El Diluvio* 6, no. 142 (August 3, 1918): 4–5.

72. Rosen, *Lost Sisterhood,* 35.

73. Ibid., n. 50, pp. 619 and 647, respectively.

74. Payne, "Vice Problem in Porto Rico," 234.

75. "Sección editorial," in *PRE* 7, no. 5 (September 10, 1918): 1.

76. Ibid.

77. M.F. Vilá, "La ley no es suficiente para poner fin al mal de la prostitución en Puerto Rico," in *PRE* 7, no. 7 (October 10, 1918): 17–18.

78. José Santana, "Por una institución rehabilitadora," in *PRE* 7, no. 7 (October 10, 1918): 18–19.

79. "Campaña educativa acerca de la vida sexual," in *PRE* 7, no. 18 (April 10, 1919): 10–11.

80. "Cinco razones en favor de la pureza personal," in *PRE* 7, no. 7 (October 10, 1918): 18.

81. Pedreira, *El periodismo en Puerto Rico,* 343. "Bleeder articles" refer to the stabbing satire of the author.

82. Figueroa, "Diccionario histórico-biogr⸱fico," 14: 385.

83. Ananké, "El juicio contra el compañero Dalta," in *El Diluvio* 4, no. 151 (October 5, 1918): 1.

84. Ibid., 2.

85. Pablo Sastre Robles, "Los defensores de la luz roja Luis Dalta," in *PRE* 7, no. 10 (November 25, 1918): 11.

86. Luis Dalta, "De domingo a domingo," in *El Diluvio* 4, no. 150 (September 28, 1918): 1.

87. Ibid., 8.

88. Ibid., 7.

89. Luis Dalta, "De domingo a domingo," in *El Diluvio* 4, no. 133 (June 1, 1918): 1.

90. Ibid.

91. "Pedimos justicia," in La *Correspondencia de Puerto Rico* (May 21, 1918): 1.

92. Ibid.

93. "Leonor Crespo, absuelta libremente," in *La Correspondencia de Puerto Rico* (May 21, 1918): 1.

94. *La Correspondencia de Puerto Rico* (May 28, 1918): 3.

95. "No estamos solos," in *La Correspondencia de Puerto Rico* (May 25, 28, 31, 1918, and June 1, 4, 5, 8, 1918).

96. "No estamos solos," in *La Correspondencia de Puerto Rico* (June 11, 1918): 3.

97. Luis Dalta, "De domingo a domingo," in *El Diluvio* 4, no. 150 (September 28, 1918): 7.

98. Luis Dalta, "De domingo a domingo," in *El Diluvio* 5, no. 181 (May 10, 1919): 6.

99. Ibid.

100. *El Diluvio* 5, no. 173 (March 15, 1919): 5.

101. Luis Dalta, "De domingo a domingo," in *El Diluvio* 5, no. 165 (January 18, 1919): 1.

102. John Worth Kern was a Democratic politician elected to the U.S. Senate representing the state of Indiana. He served in that position from March 4, 1911, until March 3, 1917. He did not obtain the renomination for re-election. For more information, see *Biographical Directory of the United States Congress 1774–1989,* bicentennial ed. (Washington, DC: GPO, 1989), 1303–4.

103. "Adiós for . . . ever!," in *El Diluvio* 5, no. 167 (February 1, 1919): 5.

104. *Report of the Governor of Porto Rico to the Secretary of War* (Washington, DC: GPO, 1919), 637.

105. Ibid.

106. Payne, "Vice Problem in Porto Rico," 234.

107. Luis Dalta, "De domingo a domingo," in *El Diluvio* 4, no. 161 (December 14, 1918): 1.

108. Fernando Picó, *Historia general de Puerto Rico,* 236.

109. AGPR, FM, SJ, Departamento de Hospitales, Archivo 65 (PII), 50b, "Registro de la carta del alcalde anejada a un articulo publicado en el periodico *El Mundo,* en la que el sugiere la necesidad de reabrir el Hospital Especial de Mujeres," August 4, 1919.

110. The Municipal Law of 1919 created a space for greater democratic participation in the municipality surroundings. This law established a local government constituted by municipal assemblies elected by the people, which also designated an administrative council in charge of the executive and administrative functions. The commission formed a council that was practically a government cabinet under the supervision of a public service commissioner. The cabinet responded to the popular assembly, "constituting in this way, a picturesque municipal government with parliamentary disposition, European style." By 1920, this law was amended to return to the organizational structure of a mayor and a municipal assembly. Both were elected.

However, more restrictions for the municipalities were created. For more information, see Bolívar Pagán, *Ley municipal revisada, anotada y comentada* (San Juan: La Correspondencia, 1925), vii–xi.

111. AGPR, FM, SJ, Departamento de Hospitales, Archivo 65 (PII), 50b, "Registro de la carta del alcalde anejada a un artículo publicado en el periódico *El Mundo,* en la que el sugiere la necesidad de reabrir el Hospital Especial de Mujeres," August 4, 1919.

112. For a detailed discussion of the failure of the prohibitive measures, refer to Rosario Urrutia, "Hacia un mundo abstemio. . . ."

113. Jorge Camacho Torres, "Comentos sobre la protitución y apuntes de su desarrollo en la capital de Puerto Rico," (unpublished manuscript, 1969), 21.

5

Gender and the Decomposition of the Cigar-Making Craft in Puerto Rico, 1899–1934

Juan José Baldrich

After the American invasion in 1898, Puerto Rican tobacco factories expanded impressively as manufacturers, until that time oriented to the domestic market, and began exporting cigars in vast numbers. Additionally, tobacco leaf exports posted significant gains and by 1910 tobacco factories employed more workers than sugar mills. They comprised 45.1 percent of employment in factories while mills comprised 32.5 percent.[1] Tobacco manufacture expanded remarkably as employment increased by more than 50 percent during the second decade of the century.

The expansion of tobacco manufacture provoked profound changes within the industry, in household composition, and in labor organizations. Tobacco shop workers became instrumental in trade unions and in socialist and anarchist groups including the Socialist Party. Large-scale recruitment of women into factories, trade unions, and the Socialist Party provoked intense contemporary discussions. For example, the employment of women became a salient issue in assemblies of cigar-makers' unions held in the 1910s. As delegates struggled to articulate the unions' position, the local organizer of the Cigar Makers International Union,[2] Prudencio Rivera Martínez, summarized the issue in the 1913 assembly as follows:

> [S]ince it is no longer feasible to stop completely the access of women to the industry, easy and practicable resolutions should be adopted to organize them in their work centers, and to stop where possible the growth of women in the

cigar industry in Puerto Rico. Women, organized with us, struggling with us, and prepared with us are not fearsome, cannot be our enemy, on the contrary, have to be our allies.[3]

Such discussions and changes, important at the time, have attracted the attention of historians and sociologists. Recent work, such as that of Yamila Azize Vargas, Gervasio L. García, and A.G. Quintero Rivera, examines elements taken from past discussions on gender and class conflict to shed light on present inequalities.[4] Early works and previously unpublished documents—many written by tobacco workers—have become available in print and thus shed light on this discussion.[5] This essay attempts to build upon past and present discussions, for the identities and the type of work of those employed in this industry can yield valuable insights into gender relations.

This research examines the transformation of cigar-making as it relates both to the labor process and to gender. Little work has dealt with cigar-making in terms of its reorganization along gender lines.[6] While researchers have recently examined gender role changes and transformations, such as the notable increase of women in tobacco manufacture as a whole, this essay emphasizes the technical division of labor in the main occupations within the industry, stemmers and cigar-makers, paying special attention to the decomposition of cigar-making as a craft.

The investigation addresses the articulation between the labor process and gender as regards five factors. First, most occupations within the tobacco industry were segregated by sex. The increase of women, in this sense, did not signify a restructuring of the industry away from late-nineteenth-century standards as far as gender is concerned because men kept to occupations socially considered masculine and women to feminine occupations. During the first few years after the invasion of 1898, occupations hiring women expanded at a faster pace than those employing men. After World War I, the main male occupation, cigar-maker, declined, while occupations employing women increased. While sex segregation remained unaltered, more women became wage earners.

A second factor addressed in this essay is the decomposition of the craft itself. While manufacturers mechanized the production of many mass-consumption commodities, cigar-making resisted for a long time the application of machinery. As an intermediate step, manufacturers divided the craft into two occupations and then introduced devices and machines to help workers increase production. Automatic machines came years later.

Third, successive reorganizations exacted fewer skills from the new type of worker now making cigars. De-skilling reduced the apprenticeship period. Consequently, the number of possible employees expanded considerably. Gender played a determinant role in the restructured craft because fabricants hired women into the new occupations to break the monopoly men held on the craft.

Fourth, the wage structure in the industry devalued work done by women. Manufacturers employed women in the new occupations because they worked for lower wages than men. Fabricants applied the same policy to machine operatives later. However, the wage differential for men's benefit was not permanent. Much later—that is, by the 1930s—men crafting cigars by hand earned less than women employed as machine operatives; men did not work as operatives. Women cigar-makers earned less than men in the same craft. Proprietors and managers carried this devaluation of women's work within the same factory. Men earned more in the same factory and the same occupation.

Fifth, class pulled men and women together while gender pushed them apart. Class brought them together as workers in their common opposition to the fabricant. Gender kept them apart because cigar-making became a male domain once men excluded women at the beginnings of the factory system during the last quarter of the nineteenth century. Cigar-makers' unions reflected these conflicting tendencies. Unions encouraged women to organize as stemmers, classers, and the like. Men did not stimulate women to become cigar-makers and had misgivings before accepting them in the occupations of the reorganized craft.

Women in Tobacco Manufacture

Mainly under the aegis of late-nineteenth-century merchants, the manufacture of both cigars and cigarettes experienced a radical transformation. Factories, operated by wage labor, gained steadily on the artisan shop run by independent craftspeople. Several factories, a few employing hundreds of workers, were already in operation at the turn of the century. Tobacco manufacture continued the concentration of capital initiated during the last quarter of the nineteenth century with an extraordinary momentum after the U.S. invasion.

The expansion of American Tobacco Company (ATC), the tobacco "trust" in Puerto Rico, altered the domestic bourgeois impulse of previous decades. At the turn of the century, Porto Rican–American Tobacco Company (PRATC), a "trust"-controlled firm, bought the two largest cigarette manufacturing companies in Puerto Rico. ATC's control of the cigarette market was nearly absolute from the beginning.

ATC's policy of expansion outside the United States lay in the acquisition and establishment of cigarette manufacturing plants. After 1901 ATC, in a policy reversal, tried to monopolize the U.S. market with cigars from the United States, Cuba, and Puerto Rico. When PRATC bought the largest cigarette plants in Puerto Rico, one of them, La Internacional, had a cigar-making division. PRATC expanded the division and in 1903, ATC-controlled corporations and their partners established the Industrial Company of Porto Rico for the manufacture of cigars and cigarettes. After 1901, the trust became the leading manufacturer of cigars for export and held a sizable portion of the domestic market. By 1903 trust-controlled factories accounted for 42.7 percent of cigar exports from Puerto Rico. Subsequently its market share showed small gains until it reached 56.3 percent in 1925.

Despite the trust, a sizable part of the cigar business remained outside ATC. Its share of the domestic market was smaller. Independent factories held their ground despite the massiveness of the trust. Portela's La Ultramarina, Infanzón y Rodríguez's La Habanera, Rucabado's La Flor de Cayey, and Casals's La Nueva Indiana, all nineteenth-century establishments, remained among the largest factories.[7] U.S. entrepreneurs not related to the trust established others such as the Cayey-Caguas Tobacco Co. in 1904.[8] Concentration of capital did not reach the same levels in other realms of tobacco production. Consequently, leaf stemming and classing never faced strong business concentration as did cigar manufacturing.[9]

The expansion of manufacture and the reorganization of the business structure of the industry after the invasion in 1898 brought a large increase of salaried women. Employment of women mainly as stemmers and leaf-classers represented, for the most part, their first contact with capitalist relations of production. This change meant a transition away from work within family and household. Fernando Picó sums up concisely the implications when he writes that wage labor represented a break with traditional domestic life. It brought stemmers into contact with others in the same shop, and provided the bases to uphold their positions in strikes and unions.[10] As of 1910, perhaps earlier, tobacco factories were the largest employers of salaried women.

Employment of women outpaced that of men during the first decades of the century. Table 5.1 presents the sizable proportion of women in the industry at the onset of the century, the eclipse of male employment in the 1910s, and the subsequent preponderance of women.[11] In this sense, tobacco manufacture became feminine.

Table 5.1, seen as a whole, may give the impression that increasing employment for women took place across the board and that in due time they became a majority in all sectors. It did not happen in this fashion. The expansion did not modify the occupational structure within the industry in terms of gender—that is, late-nineteenth-century patterns of occupational segregation remained unchanged. William Dinwiddie, a U.S. journalist who surveyed Puerto Rico soon after the invasion, reported that cigar-classers and cigar-makers were men while stemmers "are usually girls."[12] According to Blanca Silvestrini and Caroline Manning, the same gendered division of labor was still in place in the 1930s.[13]

The proportion of women in tobacco manufacture increased because the occupations for which they were hired posted gains while men's occupations declined significantly. Two changes to cigar-making account for the decline of men in the industry. First, factories either closed or made fewer cigars and, second, employers succeeded in mechanizing production. In terms of women's employment, tobacco stemming exhibited large gains throughout the period.[14] The following section of this chapter documents that transition.

Published census data are inadequate to explain the reversal of the sex ratio in the industry because they fail to differentiate major occupations, such as cigar-maker and stemmer, in the industry. Consequently, another methodology be-

Table 5.1

Employment in Tobacco Manufacture by Sex, 1904–1935

	Census data			Factory surveys[a]	
Year	Percentage women	Total	Year	Percentage women	Total
			1904	20.5	
1910	30.9	11,118	1912	42.8	1,118
1920	52.9	16,561	1913	59.7	6,332
1930	61.0	15,508	1920	62.3	8,109
1935	73.2	14,712	1926	71.5	23,801

Sources: Administración de Reconstrucción de Puerto Rico, *Censo de Puerto Rico, 1935. Población y agricultura* (Washington, DC: GPO, 1938), 91. Governor of Porto Rico. *Annual Report, 1920.* Washington, DC: GPO, 1920), 547. Negociado del Trabajo, *Informe especial, 1912* (San Juan: Bureau of Supplies, Printing, and Transportation, 1913), 61–66. Negociado del Trabajo, *Segundo informe anual, 1913* (San Juan: Bureau of Supplies, Printing, and Transportation, 1914), 27–47. Negociado del Trabajo, *Undécimo informe anual, 1926* (San Juan: Negociado de Materiales, Imprenta y Transporte, 1927), 42–43. U.S. Bureau of the Census, *Thirteenth Census of the United States: 1910*, Occupation statistics, vol. 4 (Washington, DC: GPO, 1914), 295. U.S. Bureau of the Census, *Fourteenth Census of the United States: 1920*, Population 1920 Occupation, vol. 4 (Washington, DC: GPO, 1922), 1288. U.S. Bureau of the Census, *Fifteenth Census of the United States: 1930*, Outlying Territories and Possessions (Washington, DC: GPO, 1932), 171. Walter Weyl, "Labor Conditions in Porto Rico," *Bulletin of the Bureau of Labor* 61 (1905): 723–856.
[a]Based on factory inspections.

comes necessary. As an alternative, total cigar production serves as an indicator of men cigar-makers, and tobacco leaf exports indicates for women as stemmers.[15] Figure 5.1 presents the five-year moving averages for all cigars manufactured and leaf exports for 1909 to 1936. It shows that leaf exports experienced a strong secular increase that peaked during the second half of the twenties and declined after that. Recuperation came a couple of years after the tobacco grower's boycott against the Porto Rico Leaf Tobacco Co. in 1931–32.[16] To the extent that leaf exports suggest stemmers, they posted strong gains all the way to the late twenties.

Cigar manufactures went through a trend altogether different from leaf exports. Figure 5.1 presents small increases from 1909 to the end of World War I and then slight decreases. After that came a sharp and prolonged drop after the 1926 strike against PRATC. Stemming savored an expansion unparalleled by cigar-making. According to the export data presented in the figure, decline for stemmers was steep and brief, not the precipitous drop for cigar-makers.

The sex ratios within the industry endured a significant modification. From an industry where about one in five workers was a woman in 1904 it changed to one

Figure 5.1 **Leaf Exports and Cigar Manufacture, Five-Year Moving Averages, 1909–1936**

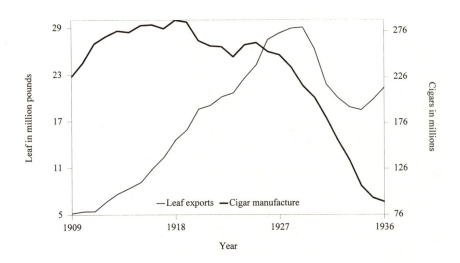

Sources: P.R., Department of Agriculture, *Annual Book on Statistics of Puerto Rico, 1941–42* ([San Juan]: n.p., 1942), 91. Sol Luis Descartes, *Basic Statistics on Puerto Rico* (Washington, DC: Office of Puerto Rico, 1946), 54.

where three of four workers were women by 1935. The feminization of tobacco manufacture, however, did not imply a restructuring along gender lines. It showed the increase of stemmers as women and the contraction of cigar-makers as men. Late-nineteenth-century schemes of gender segregation remained unchanged.

Decomposition of the Cigar-Making Craft

The traditional way of making cigars, the "Spanish method," remained until the beginning of the twentieth century the only way to make a cigar in Puerto Rico[17] and in much of the Caribbean. A single person hand-crafted the complete product from beginning to end. The artisan "bunched," as they said in the trade, the *tripa* or filler leaves that formed the inner core of the cigar inside the binder leaf, or *capote.* Then, the same person covered the bunch with the wrapper leaf, or *capa.* Finally, the head, or *perilla,* if used, covered one or both extremes of the cigar depending on the style, or *vitola.*[18]

Fabricants found this process to be expensive. Cigar-making was a skilled craft that required a long apprenticeship of up to three years where speed and skills in some styles took longer to develop.[19] The nineteenth and early twentieth centuries provided an advantage to the craftsperson because cigar consumption expanded throughout the world.[20] While cigar-makers had a scarce commodity whose production took long to master, manufacturers, in turn, sought to reduce labor costs. Nineteenth-century fabricants and mechanics in Cuba, the United States, and Europe developed machines that proved successful only with cigarette manufacture. Employers tried to fragment the craft into simpler occupations to reduce skill levels and hire low-paid workers.

The wooden mold became one of the most successful devices adopted by manufacturers to fragment the cigar-making craft. This device reduced considerably the skill needed to prepare the bunch or inner core of the cigar.[21] Originating in Germany, it came to twentieth-century Puerto Rico by way of the United States.[22] The mold eased the fragmentation of the craft into bunch-making as a distinct operation from wrapper-rolling the finished bunch. Manufacturers introduced teamwork to make the cigar, usually two rollers for each buncher, so that nobody had to master the complete craft anymore. Furthermore, hand-operated devices and rudimentary machines for both bunch-making and rolling began to appear in the 1880s.[23]

The first reference to the decomposition of the craft in Puerto Rico appears in 1905. Some manufacturers, possibly corporations under control of the tobacco "trust," introduced the mold, separated buncher from wrapper-roller, and made the cigar the collective product of teamwork. However, none used mechanical devices in bunching or rolling.[24]

By 1912 the fragmentation of the craft in Puerto Rico advanced more as wrapper-rollers used mechanical devices such as suction tables.[25] These artifacts required fewer skills from the worker as they mechanized operations previously done by hand. For instance, suction tables mechanically held firmly the stretched wrapper, or *capa,* thus freeing both hands to handle and wrap the finished bunch. Additionally, entry into the trade was easier as it took less time to master the skill because these machines reinforced the separation of bunchers from rollers. A 141-factory inspection carried out by the Labor Bureau in 1913–14 identified several hundred bunch-makers, machine-assisted cigar-makers, and wrapper-rollers, that is, occupations denoting team workers.[26] While most cigars were still made by the Spanish method, the Labor Bureau inspected two factories that successfully fragmented the cigar-making craft by the 1910s.

The American Machine and Foundry Company developed an apparatus that integrated many previous developments into a single device. Tested in 1915, perfected by 1919, the long-filler machine combined bunching and rolling in a single mechanical process. Four operators attended each machine, effectively eliminating the craft save for the small niche of expensive styles.[27] The Porto Rican–American Tobacco Company introduced the cigar-making machine to Puerto Rico in 1921.[28] Machine operators had replaced innumerable cigar-makers by the 1926 strike against the company. Thirty-eight percent of all strikers engaged directly in cigar-making used contrivances such as suction tables or fully automatic machines; had mold workers been included, the percentage would have been even higher.[29] Large-scale substitution of craftspeople by machine operators continued unabated during the late twenties.[30]

In 1930, the PRATC announced its intention of doing away completely with the craft; it planned to mechanize its production entirely.[31] By 1931, 75 percent of local production was machine-made.[32] In a quarter of a century, the once-dominant Spanish method of making a cigar disappeared from the export market of the largest manufacturer, PRATC. Their cigars for domestic consumption remained handmade only in La Habanera factory.[33] The craft first gave way to bunchers and wrapper-rollers, in second place to the partial mechanization of both occupations, and lastly, to their complete substitution by machine operatives. PRATC successfully de-skilled the tobacco artisan into oblivion.[34]

Teamwork and Gender

The reorganization of the labor process reduced the skill levels required to enter the new occupations and wrested control of the craft away from cigar-makers, placing it in the hands of the fabricants. The number of potential workers increased to include women, whom manufacturers readily hired in the restructured craft. Upon full mechanization, employers retained the women.

At the turn of the century, before the mold and teamwork, only 1.6 percent of cigar-makers were women; later, a four-factory inspection in 1904 yielded none. However, by 1912, 9.8 percent of cigar-makers were women and in 1913–14 they reached 15.9 percent.[35] While still a minority, women showed considerable gains in cigar manufacturing as bunchers and wrapper-rollers.

Most women worked in factories where the PRATC decomposed the craft, representing a clear policy to employ women in tasks until then performed by men. Table 5.2 presents the percentages of men and women by the two methods of making cigars, namely, teamwork and the Spanish method.

Table 5.2 clearly suggests that factories relying on teamwork hired only women.[36] Prevailing tendencies of gender segregation became inverted as women intruded on the exclusive domain of men and threatened men's control over the craft.[37]

Women in the Spanish method worked in very small shops known as *chinchales* and were commonplace in mid-nineteenth-century Puerto Rico.[38] However, the introduction of the factory system during the last quarter of the nineteenth century privileged men in the cigar-making craft to the extent that manufacturers and male cigar-makers successfully excluded women from the craft in a factory setting.[39] By the turn of the century, the scant number of women cigar-makers worked in *chinchales* hand-rolling inexpensive *vitolas* that went by the name of the inferior leaf employed, *boliche,* posing no threat to male domination.[40]

Table 5.2

Cigar-Making Methods by Sex, 1913–1914

	Women (%)	Men (%)	Total (%)	Cases
Spanish method	3.1	96.9	100	(2,324)
Teamwork	100.0	0.0	100	(354)

Source: Negociado del Trabajo, *Segundo informe anual, 1913* (San Juan: Bureau of Supplies, Printing, and Transportation, 1914), 27–47.

Figure 5.2 graphically illustrates this point. It presents the proportion of women working by the size of the cigar-making department in 1913–14. The hyperbola in the figure shows a precipitous drop in the proportion of women hired as the number of cigar-makers in the factory increased from shops employing one to two rollers to factories hiring around fifteen. On the average, very small shops, *chinchales,* employing fewer than three rollers, hired many women, from 12 to 33 percent of their labor force. Women made up less than 4 percent of all cigar-makers in factories employing fifteen hand-rollers. Factories with over 100 cigar-makers employed 2 percent or fewer women.

Figure 5.2 presents a much shorter curve joining two factories employing exclusively women in cigar-making. These cigar-makers did not employ the Spanish method, with each craftsperson preparing the complete cigar. Team workers were exclusively women and they did not work alongside traditional cigar-makers in the same factory. Teamwork was a large factory endeavor.

Regression analysis is another way to identify the type of factory employing women as cigar-makers. The proportion of women cigar-makers employed in each factory serves as dependent variable. It has two regressors or independent variables: the reciprocal, in its mathematical sense, of the number of cigar-makers per factory is one, and teamwork, a dummy variable standing for the presence or absence of teamwork in a given factory, is the other. Ninety-eight factories employed cigar-makers. The regression coefficients and standard errors of the estimates are:

Prop Women =   +0.02   +0.32/Cigar-makers   +0.98* Teamwork
Std Error   (0.10)   (0.02)

Teamwork and cigar-making department size have a strong relation to the proportion of women in a given establishment. The regression coefficient for cigar-makers is three times its standard error. Teamwork's coefficient is over forty times its standard error. The fit between the data and the mathematical model is remarkable.[41] Regression results show that as factories using the Spanish method employed larger numbers of cigar-makers, there was a pre-

Figure 5.2 **Percentage of Women by Size of Cigar-Making Department, 1913–1914**

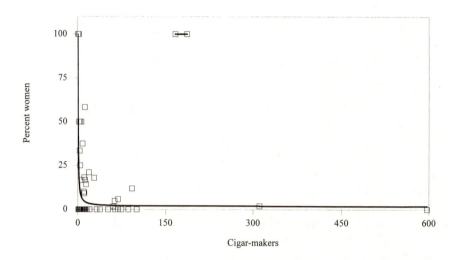

Source: Negociado del Trabajo, *Segundo informe anual, 1913* (San Juan: Bureau of Supplies, Printing, and Transportation, 1914), 27–47.

cipitous drop in the proportion of women. Teamwork, the dummy variable, unmistakably identifies the incorporation of women as bunchers and wrapper-rollers exclusively.

Decomposition of the craft allowed less-skilled workers to manufacture cigars. It broke the privileged access to skills held by men by restricting women to *chinchales.* Upon breaking the craft into bunchers and wrapper-rollers, manufacturers substituted men with women. From the introduction of the mold to the automatic cigar machine, employers segregated cigar-making away from men to women.

Salaries and Gender

Education, property, lifelong commitment to a job, skills, and social class affect salaries. Aside from these factors, this research explores the effects of gender on wages. It examines the hypothesis that wage differences between genders reflect perceptions that work done by men is more valuable. The social appraisal of work has a gender dimension. Social considerations devalue women's work compared to what men do. This proposition guides the examination of the gender wage gap in the manufacture of cigars. Gender affected wages in cigar manufacture in specific ways. This investigation examines three distinct mechanisms that affected the gender wage gap and the long-term trend in the relation between gender and wages.

First, the new division of labor privileged women because manufacturers found it more economical to hire them as team workers since women worked for less pay than men. While teamwork represented a pay raise for women, for men it embodied a demotion. Bunchers and wrapper-rollers required a short apprenticeship. Fabricants at last succeeded in expanding notably the universe of possible employees. It was easier to enter the new occupations than the old one. Short of full mechanization, the fragmentation of the craft paved the way for a reduction in labor costs.[42] Fabricants preferred women to men since women worked for less pay in the restructured occupation. The new division of labor proved disastrous for the men who until now controlled the craft. It broke their near monopoly over the trade.

The Labor Bureau inspected 141 tobacco factories at a time when the mold and other devices had been in use for about a decade, but before the introduction of the fully automatic cigar-making machine. Inspections took place in an intermediate stage of decomposition. These data are timely because the Bureau obtained them when the Spanish method still dominated the trade and teamwork was on the rise. Machine operatives were still to come.

Table 5.3 presents the average daily wages of the cigar-making occupations by sex during 1913 and 1914. It shows that manufacturers maintained large gender-based differences in wages. Craftsmen had the highest wages, team workers stood in the middle, and craftswomen earned the least. In terms of wages, women team workers stood between men and women engaged in the Spanish method.

Higher wages for teamwork attracted women from other occupations within tobacco manufacture.[43] For instance, estimates from Labor Bureau data show that women stemmers and leaf-classers earned US$0.39 and US$0.57 per day respectively.[44] Teamwork wages were also attractive to women working the Spanish method because, as Table 5.3 indicates, team workers earned more than women in the Spanish method. By raising women's pay, yet keeping it below what men earned in the Spanish method, fabricants enlarged the labor pool and saved money on wages. Manufacturers used the prevailing devaluation of women's work to their benefit.

Second, gender affected wages in the same occupation and within the same factory. Table 5.3 identifies the wage gap among cigar-makers on the Spanish method. Women earned less than men in the same occupation—on the average, 62 percent of men's wages.[45] A possible interpretation of the table suggests that women cigar-makers earned less than men because most women worked in exceedingly small factories, *chinchales,* where pay was notoriously low. How-

Table 5.3

Daily Wages of Cigar-Makers by Sex, 1913–1914

	Women	Cases	Men	Cases
Spanish method	0.65	(71)	1.05	(2,253)
Wrapper-rollers	0.87	(207)	—	—
Bunchers	0.88	(147)	—	—

Source: Negociado del Trabajo, *Segundo informe anual, 1913* (San Juan: Bureau of Supplies, Printing, and Transportation, 1914), 27–47.

Note: Wages in U.S. dollars.

ever, concentration in *chinchales,* making low-grade cigars, does not fully explain their inferior wages because the appraisal of work was gendered. Women's work was devalued compared to the reputed worth of men's labor. Unequal wages persisted within the same factory.

The Labor Bureau data for 1913–14 support this hypothesis. Out of 141 establishments, 25 factories employed both men and women on the Spanish method. Craftsmen earned more than women in the same craft in 72 percent of the factories. Craftswomen earned more than men in 16 percent while wages were the same in the remaining 12 percent of the factories.

A regression equation allows further analysis of the wage structure in these enterprises. The average daily wage for women per establishment, in U.S. dollars, serves as dependent variable. It has two regressors or independent variables: the average daily wage for men in each factory is one repressor, and the proportion of women cigar-makers employed in a given factory the other. All data refer exclusively to wages of cigar-makers on the Spanish method. The regression coefficients and standard errors of the estimates are:

Wage Women = +0.25   +0.57* Wage Men   -0.37* Proportion Women
Std Error   (0.10)   (0.13)

Men's wages and the proportion of women in a given establishment have a strong relation with women's wages. Again, the fit between the data and the mathematical model is strong.[46] The regression coefficients are several times their standard errors, with the coefficient for men's wages being nearly six times its standard error, while the proportion of women's coefficient is close to three times.

Wage increases for men cigar-makers translate far below par (0.57) for women in the same craft and in the same business. The regression equation strongly suggests that the differences in wages between men and women cannot be attributed to the fact than men tended to work in well-paid factories and women in low-paying *chinchales* because strong wage differences persisted for men and women doing the same job and in the same establishment.[47]

Third, gender affected wages in still another way. The higher the proportion of women in a factory, the lower the wages for those very same women. Stated in another way, factories that employed mostly men and few women paid these women higher wages than factories employing mostly women. Feminized factories implied devalued wages for women cigar-makers.

The regression results just reviewed examine the relation between the sex ratio in factories and wages for women. The coefficient for the proportion of women in a factory is –0.37. It means that wages for women were lower in establishments that employed more women, proportionally speaking. In other words, wages diminished as the proportion of women in the factory increased. Cigar-making for women lost worth as their workplace became more feminine. Earnings were gendered.[48]

The three points just examined refer to the wage structure and its relation to gender halfway through the breakdown of the craft. Emphasis has been on structure, not on movement. The last point on the wage–gender relation bears on the decomposition of the craft as a process. Long-term tendencies in policies of employment continued to favor women at the expense of men. In time, mechanization led to the end of the well-paid craftsperson, male or female.

PRATC started the final stage in the decomposition of the craft with the 1921 introduction of the fully automatic cigar-making machine. De-skilling advanced as the craft character of the trade gave way to machine operatives. Factories employed them for the same reason they hired bunchers and wrapper-rollers before: lower salaries.

The Spanish method had decayed much by the 1930s because, *chinchales* aside, only La Habanera, a PRATC-owned factory, hand-crafted cigars.[49] Men on the Spanish method, mostly employed in *chinchales,* earned $5.82 a week on the average. Women machine-operators, always working in large factories, earned more, around $8.00 weekly, for a shorter week.[50] From the first factories in the 1870s to the 1930s there was a complete reversal in the position of cigar-makers in terms of gender. By the 1930s, men earned less than women and worked in small shops.

In summary, this study shows gender was a powerful determinant of wages among cigar-makers in several ways. First, manufacturers successfully decomposed the cigar-making trade. Women became team workers in the new division of labor because they worked for less money. Second, men earned higher wages than women in factories employing the Spanish method. This wage gap persisted even when men and women worked in the same factory. Third, establishments with many women cigar-makers paid women lower wages than factories employing mostly men. The feminization of factory work implied the devaluation of wages for women cigar-makers. Finally, the trends initiated with the introduction of the mold and completed with the fully automatic cigar-making machine brought a full turnaround in the positions held by men and women in the manufacture of cigars.

Trade Unions

Cigar-makers were not passive bystanders to their own demise; they sustained a strong defense, for example, over control of the means of production, the value of piecework, the institution of the reader. Men successfully excluded women from cigar-making in factories during the last quarter of the nineteenth century and, concomitantly, developed a powerful ethos that tied them together in trade unions, *centros de estudios sociales, casinos de artesanos,* and the Socialist Party. Cigar-makers faced their employers militantly and, at times, with considerable success.

Trade unions reacted to women in the industry with an uneasy combination of enthusiasm and hesitancy. A shared adversary, the capitalist, brought men and women together while the antagonism created by gender relations kept them apart. Whereas in the United States, on occasion, cigar-makers opposed all women in the industry,[51] domestic cigar-makers did not oppose the massive employment of women as stemmers and leaf-classers. The Federación Libre de Trabajadores (FLT) and the cigar-makers' unions encouraged and recruited them into trade unions.

For instance, in 1910 a cigar-makers' union from the highland municipality of Cayey initiated a drive to enroll more cigar-makers and to organize other wage earners.[52] An assembly elected a provisional board of directors of a stemmers and leaf-classers' union in May.[53] In June, a cigar-maker denounced a PRATC officer for threats to move the leaf-classing establishment to another district if women joined the union.[54] Two members of the local cigar-makers' union became instructors to the newly founded stemmers' union September.[55] Stemmers, many of them union members, went on strike against the León Candelas factory in December. Cigar-makers in the same factory joined in solidarity.[56] Two women joined Bernardo Vega and other cigar-makers in preparations for the Labor Day activities in 1911. One of them, Maximina Rivera, was a founding member and officer of the stemmers' union.[57] The statement from a local trade unionist and cigar-maker shows the interest in recruiting more stemmers and leaf-classers:

> a large number of pale-faced women and girls, as if withered roses, covered their shoulders with mantles and shawls as they marched hurriedly in different directions, away from the jails with names of warehouses; some left to town and others to the countryside, until that human wave similar to a procession of corpses, disappeared They were so pale! . . . My friend was against the workers because they knew not how to defend their jobs; I was against the bourgeoise because they showed no conscience in treating those whose work, giving their life and blood, to increase their wealth; I was also against the LEADERS of the working class movement because they do nothing to get workers out of the inertia to which they are submitted.[58]

This was a common initiative. It was part and parcel of a large unionization drive, the *cruzada del ideal,* organized by the FLT between 1906 and 1915 with cigar-makers as its major driving force.[59]

Organized stemmers and leaf-classers benefited cigar-makers on two counts. Trade union women could possibly gain wage increases through collective bargaining and strikes. If well paid, they would probably remain in their own trades, for well-paid stemmers presumably had no interest in becoming bunchers or wrapper-rollers or, for that matter, cigar-makers. Cigar-makers were conscious that unionized women contributed to a stronger and larger block of workers in their opposition to manufacturers. For instance, cigar-makers' unions planned for years a general strike in the industry; they struck PRATC in 1914.[60] Organized stemmers and leaf-classers joined to strengthen the position of the cigar-makers.[61]

Uneasiness with women lay in their entry into the trade itself or, worse, with their fundamental role in the disintegration of the craft. Cigar-makers attempted to maintain their hold over the *oficio,* the craft. They had successfully excluded women and stood guard against the unskilled. These fears came to the fore in the 1913 assembly of cigar-makers. "These companions in this manner, with the cigar-making machines . . . threaten us all."[62]

They perceived the entry of women as capital's initiative to devalue their own work. Opposition to the employment of women was part of their struggle against capital. Their uneasiness with women in cigar-making was tinged with the same paternalism that manufacturers considered in hiring them: the devaluation of labor. They perceived women as instruments of capital to downgrade their labor. Cigar-makers debated whether to oppose the entrance of women or to stimulate them to form trade unions. In 1911 cigar-makers called "upon women that worked the craft to organize and to begin right away, and if this is done, these companions refuse to organize and attempt to destroy the craft, then be it resolved to remove the ailment by preventing their apprenticeship and practice of the craft."[63] Bunchers and wrapper-rollers were still an issue in the 1913 assembly. An important labor leader made a plea "to stop where possible the growth of women in the cigar industry" or to "organize them" so that they did not become "fearsome" or the "enemy"; the assembly opted for organization.[64]

De-skilling and low wages alone do not account for women in teamwork first and later as operatives. The reasons manufacturers hired women, and men cigar-makers opposed their hiring, were similar. A possible explanation might be their supposed pliability and docility in contrast to men's perception of themselves as strikers,[65] union organizers, and anarchists during these years.[66] Despite such notable exceptions as the well-known Luisa Capetillo and nearly faceless women like Maximina Rivera, it was men cigar-makers who directed most strikes and organized most unions.[67] PRATC blamed men cigar-makers for reduced profits with statements like: "Our business suffered a lot materially during the year from strikes,"[68] and the year 1919 "has been the worst in the history of the Company."[69] A PRATC board member complained about the cigar-makers' militancy.[70] Years later, women, who were said to work "for salaries infinitely lower than those of cigar-makers and who gave virtually no labor trouble at all, superseding the craftsman."[71]

Conclusions

The period between the American invasion in 1898 and the depression of the 1930s radically accelerated previously existing trends in domestic tobacco manufacturing. This study attempted to explain the change from an industry dominated by men to the powerful presence of women later and the consequences of such changes. Its discussion followed five interrelated topics.

First, the feminization of the industry did imply the integration of men and women to the same occupations because occupational sex segregation maintained its late-nineteenth-century patterns. The proportion of women increased because the occupations that hired women posted gains while men's occupations declined significantly. Cigar-making suffered two changes. First, factories either closed or made fewer cigars and, second, employers succeeded in breaking up the craft. In terms of women, tobacco stemming exhibited large gains throughout the period.

The second factor is the decomposition of the cigar-making craft. Manufacturers used the wooden mold to divide the craft into two simpler occupations, buncher and wrapper-roller. Fabricants and mechanics added other devices and simple machines that deepened the fragmentation of the craft. Years later, operatives superseded craftspeople completely with automatic machines.

Third, the reorganization of the work process effectively de-skilled the craft. Bunchers and wrapper-rollers, and later, operatives, required ever shorter apprenticeship periods. Fragmentation broke the privileged access to skills imposed by men over cigar-making during the establishment of the factory system because manufacturers successfully linked de-skilling to gender by employing women exclusively in teamwork. From the introduction of the mold to the automatic cigar machine, employers reversed the segregation in cigar-making, changing it from an occupation of men to one of women.

Fourth, gender proved to be a powerful determinant of wages among cigar-makers in three ways. First, women entered more positions in the factory under the new division of labor because they worked for lower wages. Second, men earned more than women under the Spanish method. This wage gap persisted even when they worked in the same factory. Third, establishments with large proportions of women cigar-makers paid women lower wages than factories with a high ratio of men. The feminization of factory work implied the devaluation of wages for women cigar-makers. Finally, the trends initiated with the introduction of the mold and completed with the fully automatic cigar-making machine brought a complete reversal in the positions held by men and women in the manufacture of cigars.

Fifth, while cigar-makers encouraged women to organize as stemmers, classers, and the like, they discouraged women from cigar-making; years before, men had successfully excluded women from factory work, leaving them restricted to small shops. Men in tobacco manufacture had serious misgivings about women in the occupations that came with the reorganization of the work process. However, after much discussion, cigar-makers gave in and contributed to women's syndication.

Notes

The author acknowledges the advice and suggestions of Félix V. Matos Rodríguez, María del Carmen Baerga, Humberto García, Melanie M. Domenech, Guillermo A. Baralt, and the research assistance of Lynnette Rivera. The Department of Sociology and Anthropology and the Fondo Institucional para la Investigación of the University of Puerto Rico sponsored this work. This is a revised version of a paper presented at the conference of the Latin American Studies Association, Washington, DC, September 28–30, 1995.

1. U.S. Bureau of the Census, *Thirteenth Census of the United States: 1910,* Manufactures, vol. 9 (Washington, DC: GPO, 1912), 1394.

2. Federación Libre de Trabajadores, *Informe general de cuentas del Comité Central de la Huelga de Tabaqueros de Puerto Rico* (San Juan: Porto Rico Progress, 1914), 27-28.

3. Federación Libre de Trabajadores, *Actuaciones de las segunda y tercera asambleas regulares de las uniones de tabaqueros . . .* (San Juan: Porto Rico Progress, 1914), 49.

4. Yamila Azize Vargas, "Luchas de la mujer en Puerto Rico, 1898-1919," 1979. Gervasio L. García and A.G. Quintero Rivera, *Desafío y solidaridad* (Río Piedras: Huracán, 1982). The best bibliography on the working-class movement is Erick J. Pérez Velasco and David Baronov, *Bibliografía sobre el movimiento obrero de Puerto Rico, 1873–1996* (San Juan: CILDES, 1996).

5. Luisa Capetillo, once a reader in tobacco factories, articulates many ideological strains of working-class feminism in Julio Ramos, ed., *Amor y anarquía* (Río Piedras: Huracán, 1992). The autobiography of a cigar-maker offers deep insight into the trade. See César Andreu Iglesias, ed., *Memorias de Bernardo Vega,* 3d rev. ed. (Río Piedras: Huracán, 1984). Rubén Dávila Santiago, *Teatro obrero en Puerto Rico (1900-1920)* (Río Piedras: Edil, 1985). Ángel Quintero Rivera, *Workers Struggle in Puerto Rico: A Documentary History* (New York: Monthly Review Press, 1976).

6. For a partial exception, see Amílcar Tirado Avilés, "Notas sobre el desarrollo de la industria del tabaco en Puerto Rico y su impacto en la mujer puertorriqueña, 1898–1920," *Centro de Estudios Puertorriqueños Bulletin* 2, no. 7 (1989–1990): 18–29.

7. Juan José Baldrich, "Growth and Americanization of the Puerto Rican Tobacco Industry, 1847-1902," 1997.

8. Cayey-Caguas Tobacco Company, "Informe Anual," 1903-1919, Archivo General de Puerto Rico, hereafter AGPR, Departamento de Estado, Corporaciones foráneas con fines de lucro, caja 5, ex 86; and Negociado del Trabajo, *Segundo informe anual, 1913* (San Juan: Bureau of Supplies, Printing, and Transportation, 1914), 21.

9. Juan José Baldrich, *Sembraron la no siembra* (Río Piedras: Huracán, 1988), 39–46.

10. Fernando Picó, "Las trabajadoras del tabaco en Utuado según el censo de 1910," in *Al filo del poder: Subalternos y dominantes en Puerto Rico, 1739-1910* (Río Piedras: Editorial de la Universidad de Puerto Rico, 1993), 194. See also Ángel Quintero Rivera, "Socialista y tabaquero: La proletarización de los artesanos," *Sin Nombre* 8, no. 4 (1978): 100-37.

11. Table 5.1 excludes 1899 because the data refer exclusively to cigar-makers. See U.S. Departamento de la Guerra, *Informe sobre el censo de Puerto Rico, 1899* (Washington, DC: Imprenta del Gobierno), 1900, 330. Later censuses give numbers for workers in "cigar and tobacco factories," effectively including all occupations in the industry. The sex ratios within crafts were not balanced. Most cigar-makers were men. Women tended to work as stemmers and leaf-classers. Thus, 1899 sex ratios are not comparable to those of 1910. In 1899, 1.6 percent of all cigar-makers were women. In 1910, 30.9 of all workers "in cigar and tobacco factories" were women. A comparison exaggerates women's increase, which, unfortunately, is common.

12. William Dinwiddie, *Puerto Rico, Its Conditions and Possibilities* (New York: Harper & Brothers, 1899), 125. Apprentices to cigar-makers, mostly men, also stemmed in La Ultramarina, a San Juan factory. Cigar-makers did not. The transition to an exclusive woman's occupation was not complete yet. See *La Correspondencia,* 17 and 19 August 1897, unnumbered. Olga Cabrera examines the transition of stemming from a predominantly male occupation to a female one in "Cuba y la primera experiencia de incorporación fabril de la mujer," *Revista de Indias* 49, no. 185 (1989): 227–29.

13. Caroline Manning, *The Employment of Women in Puerto Rico* (Washington, DC: GPO, 1934), 28. Blanca Silvestrini de Pacheco, "La mujer puertorriqueña y el movimiento obrero en la década de 1930," *Cuadernos de la Facultad de Humanidades* 3 (1979): 88.

14. According to David S. Campbell, "low wage scales and the inadaptability of the small-sized Puerto Rican tobacco leaf to machine stripping have been very influential in keeping the industry from moving to the States." See "Puerto Rico Tobacco Region Area Analysis," 1942, 19. University of Florida Archives, Raymond E. Crist Papers.

15. Tobacco leaf statistics for domestic consumption are not available.

16. Baldrich, *Sembraron la no siembra.*

17. While the mold was the major innovation to cigar-making during the nineteenth century, local artisans did not use it. See Dinwiddie, *Puerto Rico,* 124; and *Sketches: Porto Rico* (Porto Rican–American Tobacco Company, 1904).

18. José Enrique Perdomo and Jorge J. Posse, *Mecanización de la industria tabaquera* (Havana: Talleres de "La Milagrosa," 1945), 33, 173–78, describes the Spanish method in detail.

19. Mark J. Prus, "Mechanisation and the Gender-based Division of Labour in the U.S. Cigar Industry," *Cambridge Journal of Economics* 14 (1990): 65; and Patricia A. Cooper, *Once a Cigarmaker* (Urbana: University of Illinois Press, 1987), 48.

20. Juan José Baldrich, "Cigars and Cigarettes in Nineteenth Century Cuba," *Revista/Review Interamericana* 24, nos. 1-4 (1994): 8–35.

21. The mold was a wooden device full of cigar-shaped grooves. The worker arranged the filler leaves inside the grooves, pressed them, and extracted the bunch in the desired shape.

22. Dorothee Schneider, *Trade Unions and Community: The German Working Class in New York City, 1870–1900* (Urbana: University of Illinois Press, 1994), 57–58.

23. Cooper, *Once a Cigarmaker,* 170–71.

24. Walter Weyl, "Labor Conditions in Porto Rico," *Bulletin of the Bureau of Labor* 61 (1905): 759.

25. Negociado del Trabajo, *Informe especial* (San Juan: Bureau of Supplies, Printing, and Transportation, 1913), 62.

26. Negociado del Trabajo, *Segundo informe anual, 1913*, 31.

27. Reavis Cox, *Competition in the American Tobacco Industry, 1911-1932* (New York: Columbia University Press, 1933), 49–51; and Perdomo and Posse, *Mecanización de la industria tabaquera*, 33–37.

28. Bailey W. Diffie and Justine Whitfield Diffie, *Porto Rico: A Broken Pledge* (New York: The Vanguard Press, 1931), 96; and "A Dying Art," *Revista Económica* (September 1937): 22. PRATC was by a large stretch the biggest cigar manufacturer; by 1925 it accounted for 56.3 percent of all domestic cigars. See Cox, *Competition in the American Tobacco Industry*, 87–88.

29. The basis for the percentage consists of the 2,000 workers directly employed in cigar-making, thus excluding 350 leaf-classers, binder-stemmers, and "others" from the total. See Comité Central de la Huelga General de los Tabaqueros de Puerto Rico, *Manifiesto* (San Juan: La Democracia, 1926), 8. Negociado del Trabajo, *Undécimo informe anual, 1926* (San Juan: Negociado de Materiales, Imprenta y Transporte, 1927), 26.

30. Victor S. Clark, et al., *Porto Rico and Its Problems* (Washington, DC: The Brookings Institution, 1930), 465.

31. Cox, *Competition in the American Tobacco Industry*, 57.

32. Diffie and Diffie, *Porto Rico: A Broken Pledge*, 96. According to Manning, the "vast bulk of cigars" were machine-made by 1934. See *The Employment of Women in Puerto Rico*, 27.

33. Cámara de Comercio de Puerto Rico, "Tobacco Culture," *Boletín Oficial* 10, no. 6 (1934): 62. PRATC bought Infanzón and Rodríguez's La Habanera earlier in an unpublicized deal. See Luis Muñoz Morales, "Compraventa de fábrica," 10 May 1915, AGPR, Protocolos Notariales, Siglo XX, San Juan, caja 763, fols. 127-40.

34. Bernardo Vega, a cigar-maker, migrated to the United States seeking better economic opportunities within his craft. His memoirs depict his struggle to remain a cigar-maker in the New York of the twenties and thirties. See Andreu Iglesias, *Memorias de Bernardo Vega*.

35. Negociado del Trabajo, *Informe especial*, 61. Negociado del Trabajo, *Segundo informe anual, 1913*, 28–47. U.S. Departament of War, *Informe sobre el censo de Puerto Rico, 1899*, 330. Walter Weyl, "Labor Conditions in Porto Rico," 823–25.

36. The Commissioner of Labor inspected 141 tobacco factories during 1913 and 1914. He published detailed statistics for each factory giving precise occupations, the number of women, men, and children in each occupation, the daily wage for each, etc. Analysis of these data informs much of what follows. Refer to Negociado del Trabajo, *Segundo informe anual, 1913*, 27–47.

37. Among the 354 women employed in teamwork factories, 159 were wrapper-rollers, identified in the report as cigar-makers, 147 bunch-makers, and 48 machine-cigar-makers, the latter probably using suction machines to stretch the binder leaf.

38. Félix V. Matos Rodríguez, "Economy, Society and Urban Life: Women in Nineteenth Century San Juan, Puerto Rico (1820-1870)" (Ph.D. diss., Columbia University, 1994), 240. No tobacco factories appear in the literature until the 1870s. The women cigar-makers identified by Matos Rodríguez had fathers in the craft. This phenomenon was not exclusive to Puerto Rico. For the United States refer to Edith Abbott, "Employment of Women in Industries: Cigarmaking—Its History and Present Tendencies," *Journal of Political Economy* 15, no. 1 (1907): 4. In France, Spain, and other countries in Europe, women were cigar-makers from the beginnings of the factory system. See José Pérez Vidal, *España en la historia del tabaco* (Madrid: Consejo Superior de Investigaciones Científicas, 1959), 255–64; and Louise A. Tilly, "Paths of Proletarianization," *Signs* 7, no. 2 (1981): 400-17.

39. Stemming remained, then and later, mostly a woman's craft.

40. A similar situation occurred in Cuba. See Olga Cabrera, "Cuba: Mujer y familia en

la industria tabacalera," paper presented at the Society for Caribbean Studies, Institute of Commonwealth Studies, London, July 5–7, 1995; and Jean Stubbs, "Gender Constructs of Labour in Prerevolutionary Cuban Tobacco," *Social and Economic Studies* 37 (1988): 247.

41. Figure 5.2 and the regression equation that generated it do not present statistical difficulties. However, the variance of the residuals obtained from the regression is not even for all values of an independent variable, thus violating an assumption of regression analysis. The variable in question is the reciprocal of the number of cigar-makers in each factory. The variance of the error term is large for factories with few cigar-makers and decreases as the number of cigar-makers increases. This problem goes by the name of heteroskedasticity in the statistical literature. Technically it means that the estimates of the regression are unbiased and consistent but inefficient. That is, the variance of the estimates is larger than the value of the population or true value. This problem affects aggregate data like those under examination. See Eric A. Hanushek and John E. Jackson, *Statistical Methods for Social Scientists* (New York: Academic Press, 1977), 143, 175. Weighted least squares (WLS) corrects the problem. The regression coefficients and standard errors presented above are WLS.

42. Decomposition did not result in gains in efficiency or speed in cigar-making. It reduced labor costs. See Cooper, *Once a Cigarmaker,* 169–70; and Prus, "Mechanisation and the Gender-based Division of Labour," 68.

43. Its attraction to women in other industries was so strong because the tobacco industry as a whole paid women the highest wages of any industry. Negociado del Trabajo, *Cuarto informe anual, 1915* (San Juan: Bureau of Supplies, Printing, and Transportation, 1916), 32–34.

44. Stemmers included *caperas* and *capoteras.*

45. Wage discrimination against women cigar-makers in Puerto Rico was very strong. Comparable data for the U.S. in 1913 show that women earned between 79 percent and 96 percent of men's wages. See Cooper, *Once a Cigarmaker,* 176–77.

46. The multiple regression coefficient for the equation is 0.84. I eliminated the single outlier from the regression, so the actual number of cases, or factories, for the regression is 24.

47. Patricia Cooper reports equal pay for the same occupation in the same factory. Only occasionally did factories pay women less. See *Once a Cigarmaker,* 175. In contrast to the Cigar-Makers' International Union, a U.S. trade union that was squarely opposed to different scales, in Britain there was a 25 percent difference for the same work in the same factory. See Abbott, "Employment of Women in Industries: Cigarmaking," 18.

48. Despite the sizable difference in time and space, Barbara Stanek Kilbourne et al. reach a similar conclusion. See their "Returns to Skill, Compensating Differentials, and Gender Bias," *American Journal of Sociology* 100, no. 3 (1994): 689-719. Their analysis is not based on gender ratios within workplaces for a given occupation as is this research; it relies on the wage gap between different occupations.

49. Cámara de Comercio, "Tobacco Culture," 62.

50. Manning, *The Employment of Women in Puerto Rico,* 27–28.

51. Abbott, "Employment of Women in Industries: Cigarmaking," 17. Cooper, *Once a Cigarmaker,* 115, 219. Prus, "Mechanisation and the Gender-based Division of Labour," 69.

52. Eusebio Colón, "No hay peor cuña . . ." *Unión Obrera,* 16 April 1910, unnumbered. Eusebio Colón, "Cayey también se prepara," *Unión Obrera,* 12 May 1910, 1.

53. Ramón L. Fraguada and Eleuterio Sierra, "Acta," *Unión Obrera,* 11 June 1910, unnumbered.

54. Ramón L. Fraguada, "Notas de Cayey," *Unión Obrera,* 16 June 1910, unnumbered.

55. Vicenta Barrera and Francisca Gandía, "Acta constitucional," *Unión Obrera,* 5

October 1910, unnumbered. Ramón L. Fraguada, "Desde Cayey," *Unión Obrera,* 31 August 1910, unnumbered.

56. Titán, "De Cayey," *Unión Obrera,* 22 December 1910, unnumbered.

57. Arturo de Santiago, "Labor Day en Cayey," *Unión Obrera,* 20 July 1911, 1.

58. Luis Barrera, "Impresiones de un paseo," *Unión Obrera,* 11 October 1910, unnumbered.

59. Angel G. Quintero Rivera, "El Partido Socialista y la lucha política triangular de las primeras décadas bajo la dominación norteamericana," *Revista de Ciencias Sociales* 19, no. 1 (1975): 60.

60. García and Quintero Rivera, *Desafío y solidaridad,* 49–50, 60. Federación Libre de Trabajadores, *Actuaciones de las segunda y tercera asambleas,* 21, 89.

61. Prudencio Rivera Martínez to Samuel Gompers, 29 July 1914, in *Informe general de cuentas del Comité Central de la Huelga de Tabaqueros de Puerto Rico,* Federación Libre de Trabajadores (San Juan: Porto Rico Progess, 1914), 27–28, AGPR, Fortaleza, caja 593, ex 746, documento 20. José Dieppa and others to Arthur Yager, 23 April 1914, AGPR, Fortaleza, caja 593, ex 746, documento 19.

62. Federación Libre de Trabajadores, *Actuaciones de las segunda y tercera asambleas,* 48.

63. Ibid., 105.

64. Ibid., 49.

65. Quintero Rivera, "Socialista y tabaquero," 133–37.

66. Rubén Dávila Santiago, *El derribo de las murallas* (Río Piedras: Cultural, 1988), 180–216.

67. Capetillo participated actively in the FLT unionization drive known as the *Cruzada del Ideal.* See Ramos, *Amor y anarquía,* 65. Rivera helped charter a local stemmers union in Cayey during the *Cruzada del Ideal* and later became an elected official of the same union. She was active in the organization of Labor Day festivities. See Barrera and Gandía, "Acta constitucional." Fraguada and Sierra, "Acta." De Santiago, "Labor Day en Cayey."

68. PRATC, *Annual Report, 1918* (Jersey City: n.p., 1919).

69. PRATC, *Annual Report, 1917* (Jersey City: n.p., 1918).

70. José María González to Pedro Giusti, 28 May 1919, papers of Juan Giusti Cordero.

71. "A Dying Art," 22.

6

Halfhearted Solidarity: Women Workers and the Women's Suffrage Movement in Puerto Rico During the 1920s

María de Fátima Barceló-Miller

*There are two suffrage associations on the island, one organized by
female workers and our own, in which the most intellectual feminine
elements of Porto Rico are to be found.*

—Milagros Benet de Mewton, President, Suffragist Social League

Introduction

In 1921, Milagros Benet de Mewton, president of the Suffragist Social League,
included the above epigraph in the text of her letter to Frank McIntyre, director
of the Bureau of Insular Affairs in Washington. In that letter she thanked him for
his promise to acquaint the new governor, E. Montgomery Reilly, with the
suffragist crusade in Puerto Rico. She did not miss the opportunity to point out
that, although the suffragist movement had two organizations, the one in which
she was active and over which she presided was the one that convened the most
distinguished Puerto Rican women.[1] The class division within the suffrage
movement was more than evident.

However, the literature on the suffrage movement in Puerto Rico[2] maintains
that the 1924 coalition between the Suffragist Social League (Liga Social

Sufragista) and the Popular Feminist Association of Women Workers of Puerto Rico (Asociación Feminista Popular de Mujeres Obreras de Puerto Rico) allowed for a close collaboration among women of different social classes, represented by these two associations, in the struggle for women's right to vote. Furthermore, the generalized perception is that the Suffragist Social League, through this pact or alliance, adopted the demands and clamors of the female workers, and that the issues raised by the labor sector set the stage for the Puerto Rican feminist movement of the day.[3]

A careful analysis of the feminist press and workers' literature of the early part of the century illustrates the abysmal differences between the working-class women and the upper- or middle-class women, differences that posed an insurmountable obstacle to the development of a united suffrage movement. These differences also reveal the important role played by political influences, socioeconomic conditions, and educational levels in the development of a right-to-vote movement within each social class. Poverty, illiteracy, and an identification with the Socialist Party are some of the factors that help us understand the actions of working women—their militancy during labor strikes, their defense of socialism, and their rejection of the traditional image of women. For female workers, the specificity of their problems as women was contained within the broader context of a class struggle. They denounced the capitalist interests that exploited them as workers and made them victims of dire misery, injustice, and hunger. Suffrage was just one more weapon in their battle against oppression and their struggle for a better life. For the women of the elite, social origin and academic background shaped their views of social problems and insular politics. Their ideology stemmed from classic bourgeois liberalism. Their weapons were democracy and liberal social institutions. They endorsed social reforms, such as health programs for the indigent, care for the elderly, rehabilitation for prostitutes and vagrants, and so forth. However, this impulse toward reform did not necessarily include a commitment to an egalitarian social system. The main objective was to create a modern and progressive society in which educated women, as part of the propertied, professional, and intellectual class on the Island, played a high-profile role and shared equally in the rights and responsibilities of their male counterparts.[4]

In this essay I intend to explore the socioeconomic and ideological differences between elite and proletarian women within the suffrage movement. In addition, I will take a close look at the differences in gender relations within each social class and the implications such differences may have had for the suffrage movement in Puerto Rico in the 1920s. My purpose is to unravel the interaction between these elements and weigh their influence in the different meanings each social sector ascribed to the suffrage movement. From this vantage point, the study of women's suffrage also helps us understand how both men and women in the two social sectors looked at the notion of "woman" and her social roles.

The Suffragist Social League

In 1921, the Puerto Rican Feminine League (Liga Femínca Puertorriqueña), the first suffrage association in Puerto Rico that we know of, changed its name to Suffragist Social League. Both the Feminine League and the Suffragist Social League comprised the women of the propertied, professional, and intellectual elite. Their social extraction and economic affluence gave them access to a formal education that, in turn, enabled them to work in science and liberal arts professions and to exercise the highest of social functions within the country, such as public service and public administration. Consider the following distinguished members of the Social League between 1921 and 1924: Ana Roqué de Duprey, Ana López de Vélez, Isabel Andreu, Beatriz Lasalle, Carmen Gómez, and Carlota Matienzo were teachers; Dolores Pérez Marchand, Elisa Rivera de Díaz, Marta Robert, and Josefina Villafañe were medical doctors; Luisa Amelia de Hostos was a writer; Trinidad Padilla de Sanz and María Cadilla de Martínez were renowned poets within the country's intellectual circles; classical pianist Elisa Tavárez de Storer and sopranos Margarita Callejo and Amalia Paoli were outstanding artists in the music field. [5]

All these women had the economic means and education needed so that their appeals would be heard in the highest centers of power in the country. In addition, several of them were part of the Puerto Rican intellectual and liberal political leadership and had close ties to the national heroes of the day. A few examples will suffice. Amparo Fernández Náter, cofounder of the Suffragist Social League, was the daughter of Manuel Fernández Juncos.[6] Trinidad Padilla de Sanz was the daughter of Dr. José Gualberto Padilla, "El Caribe," a nineteenth-century Puerto Rican poet and political figure.[7] Soledad Lloréns Torres was the sister of poet Luis Lloréns Torres.[8] Milagros Benet de Mewton was the sister of the Republican Party's House delegate, José Benet.[9] Luisa Amelia de Hostos was the daughter of Eugenio María de Hostos, and Carlota Matienzo Román was the daughter of Rosendo Matienzo Cintrón.[10] The family ties with these men influenced the ideological stance of these suffragists. For example, Amparo Fernández Náter acknowledged her father's influence in her militancy as a suffragist:

> I have been a suffragist ever since I can remember. Having a father with such progressive ideas, I could not be too far behind. When my father founded and directed the *Revista Puertorriqueña de Literatura, Ciencias y Artes* back in 1899, for which he had the most illustrious men in this country and abroad as collaborators, he appointed me to be the manager of that journal. My father used to say women should partake in all of this country's affairs, and since then the ideas about women's freedom have taken root in me.[11]

Other suffragists such as Trinidad Padilla de Sanz, Soledad Lloréns Torres, and Carlota Matienzo also acknowledged their fathers' and brothers' influence in the formation of their liberal ideologies and in their militancy as suffragists.[12]

The name change, from Puerto Rican Feminine League to Suffragist Social League, was not merely cosmetic; it expressed the expansion of their goals and adoption of new strategies. In addition to the right to vote, the Suffragist Social League aspired to civil and political equality with men through legislation that would grant them equal rights in the political system.[13] The right to hold legislative office and other public positions was a central issue.

The arguments raised to defend this right stemmed from the very nature and experience of women as mothers and educators. Given their special sensibilities, they could understand and act on the problems of home, youth, health, and poverty. Their roles as mothers and educators within the home qualified them as the best persons to render opinions, to legislate, and to make decisions that concerned the problems of infancy, education, and motherhood. The following quotation brings out this argument: "women in politics have a broader range of action as mothers because a female Senator takes into account and will always take into account childhood and its misery."[14] These arguments highlighted woman's nature and attributes as elements that qualified her to legislate for social problems ranging from crime to children:

> Women, endowed with a noble spirit, will always try to purify our social surroundings, from the House, where only fair and equitable laws will meet with her approval, to the streets, where homeless orphans and fallen women lead a miserable life.[15]

Ana Roqué de Duprey defended women's franchise and women's incursion into politics as an extension of motherhood:

> A woman is a mother every minute of her life. And when she goes to legislate in the House, she does so in compliance with her divine duty as a mother, in the highest sense of the word. Her actions there are more extensive, as she works for the good of all society's children, whose mothers gave her their vote and elected her as their representative to this grand assembly of our people's government.[16]

These quotations reveal much about the nature of the struggle for women's suffrage of the propertied, professional, and intellectual elite of the country. Social feminism, a movement that sought to increase women's influence and autonomy in the family, the community, and society, provided the framework for their ideology. Social feminism acknowledged the differences between men and women, while allowing for a compatibility between the sexes that made feasible, and indeed necessary, a society in which women, albeit with their particular qualities and characteristics, worked side by side with men for the common good.[17] From this vantage point, social feminism was useful in the reformulation of gender relations. This was expressed more than once by suffragists, first within the Feminine League and later within the Suffragist Social League:

> Feminism is the doctrine that sustains and proves women's capacity to collaborate with men in the work of improving humanity. . . . Keep that in mind, fellow citizens: we are women, always women, but we march with men as their true companions; we share their active lives; shoulder to shoulder we cooperate to make better our beautiful Island."[18]

Furthermore, this ideology was an integral part of the reformist discourse and of the project of modernization promoted by the liberal political sector. The modernization of society entailed a readjustment of women's roles. The growth and reorientation of the educational system would give women better educational opportunities. The expansion of government services in areas such as health, education, and social services would provide the ideal architecture for new professional women to join public service. Women would have to adjust their image and role to the new conditions surrounding them; they could no longer remain secluded or limited by society's traditional structures, ideologies, and mentalities. Social feminism was the vehicle that enabled them to expand their breadth of action and also channel and further the feminine project of modernizing women's roles and social position hand in hand with society's overall modernization.

We cannot lose sight of the suffragists' need for support from the more liberal men. With social feminism, suffragists paved the way to get that much-needed support from the male elite. The readjustments of social roles for the "new woman," as espoused by the liberal men, were highly compatible with the social-feminist demands made by women suffragists. Consider, for example, these words by Manuel Fernández Juncos:

> In every society, assembly, or convention in which women participate, men behave in a more circumspect and noble manner, being more careful with the language they use and more moderate in both their thoughts and actions. I believe that granting women the right to vote will be not only an act of justice, but a great political and social benefit. Legislation influenced by women will be more humane, visionary, expedient, and transcendental. Our country's government, public administration, and culture will have much to gain from this![19]

Social feminism allowed suffragists to take advantage of the very system men controlled to further women's interests. Suffragist Agueda Aponte once said:

> There is no shortage of men in love with progress and who are champions of justice, so, as it turns out, we feminists are not marching alone, as many seem to believe . . . . In this dawn of enlightenment . . . women are doing nothing but taking advantage of an opportunity provided by an age which is new born and very much alive.[20]

Contrary to the Feminine League, which favored from the very beginning a voter literacy qualification, the Suffragist Social League kept silent during its first three years of existence, although internal discussions continued to favor restricted suffrage.[21] It was not until 1924, after the division of the Suffragist Social League and its coalition with the Popular Feminist Association of Working Women of Puerto Rico (Asociación Feminista Popular de Mujeres Obreras de Puerto Rico), that universal suffrage was openly advocated.

The Breakup of the Suffragist Social League

The Suffragist Social League held an Extraordinary General Assembly in August 1924 to "report on all the facts and circumstances that have brought about the current crisis within the League."[22] The crisis arose due to the partisan preferences of the membership. This assembly resulted in the resignation of the president, Rosario Belber, followed by the resignation of María Cadilla de Martínez, Ana López de Vélez, Ana Roqué, Isabel Andreu, Beatriz Lasalle, Amina Tió de Malaret, and Luisa Callejo.[23] Among those reasons stated for their "irrevocable exodus" was to prevent the suffragist cause from losing prestige due to "morbid, sectarian, and partisan controversies."[24]

The Suffragist Social League elected a new board of directors as follows: Marta Robert, president; Olivia Paoli de Braschi, vice president; and María Luisa Ortíz, secretary.[25] Upon a closer look at the members of this new board of directors and of the membership list of those who remained in the League, it becomes evident that the bulk of those suffragists who did not abandon the association were sympathizers and partisans of the Pure Republican Party (Partido Republicano Puro) and the Republican–Socialist Coalition. Indeed, Marta Robert, Ricarda L. de Ramos Casellas, Milagros Benet, Ángela Caldas de Miró, María Luisa Arcelay, Carmen Gómez de Grosas, and Irene F. de Thordsen, among many others, were militant Republicans. Dr. Robert was the first vice president for that party's Territorial Central Committee. Ricarda de Ramos Casellas presided over the Women's Bloc of the Republican Union for several years. Olivia Paoli de Braschi was a collaborator of Santiago Iglesias Pantín within the Socialist Party.[26]

The dissidents, led by Isabel Andreu de Aguilar and Ana Roqué, founded another organization in November 1925: the Puerto Rican Association of Women Suffragists (Asociación Puertorriqueña de Mujeres Sufragistas). The new association recruited its membership from sympathizers of the Union Party and the Republican–Unionist Alliance. Amina Tió de Malaret, Ana Roqué, Trinidad Padilla de Sanz, Isabel Andreu de Aguilar, Ángela Negrón Muñoz, Adela Newman de Gerardino, Ana López de Vélez, and many others who joined the Association were Alliance partisans.[27] The partisan lines drawn by women suffragists evidently had repercussions in their goals and strategies. The discussion of limited versus universal suffrage was the one issue that divided them the most.

The Suffragist Social League, akin to the Republican–Socialist Coalition, defended the universal vote, and the Association, identified with the Alliance, proposed a restricted franchise.

The Popular Feminist Association of Women Workers of Puerto Rico

The Popular Feminist Association of Women Workers of Puerto Rico was formed mainly by women tobacco strippers (despalilladoras). Most of them were illiterate and heads of families whose material conditions were extremely precarious. The Popular Feminist Association's leadership was recruited from among those women who were union leaders and militants within the Free Federation of Labor (Federación Libre de Trabajadores). Thus we find Carmen Puentes, president of the San Juan Tobacco Strippers Union; Genara Pagán, president of a union in Aguadilla; Franca de Armiño and Carmen Gaetán, leading organizers in several tobacco strippers unions in different towns throughout the Island; Petra Aybar, an outstanding Free Federation leader; and Amparo Miranda, a collaborator with the working-class newspaper, *Unión Obrera*.[28]

The Free Federation of Labor had an interest in organizing women workers since its creation in 1899. Labor leaders were concerned about men's jobs being taken over by women who were willing to accept lower pay for unskilled labor, which in turn could lower every worker's salary. The urgency of organizing and educating women arose from the effort to eliminate their threat as cheap labor.[29] From the 1900s to the 1920s, the Federation made great strides in unionizing women. Committees were created to organize the workers and unions were formed in nearly every town on the Island. Furthermore, the Federation made demands regarding the issues of minimum wages, better health care, and improved safety on the job.[30] Female workers made their first claims for suffrage in the assemblies and work groups affiliated with the Federation and its political arm, the Socialist Party. Their militant participation in the union played an important role in the female wage workers' awareness of their rights and rightful place in society.

Emilia Hernández organized the first Women Workers Congress in 1919 to protest the exploitation of women in the tobacco industry and to demand women's vote.[31] In order to organize the struggle and reach those objectives, the Popular Feminist Association of Women Workers of Puerto Rico was created in 1920 under the presidency of Franca de Armiño and with the guidance of U.S. suffragist Betty Hally and Luis Muñoz Marín.[32]

Proletarian women's defense of suffrage was a first step in their struggle for social justice. Carmen Puentes, a renowned labor leader, put it in these words: "we understand that suffrage is not simply a matter of women's vote, but a matter of the highest principles of liberty for us all."[33] These principles and rights included general well-being and progress for those female Puerto Rican workers that suffered the exploitation of capitalist expansion on the Island. On those grounds, demands were made to revise the Minimum Wage Law, enforce compliance with the Women's and Children's Labor Protection Law, supervise more closely the applicability of health laws inside the shops where women were employed, and to have greater female participation whenever the Legislature discussed matters that affected women's work.

Whereas for the suffragist of the propertied, professional elite the right to vote and political emancipation were ways to greater social participation, for the workers, suffrage was an instrument to fight against injustice, hunger, and the misery brought about by U.S. capitalist exploitation on the Island:

> We will no longer allow the capitalist to abuse us. How can we achieve this right to which we are entitled? Well, it's very easy: by means of union and brotherhood [sic] in the workplace and by means of a good organization. . . . Start a labor-organizing campaign, join the Free Federation, and you will have begun to earn respect, to acquire a collective personality, to make progress, and to be free.[34]

The specificity of these workers' problems as women was framed by the broader context of a class struggle. They denounced the hunger and misery that capitalist exploitation brought upon them as laborers. Suffrage was just one way to fight for improved life conditions and to do battle against the oppression that victimized them:

> We cannot go on living as slaves within the terrain of oppression, because we have been tyrannized for many years, because we understand that the labor movement is moving forward in giant strides. We are already knowledgeable in the political, physical, intellectual, and economic arenas; we can embrace innumerable doctrines in order to undertake our own defense . . . and we will continue to espouse these as we prepare for this suffrage campaign.[35]

The female workers' discourse included a cult of domesticity, but it was far from being the argumentative strategy used by the elite suffragists. The workers' arguments were tied to their reality as mothers lacking food for their children, and from this arose the urgency to take part in public life in order to remedy their situation. Males were seen as solidarity partners in a battle against shared problems:

> The time has come to raise our voice . . . and we will go wherever we must to ask justly for what is legitimately ours: the hope of work, of vanishing from our homes the misery and hunger that have been haunting us for so long.[36]

> The country needs her daughters, the self-sacrificing women laborers who struggle just like their men companions for that stale crust of bread they must feed their children. . . . [37]

Finally, the discourse of women workers also included the role of mother–

educator, who was to form future citizens useful to society. However, this function was also framed by the class struggle:

> Are you or will you not be the mothers of those men who will fight in the glorious tomorrow of social dawning? Yes, you are all of that. You bear upon your shoulders that enormous moral and material burden; all that responsibility; all that pain.[38]

Halfhearted Solidarity: The Social League and Its Relation to the Popular Feminist Association of Women Workers of Puerto Rico

The Pure Republican Party, under the leadership of Rafael Martínez Nadal, and the Socialist Party, under the direction of Santiago Iglesias Pantín and Bolívar Pagán, ratified a pact for the 1924 elections. This Coalition, once in power, was committed to universal suffrage.[39] Among many other reasons, the Coalition leadership endorsed universal suffrage with the hope of attracting as many as possible of the estimated 300,000 future women voters. Most of these were illiterate workers active in the Free Federation and the Socialist Party.[40] Ignoring this constituency would have had a very high political price tag; it would have been the equivalent of excluding a force that could potentially decide future electoral results. The atmosphere of agreements and arrangements between the principal political groups in the country set the stage for the rapprochement of the Suffragist Social League and the Popular Feminist Association in September 1924.

Once the Republicans and Socialists ratified their Coalition pact in August 1924, Republican and Socialist women suffragists decided to join in and help out with the Coalition's electoral campaign. In September of that same year, the leaders of the Suffragist Social League and Popular Feminist Association met in Puerta de Tierra and agreed to work together for the Coalition's triumph and to demand universal suffrage.[41]

Nevertheless, this proposed collaboration never materialized. There were very few activities held jointly by these two groups, limited to two or three conferences and talks on suffrage offered at the Puerta de Tierra Seamen's Federation.[42] The Suffragist Social League did not incorporate women workers in the campaigns organized as of September 1924, either. After this date the League's strategies concentrated on these fundamental areas: recruitment of new members and gathering support from other feminist groups in the United States and Latin America.

As to the first issue, the League became more flexible in the admission policies, eliminating dues for first-time membership and monthly dues.[43] It also eliminated the membership requirements under Article 7 of the Foundational Clauses, which laid out the terms and conditions for admission: "to be eighteen years old, be of good moral character, and be introduced by two members of the Local Committee."[44] This opening of the League had well-defined political purposes: to attract the greatest number possible of women who favored women's right to vote. In Ricarda L. de Ramos Casellas's own words: "The Suffragist Social League needed a large number of members, just like any political party, regardless of class, regardless of the private affairs of those applying for membership."[45]

One could get the impression that the new strategy sought to facilitate workers' access to the Suffragist Social League. However, this was not the case. In spite of the agreement reached in September 1924, the League was reluctant to collaborate with women workers. Several episodes confirm this. First, the League refused to gather signatures and engage in a membership drive during an activity sponsored by the Socialist women at the Municipal Theater in November 1924.[46] Second, the League ignored the suggestion made by the Federation's Santurce Organizing Committee for the League to organize a ladies' committee that would help the Free Federation of Labor organize women workers in shops and factories.[47] Third, Milagros Benet de Mewton's visit to the Free Federation's offices in December 1924 revealed many of the League's apprehensions in terms of their affiliation with that union. The visit was made to deliver a set of questionnaires, prepared by the Pan-American Women's Association based in Washington, intended to gather data on the life and activities of Puerto Rican women. She delivered the questionnaires and left quickly. An extract of this episode, covered by the local press, revealed Benet's attitude toward her relationship with the Free Federation of Labor:

> [S]he provided us with some details about the work she was doing, but first she asked that we mention nothing about having met at the Free Federation offices, but to say instead that we had met with her at the Department of Education. . . . Later, trying to provide an explanation, she said that such a precaution was simply to avoid the attacks of those who mistook her for an advocate of certain political factions.[48]

Add to this episode Benet's refusal, once again, to meet with suffragists in La Perla in 1928, arguing that while they would not go into this sector, the women under her leadership would be willing to find a more suitable location in San Juan to hold that meeting.[49]

Finally, it is important to note that the League's official discourse heralded its members as the "unquestionable defenders" of universal suffrage.[50] However, in their lobbying activities with local politicians, the League's leaders were willing to make broad concessions. For example, when Ricarda L. de Ramos Casellas, the League's representative, testified before the Puerto Rican Senate's Government and Elections Committee, she pointed out that

> the League asked for universal suffrage, for men as well as women, but would be grateful for whatever the Senate could do, since any legislation approved by the Legislature would be a step forward, considering that it would endow a group of women with an opportunity that would open the doors for the rest of

the group. . . . [E]very Puerto Rican women wanted earnestly to enjoy this right, even though the groundwork to achieve this was left in the hands of a very few.[51]

Likewise in 1929, when the Senate approved the bill of law granting literate women the right to vote, the Suffragist Social League directors met with the Coalition's Supreme Council and asked that the Coalitionist legislators not revoke it.[52]

The Popular Feminist Association was left out of these suffragist debates. The women workers denounced the situation one year after their pact with the Suffragist Social League:

> The feminist movement on our Island is excessively academic and dogmatic. We need a strong campaign to disseminate the greatness of our principles. We must make use of the press and all public means available, in order to bring about the victory of our magnificent ideas. The creation of committees in different communities throughout the Island, that attempt to break the stale social molds, will bring excellent results. A sweeping movement is called for.[53]

Evidently, women workers felt alienated from the suffragist coalition and demanded a more energetic action and greater participation in the forthcoming battles. However, the League's strategies and activities focused on gathering support for their cause in the United States and Latin America. The Puerto Rican legislature had ignored for eleven years their demand for the franchise and so they sought support in international feminist organizations. In fact, they were not alone. In 1920, the congress of the International Alliance of Women Suffragists decided to struggle for women's suffrage throughout the world. The League lost no time in mobilizing its contacts and influences to lobby in favor of the electoral franchise for Puerto Rican women.[54] In 1925, Dr. Marta Robert was commissioned to represent Puerto Rico's women before the Pan-American Congress held in Washington. At this meeting the League was able to get the support from three U.S. suffragist groups: the Women's National Party, the International League of Women Voters, and the National League of Women Voters.[55] Affiliation with these organizations accelerated the League's lobbying efforts before the U.S. Congress. In November 1927, the Women's National Party, through Senator Hiram Bingham, filed a bill of law granting suffrage to all women in Puerto Rico.[56] That same year the League's suffragists sent a letter to President Calvin Coolidge asking for legislation, as part of his message to Congress, to extend the right to vote to women in Puerto Rico.[57] The same petition was then made to the governor of Puerto Rico, Horace Mann Towner.[58] These efforts apparently were successful, since Governor Towner, in his 1928 message to the Legislature, recommended that legislation be approved granting the right to vote to women who could read and write.[59]

Finally, on April 1929, after heated debates and political maneuvers, restricted suffrage was approved.[60] The Suffragist Social League announced that the law did not meet its expectations because it granted the franchise only to literate women and that it would continue to fight until the ideal of universal suffrage was achieved.[61] In reality, that never happened. During the League's annual meeting, held in May 1929, one month after restricted suffrage had been approved, a delegate from Cayey, identified only as Miss Nogueras, presented a motion to ask Governor Towner for a revision of the law, and to recommend to the Legislature in his address that they extend the right "to all citizens, men and women, whether or not they can read or write." The motion was put to a vote and defeated by the majority.[62]

Although the Suffragist Social League remained registered with the State Department until the 1940s, membership dues were neglected, and as of 1934 certain irregularities appeared in the elections of the board of directors.[63] Idleness and neglect characterized the League in the years that followed the approval of restricted suffrage, as can be confirmed by the reports in the press. Indeed, newspapers and magazines between 1930 and 1940 have few, if any, news items or articles about the League's activities, programs, or endeavors. In contrast, the names of its leaders often appear in the press as leaders of the Pure Republican Women's Bloc and later of the Republican Union Women's Bloc.[64] Once the right to vote was obtained, the League abandoned its proletarian "brethren" and members became immersed in the struggles of party politics.

Epilogue

The first issue on the agenda of the elite feminists during the 1920s had been to obtain a voting franchise. Once that was obtained, former members of the Suffragist Social League and of the Puerto Rican Association of Women Suffragists channeled their efforts in favor of their own political ideologies and party interests.

The Republican Union Women's Association (Asociación de Mujeres de la Unión Republicana) was created in 1932. Their Articles of Incorporation specified their purpose to "[w]ork towards the achievement of an Ideal State in Puerto Rico, and for the glory of the Republican Union, providing our assistance to its official agencies."[65] The leaders of this new group, most of them members of the idle Suffragist Social League, said the time had come to join efforts to win the 1932 elections.[66] A vigorous campaign was started in every town for Republican Union women to participate in the party's primaries and support María Luisa Arcelay, the group's candidate for the House of Representatives.[67] The campaign stressed that she should not be supported solely on the basis of her sex, but on the basis of her Republican convictions and beliefs, as well as her commitment to the struggle for federated statehood for the Island. In the words of Ricarda L. de Ramos Casellas, at that time president of Republican Union Women's Association: "[w]omen cannot vote for a candidate merely because she happens to be a woman."[68] Ramos Casellas was making a direct reference to the candidacy of Isabel Andreu de Aguilar, a member and outstanding leader of the former Republican Union Women's Association, who was running for a Senate seat in San Juan under the Liberal Party. Her campaign stressed the distinguished role she had played in the suffragist battles, and urged all women to vote for her.[69] As far as Ramos was concerned, Liberals defended very different ideals from those of the Republican creed. For that reason, an opponent's candidacy could not be supported simply because she was a woman.

Arcelay was in fact elected in 1932 and re-elected in 1936. Interestingly enough, she showed no interest whatsoever in women's issues. On the contrary, in her role as legislator she fought against minimum wages for the women of the needlework industry. Of course, her own economic interests were at stake, since she was one of the most prominent shop owners in this industry in the western part of Puerto Rico.[70] Her class interests were above her gender interests.

Nevertheless, suffragists who identified with the Liberal Party created the Sisterhood of Liberal Women (Hermandad de Mujeres Liberales) in April 1932. The purpose of this association was to initiate "a vigorous campaign to raise funds for campaign expenses to ensure the success of our party in the next elections."[71] Two Liberal women candidates ran for legislative positions in the 1932 elections: Adela Ramírez de Ramírez for the House and Isabel Andreu de Aguilar for the Senate.[72] Their respective campaigns focused on the defense of the party's ideals, and more specifically on the solution to the Island's political status. For Isabel Andreu de Aguilar, the Liberal Party bore the responsibility of validating the national dignity by voting for the only party that defended the highest values of Puerto Rican nationality.[73] Likewise, Adela Ramírez de Ramírez pointed out that she accepted the candidacy in order to contribute to the Party's triumph in the western part of the Island, since coalitionist adversaries had strengthened their hold in that region.[74] Just like their Republican counterparts, Liberal women moved away from the goals of their proletarian "brethren," who did not qualify to vote since they were, for the most part, illiterate.[75]

In contrast, the Socialist Party, in an attempt to forward the cause of universal suffrage, began once more to organize its women militants. In 1929, a massive campaign began to create committees and Socialist women's unions in every town on the Island. From then on, all proletarian actions and activities in favor of women's vote came from the Socialist Party and its women's sections and committees. In 1930, the Socialist Party's Executive Territorial Committee rejected and disapproved of all female political activity "that did not take place within the genuinely socialist organizations."[76] When the Republican–Socialist Coalition won the 1932 elections and took power, Socialist leader and legislator Bolívar Pagán submitted a bill of law granting universal suffrage. It was approved in 1935. Illiterate women exercised their new right for the first time in the 1936 elections.

Notes

The author wishes to thank María del Carmen Baerga Santini for her valuable comments and Ángel Quintero Rivera for his suggestions. Of course, the responsibility for the final result is entirely the author's. She also thanks Janice Palma for the translation and Lanny Thompson for editing the text.

1. *National Archives*, R.G. 350, File 27260–14, Box 1217.

2. See, for example, Yamila Azize, *La mujer en la lucha* (Río Piedras: Editorial Cultural, 1985); Isabel Picó, *La mujer y la política puertorriqueña* (Rio Piedras: Centro de Investigaciones Sociales, UPR, 1983); Gladys Jiménez-Muñoz, " 'A Storm Dressed in Skirts': Ambivalence in the Debate of Women's Suffrage in Puerto Rico, 1927–1929" (Ph.D. diss., State University of New York at Binghamton, 1994).

3. Azize, *La mujer,* 134.

4. Isabel Picó, "Women in Puerto Rican Politics before Enfranchisement," *Homines* 4 (1987): 413. See also Julio Ramos, ed., *Amor y anarquía. Los escritos de Luisa Capetillo* (Río Piedras: Ediciones Huracán, 1992), 47–58

5. "Women Who Have Gained Renown in the Arts, Science, and Professions," *National Archives,* Washington, DC, General Records, Record Group 350, Bureau of Insular Affairs, File 27260–13, Box 1217; *La Mujer del Siglo XX,* June 30, 1919, 5.

6. Ángela Negrón Muñoz, "Figuras sobresalientes del feminismo insular. Amparo Fernández Nater," *Puerto Rico Ilustrado,* August 24, 1939, 36.

7. Ángela Negrón Muñoz, "Figuras sobresalientes del feminismo insular. La Hija del Caribe," *Puerto Rico Ilustrado,* June 8, 1929, 38.

8. Ángela Negrón Muñoz, "Conversando con las principales feministas del país. Soledad Lloréns Torres," *El Mundo,* April 20, 1930, 1.

9. *La Mujer del Siglo XX,* August 15, 1919, 8–9.

10. Ángela Negrón Muñoz, *Mujeres de Puerto Rico* (San Juan: n.p., 1935), 219–20.

11. Ángela Negrón Muñoz, "Conversando con las principales feministas del país. Amparo Fernández Nater," *El Mundo,* June 8, 1930, 1.

12. See Negrón Muñoz, "Figuras sobresalientes del feminismo insular. La Hija del Caribe," 38; Angela Negrón Muñoz, "Figuras sobresalientes del feminismo insular. Soledad Lloréns Torres," *Puerto Rico Ilustrado,* April 20, 1930, 38; Ángela Negrón Muñoz, "Figuras sobresalientes del feminismo insular. Carlota Matienzo," *Puerto Rico Ilustrado,* July 9, 1929, 7.

13. Archivo General de Puerto Rico (hereafter quoted as AGPR), Fondo: Departamento de Estado; Serie: Corporaciones sin fines de lucro, "Arts. de incorporación de la Liga Social Sufragista de Puerto Rico," File 236, Box 17–A.

14. Librada Rodríguez de Ramos, "Voz femenina," *La Mujer del Siglo XX,* October 1920, 12.

15. Ana Roqué de Duprey, "Apreciaciones falsas," *La Mujer del Siglo XX,* September 1917, 3.

16. Ana Roqué de Duprey, "Fulguración," *Heraldo de la Mujer,* October 1919.

17. Naomi Black, *Social Feminism* (Ithaca: Cornell University Press, 1987), 324–48. Research in Asia, Europe, the United States, and Latin America has shown that social feminism was useful in expanding the support for the movement without challenging the traditional vision of women's roles in society. See Barbara Southard, *The Women's Movement and Colonial Politics in Bengal: The Quest for Political Rights, Education, and Social Reform Legislation, 1921–1936* (New Delhi: Manohar, 1995); Ross Evan Paulson, *Women Suffrage and Prohibition: A Comparative Study of Equality and Social Control* (Glenview: Scott, Foresman, 1973); Kathryn Lynn Stoner, "Women's Rights and the Cuban Republic," *Cuban*

Heritage, 2, no. 1 (1988): 13–22; María de Fátima Barceló Miller, *La lucha por el sufragio femenino en Puerto Rico, 1896–1935* (Río Piedras: Ediciones Huracán and Centro de Investigaciones Sociales, 1997).

18. Liga Femínea Puertorriqueña, Propaganda Committee, "Feminismo," *La Mujer del Siglo XX,* January 31, 1918, 13.

19. Manuel Fernández Juncos, "Opinión," *La Mujer del Siglo XX,* October 31, 1918, 1.

20. Agueda Aponte, "No desmayemos," *La Mujer del Siglo XX,* February 28, 1918, 5.

21. "Liga Social," *National Archives,* Record Group 350, File 272607–C, Box 1217.

22. "La Asamblea de la Liga Social Sufragista celebrada en el Ateneo. La nota escandalosa dada por la Sra. Mewton y su grupo," *La Democracia,* August 6, 1924, 4.

23. Centro de Investigaciones Históricas (CIH), *Libro de Actas de la Liga Social Sufragista, año 1923–24,* "Acta de la Asamblea General de la Liga Social Sufragista, de Puerto Rico, celebrada en el Ateneo Puertorriqueño, 4 de agosto de 1924."

24. "Un telegrama de la Dra. Pérez Marchand," *El Mundo,* Thursday, August 21, 1924, 1.

25. AGPR, Fondo: Departamento de Estado; Serie: Corporaciones sin fines de lucro, "Informe de cambios de vacantes habidas en la Directiva de esta Liga, cubiertas según dispone nuestro reglamento," File 236, Box 17–A.

26. "El Bloque de Mujeres de la Unión Republicana constituye sub-comités en diversos barrios de San Juan," *El Mundo,* May 14, 1932, 1; "Organiza un recibimiento la Vanguardia femenina de San Juan," *El Mundo,* August 12, 1932, 2; "Actividades de la Unión Republicana de Puerta de Tierra: Una reunión femenina," *El Mundo,* April 19, 1932, 12; "Se reunió la Directiva insular del Bloque de Mujeres de la Unión Republicana," *El Mundo,* May 18, 1932, 2; Ángela Negrón Muñoz, "Figuras sobresalientes del feminismo insular. Olivia Paoli de Braschi," *Puerto Rico Ilustrado,* June 29, 1929, 40.

27. Barceló Miller, *La lucha,* chapter 2.

28. "A las mujeres de Santurce," *Unión Obrera,* December 14, 1920, 1; "Mujeres Puertorriqueñas," *Unión Obrera,* February 14, 1920, 2; Azize, *La mujer,* 61–88.

29. Alice Colón, Margarita Mergal, and Nilsa Torres, *Participación de la mujer en la historia de Puerto Rico (Las primeras décadas del siglo XX)* (Río Piedras: Centro de Investigaciones Sociales/ CERES, 1986); Azize, *La mujer,* 61–91.

30. Colón, et al., *Participación,* 32–35; Azize, *La mujer,* 61–91.

31. Isabel Picó, *La mujer y la política,* 33.

32. "A las mujeres de Santurce," 1.

33. *Unión Obrera,* February 7, 1920, 3.

34. Elvira Matos, "A las trabajadoras de Cidra," *Unión Obrera,* January 11, 1920, 1.

35. Carmen Puentes, "La mujer puertorriqueña pide el sufragio," *Unión Obrera,* February 7, 1920, 3.

36. Josefa G. de Maldonado, "Manifiesto obrero," in Julio Ramos, ed., *Amor y anarquía. Los escritos de Luisa Capetillo* (Río Piedras: Ediciones Huracán, 1992), 219–20.

37. "Mujeres puertorriqueñas," 3.

38. "A las mujeres de Santurce," 11.

39. For greater detail about the Coalition, see Bolívar Pagán, *Historia de los partidos políticos puertorriqueños,* 2 vols. (San Juan: 1959), II, 32–41.

40. Azize, *La mujer,* 103.

41. "A la mujer socialista y republicana pura," *Unión Obrera,* September 10, 1924; "Reunión," *Unión Obrera,* September 24, 1924; Azize, *La mujer,* 131.

42. These talks and gatherings for women workers were not exclusive to the Social League. The Puerto Rican Association of Women Suffragists also sponsored similar activities for proletarian women. See Azize, *La mujer,* 134–35.

43. CIH, Ricarda L. de Ramos Casellas Collection, *Libro de Actas de la Liga Social Sufragista,* Box 2, Minutes 59, December 7, 1924; Minutes 80, February 27, 1926.

44. CIH, Ricarda L. de Ramos Casellas Collection, *Libro de Actas de la Liga Social Sufragista,* Box 2, Minutes 67, March 29, 1925.

45. Ibid.

46. CIH, Ricarda L. de Ramos Casellas Collection, *Libro de Actas de la Liga Social Sufragista,* Box 2, Minutes 54, October 30, 1924.

47. CIH, Ricarda L. de Ramos Casellas Collection, *Libro de Actas de la Liga Social Sufragista,* Box 2, Minutes 59, December 7, 1924.

48. "La líder del sufragismo, la Sra. de Mewton, visitó ayer la Federación Libre," *El Mundo,* December 6, 1924, 3.

49. "Las damas sufragistas se niegan a ir al Barrio La Perla," *La Correspondencia,* March 29, 1928, 3.

50. "La Liga Social Sufragista nunca ha prestado ni podrá prestar apoyo a una petición de sufragio restringido," *El Mundo,* December 8, 1927, 3.

51. CIH, Ricarda L. de Ramos Casellas Collection, *Libro de Actas de la Liga Social Sufragista,* Minutes Book, Box 2, Minutes 65, March 14, 1925.

52. CIH, Ricarda L. de Ramos Casellas Collection, *Libro de Actas de la Liga Social Sufragista,* Box 2, Minutes 101, April 24, 1929.

53. "Feminismo regional," *Unión Obrera,* September 19, 1925.

54. "La única asociación sufragista que desde 1924 hasta ahora ha trabajado en Washington la franquicia electoral es la Liga Social Sufragista," *El Mundo,* July 31, 1928, 3; "La Dra. Robert y la Srta. Emanuelli fueron las únicas mujeres que defendieron valientemente nuestro derecho ante los poderes nacionales," *Mundo,* May 16, 1928, 3; "La Liga Social Sufragista está representada en la Conferencia Panamericana," *El Mundo,* January 20, 1928, 3. "Documento interesante," *La Mujer del Siglo XX,* n.d., 12.

55. "Liga Social Sufragista adquiere la protección de las tres agrupaciones más fuertes en la historia del sufragio femenino," *El Mundo,* May 25, 1925, 3.

56. "En la próxima sesión del Congreso se presentará nuevamente el proyecto concediendo el voto a la mujer puertorriqueña. El Partido Nacional de Mujeres ya ha hecho las gestiones en ese sentido," *El Mundo,* October 11, 1927, 1.

57. "Fue un éxito la asamblea anual de la Liga Social Sufragista. Se acordó enviar un cablegrama a Coolidge pidiéndole que recomiende al Congreso la concesión del voto a la mujer puertorriqueña," *El Mundo,* September 8, 1927, 11.

58. "No veo razón por qué las mujeres de Puerto Rico no han de tener el voto lo mismo que si residieran en los Estados Unidos," *El Mundo,* November 28, 1927, 3.

59. "Mensaje del Gobernador Towner," *La Democracia,* February 17, 1928, 5–7.

60. See Barceló Miller, *La lucha,* chapters 2 and 3.

61. "La Liga Sufragista define su actitud," *El Mundo,* April 26, 1929, 5.

62. CIH, Ricarda L. de Ramos Casellas Collection, *Libro de Actas de la Liga Social Sufragista,* Box 2, Minutes 102, May 19, 1929.

63. AGPR, Fondo: Departamento de Estado; Serie: Corporaciones sin fines de lucro; "Informes anuales," File 236, Box 17–A.

64. Between 1930 and 1932 the press is inundated with news items about these groups: "Organiza nuevos comités en distintas pártes de la Isla el Bloque de Mujeres de la Unión Republicana," *El Mundo,* August 13, 1932, 2; "La participación del Bloque de Mujeres de la Unión Republicana en la parada del último domingo," *El Mundo,* December 10, 1932, 2; "Organizado el Comité de Damas de la Unión Republicana en Comerio," *La Correspondencia,* September 1, 1932, 3; "El Bloque de Mujeres de la Unión Republicana urge que sus correligionarias participen en las primarias del partido," *El Mundo,* July 2, 1932, 2; "Se constituyó en Santa Isabel un Comité del Bloque de Mujeres republicanas puras de Puerto Rico." *El Mundo,* October 7, 1930, 1; "Un llamamiento a las mujeres republicanas puras," *El Mundo,* January 22, 1931, 1.

65. "Artículos de Incorporación de la Asociación de Mujeres de la Unión Republicana," AGPR, Fondo: Departamento de Estado; Serie: Corporaciones sin fines de lucro; Box 40–A, File 646.

66. "Nos sentimos orgullosas de nuestro pueblo," *El Mundo*, May 1, 1932, 1.

67. "El Bloque de Mujeres de la Unión Republicana urge que sus correligionarias participen en las primarias del partido," *El Mundo*, July 2, 1932, 2; "Organizado el Comité de Damas de la Unión Republicana en Comerío," *La Correspondencia*, September 1, 1932, 3; "Espero que todos habrán de cooperar conmigo," *El Día*, December 2, 1932, 8.

68. "Doña Ricarda Ramos Casellas se dirige a las mujeres de la Unión Republicana," *La Correspondencia*, October 28, 1932, 1.

69. "Un grupo de damas liberales lanzan un manifiesto," *El Mundo*, October 24, 1932, 1.

70. Azize, *La mujer*, 163–64.

71. "Se constituye la Hermandad de Mujeres Liberales," *El Mundo*, April 1, 1932, 7.

72. "Un grupo de damas liberales lanza un manifiesto," *El Mundo*, October 24, 1932, 1; "Hablando con Adela Ramírez de Ramírez," *El Mundo*, October 23, 1932, 1.

73. Isabel Andreu de Aguilar, "Al electorado femenino," *El Mundo*, October 21, 1932, 2.

74. "Hablando con Adela Ramírez de Ramírez," *El Mundo*, October 23, 1932, 1.

75. Barceló Miller, *La lucha*, 96–113.

76. "Declaración del Comité Ejecutivo Territorial del Partido Socialista aprobada unánimemente en su sesión de septiembre 28 de 1930," in Azize, *La mujer*, 177–79.

7

Literacy, Class, and Sexuality in the Debate on Women's Suffrage in Puerto Rico During the 1920s

Gladys M. Jiménez-Muñoz

[C]olonial mimicry is the desire for a reformed, recognizable Other, as a subject of a difference that is almost the same, but not quite. Which is to say, that the discourse of mimicry is constructed around an ambivalence. . . .

—Homi Bhabha
Of Mimicry and Man: The Ambivalence of Colonial Discourse (1994)

Considerations of power are central to the interaction of the physical body and the body of language. Sexuality produces power, at the same time as the discourse of the powerful constructs sexuality. We must not collapse sexuality, power, and discourse upon each other. It is their interpenetration not their interchangeability that is critical within the abstractions of post-structural debate, within the affective world of the emotions—and within the political arena.

—Carroll Smith-Rosenberg
The Body Politic (1989)

In the U.S. colony of Puerto Rico, the struggle for women's suffrage erupted onto the Island's political scene from social elements that had been accumulating during the first three decades of the twentieth century. The focal point of the debate on this issue was from 1927 to 1929, when there was a prolific and heated exchange of views in the local press. The principal goal of this essay is to explain how the social contradictions rocking Puerto Rico's colonial society in the 1920s cut through the debate over granting voting rights to Island women. In particular, I examine how urbane public opinion in Puerto Rico perceived the demands for women's suffrage as an integral component of chaotic modernity and of the masses of illiterate laborers who supposedly embodied this chaos. In this manner, I hope to demonstrate the relational character of colonialism and the contested and hierarchical interdetermination of colonial subjects (dominant and subordinate). Historiographically, such relationality and interdetermination can be clarified through the various ways in which the differing sectors of the colonized population and of the colonizers regularly mirrored each other's practices, assumptions, and expectations—even as they struggled over whose socio-political (and cultural-national/racial) ontology and practices were the initial model and whose were mere imitation—in pursuit of contradictory yet overlapping objectives. Hence, my reliance on the notions of *colonial mimicry* and *colonial ambivalence* as such concepts have been theorized by critiques of colonial discourses.[1]

I begin by examining the "illiteracy panic" that took over official circles and cultured public opinion in Puerto Rico toward the late 1920s. I explore the ways in which this panic directly intersected the claims of the various sectors within the debate on women's suffrage by analyzing how this politicized anxiety, in turn, was sexualized and class-based. I include a section on the ways in which the mainstream press made sense of modernity and of its social, cultural, market, and technological effects. This is followed by an analysis of the specific fear nagging genteel Creoles: namely, that women's suffrage would blur the distinction between the Puerto Rican social body and Puerto Rican sexual bodies, thereby en-gendering chaos within the Island's political body. Such fears immediately conjured visions of political cross-dressing and gender uncertainty among those opposed to granting women the vote and among mainstream representatives within the colony's legislature. The chapter ends by exploring the meanings of these apprehensions and the way they interpellated the suffragists themselves, particularly by examining the figures that—together with the suffragist—embodied these anxieties most clearly: the prostitute and the laboring-poor woman of allegedly loose morals.

Women's Suffrage Organizations in Puerto Rico and the Approval of a Limited Women's Suffrage Bill

In early-twentieth-century Puerto Rico, the category "woman" ambivalently intersected the category of "citizenship" insofar as Island women were denied the right to vote within the local political scene. This prohibition gained even greater significance after the U.S. Congress passed the Jones Act of 1917 enabling every adult male "native" to elect the members of both houses of the local legislature.[2]

The rise of the women's suffrage struggle partially stems from this pivotal accumulation of political contradictions, as exemplified by the 1917 founding of an unstable women's rights confederation mainly composed of "native" women professionals from widely dissimilar social backgrounds and viewpoints known as the Liga Femínea Puertorriqueña that same year.[3]

Although the organization grouped widely divergent viewpoints, in 1917 the majority faction convinced the Liga to circumscribe its petition to the Island's legislature in terms of limited franchise for those women who could read and write. In 1920 the Liga Femínea became the Liga Social Sufragista, an organization openly struggling for a wider range of social reforms, women's suffrage included. According to the prominent suffragist Milagros Benet de Mewton, the new name and broader objectives "expressed more clearly the organization's goal," among other things indicating the rising clout and/or numbers of socially progressive women professionals within the Liga.[4] In 1921 the Liga promoted several legislative bills in favor of voting rights for all the Island's women, regardless of whether they were literate or not.[5]

In March of 1924, disagreements sprung up within the Liga, overlapping with the regrouping in the Island's political scene at this very moment. The dispute officially arose because one Liga faction opposed pro-suffrage court actions in open association with a common, working-class woman (Mariana Morales Bernard) and a lawyer (Bolívar Pagán) who was an outspoken member of the Partido Socialista.[6] Some of the top leaders of the Liga (e.g., Ricarda de Ramos Casellas) became publicly recognized as straightforward Jacobinist professionals.[7]

Such company was obviously anathema to women identified with patrician respectability, bourgeois high culture, and renovated cultural nationalism of the mainstream political parties—the Partido Unión (or "Unionistas") and the Partido Republicano, who joined forces that same spring to form the "Alianza." The main fear of the Alianza was that if *all* women on the Island were granted the right to vote, this would throw the election in favor of the Socialistas, who had the largest number of illiterate adherents.[8] The converging political organs of the Creole propertied and educated classes rallied against what they portrayed as the Socialista "red menace" and trade-union rabble—that is, the Federación Libre de Trabajadores (FLT)—particularly against the last two groups' purportedly unpatriotic agenda. In June of 1924 the splinter group comprised by the more refined suffragists became the Asociación Puertorriqueña de Mujeres Sufragistas.[9]

At this time, politically active working-class women were also struggling for the "emancipation of the female sex." In 1919 a FLT committee for women's organization presented a resolution at the 10th Congress of the Island's principal labor federation demanding a law guaranteeing the minimum wage for women, subsequently hand-delivering this resolution to the colonial governor.[10] Two years later some of these very same trade-union women established the Asociación Feminista Popular de Mujeres Obreras Puertorriqueñas, headed by Franca de Armiño and Carmen Gaetán, among others. This organization was aimed at both obtaining women's suffrage and the complete recognition of all civil

and public rights for Island women. The ideological kinship between this association and the Partido Socialista partially stemmed from the fact that the latter
was the only Island electoral organization to include women's suffrage in its
program.[11]

Although almost a dozen bills granting women the vote had been presented in the
Island's legislative assembly between 1920 and 1929, women's suffrage was hardly
a burning issue within local legislative polemics at this time. As the majority party in
the colony's parliament (either by itself or within the Alianza), the Unionista leadership was chiefly responsible for blocking women's suffrage bills. Between 1924 and
1929 the Unionistas (now as Aliancistas) promoted and benefited from the split
within the Liga by winning over the support of the splinter group (the Asociación
Puertorriqueña).[12] By acknowledging the growing pro-suffrage elements among
propertied and educated women, the Unionista patriarch and senator Antonio R.
Barceló resurrected the 1917 project of a restricted female vote (i.e., only for women
who knew how to read and write), convincing the Asociación Puertorriqueña that
this was the more pragmatic option. Yet, despite Barceló's formal endorsement,
most of the Unionista (now joint-Aliancista) legislative representation basically
stalled all support for even this lukewarm measure.[13]

During the Pan-American Congress of Women in 1926 the leadership of both
the Liga Social Sufragista and the Asociación Puertorriqueña de Mujeres
Sufragistas met with representatives of the U.S. National Woman's Party, although it was the Liga that established the stronger links with this North American women's rights organization.[14] Such connections soon paid off insofar as it
was the U.S. National Woman's Party that, in turn, convinced U.S. Senator
Bingham to submit a bill amending the Jones Act and granting Puerto Rico's
women the vote.[15] The short-term failure of this legislative effort led to further
lobbying efforts during 1927–28 on the part of the National Woman's Party in
Congress on behalf of the vote for the women of Puerto Rico.[16]

These efforts paid off because by late 1928 the bill had been passed in the U.S.
House of Representatives and had almost been passed in the federal Senate. All the
while, the colony's legislature had been delaying the issue, as the Alianza became
increasingly upset at yet another case of federal usurpation of Puerto Rico's official
spokesmen.[17] However, the balance of forces had decisively changed by late 1928:
"Nothing further was done or attempted by the United States Congress to push
woman suffrage into the Jones Act, but the point had been made: The Puerto Rican
legislature should get the job done, or it would be taken out of the hands of the
islanders."[18] On April 16, 1929, the Island's legislature finally passed a law granting
educated women the vote; universal suffrage was eventually granted in 1935.

Women's Suffrage as a "Constant Danger"

On Monday, February 21, 1927, the readers of *La Democracia* were able to see
the whole text of the long message delivered by colonial Governor Horace Mann

Towner to the 11th Legislative Assembly of Puerto Rico. The suffragists on the Island were particularly concerned with one of the sections, "The Elections and the Faculties of the Voters," in which Governor Towner issued some recommendations for improving the voting process on the Island while simultaneously recognizing the issue of women's suffrage:

> I assume that all of you have acknowledged the fact that, [since] the women of Puerto Rico are American citizens, suffrage should be granted to them as soon as possible *so as to in this way harmonize our political conditions with the Nineteenth Amendment to the Constitution of the United States.* This right should also be granted to women because the government of Puerto Rico is obligated to them for the cooperation and help they provide in the fields of education, hygiene, and public health, compliance with the law, and in all those measures promoting good morals, social betterment, and the general welfare of the people.[19]

Although the colonial governor is proposing that the women of the Island be granted the vote on the basis of the Nineteenth Amendment to the U.S. Constitution, this address remains ambivalent and contradictory. In the process of normalizing, not just the colonial state—both as a social situation and as juridico-political structure—but also the colonized subjects, Governor Towner additionally suggested in another part of his speech that such suffrage be limited to literate Puerto Ricans (male or female): "the requirement that the suffrage rights of every new voter, man or woman, be limited to those who know how to read and write would be completely justified in the future. . . ."[20] Towner's recommendation exempted those illiterate men who voted in the previous elections, whose already existing rights could not be taken away. Although this recommendation was never implemented, it nevertheless reflects some of the imminent concerns of the colonial bureaucracy, both North American and Creole, during this juncture. Behind the advice that, starting with the next elections, voter registration be limited to literate men, lurked the threat epitomized by the high percentage of illiterate people voting in the Island:

> An electorate, where forty out of every hundred voters does not even know how to read the voting slip that they deposit in the voting box, constitutes a constant danger. At any one moment, the results of an election may be determined by those who know how to vote on the basis of other people's advice. Undoubtedly, it would be dangerous to double the number of illiterate voters.[21]

This illustrates how hegemonic ideological representations were populated with concerns over the destabilization of colonialist authority, the issue of U.S. citizenship being a case in point.[22] As had been the case since 1898 and has continued unevenly to the present day, the colonialist identity being enacted through the colonial governor's practices and pronouncements (in this case,

Towner's speech) evidently desired a colonized subject that was sufficiently different from U.S. hegemonic identities to justify the North American republic's "civilizing mission" in the Island, yet sufficiently similar to the colonizers so as to be identifiably reassuring in the latter's eyes.[23] Since universal white suffrage already existed in the U.S. mainland, Towner's recommendation placed illiterate white North Americans at the same level as propertied and educated Puerto Ricans. Such a maneuver located the supremacy of the colonizer/Same and the subordination of the colonized/Other within the textual gridwork and social structure of colonialist politics.

By extending Nineteenth-Amendment–based voting rights to women in Puerto Rico, Towner's normative gesture of enfranchisement would have produced a new and improved colonized political space recognizable within the terms of the U.S. Constitution.[24] But, at the same time, such reforms created their own slippages and disparities by estranging the proposed voting rights of both Puerto Rican women and men from those prerogatives enjoyed by their (white) North American fellow citizens.

Two weeks before (February 5, 1927), *La Democracia* published an open letter from the president of the Senate of Puerto Rico and top leader of the Unionistas, Antonio R. Barceló, to the president of the Asociación Puertorriqueña de Mujeres Sufragistas, Isabel Andreu de Aguilar. In this letter, the renowned leader of the Creole hacendado class reaffirmed his position in favor of women's suffrage, stating that "the amendment that might succeed without difficulties is the one that gives the vote to the competent woman, that is, the woman who knows how to read and write . . ."[25] Barceló explains that the Island's government should not repeat the same mistake made by the federal government when in 1904 it bestowed universal male suffrage to Puerto Rico:

> It must be admitted that a great segment of public opinion believes that [woman's] suffrage should be limited to those who know how to read and write, because it is understood that this is precisely the cause behind the outrage by which today we cannot display with pride a proportion of literate people similar to the average found in the United States and because, additionally, said outrage constitutes an impediment to our political aspirations and even to the development of our economic matters.[26]

According to the president of the colony's Senate, to grant voting rights to even more illiterate people was akin to placing governance in the hands of strangers—literally. Puerto Rico had qualified men capable of directing it better than

> any other man who is a stranger to its customs and to its being—no matter how prominent he may be; and a system such as the one that rules us, that expels our competent elements, annulling its initiatives and diminishing its dignity within the political realm, tends to create citizens without any faith, without any abnegation, and without legitimate ambitions, which, forced to think only

about their lives in the present and to look for the best way of having a good time with the least sacrifices and complications possible, they finally turn into negative beings regarding the progress and welfare of the motherland.[27]

Barceló establishes a link between (a) U.S. colonialism, which, in authorizing the vote to illiterate Puerto Rican men, also employs such authority to impose North American administrators on the Island's inhabitants, and (b) the need to control the imminent evil of having more uneducated people vote in the case of Puerto Rican women. It seems that the president of the Island's Senate is not opposed to a "good colonialism" that would allow the educated Creoles to participate in the administration of colonial rule. Paraphrasing Thomas Babington Macaulay's vision of a "mimic man raised through our English School" in nineteenth-century India, Barceló wants to participate in the U.S. colonialist dream of a "class of interpreters between us and the millions whom we govern—a class of persons" Puerto Rican "in blood and colour, but" North American "in tastes, in opinions, in morals and in intellect."[28]

In this manner, the leader of the "native" elites attempts to transcend the mistakes of the colonizers by improving on the latter's methods of colonial(ist) governance. Such an operation would demonstrate that the educated Creoles have a claim to a greater share in the colonial administration because, like the colonizers, the identity of the Puerto Rican propertied class is also enacted in a relation of supremacy with respect to the subjectivities of the Island's dispossessed and uneducated majorities.

Like Barceló, Senator José Tous Soto (chieftain of the majority, pro-Aliancista wing of the Partido Republicano) also signaled the mistake the United States made in according voting responsibilities to illiterate Puerto Ricans, the latter being the ones "who need to be led by the hand, lacking as they are in any guiding light."[29] And similar to Barceló, for Tous Soto—the prominent sugar-corporation lawyer—the desire for increasingly disciplining the colonized majorities was being expressed by a disciplined and respectable Creole. For him, it was more appropriate to extend this "prerogative to the educated woman before reaching universal female suffrage like the one enjoyed by the man."[30] The discourses deployed by Soto and Barceló illustrate the extent to which not all the colonized subjects shared a common identity: not all the colonized were the same because there were some colonized subjects that were more equal than others. Even among the colonized there was a desire for a new and improved Other, almost the same as the educated and propertied Creole men but not quite—either for being women and/or for being dispossessed and illiterate.

The personification of these Other(ed) differences makes some privileged colonized subjects similar to the colonizer and, therefore, should give these privileged colonized subjects access to the ruling spheres of the colonialists. The colonial mimicry of restricting women's suffrage in Puerto Rico (in part or in total) would apparently verify the capacity of the educated/propertied/Creole male for ruling (the) Others. And yet the ambivalence remained in the realm of political authority—between the colonizer and the colonized, between genders, and between classes—thereby reproducing a slippage of normative structures within the existing differences of gender, race, sexuality, and class.

Creeping Modernization/Modernism and Creepy Modernity

Women's bodies became one of the terrains in which, not just women's suffrage, but many of the broader political issues were going to be debated in Puerto Rico—such as the anxiety of the privileged over more and more chaotic social change. There are many examples of how and why the Creole propertied/educated sectors saw disorder as rampant in Puerto Rico during the 1920s, but this real and imagined turbulent metamorphosis cannot be understood without briefly examining its broader social context.

The decline in the principal agricultural exports (as a proportion of all Island exports) at this time induced large property-owners (Creole and North American) to promote a number of changes that, in turn, responded to the restlessness unevenly enacted by the Island's laboring classes since World War I.[31] The decline of the hacienda system hastened the breakdown of coffee and tobacco agriculture as a whole. Coffee hacendados experienced problems obtaining enough credit to finance their operations and securing a suitable and dependable labor force, so they began exploring other options: not only decreasing cultivation, but also abandoning their haciendas in droves by migrating to the towns and cities.[32]

This migration partially accounted for the rising number of narratives (from this decade to the Second World War) expressing a desire for a "respectable city" that could somehow reconcile—or at least alleviate—the tensions between the aesthetic and lived excesses of urban modernity with the still recurring and emblematically rural sociability of the nineteenth century. It was within this "respectable city" that "Sons of the large landowners, from these 'old families' from the hinterland, are educated . . . or in other urban centers and increasingly distance themselves from the culture sired by the hacienda."[33]

In a broader semiotic sense, these unsettling transmutations occurring in Puerto Rico were part of a much larger, global context. I am using the terms *modernization, modernism,* and *modernity (*or the *modern)* as a general, elastic way of referencing the distinctions, connections, and overlap between, respectively: (1) the exceptionally rapid process of socioeconomic and technological transformations and cultural upheavals originating in—and metonymic of—the West from the Industrial (Urban) Revolution to the present; (2) the artistic and literary movements that attempt to account for, as well as personify, these turbulent shifts and metamorphoses; and (3) both the historical period (nineteenth to mid-twentieth centuries) and the ways in which these drastic transmutations and cultural disruptions have been experienced (simultaneously, as Progress and Disorder).[34] The connection between (a) the figure of "woman," (b) the subsequent urban sprawl and its emerging public sphere (and official political scene), and (c) the ways in which such dizzying changes and uncertain spaces have been imagined and lived—within perspectives informed by the West—has been already documented.[35]

Such were viewpoints associating the collapse of Creole tradition with the common-sense symbols of Advancement: it was the Age of Creeping Modernization which informed Modernist narrative and graphic forms of aesthetic representation. Take, for instance, the noted literary figure José de Diego Padró's description of the myriad cafés populated by bohemian circles in the cobblestoned streets of San Juan where "the towering and almost airborne billboards of the city, studded with electric light bulbs, flickered like gigantic fireflies."[36] While Caroline Dawes Appleton, a North American woman who had spent some time living on the Island, bore witness in 1925 to additional—and unmistakably modern—features of the colony's capital:

> New office buildings tower, and along the single road that leads from San Juan to its gracious suburbs on the mainland, new public buildings are complete or in process of construction. . . . Along this road the ancient clap-trap of crowded *guaguas* (buses] has given place to the purr of expensive motors that propel a type of omnibus that thwarts our best dream of urban transit! It is a super-bus, which clearly we build for export as the Porto Ricans grow their best citrus fruits for the Northern market. . . . Fine banks spread shadowy doorways through which gleam mosaic, bronze and marble—a department store, a new restaurant. . . . [37]

As with marketing in the U.S. mainland, where at this time "modern living" meant advertisements "constantly hammer[ing] away at everything that was [a woman's] own—bodily function, self-esteem—and offer[ing] something of theirs as a socially more effective substitute," Island ad campaigns championed modernity in similar ways—primarily concentrating on the urban population. As Stuart Ewen has observed, these promotional techniques were "[s]peaking often to women," offering them "daintiness, beauty, romance, grace, security, and husbands through the use of certain products," and intimating that "anything natural about the consumer"—such as the body's unaffected appearance—"was worthless or deplorable."[38]

Arnaldo Meyners subscribed to comparable taxonomies of deception and sophisticated-city womanhood in a 1928 article published by *Puerto Rico Ilustrado,* appropriately titled: "The Flapper: Heroine of the Century." "In our milieu also, in this a bit provincial San Juan despite its pretended cosmopolitanism—the flapper has made her strident debut."[39]

Meyners, however, was considerably more wary about what he perceived to be the ambivalent signs of female modernity emerging within Puerto Rico's urban centers:

But our flapper is only a suggestion of untroubled modernity, a timid and blushing flapper because her fear and shame is that she may be characterized as "an old-fashioned girl." This is why our girls have nothing in common with the notably revolutionary type of the foreign [i.e., U.S.] flapper, [they] smoke cigarettes even when they find the taste of tobacco to be bitter and repugnant and they play bridge even when they're bored by the game and they go to bed at dawn even when they're tortured by sleep. . . . All for the horror of looking like their grandmothers.[40]

Interestingly enough, the cover of this issue of *Puerto Rico Ilustrado* displayed a drawing of just such a contradictory "native" flapper: close-cropped hair, decked in short skirt with a man's tie and cufflinks, off-balance and startled while sitting on a sofa, with arms raised in despair at something or someone outside of the cover's frame, and flinging through the air the book she was reading. It is no accident that on the cover of the book one can clearly discern the words "women's suffrage." The image of women's suffrage and feminism in Puerto Rico as inherently disruptive and unsettling crystallized with the formation of the first suffragist organizations in 1917. In 1919, Creole writer Rafael H. Monagas stridently canonized this correlation in *Puerto Rico Ilustrado* when he described "the suffragist" as "an unyielding and ferocious being, aggressive and acrimonious like a man," adding: "feminism is a storm dressed in skirts."[41]

Hence, this tropical island's principal cities were not only seen as a veritable cornucopia of advancement: rising new buildings, bright lights, modern transportation, the latest fashions, cosmetology, and so forth. Puerto Rico's main newspapers also filled the urban terrain with other, stranger omens of modernity, many of them full of explicitly masculinist apprehension. News of U.S. aviatrix Ruth Elder's attempt to cross the Atlantic in 1927 blurred into fears of (Island) women defying the laws of gravity and nature.[42] Another overseas item (reprinted in *La Correspondencia*) about Pilar Caroaga, the first woman engineer to drive a Spanish train, recalled a previous *La Democracia* dispatch about local Prohibition agents who gave hot pursuit to a suspicious automobile "driven by a deranged woman."[43] A 1929 article on the precursors of the suffrage movement in San Juan and Ponce was framed (literally and metaphorically) by an ad placed immediately above it and spanning the same two columns. This advertisement announced a Cecil B. de Mille film titled in Spanish *La mujer sin Dios* (The Godless Woman), with a trailer that read: "The tragic, insane escapades of modern youth."[44]

For these and other reasons, the propertied and educated natives also lived and imagined the 1920s as the Age of Creepy Modernity. Privileged Creoles desired that order be restored within a city panorama they perceived as increasingly slipping from their social and semiotic grasp. In a recent essay, the literary historian María Elena Rodríguez has depicted this situation as one in which ordinary, familiar objects uprooted from the countryside become alien and ineffective within the confines of urban modernity.

The order of the city imposes its own laws on those objects that we watch become unhinged from their place and habitual function. . . . Far from summoning the amicable and harmonious image, once insistently connected to rural society, these objects become the preamble for the disorder and the dizzying urban rhythm that imposes its own dynamic on these village remnants.[45]

Such desires for order were partially informed by the rising numbers of rural laborers being simultaneously displaced to these very same towns and cities. This parallel migration, in turn, resulted from the forcible eviction of squatters and landless peasants that during this period were flocking to the many shanty-towns and densely populated workers' districts springing up in the major metropolitan areas.[46] From the viewpoint of the propertied and educated classes ("native" and U.S.-born), these other—more ominous—signs of modernity literally blanketed the entire urban landscape.

Begging is a case in point but, once more, the broader social context should not be overlooked. During the 1920s (especially in the second half of this decade) the colonized laborers and their families were increasingly afflicted by starvation and inflation.[47] On the one hand, this misery compounded the shrinking job market: according to a report commissioned by the local legislature during 1920–26, the rate of unemployment among the male laboring population rose from 20 percent to 30 percent, while the colonial governor's 1930 annual report indicated that the unemployment rate for the whole Island (both sexes) that fiscal year had been 60 percent.[48] On the other hand, the increasing taxes on the poor's consumption items—such as matches and soap—further aggravated the situation of the laboring poor majorities.

These desperate circumstances assembled growing armies of beggars roaming cities and towns. Helen V. Bary, an envoy from the U.S. Child Welfare Bureau, reported that even during the early part of this decade (when the situation had not yet deteriorated), the "northern visitor in Porto Rico is shocked at the institution of begging," because the "mendicants have their stations along the sidewalks of their regular routes through offices, restaurants, and residence districts."[49]

Sudden shifts in climate phenomena only made an already bad situation worse. In 1929, then colonial governor Theodore Roosevelt, Jr., described the results of the San Felipe hurricane of 1928 in these terms:

I have seen mothers carrying babies who were little skeletons. I have watched in a class-room thin, pallid, little boys and girls trying to spur their brains to action when their little bodies were underfed. I have seen them trying to study on only one scanty meal a day, a meal of a few beans and some rice. I have looked into the kitchens of houses where a handful of beans and a few plantains were the fare for the entire family.[50]

But the laboring poor on the Island in general and in the urban areas in particular reacted in other ways to this strife. Unwittingly, many of the social responses and survival mechanisms of the "native" working classes only served to confirm the worst fears of the educated and propertied classes (Creole and North American) about the underside of modernity in Puerto Rico with rising levels of social unrest, theft, violence, and vagabondage (particularly in the case of dependent children).

Labor resistance in the Island's factories (most of which were tobacco-products-related and located in the towns and cities) went from high absentee rates, workplace irregularity, and low levels of discipline to widespread violence during strikes.[51]

Yet there were also the growing waves of city crime enacted by these masses of landless peasants and child nomads migrating to the main urban centers. Knowlton Mixer, for example, decries in 1926 petty thieving as "very prevalent in San Juan and extremely annoying to automobile owners," because cars left "parked in front of places of amusement in the evenings" were "likely to lose everything that is removable." These unseemly feats were, "of course, the work of hoodlums," acts "so deftly done that it is extremely difficult for the police to catch the offenders."[52]

Collapsing the "Woman's" Body and the Political Body into Social Disorder

From the perspective of the anti-suffrage forces on the Island, one of the more prominent examples of modernity's social anarchy were the attempts of women's suffrage advocates to couple the realm of "the social" with the realm of "the sexual." As Smith-Rosenberg suggests in another context, "sexuality and the physical body emerge as particularly evocative political symbols."[53] Many newspaper articles and journal essays against women's suffrage collapsed "woman's" body with the political body, reading the former as a manifestation of social disorder within the latter.[54]

For example, in an article written by C. Hernández Frías in 1927, the author asserts that woman should be kept

> in the place that until this date she has been occupying, and that today, more than to advancement and progress the high modern orientation is due to imminent dangers that drive her to masculinize herself and to intervene directly in our politics, when she is the one in charge by Nature to live peacefully in a sacred home, nest of love and happiness, encouraging her husband in destiny's difficult struggles and modeling the heart of her sons for the service of her fatherland.[55]

Notice that it is only "women"—and not "men"—who ran the risk of gender blurring when as the abstractly (hetero)sexualized beings embodying reproduction and motherhood they were located within the realm of the "public." Here we see the "natural" linkages perceived to be inherent between "the sexual" and gender differences/hierarchies. "Women" can only be understood or recognized in relation to "men": without a clearly identifiable and socially obvious difference between the two, neither can be defined because one is not distinguishable from the other.

If "woman" was recognizable as a woman, among other things, because she was not, nor could be, positioned or imagined (as a heterosexualized "woman") within the public realm, then how could you distinguish a "woman" from a "man" if and when "women" were allowed to vote and hold office? As the English linguistic theorist Deborah Cameron derisively explains, "[s]ex differentiation must be rigidly upheld by whatever means are available, for men can be men only if women are unambiguously women."[56] And as C. Hernández Frías suggests, being woman can only take place in the private sphere (i.e., "in a sacred home"): it can only be enacted by "encouraging her husband" and embodied by "modeling the heart of her sons for the service of her fatherland."

Here we can also see the "natural" linkages perceived to be inherent between "the sexual" and class differences/hierarchies. Since the First World War, the all–Puerto Rico leadership of the Socialists, trade-unionists, and men from the working classes (in general) tended to see their political and economic survival as depending on "their" women being able to be in the realm of "the public": politics, the [labor] market, the streets.[57] This Island-wide perspective was still prevalent during the late twenties as is shown in a 1928 article published in the trade-union newspaper *Unión Obrera:*

> Through the opinion we have read in the press in relation to women's suffrage it seems that for these journalists there is no other criterion than that of the party leaders or the figure heads.
>
> [O]ur public men's ridiculous custom of obstructing our women in the economic and political progress is an attempt against liberty and a violation of democracy because woman has the right to organize and demand from her employer that which by justice belongs to her, and as an integral part of our people, women also have the legitimate right to elect and to be elected.[58]

After fifteen years of the uneven generalization of the capitalist wage system in Puerto Rico, men from the "native" working classes knew that having "their" women in the labor market, in the streets, and in social struggles (including political campaigns) had not changed and would not change "who wore the pants in the house": gender divisions/hierarchies could and should be reproduced in the realm of "the public" just like they were being maintained in the realm of "the sexual/private."

This outlook was still current in 1928 when Victorio Osorio, for example, remarked in *Unión Obrera:*

> There are those who have publicly stated that women's suffrage will create much discord within the matrimonial home, but I doubt it because woman with

or without suffrage has the right to be a good wife and a good mother. Virtue is established in the home by way of these good qualities, [a virtue] that is none other than the conservation and practice of marriage duties. Which is to say, that man as much as woman should live in complete harmony and according to [their] conditions but if on account of suffrage woman imposes herself, then marriage conflicts arise. If this should happen it would be denounced because the duty of the woman is to mend men's pants but never try to wear them [herself].[59]

Middle-class Unionistas and Republicanos knew that their political and economic survival did not depend on having "their" women positioned (as heterosexualized "women") in the realm of "the public." On the contrary, their class identity was built on how well they controlled, took care of, and provided for "their" women, as exemplified by the desire and ability of "their" women to stay home, administrate domestic affairs—as particularly exemplified by bearing and raising "their" children. This is why, initially (1915–21), political differences on the issue of women's suffrage were mostly class differences between the principal voting blocs. The rise of a middle-class women's suffrage movement (1917–29) transformed this situation by reproducing these political differences (over granting women the vote) within the political parties of the educated and propertied classes themselves. Women's suffrage went from being an interclass dispute to being an intraclass dispute. Initially, it was primarily a conflict between the Island-wide political and trade-union representatives of the "native" labor movement (and its middle-class, Jacobinist allies), on the one hand, and the chieftains of the Creole intelligentsia and large-property owners, on the other. But eventually it became primarily a controversy between the bourgeois and patrician leadership of Puerto Rico's suffragist movement, on the one hand, and the no less bourgeois and patrician leadership of the Alianza.

If anti-suffrage forces on the Island saw women's suffrage advocates as attempting to couple the "social" sphere with "sexual" space, how did the anti-suffrage forces imagine the repercussions of failing to maintain this necessary distinction between "the sexual" and "the social"? Within this camp, C. Hernández Frías argued in 1927 that

> it would be one of our greatest sorrows that an Angel created by Fate for sweetness, the adoration of men, should lose all its charms while pretending to argue heatedly a belief in the clubs, in saloon discussions, and in the town barbershop, while emphasizing the public stage, exposing herself in party meetings and mingling like a boor in the tumultuous groups of enthusiastic party members shouting cheers to their beliefs and leaders.[60]

That same year, another anti-suffrage author, María Dolores Polo, made analogous claims:

> Of course woman, in the naivete of peaceful life at home, does not prepare for, does not imagine the depth of the political mudhole where she wants to immerse herself. The woman suffragist goes with the purest intentions, with the

most tender feelings of contributing to cultivate her people's political goals; and I would stand by their side, being one of the most tireless and brave soldiers in their ranks, if I was sure that their politics, immaculate, for being virgin, for not having yet experienced full battle, would not yet be contaminated by the vicious germs of men's politics.[61]

For both of these anti-suffrage writers, the public sphere was replete with multiple perils for "women" (as sexualized subjects). It was a space full of "tumultuous groups" and "shouting," where women "created by Fate for sweetness" ran the risk of being mistaken for "boor[s]" and of being "contaminated by . . . vicious germs." Only "men" were capable of operating within this public space because only they were sufficiently virile, strong, healthy, and worldly to face the risks inherent to the "clubs, . . . saloon[s], . . . the town barbershop, . . . [and] party meetings": since the "public stage" was a dark and dirty space it could only be safely populated by men. No matter how "tireless," "brave," or "soldier[ly]" "women" were, "their politics, immaculate, for being virgin" could never survive the real world of concrete politics ("full battle"). This is why it was "men" who tended to be identified with the public area/part—that is, the realm of politics, the streets, the market (the place where all goods got bought and sold, particularly the labor market), the social sphere. Although propertied and educated men tended to be associated with the leadership, individuated, and superior functions in all portions of the public area/part, while men from the working classes tended to be associated with the manual, mass, and subordinate functions within this same space, "the depth of the political mudhole" was still understood as the "natural" terrain and the mostly undifferentiated characteristic of all "men" regardless of social class. Real and concrete politics were, by definition, "men's politics."

Polo's use of sexualized medical terminology to define gender differences is quite revealing. By explaining the coupling of the political body and "woman's" physical body by means of biological nomenclature ("contamination"), her text accentuates the "natural" condition of "woman" as "immaculate, for being virgin," as having "the purest intentions" and "the most tender feelings," and, hence, as only being physically suitable for the quarantined "naivete of peaceful life at home."

However euphemistically, both Polo and Hernández Frías perceived sexual propriety within the sheltered and strictly heterosexualized terms of domesticity. The "sweetness" and "charms" of "women" only existed for "the adoration of men," a union that should only materialize in the "peaceful life at home." From this perspective, "sexuality" was intrinsically associated with the private area/part—both in terms of social space (the home) and physical space (the hidden [female] genitalia). This was the abstract, indirect, chaste, sublimated, and sublime attribute of propertied and educated women. Only the latter could be identified as "virgin[s]," full of "naivete," "the purest intentions," and "tender feelings." If "women" drifted beyond this protective cocoon they ran the risk of losing their respectability by losing their virginity (metaphorically or literally) outside the home, of becoming soiled, and, hence, of no longer being recognizable as a "(proper) woman."

"Men" would only be recognizable as such if "sexuality" was something that "women" awakened or provoked in "men," i.e., by mobilizing their "adoration." Otherwise, the "man" would be perceived as an oversexed brute (by having self-originating and, hence, uncontrolled sexual energy) or, still worse, he would be identified as a non-manly "man," namely, a homosexual—in Puerto Rico's Spanish, literally, as "a crazy woman" *(una loca)*. But at the same time and within this socio-cultural universe, "sexuality" had to be a function that "men" were expected to control by subduing its source: namely, "women," "Nature" (glands), and/or "Woman-as-Nature."

When "women" deployed their "charms" to captivate "the adoration of men" but did so outside the "peaceful life at home"—i.e., "in the clubs, in [the] saloon[s]," in the "public stage," then both "sexuality" and the "woman" who embodied it became "contaminated" and debased: this was no longer the doings of a "virgin," but of one who was "mingling like a boor" among "tumultuous groups." Here, "sexuality" was associated not with the private, but with the pub[l]ic area/part. The social space being referenced was not the home but the street, while the physical space alluded to was no longer the chaste hidden genitalia of this divine creature "created by Fate for sweetness" but the uncovered pubic region of the whore: "exposing herself in party meetings" directly blurred into "exposing herself" sexually. This was the concrete, direct, vulgar, and cruel characteristic of prostitutes in particular and all working-class women in general.

According to this traditional viewpoint, the "woman suffragist," despite her "purest intentions," had only two obvious ways of entering "the public stage" as a sexualized subject. One was becoming a declassé pariah by abandoning her propertied propriety and being mistaken for a boorish woman. By becoming the object of desire and of purchase by "men" other than her husband, she automatically ventured into the world of literal and metaphoric contagion: dirt, violence, venereal disease, and loss of respectability.

But since "the public stage" was, by definition, the world of "men's politics," the other obvious choice available to the "woman suffragist" was being mistaken for a "man," namely, for a "mannish" woman or lesbian. This is what Hernández Frías had described as the "imminent dangers that drive her to masculinize herself and to intervene directly in our politics."[62]

The question still remained: how could the "woman suffragist" be allowed in the "public stage," provoking these mistaken identities, without becoming such an agent of disorder? The question needs to be raised, though I do not have the space here to provide an answer (having done so elsewhere).[63]

Women's Suffrage as Political Transvestism: Ladies of "Exquisite Customs" and Impotent Legislators

Some pro-suffragist elements saw the limited franchise (for women) as one formula for alleviating the anxieties of respectable "natives" about modernity's frighteningly rapid social changes. The arguments for limiting the franchise to educated women, however, confirmed the practice of having, as Judith Butler explains, "legal reforms in women's interests, in the hands of the paternal state, [being] turned against other marginal groups."[64] In terms of education and morals, propertied and educated Creole women were being positioned as superior to the laboring-poor women of the colonized population even as the signifier "woman" was constantly being used as an undifferentiated, homogenous, and unmarked classification in this debate. This strategy was loaded with contradictions.

People like Barceló and Soto explicitly contrasted those women who could read and write to those unfit to vote because of their lack of education. In other words, it was legitimate to allow "women" the vote, but it was unacceptable to give *every woman* such a right. Among the colonized themselves, the category "woman" appeared as a fragmented subject that embodied a multiple social difference—in this case, social class.

These dimensions of social class were also lived, desired, and imagined in similar ways by Puerto Ricans who were against women's suffrage—even by some propertied and educated women. In a newspaper article in 1927 by Carlota B. de Cabañas, the author points out that, if passed, the pro-suffrage congressional bill presented by Senator Bingham amending the colony's constitution (S-4247) would lower the current social status of "women" in Puerto Rico, as well as needlessly foster strife and rivalry among "women" themselves. But who are these "women"? For Cabañas, such a loss would be experienced by "that lady whose exquisite customs by way of dress, hair-style, gait, and behavior in society allowed her to be positioned in a very superior plane. . . ."[65]

This is in marked contrast to the way Osorio, the previously cited author of the labor journal *Unión Obrera*, defined what he understood by "women" during the late twenties:

> [O]ur public men's ridiculous custom of obstructing our women in the economic and political progress is an attempt against liberty and a violation of democracy because woman has the right to organize and demand from her employer that which by justice belongs to her, and as an integral part of our people, women also have the legitimate right to elect and to be elected.[66]

True, this laborer/author deployed the category "woman" here with certain ambiguity. On the one hand, he was invoking this category in reference to women who belonged to the working classes, while, on the other hand, he was referring to "women" as the ones who belonged to working-class men. Nevertheless, for him, these were the women who were genuinely entitled to exercise the vote and to be elected into office because, among the women from all social classes, urban-laborer and peasant women are the ones truly struggling for the social justice they deserve.

Cabañas proceeded to alert the reading public of the perils of having women from the lower social classes—such as servants—eventually reach a level of electoral participation that might determine the fate of the Island:

> Today youngsters become estranged from their parents and many of the latter (75 percent) are unaware of where their daughters are going. If women were granted the vote during the political season (the days of calamity and confusion, as I call them), it would be a rare woman who would stay at home attending to it, providing care for her children and her husband, because not even the maid would attend to her chores, she too also having the right to engage in politics, to obtain a position in the Municipal Assembly or in the Legislature and to even go or run against her Lady. What an excess of aberration![67]

Within this context, the term "aberration" is fairly significant. Once again, visions of deviation, degeneration, anomalies, and other expressions of chaos and loss of respectability are being summoned. As in many of the other passages already analyzed, the implications are that the propriety, normality, and naturalness of the Island's social order—as embodied, in this case, by colonial governance—could only be maintained if it remained exclusively in the hands of the propertied and educated "natives." At this level, the views of Cabañas differed from those of Barceló or Tous Soto merely in the ways in which such a social order should be secured vis-à-vis women's suffrage.

By re-presenting "women" as an "unmarked constituency," all three of these propertied and educated Puerto Ricans continued to recreate the existing social hierarchies within the colonized social space. If not granting *any* Puerto Rican woman the vote was the sole way of preventing *all* of the Island's riffraff (not just dispossessed men, but now also the women from the working classes) from threatening the boundaries of respectable, responsible, and natural governance, then *this* particular (propertied and educated) Puerto Rican woman was willing to forfeit even her right to vote.

This does not mean, nevertheless, that Cabañas was advocating measures that were contrary to "legal reforms in women's interests . . . [which would be] in the hands of the paternal state." On the contrary, she saw such interests as being ensured by having the paternal state protect "women" from the dangers that haunted the public sphere. And if male legislators were perceived as being too impotent and hesitant to further women's true interests by protecting them from the perils of "the days of calamity and confusion," then it was the duty of every "lady . . . [of] exquisite customs" to rise to the occasion and remind the Creole men of their responsibilities: this would verify and enact the fact that, morally, such ladies remained "positioned in a very superior plane."

> Our legislators should consider this question carefully and for now abstain from making such a concession. . . . I understand that this opinion of mine will cause some disgust to certain publicists in our Island; but it is necessary to speak clearly and without qualms [since] the men have shown themselves to be so weak on an issue of such great consequence and of such vital importance to our sex.[68]

Nevertheless, the term "aberration" is fairly significant in corollary ways. As with some of the other texts examined above, the class-based phantoms being invoked by Cabañas are specifically those of *gender* deviation, *sexual* degeneration, and *age-grade* chaos. What was at risk was the peace and morality of the respectable Puerto Rican home, which would be inevitably destroyed by granting women's suffrage.

> In previous times, the woman belonged to the home, and this was why the home was durable and lasting: Until recently, the woman was a slave of her duties, today she is [a slave] of the dressing table and of grooming; she was always found in the house, today one has to look for her in the street, in the public plaza, and oftentimes in the air, because she has left to visit the clouds in airplanes; and to complete this annihilation [she] wants to place herself at the same level as the man waiting in street line to deposit her vote in a box. For this I suggest that they change their dress putting on a good pair of pants and a long jacket, because it would be ridiculous to have women waiting in line dressed as usual.[69]

Placing in jeopardy the allegedly natural boundaries of governance that existed between the Island's social classes by advocating women's suffrage was perceived as metonymical to threatening the natural frontiers that supposedly existed between "men" and "women," between "normal" sexuality and "abnormal" sexuality, and between "children" and "adults." It was even tantamount to endangering the natural limits that were expected to exist between being earthbound and being airborne, between taking leave of one's senses and taking off from the ground in an airplane.

Within Cabañas's heteronormative and class-based perspective, a woman who crossed into the (public) space of electoral rights was not only equivalent to the wayward adolescent whose parents were oblivious of her whereabouts. Such a woman was also akin (literally, in blood and color) to the woman who crossdressed as well as to the "public woman": enter, once more, the frightening figures of the lesbian and the prostitute. In such cases, her sexuality and her respectability—indeed, her naturalness as a woman, her very womanness—were all in question.

Some pro-suffrage trade-union journalists instead inverted the symbol of the prostitute by positioning not the austere and modestly presented working-class woman, but the cosmetologically conscious and stylishly dressed woman from the propertied and educated classes as the one who would be mistaken for a whore. A 1928 *Unión Obrera* article thundered,

> If she does not know how to read or write, a woman of this type does not have the right to use the electoral franchise; and instead one who sits idle not producing anything useful[,] who is watching her husband's or lover's salary, one of these who only think of rouge and of silk stockings to show off her ankles, *and there are many who use so much makeup that any man in the street could make a mistake,* these women[,] if they know how to read and write[,] have the right to vote.[70]

"At the Same Level as Any Woman of the Street"

Gender and sexual disorder were also the specters that loomed in the political horizon of the anonymous and portentous article titled "The Sad and Bitter Truth," which appeared in *El Mundo* on March 20, 1927. In this piece, the evidently male author denounces the approaching imposition of women's suffrage in Puerto Rico by the U.S. government in no uncertain terms:

> Congress apparently tries to place in the voting registers the sacred names of our mothers, wives, and daughters *at the same level as any woman of the street.* You people may open the doors and place the government in the hands of the *vice-ridden and the criminals* if you so wish, but I claim that you do not have any right to hurl at us such an enormous insult.[71]

What was merely suggested in Cabañas becomes explicit in this article. For this stalwart champion of Puerto Rican womanhood, having the U.S. Congress decree such a privilege signified making suspect the dignity and rank of "our mothers, wives, and daughters" insofar as the latter would be sharing the identical social space of the common whore. This also raised questions about the manhood of the Creole (man), incapable of (paternalistically) protecting "his" women from being confused with streetwalkers.

Despite having the U.S. Congress expose colonial governance to the threat of the "vice-ridden and the criminals" by granting universal male suffrage in 1904, this would explain the attempt to draw the line at the ultimate outrage of debasing the honor of Puerto Rican "women" by blurring their identities with those of prostitutes. As in the case of Barceló and Tous Soto although via different proposals, the goal is still the re-creation and preservation of the Island's social hierarchies through the enactment of privileged Creole agency: here, the colonialist observer (the U.S. Congress) is submitted to the accusations of the indignant propertied and educated classes in Puerto Rico.

This is also the haunted territory traversed by Esmeralda Sainz, but from a pro-suffrage viewpoint, in her article "We Want the Vote for Obvious Reasons," which appeared in *La Correspondencia de Puerto Rico* in 1927. Such category-maintenance on the part of Sainz implicitly recognized the meaning of "woman" in general and of "women's proper sphere" in particular as key coordinates in the cultural mapping of this debate.

Sainz challenges the anonymous *El Mundo* article cited above by rhetorically raising the question that, if these men are so virtuous and such stalwart champions of women's dignity and morals, then how can the existence—and livelihood—of these "women of the street" be explained? "In a country where the men claim to be so virtuous, how and where can such women be found?"[72]

The suggestion, of course, is that there can only be "fallen women"—i.e., "women of the street"—if there are men who are not so morally upright. Sainz holds these men responsible for the virtue of such women and does not accept denying all women the vote on the basis or pretext of pointing to the moral differences that exist among women.

Although this last position continues to reproduce the "enfranchisement of 'women' as an unmarked constituency" and the pursuit of "legal reforms in women's interests . . . [as being] in the hands of the paternal state," Sainz nevertheless disputes that such measures "might require and institute a different set of hierarchies"—such as social class: "Universal suffrage is requested, is categorically demanded by the people of Puerto Rico; [and] the Puerto Rican woman, without exception; because in such matters [making] an exception is a usurpation."[73]

This, of course, was the programmatic position of the Liga Social Sufragista, of the Asociación Panamericana de Mujeres de Puerto Rico, and of the Partido Socialista. So, whenever they could, any one of the forces united against this political stance (those opposed to granting voting rights to all women or those who only resisted the enfranchisement of illiterate women) tried to advance their cause by summoning the demons of class difference within the Liga, within the Asociación Panamericana, and within the Coalición: that is, between the laboring classes and the socially progressive professionals. The sycophants of patrician culture in the mainstream press fostered Alianza goals by deliberately fabricating or distorting any incident that might call into question the sincerity of the Liga's, the Asociación Panamericana's, or the Coalición's position on women's suffrage and/or drive a wedge within the groups working toward unrestricted women's suffrage.

For instance, in a *La Correspondencia de Puerto Rico* article of 1928, an author using the pseudonym Miguel Strogoff informed his readers that the members of the "Asociación de Damas Sufragistas" rejected an invitation to come to La Perla barrio in San Juan. The invitation allegedly came from a Sr. Lorenzo Padilla, described here as an "enthusiastic defender of this Association who, in addition to being a member of the executive board of La Perla's Alianza Sub-committee, is also a member of the Alianza local committee's press corps."[74]

Under the title "Pro-Suffrage Ladies Refuse to Go to the La Perla Neighborhood," the article describes how Milagros Benet de Mewton informed Sr. Padilla that "the ladies she was convening for a meeting, WOULD NOT GO TO LA PERLA, but that they were willing to find an appropriate site in San Juan to carry out the meeting."[75]

La Perla was—and still is—of course, a notorious shantytown situated outside the walls of the old capital city. Since Mrs. Milagros Benet de Mewton was at this time the leader of the Asociación Panamericana de Mujeres de Puerto Rico as well as an outstanding member of the Liga Social Sufragista, the article's author is probably subsuming these two organizations under the name of "Asociación de Damas Sufragistas." The suggestion—or reported fact?—was that the pro-suffrage "ladies" with all probability preferred a more "appropriate site" within the safer and more respectable walls of the city, thereby raising doubts about the Liga's and the Asociación Panamericana's advocacy of laboring-poor women's interests in Puerto Rico.

However, several things suggest that this was a counterfeit report. Padilla is ostensibly what in twentieth-century Puerto Rican politics is known as a *comisario de barrio:* a local-neighborhood political boss for the party that controls the colony's legislature—in this case for the Alianza. We should bear in mind that in 1928 the Alianza representatives were still divided between those who opposed any kind of women's suffrage (the majority) and those who favored granting the vote only to educated women (the minority). We should also remember that this last position was, typically, the one espoused by the Asociación Puertorriqueña de Mujeres Sufragistas, which was politically allied to the Alianza.

Therefore, what had Padilla done in order to win him the title of "enthusiastic defender" of the group(s) headed by Milagros Benet de Mewton—namely, the Liga and the Asociación Panamericana? Why was this neighborhood Alianza party boss "enthusiastically defending" those who trumpeted unrestricted women's suffrage in Washington, DC, as well as in Puerto Rico, much to the embarrassment and aggravation of the Alianza?!? Real or—probably—fictitious, the author's article clearly attempts to both transform and promote social class as an impediment to the organizational efforts of these Jacobinist women's rights advocates by illustrating the inconsistent political practice of such suffragism.

Yet, if true, such reports would have only confirmed some of the class markers of the principal women's suffrage forces: in particular, the Asociación Puertorriqueña and, to a lesser degree, the Liga and the Asociación Panamericana. As we have seen, many of the women who championed suffrage were very wary of jeopardizing the allegedly natural boundaries of governance by, in this case, crossing the physical boundaries that marked the gulf between San Juan's social classes. The textual groundwork being covered by these "mothers, wives, and daughters," who in this case upheld women's voting rights, came full circle inasmuch as it returned to the ideological domain of the anonymous author of "The Sad and Bitter Truth." After all, weren't places like La Perla the very sites where such ladies expected to find "any woman of the street" as well as the "vice-ridden and the criminals"?

By simultaneously locating those women/Others belonging to the Island's working classes as the subject of difference for these propertied and educated suffragists (mostly but not exclusively identified with the Asociación Puertorriqueña), weren't these privileged "native" women positioning themselves as the reassuring and recognizable analogues of Creole men and of the North American colonizers? But by stressing the need for this sort of distance and disclaimer, such privileged "native" women unwittingly ended up verifying that (within the—propertied and educated—realm of "common sense" and "public opinion") there was some truth to the charge that demands for women's suffrage were indeed part and parcel of chaotic modernity and of the masses of illiterate laborers who supposedly embodied this chaos.

As we have seen, such maneuvers were closely linked to the "illiteracy panic" and to its rapid sexualization and class-designation by blurring the distinctions between the Puerto Rican social body and Puerto Rican sexual bodies, as a way of supposedly engendering disorder within the Island's political body. Together, all of these forms of unease illustrate to what extent some of the political practices among the colonized population not only mirrored each other across the gulf of gender inequalities and political difference, but also mirrored those of the colonizers across the gulf of social and cultural-national/racial inequalities. Such maneuvers further illustrate the hierarchically interdetermined and grossly asymmetrical ways in which all of these colonial subjects (dominant and subordinate—across gender, class, and race/national-culture) struggled to establish the (ahistorically) moral, truthful, and—more importantly—authentic and unique legitimacy of their interests and exigencies from which all other—adversarial—claims derived as simple forgeries, impersonations. This is one of the important and seldom explored ways in which Puerto Rico's social contradictions in the 1920s overwhelmed the debate over granting voting rights to Island women.

Notes

1. Although the specific terminology deployed here is borrowed from Homi Bhabha, "Of Mimicry and Man: The Ambivalence of Colonial Discourse," *October* 28 (Spring 1994): 125–33, current conceptual work in this regard has much broader origins. See, for example: Edward Said, *Orientalism* (New York: Vintage, 1979); Trinh T. Minh-ha, *Woman, Native, Other: Writing Postcoloniality and Feminism* (Bloomington: Indiana University Press, 1989); Ashis Nandy, *The Intimate Enemy: Loss and Recovery of Self under Colonialism* (Delhi: Oxford University Press, 1989). Historically, though, the original theorization in this regard harks back to the work of W.E.B. DuBois (*Souls of Black Folk*), Frantz Fanon (*Black Skin, White Masks*), Albert Memmi (*The Colonizer and the Colonized*), Octave Mannoni (*Prospero and Caliban*), and Roberto Fernández Retamar (*Calibán*). For a recent application and further development of these concepts in the historiography of Puerto Rico, see Kelvin Santiago-Valles, *"Subject People" and Colonial Discourses: Economic Transformation and Social Disorder in Puerto Rico, 1898–1947* (Albany: SUNY Press, 1994).

2. See Sec. 5 of Jones Act (Puerto Rico) 1917 in *Documentos históricos relacionados*

con el Estado Libre Asociado (Oxford, New Hampshire, 1974), 82–86. Island "natives" were still barred from electing the colonial governor, a right that was only granted in 1948.

3. Women's suffrage in Puerto Rico has become an object of historical inquiry only relatively recently and the existing body of work is not very extensive. The published research in this respect is comprised of the following: a third of one chapter of Truman Clark's *Puerto Rico and the United States, 1917–1933* (Pittsburgh: University of Pittsburgh Press, 1975), 39–46; Norma Valle's "El feminismo y su manifestación en las organizaciones de mujeres en Puerto Rico," in *La mujer en la sociedad puertorriqueña,* ed. Edna Acosta-Belén (Río Piedras: Ediciones Huracán, 1980), 91–108; Marcia Rivera's "El feminismo obrero en la lucha de clases (1900–1920)," mimeographed document, 1981; one chapter of Isabel Picó's *La mujer y la política puertorriqueña* (Río Piedras: Centro de Investigaciones Sociales, Universidad de Puerto Rico, 1983), 21–40; two chapters of Yamila Azize's *La mujer en la lucha* (Río Piedras: Editorial Cultural, 1985), 92–153; and some portions of Alice Colón, Margarita Mergal, and Nilsa Torres, *La participación de la mujer en la historia de Puerto Rico (las primeras décadas del siglo veinte)* (New Brunswick: Centro de Investigaciones Sociales de Puerto Rico/State University of New Jersey–Rutgers, 1986), 39–68. There are also three unpublished documents on the topic of women's suffrage in Puerto Rico: Magda Grisell Rosa, "El sufragio femenino en Puerto Rico," Tesina, Programa de Estudios Intensivos, Facultad de Ciencias Sociales, Universidad de Puerto Rico, Río Piedras, 1977; María de F. Barceló Miller, "Voto, colonialismo y clase: la lucha por el sufragio femenino en Puerto Rico, 1896–1935" (Ph.D. diss., Universidad de Puerto Rico, Río Piedras, 1993), recently published as *La lucha por el sufragio femenino en Puerto Rico, 1896–1935* (Rio Piedras: Ediciones Huracán y Centro de Investigaciones Sociales, 1997); and Gladys M. Jiménez-Muñoz, " 'A Storm Dressed in Skirts': Ambivalence in the Debate on Women's Suffrage in Puerto Rico, 1927–1929" (Ph.D. diss., State University of New York at Binghamton, 1994). The issue of allowing Island women to vote had surfaced in passing since the late nineteenth century. See, for example, Rafael M. Labra, *La mujer y la legislación castellana* (Madrid: Imprenta y Estereotipia de M. Revadenegra, 1869), 11. In relation to Latin America see: K. Lynn Stoner, *From the House to the Streets: The Cuban Women's Movement for Legal Reform, 1898–1940* (Durham: Duke University Press, 1991); June E. Hanner, *Emancipating the Female Sex: The Struggle for Women's Rights in Brazil, 1850–1940* (Durham: Duke University Press, 1990).

4. "Estamos pidiendo los derechos políticos aquí y allá," *El Mundo* (February 7, 1929): 8; this and all subsequent translations, unless otherwise noted, are mine. Although Yamila Azize gives 1921 as the year in which the Liga Social Sufragista was organized, she does not disclose the source of her information in this respect. See Azize, *La mujer en la lucha,* 117. According to Azize, in 1921 another "Liga Femínea" was formed by Librada R. de Ramos, María Cadilla de Martínez, and by the renowned Creole intellectual Trina Padilla de Sanz. Although this second Liga Femínea had goals similar to those of the Liga Social Sufragista and published a women's rights and cultural issues newspaper—*Iris de Libertad y Democracia*— the organization folded a year later (ibid., 123–24).

5. See Ricarda L. de Ramos Casellas and Marta Robert de Romeu, "A la legislatura de P. Rico," *La Correspondencia de Puerto Rico* (March 11, 1927): 4; "Estamos pidiendo los derechos políticos aquí y allá," 1, 8, 13. Ángela Caldas, "Movimiento sufragista ¡Alerta señores legisladores!" *La Correspondencia de Puerto Rico* (March 2, 1927): 4.

6. Azize, *La mujer en la lucha,* 130.

7. See, for example, "El sufragio femenino y 'La Democracia,' " *La Democracia* (March 25, 1929): 4; R. Rodríguez Cancel, "Las mujeres socialistas," *La Democracia* (November 2, 1928): 4.

8. Between 1924 and 1929, the Socialistas joined forces with a small group of

Republicano nonconformists to form the "Coalición." Nevertheless, the dissident Republicanos were not of much help to the suffragists because the former were divided over the votes-for-women issue. Only the Socialista faction of the Coalición remained consistently pro–universal suffrage. Ángel G. Quintero Rivera, *El liderato local de los partidos políticos* (Río Piedras: Centro de Investigaciones Sociales, 1970), 105.

9. Isabel Andreu de Aguilar, "Reseña histórica del movimiento feminista en Puerto Rico," *Revista Puerto Rico*, 1 (June 1935): 266. After 1929 the organization changed its name to Asociación Insular de Mujeres Votantes (Island Association of Voting Women). Some Puerto Rican women's historians have characterized the Liga and the Asociación Puertorriqueña as the collective expression of the liberal-reformist tendency within the women's movement of that period, perceiving both organizations as tacitly speaking for middle- and upper-income, as well as well-educated, women. (See, for example, Azize, *La mujer en la lucha*, 118–119, 141–142.) Here I have tried to offer a more nuanced explanation of the roles and ideological tendencies among "native" women professionals within these two suffragist organizations.

10. "Las mujeres piensan dirigirse al Gobernador para pedir el sufragio femenino," *El Mundo* (December 16, 1919): 1, 3; "Las mujeres se dirigen al Hon. Gobernador Yager," *El Mundo* (December 17, 1919): 1, 3. See also, Alice Colón, Margarita Mergal, and Nilsa Torres, *La participación de la mujer en la historia de Puerto Rico*, 43.

11. Asociación Feminista Popular de Mujeres Obreras Puertorriqueñas, "Mujeres Puertorriqueñas," *Unión Obrera* (February 8, 1921): 2. The Socialistas had included this demand since the party was officially founded in 1915. Santiago Iglesias Pantín and Manuel F. Rojas, "Al electorado y pueblo en general de Puerto Rico," *Justicia* 7, no. 236 (October 11, 1920): 9. Although I have not been able to find any leading sign of this Asociación Feminista Popular after 1922, many of its members participated in pro-suffrage activities with the Liga—before and particularly after the formation of the Coalición in 1924. This convergence between the Liga and the Asociación Feminista can once again be understood in terms of the already mentioned affinity between politically active members of the working classes and the socially progressive urban professionals.

12. Azize, *La mujer en la lucha*, 130–31, 138–44.

13. Clark, *Puerto Rico and the United States*, 42.

14. These closer ties were due, in part, to the fact that the Liga Social Sufragista was not programatically and politico-personally obligated to the Alianza—as was the case of the Asociación Puertorriqueña de Mujeres Sufragistas—in opposing any further congressional intervention regarding (a) insular affairs in general, and (b) Aliancista control over the decisions of the colony's legislature in particular. I have examined the details of such coalition politics in chapters 4–6 of my doctoral dissertation: " 'A Storm Dressed in Skirts': Ambivalence in the Debate on Women's Suffrage in Puerto Rico, 1927–1929."

15. Azize, *La mujer en la lucha*, 142.

16. "La doctora Marta Robert embarca hoy para Estados Unidos en representación de la Liga Social Sufragista," *La Correspondencia de Puerto Rico* (April 5, 1928): 1, 6.

17. Clark, *Puerto Rico and the United States*, 44; and, Azize, *La mujer en la lucha*, 138–414.

18. Clark, *Puerto Rico and the United States*, 45.

19. "Texto íntegro del mensaje del Gob. Towner a la 11a. Asamblea," *La Democracia* (February 21, 1927): 5, my emphasis.

20. Ibid.

21. Ibid., 4.

22. According to Homi Bhabha, "the effect of mimicry on the authority of colonial discourse is profound and disturbing." Homi Bhabha, "Of Mimicry and Man: The Ambivalence of Colonial Discourse," 126.

23. In Homi Bhabha's words, the colonizer desires a "subject of a difference that is almost the same, but not quite," ibid.

24. "For in 'normalizing' the colonial state or the subject," Homi Bhabha has noted, "the dream of post-Enlightenment civility alienates its own language of liberty and produces another knowledge of its norms," ibid.

25. "Carta: Hon. Antonio R. Barceló, Presidente del Senado de P.R. a la Asociación Puertorriqueña de Mujeres Sufragistas," *La Democracia* (February 5, 1927): 1.

26. Ibid.

27. Ibid.

28. Quoted in Bhabha, "Of Mimicry and Man," 128. Such a shift requires that the colonized be presented as a subject that can partially displace the gaze/practice of the colonizer, transforming that gaze/practice in the process "by which the look of surveillance returns as the displacing gaze of the disciplined, where the observer becomes the observed" (129).

29. F.J.R., "El debate sobre el proyecto del sufragio femenino en el Senado," *La Democracia* (April 28, 1927): 5.

30. Ibid.

31. See Sol Luis Descartes, *Basic Statistics on Puerto Rico* (Washington, DC: Office of Puerto Rico, 1946), 50, 53–58; Harvey Perloff, *Puerto Rico's Economic Future: A Study in Planned Development* (Chicago: University of Chicago Press, 1950), 136–137; Ángel G. Quintero Rivera, "La clase obrera y el proceso político en Puerto Rico—I" *Revista de Ciencias Sociales* 18, nos. 1–2 (March–June, 1974): 180–82.

32. Victor Clark, ed., *Porto Rico and Its Problems* (Washington, DC: Brookings Institution, 1930), 521–22.

33. María Elena Rodríguez, "Tradición y modernidad: El intelectual puertorriqueño ante la década del treinta," *Op. Cit.* 3 (1987–88): 49, 52, 53–54. See also Arcadio Díaz Quiñonez, "Recordando el futuro imaginario: la escritura histórica en la década del treinta," *Revista Sin Nombre* 14 (April–June, 1984): 16–35; Arcadio Díaz Quiñonez, "Tomás Blanco: La reinvención de la tradición," *Op. Cit.* 4 (1988–89): 147–82.

34. See, for example, Marshall Berman, *All That Is Solid Melts into Air: The Experience of Modernity* (New York: Penguin Books, 1982).

35. See, for instance, George Mosse, *Nationalism and Sexuality: Middle-Class Morality and Sexual Norms in Modern Europe* (Madison: University of Wisconsin Press, 1985); Elizabeth Wilson, *The Sphinx in the City: Urban Life, the Control of Disorder, and Women* (Berkeley: University of California Press, 1991).

36. Quoted in Rodríguez, "Tradición y modernidad," 49–50.

37. Caroline D. Appleton, "Porto Rico: A Study in Colonial Courtesies," *American Review of Reviews* 72 (September, 1925): 303–4.

38. Stuart Ewen, *Captains of Consciousness: Advertising and the Social Roots of the Consumer Culture* (New York: McGraw-Hill, 1976), 46–48.

39. J. Arnaldo Meyners, "La flapper: heroína del siglo," *Puerto Rico Ilustrado* 965 (September 1, 1928): 2.

40. Ibid.

41. Rafael H. Monagas, "La plaga del sufragismo," *Puerto Rico Ilustrado* 482 (May 19, 1919): n.p.

42. "La Sra. Cabañas no es partidaria del sufragio femenino," *La Democracia* (February 7, 1927): 5.

43. "Tren guiado por una señorita," *La Correspondencia* (February 14, 1929): 144; "Agentes de la Prohibición tirotean a un automóvil que conducía una demente," *La Democracia* (February 14, 1927): 1.

44. *La Correspondencia* (May 6, 192): 3.

45. Rodríguez, "Tradición y modernidad," 55.

46. Clark, ed., *Porto Rico and Its Problems,* 39–42, 353–54; Robert William Stevens, "Los arrabales de San Juan: Una perspectiva histórica," *Revista de Ciencias Sociales* 24, nos. 1–2 (January–June 1985): 167–69.

47. W. Bailey and Justine Diffie, *Porto Rico: A Broken Pledge* (New York: Vanguard Press, 1931), 174–175, 182; Carmelo Honoré, *Problemas sociales* (San Juan: Negociado de Materiales, Imprenta y Transporte, 1925), 14.

48. Asamblea Legislativa de Puerto Rico, *Primer informe de la Comisión Legislativa para investigar el malestar y desasosiego industrial y agrícola y que origina el desempleo en Puerto Rico* (San Juan: February 3, 1930), 61; Theodore Roosevelt, Jr., *Report of the Governor of Porto Rico* (Washington, DC: Government Printing Office, 1930), 2.

49. Helen V. Bary, *Child Welfare in the Insular Possessions of the United States, Part I: Porto Rico* (Washington, DC: U.S. Child Welfare Bureau, Government Printing Office, 1923), 26.

50. Theodore Roosevelt, Jr., "Children of Famine," *The Review of Reviews* 81, no. 1 (January, 1930): 73.

51. Clark, ed., *Porto Rico and its Problems,* 461–62; Clark, *The United States and Puerto Rico,* 125; Fernando Picó, *Los gallos peleados* (Río Piedras: Ediciones Huracán, 1983), 94–98, 121; Horace M. Towner, *Twenty-seventh Annual Report of the Governor of Porto Rico* (Washington, DC: Government Printing Office, 1928), 32.

52. Both quotes come from Knowlton Mixer, *Porto Rico and Its Conditions* (New York: Macmillan, 1926), 195.

53. Carroll Smith-Rosenberg, "The Body Politic," in *Coming to Terms: Feminism, Theory, Politics,* ed. Elizabeth Weed (New York: Routledge, Chapman and Hall, 1989), 103. In the case of Puerto Rico, see Eileen Jean Findlay, "Domination, Decency, and Desire: The Politics of Sexuality in Ponce, Puerto Rico, 1870–1920" (Ph.D. diss., University of Wisconsin–Madison, 1995).

54. See, for example, C. Hernández Frías, "Sufragio Femenino," *La Democracia* (March 26, 1927): 6; Rafael Rodríguez, "La mujer no es igual al hombre," *La Correspondencia de Puerto Rico* (April 8, 1927): 8; *La Democracia* (August 22, 1928): 5, 8; V.S.J. "La hombría del feminismo," *La Democracia* (May 28, 1928): 5; "Tal medida ocasionaría un desastre en nuestra política y en nuestra sociedad," *El Mundo* (January 16, 1929).

55. Hernández Frías, "Sufragio femenino," 6.

56. See Deborah Cameron, *Feminism and Linguistic Theory* (London: Macmillan, 1985), 155–156.

57. Whether this was common knowledge among the local leaderships and rank-and-file of the Socialist and trade-union movements or not remains an open question. For a different viewpoint, see the contribution by Juan José Baldrich in this anthology.

58. "Sobre el sufragio femenino" *Unión Obrera* (May 14, 1928): 1.

59. Victorio Osorio, "Sobre el sufragio femenino" *Unión Obrera* (May 17, 1928): 1.

60. Hernández Frías, "Sufragio femenino," 6.

61. María Dolores Polo, "¡Oíd Sufragista!" *La Correspondencia de Puerto Rico* (February 15, 1927): 5.

62. Hernández Frías, "Sufragio femenino," 6.

63. See chapters 8–11 of " 'A Storm Dressed in Skirts.' "

64. Judith Butler, "Disorderly Woman," *Transitions* 53 (1991): 88.

65. "La Sra. Cabañas no es partidaria," 5.

66. "Sobre el sufragio femenino," 1.

67. "La Sra. Cabañas no es partidaria," 5.

68. Ibid.

69. Ibid.

70. "Sobre el sufragio femenino," 1, my emphasis.

71. "The Sad and Bitter Truth," *El Mundo* (March 20, 1927), my emphasis.

72. Esmeralda Sainz, "Queremos el voto por razones obvias," *La Correspondencia de Puerto Rico* (March 29, 1927): 10.

73. Ibid.

74. Miguel Strogoff, "Las damas sufragistas se niegan a ir al Barrio La Perla," *La Correspondencia de Puerto Rico* (January 3, 1928): 3.

75. Ibid., capital letters in original.

8

Rufa Concepción Fernández: The Role of Gender in the Migration Process

Linda C. Delgado

In an essay entitled "Transnationalism: A New Analytic Framework for Understanding Migration," Nina Glick Schiller, Linda Basch, and Cristina Blanc-Szanton defined transnationalism as the "processes by which immigrants build social fields that link together their country of origin and their country of settlement." They added that "transmigrants develop and maintain multiple relationships—familial, economic, social, organizations, religious and political that span the borders" and that they "take actions, make decisions, and feel concerns and develop identities within social networks that connect them to two or more societies simultaneously."[1] While Schiller, Basch, and Blanc-Szanton applied their framework to an analysis of contemporary immigration/migration, this framework also reflects the lived experiences of many U.S. migrants. This seems to be an appropriate description applicable to Puerto Ricans. One foot in two cultures—that is, one foot in the U.S. culture while steadfastly retaining one foot in the island's culture—describes the working perimeters for many Puerto Ricans as well as other Latinos living in the United States. It is through the prism of this dual identity, Puerto Rican and American, that a clearer view of how this group of people navigates through systems, structures, and institutions on and off the Island. One way in which that duality was maintained and, in fact, nurtured, was through stories and news from "home." Whether they were a reminder of the upcoming feast of "Los Reyes" or a wedding announcement or a telling of who left Fajaldo, Puerto Rico, for Brooklyn, New York, it was through these stories related on paper or told by a visitor that the linkage between home culture and host culture was sustained.

We know that there existed commercial and trade relations as well as political entanglements between Puerto Rico and the United States during the early nineteenth century. The first Cuban and Puerto Rican Benevolent Society operated in New York City during the 1930s. In 1868 at Claredon Hall in New York City, plans were made for "El Grito de Lares." This was a failed attempt by Puerto Ricans at gaining independence from Spain.[2] This was also a period of intellectual growth, the rise of a separatist movement and a coalescing of the Cuban-Puerto Rican Revolutionary Army based in New York City. Spanish speaking newspapers such as *la democracia*, carried articles and illustrations that chronicled the life of Puerto Ricans living in New York. Women's voices in their traditional tones were expressed and recorded in may ways—a recipe from Ponce, a children's story, "modern" dress patterns for home sewing, and ads for beauty products. These all communicated the changing role of Puerto Ricans in their new environment. By the 1870s approximately 68.6 percent of the Island's sugar was being imported into the United States while only 7 percent was going to Spain. Many of these *pioneros* emigrated to the mainland almost exclusively to New York City during this revolutionary phase of the island's history.[3]

After 1898 the pattern of emigration changed as Puerto Ricans became part of a labor migration reflecting growing industrialization, modernization, and the expansion of capitalism. These early settlements lay the foundation for future migrations by establishing links among the commercial enterprises in the United States and in Puerto Rico. By 1917, contract labor agents had moved Puerto Rican workers to Hawaii, the Philippines, Panama, Arizona, Philadelphia, and, especially, New York.[4]

In 1917 a young man by the name of Jesús Colón left Puerto Rico on the *Cuomo* and headed to New York City. Colón was born in Cayey, Puerto Rico, in 1901. Cayey was also the birthplace of the Socialist Party in Puerto Rico, and in 1914 Colón became one of the leading members of that organization. He came to America to take his place among the people in the land where "we, the people" had rights, inalienable rights.[5] In a collection left to the Centro de Estudios Puertorriqueños at Hunter College in New York City, I found a series of letters that illustrate the roles gender played in the process of migration.

During the 1920s and 1930s Jesús Colón and his fiancée, Rufa Concepción Fernández (Concha), lived a life that Schiller et al. would call transmigrant. Their personal relationship not only became the link across the miles between Puerto Rico and New York City, but it was also a conduit of information for two communities creating an interlocking web between home culture and host culture. In a series of letters from Concha to Jesús we find the struggles and frustrations that were part of the processes of migration and a clearer picture of the pains of acculturation. The personal, subjective experiences of this couple reflect the objective conditions that produce and/or nurture these experiences.

In the following essay I present these letters by Concha Fernández sent from

Puerto Rico to Jesús Colón in New York City and how they reflect Schiller et al.'s position and analysis. I will conclude with some implications.

July 26, 1923

Concha wrote that while her letters were long and full of detail, Jesús Colón's letters were mostly short, crisp, and to the point—like a telegram. She told him about daily life at home, complained about the distance between them and her desire to hear his voice and not just to read his words. He did not write as often as she did (each day) and this, for her, was torture. What could he possibly find so riveting in New York City? However, she would continue to wait for him to find time enough to write to her, even if his letter was very short.[6]

> Each time a boat arrives, I wait to see your face coming home again. Tell me, what would you like for me to cook for you when that happy day arrives? Something criollo of course, something you cannot get in New York City. If you weren't so mean, you would give me the date of your return. Meanwhile you encourage me to read as much and as many things as I can. Do you know that I actually hate to read. I like novels, love stories, stories about the lives of different men and women but in general, I love to talk, to have a discussion rather than to read about it. Sometimes I write you short notes but I write often and then I wait for your return letter and hope that it is a long letter telling me of your life in New York City.

March 5, 1924

Concha wrote about *las fiestas carnavalescas.* She noted that life was too short and stated that this is why she decided to enjoy herself at Carnival. She also wrote messages for other members of the New York City community from people that she had seen at the dance. She relayed their greetings and family news as well as information on a Puerto Rican life insurance agent moving into their area in New York from Puerto Rico. At the *baile* (dance) she also saw several people who were mutual acquaintances; she described them as looking well and enjoying the evening in her letter to Colón.

By then, Colón's politics were quite clear to all who knew him and his commitment was expressed in his battle for equality for the Puerto Rican worker in New York City. Thus, we find Concha's salutation in this and in subsequent letters as "Mi siempre socialista" (My always socialist). In an undated letter but one that seemed to come on the heels of this March 5th letter, Concha related how a cousin who visited New York City described Jesús. Concha wanted all the details of how her beloved looked and she apparently got them. She expressed concern about whether this cousin had given him an accurate picture of her. She also asked for information on his activities with the "Alianza."[7]

Concha later became as politically active as her husband. She was the secretary to several organizations that Colón was involved with or that he started. She became the keeper of many of Colón's records. In closing, Concha wrote, "Well, my love, this is a short note. I do not want to take up too much of your time, time that could be served further enhancing any of the many causes that you are involved with. I do not want to be a distraction while you write your important articles."[8]

"5/6/25"

Concha wrote "My dear Jesús." She was writing from her office job in San Juan and was describing to Jesús, who was in New York City, the many changes in the city. This letter was interesting in that she code-switched in several places, using a word in English to complete her thought. By the "7/8/25" letter, she was comfortably using the typewriter on a regular basis. As Colón's political activities increased, the poetry of his letters became less and less and she missed his old style of writing, but she did not notice how her letters too had changed.

July 14, 1925

Here was an intense discussion involving a misunderstanding between Colón and his sister and its effects on Concha's friendship with his family. With only one side of the story, I could not tell what started this problem. However, the argument clearly led to feelings of alienation and mistrust between Concha and Colón's sister. Concha grew up with Colón's family as neighbors; his sister and brother-in-law were childhood friends, so she tried to help settle the argument— but to no avail. She stated that, of course, she would stand by whatever and however Colón chose to resolve the issue. When Colón told her to sever her relationship with his sister and his sister's husband, Concha acquiesced. She swore that she would be more than willing to end contact with these friends in order to give him peace of mind. She closed the letter by stating that she had, indeed, broken the relationship and that he should rest easy. Her happiness was with him and not with old family ties.

In the same letter Concha expressed concern about Jesús's description of a few parties he had recently attended. She told him that this news disturbed her for several reasons. She admitted that she always was a little jealous of what went on in his New York City life, but more importantly, being out late was not good for his health. It will only make him drawn and thin. She liked him the way he used to look when he was a student and living on the island. She reminded him that as an engaged woman, she was not allowed out without a chaperone by her family and that things got stricter at home as they got closer to the wedding date.

She added a postscript that explained how she dreamt he had gotten sick. She warned him of the winter cold and the need for him to stay healthy and strong. She also sent him the name and address of another friend who had recently moved to New York City so that they could connect with each other.

In the Jesús Colón papers, there are disparate notes to Concha written by Colón, but not the direct responses to her letters. Those notes that appear in his collection are mostly typed. In his earlier letters, he told Concha about city life and about long, hard working hours.[9] In what seems to be a response to a letter from her in which she apologized for not being a smarter woman, he told her that pieces of paper (academic degrees) did not impress him and that she was far from being a stupid woman. He affirmed that he loved her exactly the way she was. However, he then went on to tell her that in coming to America, she would discover that things were different; degrees did matter and that here [New York City], people would expect her to only be qualified to do manual work. Having no degree would only complicate the situation. He urged her to go back to school because that would allow her to find the kind of job she might like.

Colón himself went back to night school at St. John's University but never actually earned a degree. He was self-taught and became fluent in English. He considered himself an intellectual and the chronicler of the Puerto Rican worker in New York City, writing and publishing over 240 essays and articles over a fifty-year period. In the 1950s and 1960s Colón was more than a political voice of the Puerto Rican laborer. He ran for the public office of comptroller in New York City and was supported by the American Labor Union.

The Colón papers constitute what Colón called a *testimonio*.[10] He had a keen sense of history and wanted the story of Puerto Ricans in New York to be "accurately" told. There are no wills, diaries, or other legal documents in the Colón papers—only letters, articles, clippings, essays, and a photo collection. These are part of an official legacy, the *testimonio* left behind by Jesús Colón and his wife, Rufa Concepción Fernández.

In the few personal letters we read how Concha kept Colón abreast of daily life on the island and passed along information from New York City to other relatives and friends on the island, and in so doing kept him grounded in the roots of his people back home. Colón came to New York City carrying with him traditions of his native town. The decisions to travel to New York City, to find work, and to remain in New York City were influenced by home values as well as the host values influencing Colón in New York City. He came to America to find his place within the concept "we, the people" and Concha supported him. As Schiller et al. point out, the relationship to the home culture and its influence was "not in contradiction to but in conjunction with . . . host culture." It was Concha who kept the circular flow of information going even to the point of chastising Colón when he sent short, telegram-like notes.

In Colón's letters we get a glimpse of labor conditions for Puerto Rican males in the interwar years in the United States and how changing industrial needs in America fueled and supported the emigration of women workers as the U.S. labor market needed more hands. We also see economic stress and loneliness attached to these processes on both sides of the divide. Colón focused mainly on his life in New York as a worker, as a representative of the Puerto Rican community in the city's labor force. Concha focused on her role as the dutiful betrothed living a very traditional life on the island. However, we see transitions occurring in both of these people as U.S. influence becomes more prominent in their lives. Concha, who complained about Colón's terseness in her earlier letters, resorts to similar patterns as she learns to handle the typewriter better and as she later becomes more competent in office work.

In 1991, sociologist Silvia Pedraza called our attention to the "neglected role of women in migration." She asked a series of questions including how was gender related to the decision to migrate; what were the causes of male/female dominated flows of migration; what were the patterns of the labor market that shaped migration? She also asked how did migration impact interpersonal relationships and how did work impact the family unit? By looking at the transmigrational aspects of the migration of Jesús Colón to New York City as logged by Concha Colón and chronicled by him, we can begin to answer some of Pedraza's questions, at least in the case of these Puerto Ricans' movements and their political involvement in New York City. In her essay "Women in Migration: The Social Consequences of Gender," Pedraza argues that it was in the daily lives, in the routine, uneventful experiences of those who migrated and those who stayed behind, that can be found some understanding of the role gender played in migration. Concha was the communicator of information, of ideas, and of comfort to Colón. This became an expression of their relationship and, in times of stress, what Colón came to rely on to keep him strong and to keep him focused on the political and social issues of the day.[11]

In a July 25, 1925, letter, it was clear that while Concha understood the monetary cost of returning to the island, their time apart caused many anxieties for her. She gave Colón a list of contacts including addresses and phone numbers that provided him with information on insurance brokers, movers, and possible job contacts. It was by networking, not necessarily through kinship, that survival was made possible and more probable.

Colón described and analyzed the link between the colonial status of Puerto Rico and the socioeconomic condition of the Puerto Rican worker in New York City. As he became more disillusioned he asked what happens in a country where a second-class citizenship is legitimated through the passage of such laws as the Jones Act of 1917.[12] Concha's letters helped him to sort out his place in Jim Crow America as a man who saw himself as a Puerto Rican who happened to be black rather than a black man who happened to be Puerto Rican, as did his contemporary Arturo Schomberg.[13]

We also see in these letters conflict between Old World traditions and those changing as a result of modernity. Colón and Concha sort out their views on women and their role in American culture. In an essay entitled "My Wife Doesn't Work" (1961), Colón wrote that this little phrase actually said volumes about male/female relationships: "with this tiny phrase, men make slaves of the women who serve them twelve to fourteen hours a day without salary and most often without love."[14]

While these letters were written for personal reasons by Concha to Colón, they also provide insight into the political world that they both lived in. Concha later became an important player in that world. In 1925 the Colóns were married and Concha came to New York City to live with her husband. During the 1930s Colón was creating and developing many organizations. It was Concha Colón who was his secretary and typist and who did much of the business writing for and to social, political, and labor organizations. The two were a team as Colón became an increasingly important member of the fledging *colonia*.

In more recent scholarship, it is argued that individuals have used collective strategies including those produced by family ties, class, and ethnic grouping to make their way through the processes of Americanization. Virginia Yans McLaughlin argues that instead of free labor markets, as touted, it was the unequal positioning of different ethnic groups that fashioned the socioeconomic condition of new migrants and immigrants in the United States, and that it was the alliances between capital and labor that restricted the upward mobility of the migrant and immigrant labor force and reshaped the dreams of these individuals. The changing global economy directly and indirectly created many of the perimeters that defined the work that the immigrant and migrant labor force engaged in. As early as the 1920s Jesús Colón tried through his many articles to make Puerto Rican workers understand their place in this larger context[15] just as he also tried through his union activities and organizing to make labor understand the importance of Puerto Rican workers. In the 1920s and in the subsequent two decades, Puerto Rican families made migration part of their survival strategy. As transportation and mail service improved between Puerto Rico and the United States, networks on both sides of the Caribbean were strengthened.

Records of Puerto Rican women's participation in these networks is limited if we look only to traditional sources for research.[16] Concha did not leave behind a will or other documentation of her journey through life. She left letters, clippings, pictures, poems and stories. She left correspondence that referred to her husband's union activities, his politics. She left letters that fully expressed the frustrations, anxiety, and pain of racism. After the 1930s, Concha's signature appears on several documents authored by Jesús Colón. As he advocated more and more for recognition of Puerto Rican workers' rights, it was Concha who was his typist.[17]

While Puerto Ricans have been heavily researched, they are one of the least understood people in the United States.[18] They do not conform to the generally accepted definition of assimilation nor of the melting pot model, which predicted that over time and generations they would gradually assimilate into the dominant culture and the seemingly monolithic solidarity of their ethnic community would erode. The concept of assimilation concentrates on the end product and pays little attention to the socioeconomic conditions that give rise to it.[19] The scope of the research on Puerto Ricans, in general, has been limited to viewing the mechanisms through which individuals have attempted to cope with what seemed to them an unchangeable structure of opportunity distributed unequally. While push/pull theories represent a counterpoint to assimilation, they do not transcend these limitations. In contrast, a broader understanding of structural and institutional arrangements within and across borders can provide the kind of understanding that Jesús and Concha Colón were seeking during the interwar years.

The domestic division of labor through which wealth was produced and the position of national "others" that reflect the inequality of opportunity can be interrogated by entering through a different door into the political, social, and economic world of Puerto Ricans in New York City. The Colóns did not have a nostalgic view of their past nor of their life in Puerto Rico. At no point in his correspondence with Concha does he state a desire to return to the Island. In 1915 while still in Puerto Rico, he wrote:

> Thumbing through the [history] book I chanced upon a phrase at the end of the book. That phrase was, "we, the people of the United States. . . ." That phrase somehow evoked a picture of all those people we had been studying in our creme colored pages of our geography book. The people who picked cotton in the South, raised wheat in the Dakotas, grew grapes in California . . . the people in Brooklyn who build great ships that plied the waters of the Caribbean. All of these people and I and my father and the poor Puerto Rican sugar workers and tobacco workers, we were all together, the people of the United States. We all belonged.[20]

By 1948, Colón had readjusted his "imagined community" and wrote:

> In the phrase *we, the people of the United States,* that I admired so much were there first and second class citizens? [In New York City] the workers told me that we [Puerto Ricans] were from a colony. A sort of storage house for cheap labor and a market for second class industrial goods. Colonialism with its agricultural slavery, monoculture, absenteeism and rank human exploitation are making young Puerto Ricans of today come in floods to the U.S.[21]

For the Colón family, being American citizens meant involvement and participation in their host society. How these two people perceived themselves and the circumstances of their existence seemed to be linked to broader forces at play in the United States. Race, class, ethnicity, and changing gender roles influenced these perceptions and defined the world that they lived in.

Dynamic forces such as institutions, demographic trends, economic and occupational patterns, ideological changes, and other variables were explained and chronicled by Jesús Colón. These forces largely determined the trajectory of the social history of his compatriots living on and off the island. The relationship among such concepts as political activism and citizenship, nationality, nationhood, and transnationalism are part of the people-making process. In this case, they also were shaped by the transmigrant existence of Jesús and Concha Colón. The letters and other such materials in this collection tell us as much about the writer and those in his life, especially his wife, as they do about New York City from 1917 to the 1970s.

Notes

1. Nina Glick Schiller, Linda Basch, Cristina Blanc-Szanton, "Transnationalism: A New Analytical Framework for Understanding Migration," in *The Annals of the New York Academy of Science*, 645, July 26, 1972.

2. Linda Delgado, "Puerto Ricans in Late 19th Century New York," paper presented at Graduate Seminar in 1992 at CUNY Graduate Center.

3. Virginia Sánchez Korrol covers this material in *From Colonia to Community: The History of Puerto Ricans in New York City*, updated and revised edition (Berkeley: University of California Press, 1994), chapters 2 and 5.

4. For more on this subject and alternative perspectives, see Shari Baver, *The Political Economy of Capitalism: The State and Industrialization in Puerto Rico* (Westport, CT: Praeger, 1993); Stanley Freidlander, *Labor Migration and Economic Growth: The Case of Puerto Rico* (Cambridge: MIT Press, 1965); Andreau Cesar Iglesias, ed., and Juan Flores, trans., *Memories of Bernardo Vega: A Contribution to the History of the Puerto Rican Community in New York* (New York: Monthly Review Press, 1984).

5. Jesús Colón, "Bitter Sugar," box 1, 1948 folder, in The Jesús Colón Papers at the Centro de Estudios Puertorriqueños at Hunter College in New York. These papers were a gift to this archive from the Communist Party in the early 1990s.

6. I refer to Rufa Concepción Fernández's (Concha's) letters throughout this essay. These letters are found in "Correspondence," box 5, folders 3–8 in The Jesús Colón Papers.

7. Colón was the founder of Alianza Obrera and was its first secretary.

8. See "Correspondence," box 5, folder 3–8 in The Jesús Colón Papers.

9. Ibid.

10. Virginia Sánchez Korrol and Edna Acosta Belén explain *testimonio* in the Introduction to *The Way It Was and Other Writings: Jesús Colón* (Houston, TX: Arte Público, 1993).

11. Silvia Pedraza, "Women in Migration: The Social Consequences of Gender," in *The Annual Review of Sociology* 17 (1991). Also see Pedraza, *Political and Economic Migrants in America* (Austin: University of Texas Press, 1985).

12. In 1917, the Jones–Shaforth Act made Puerto Ricans citizens of the United States. This gave them the right to travel freely to the United States (although visa-type cards or birth certificates were required to distinguish them from other Spanish-speaking non-citizens). Those living on the U.S. mainland could vote like the native born. For those living on the island, a different kind of voting right was established. The passage of this law meant that all male Puerto Ricans were immediately eligible for the draft (of prime interest to the United States in 1917) and, among other things, it did not include the right to trial by jury. The only option given on the referendum was "no." Thus, a non-vote was an automatic yes. Refusal of citizenship would make Puerto Ricans aliens in their own homeland and would deprive them of holding any local political office. Many had no idea what this vote meant, only that it required a long journey by horse or mule or on foot into the city of San Juan to cast the vote. For more, see Alfredo López, *The Puerto Rican Papers: The Re-Emergence of a Nation* (New York: Bobbs-Merrill, 1973); Kal Wagenheim, *The Puerto Ricans: A Documented History* (New York: Praeger, 1973); and *Documents on the Constitutional Relationship of Puerto Rico and the United States*, ed. Marcos Ramírez Lavandero (for the Puerto Rico Federal Affairs Administration, 1988).

13. For more on Schomberg and his contemporary Jesús Colón, see Winston James, "Afro-Puerto Rican Radicalism in the U.S.: Reflections on the Political Trajectories of Arturo Schomberg and Jesus Cólón." *The Journal of the Centro de Estudios Puertorriqueños* (Spring 1996).

14. See Jesús Colón, "My Wife Doesn't Work," in Korol and Belén, *The Way It Was and Other Writings.*

15. Virginia Yans McLaughlin, ed., *Immigration Reconsidered: History, Sociology and Politics* (New York: Oxford University Press, 1990), Introduction.

16. Jesús Colón wrote more than 200 essays and published one book, *A Puerto Rican in New York and Other Sketches;* a second book, edited by Korrol and Belén (see note 10 above), was published posthumously.

17. I refer to the letters and the entire *testimonio* here. Also see Charles Tilly, "Transplanted Networks," in McLaughlin, ed., *Immigration Reconsidered.*

18. It is impossible to tell from Colón's correspondence if Concha initiated any of the plans discussed in the letters she typed. She signed as typist. However, understanding the working relationship between these two people and the fact that Concha's circle of friends included women who were members of the Socialist and later, Communist, Party, it seems likely that she and Colón had several discussions on the matters about which she typed for him.

19. Clara Rodríguez, *Russell Sage Working Paper #57,* (New York: Russell Sage Foundation, 1992); "Introduction."

20. The processes of assimilation are explained by many scholars, including Leonard Dinnerstein, Roger L. Nichols, and David M. Reimer, eds., *Natives and Strangers: Blacks, Indians, and Immigrants in America,* 2d ed. (New York: Oxford University Press, 1990); Milton Gordon, *Assimilation in American Life: The Role of Race, Religion and National Origins* (New York: Oxford University Press, 1964); Nathan Glazer and Daniel Patrick Moynihan, *Beyond the Melting Pot: The Negroes, Puerto Ricans, Jews, Italians and Irish in New York City,* 2d ed. (Cambridge, MA: MIT Press, 1970); also see Ronald Takaki, "Reflection on Racial Patterns in America: An Historical Perspective," in *From Different Shores: Perspectives on Race and Ethnicity in America,* 2d ed. (New York: Oxford University Press, 1990); E. San Juan, *Racial and Ethnic Formations in the United States* (Albany, NY: SUNY Press, 1992).

21. Colón, "Bitter Sugar," box 1, 1948 folder, in The Jesús Colón Papers.

9

Gender, Work, and Institutional Change
in the Early Stage of Industrialization:
The Case of the Women's Bureau and
the Home Needlework Industry in
Puerto Rico, 1940–1952

Félix O. Muñiz-Mas

Introduction

Gender and work played an important role in the early stages of the process of industrialization in Puerto Rico. During the 1940s the Popular Democratic Party (PPD) started several reforms based in specific gender constructions that defined women as mothers and wives, and men as breadwinners and workers.[1] These interpretations of gender, combined with the ideology of modernization, led to the regulation of working-class labor, especially the home needlework industry. The creation of state institutions like the Women's Bureau (1945) responded to the increasing participation of women in the economy, and intended to defend the rights of the working class. Unfortunately, the colonial state gave emphasis to the protection of sugar workers, and favored factory workers and not home needleworkers.

The study of gender and work in twentieth-century Puerto Rico has received special attention from sociologists and anthropologists.[2] However, many of these studies have not addressed a fundamental issue: What was the role of the colonial state in the creation of gender subjectivity? This question is important because it helps us to go beyond the view of the state and its policies as protecting or oppressing women, as if this gender category were pre-given. Instead, we can show how gendered subjectivity is produced and hierarchically organized by state discourses and practices. In other words, it involves looking conversely, not just showing that women have been excluded from historical definitions of worker, for example, but also showing how the fundamental categories of social, economic, and political analysis came to be supported by gender assumptions. Gender constructions are then constituted within and by the official discourse, by administration practices, within the social spaces defined and delineated by state policy, and by state formation itself.[3]

In Puerto Rico during the 1940s, gender categories of women were constructed in various ways—as mothers and wives, and not as workers. This study will focus on the following questions: Why did the disintegration of the family lead to the reproduction and reconstruction of gender meanings? Why did state policies lead to particular constructions of gender? How were gender difference and subordination regulated in Puerto Rico? It is with these questions in mind that I want to study the Women's Bureau and the home needlework industry in Puerto Rico from 1940 to 1952.

First Attempts: The Bureau for Women and Children in Industry, 1933–1941

One problem in this study was the lack of previous research on the role of the colonial state in the construction of gender subjectivity in Puerto Rico.[4] My analysis, therefore, begins by exploring the role of the state during the 1930s. Any study of this period should take into consideration the development of the needlework industry as a primary employer of Puerto Rican women, the colonial state, the New Deal administration, and home needleworkers.

Soon after the outbreak of World War I, a severe interruption of commercial relations between the United States and the Philippines—the main supplier of cheap labor for American needlework industries, led to a major development of the needlework industry in Puerto Rico.[5] The island started to receive embroidery material from needlework centers like New York; once finished, the product returned to the United States where it was sold in retail stores.[6] In this production system, the salaries for home needleworkers were very low. Almost 60 percent of the homeworkers received wages between one and two cents per hour during the 1930s.[7] Consequently, during the Great Depression home needleworkers' living and working conditions deteriorated, leaving workers with no other alternative but to strike.

Several strikes by factory needleworkers during the 1930s led to violent repression of female workers. The first strike erupted in 1933. Industry salaries hit their lowest point during this year, and the workers demanded higher wages. An investigation made by the Insular Department of Labor in the same year found that 19 percent of the women earned less than 25 cents per bundle, that 23 percent earned between 25 cents and 50 cents per bundle, and that 27 percent earned between 50 cents and a dollar per bundle.[8] In 1933, factory workers started the most important strike for the needlework industry in the town of Mayagüez.[9] This strike quickly led to repression when police fired upon the strikers. It should be no surprise that police officials' quick response in repressing the strike was related to the identity of the shop's owner, Representative María Luisa Arcelay.

State initiatives tried to address working-class problems by enforcing Act 45 (of June 9, 1919), which established minimum wage laws, and a 1932 law providing insurance for workers in case of an accident in the workplace.[10] By arguing that the application of the minimum wage laws could severely threaten the needlework industry, the owners of needlework factories pressed the Republican Party in 1933 to reject any attempt by the Socialist Party to increase needlework salaries. Since the original proposition of accident insurance was considered too expensive for factory owners, the law that passed gave factory owners lower insurance payments and fewer benefits for workers.[11] These laws remained on the books only, because there was no state agency that could oversee them.

In 1933, the Insular Department of Labor created the Women and Children's Bureau (WCB) with the purpose of enforcing minimum wage, accident insurance, and age verification laws. The initial investigations of the WCB centered on the violation of minimum wage laws and employment age laws.[12] In the 1937–38 fiscal year the WCB investigated 641 establishments and found that 16.2 percent of these establishments (104) violated these laws.[13] The investigations showed that only 19.2 percent of the employers who violated labor laws were forced to correct violations. The government took only 10.5 percent of the employers to court while the rest were not forced to correct the violations.[14] Workers were unwilling or unable to come forward with evidence, which presented some obstacles for corrective action. Labor coercion and the economic structure of the homework needlework industry gave workers little chance to provide any evidence against their employers. Unfortunately, there were many examples of employers paying homeworkers with groceries or in cash. Other workers received their wages from several subcontractors, making complaints difficult to prove.

The best example of the obstacles placed on federal reforms was the application of the National Industrial Recovery Act (NIRA) in 1934.[15] NIRA codes caused an uproar in the manufacturing community because they provided workers the right to a minimum wage and to collective bargaining. A local battle over the limits of the law launched commercial and industrial interests to fight against its application to the Island. In a letter to Governor Gore, Lupercio Colberg, president of the Puerto Rico Manufacturers' Association, requested the governor's intervention to prevent the application of the NIRA in Puerto Rico.[16] Resident Commissioner Santiago Iglesias Pantín went to Washington with a group of manufacturers to meet with the secretary of war to request the exclusion of the Island from the legislation. Morris E. Storyk, in charge of the NIRA in Puerto Rico, met with the owners of the needlework industries. In this meeting, Storyk supported some of the arguments brought forth by the owners.[17]

Neither the Garment Workers Union (GWU) of the United States nor the Federation of Free Labor (FLT)—who was the leader of the labor movement for much of the 1930s—disputed the exclusion of NIRA codes in Puerto Rico.[18] GWU officials were concerned that the application of the law might force industries to close down leaving many people, mainly women, unemployed.[19] Officials in the FLT and the PS had their hands tied when supporting the exclusion of Puerto Rico from the NIRA codes. The FLT and PS did many things in benefit of the working class, yet after 1932 the Socialist Party confronted an important issue: either gain access to the colonial state, or continue to fight for the Puerto Rican working class. The Socialist Party chose the former. As a result, factory owners were successful in preventing the full application of the NIRA codes to the Island.[20]

Another major obstacle in the defense of the working class by the WCB was the debate over the applicability of the Fair Labor Standards Act (FLSA) in 1938.[21] As they had done in the past, the members of the Socialist-Republican Coalition attempted to prevent its application in Puerto Rico. Metropolitan agencies like the Department of Labor assigned a Special Industry Committee (SIC) to evaluate the impact of the FLSA on the needlework industry.[22] This commission excluded Puerto Rico from the FLSA in 1939. Some of the reasons given by the SIC were related to the actions of needlework employers.[23] Finally, in the 1940–41 fiscal year a determination made by the SIC established wage structures for the needlework industry. This decision modified the wage rates for the needlework industry using the minimum wage law (1919) as its precedent.[24] The only problem encountered with this law was that a 1940 exemption for hardship allowed needlework industries in Puerto Rico to set lower minimum wages.[25]

In the 1940–41 fiscal year the report of the WCB paid little attention to the number of investigations and violations of labor laws. One reason for this omission was the production halt of some needlework industries.[26] The WCB, however, began to investigate the elimination of subcontractors in the distribution of work directly to the homeworkers. This trend reflected a decline in the number of subcontractors renewing their permits. From the 2,793 permits issued to subcontractors in 1939–40, the number declined to 733 in the 1940–41 fiscal year.[27] However, the war cannot be held responsible for all of the changes in the industry. During the last part of the 1930s, there was an increasing trend in mechanization.[28] Some tasks previously sewed by hand were now done with sewing machines in the factories. My study found no evidence, however, that the elimination of subcontractors changed the payment structure established by the corporations. In other words, the disappearance of subcontractors was not transformed into higher salaries for homeworkers.

The Myth of the Male Breadwinner: Populism and the Populist State

In order to win the 1940 election, the PPD started a series of reforms based on a populist program that emphasized agrarian reform and industrialization as its basic principles.[29] The PPD incorporated many issues raised in the political market by the rural peasantry, the middle class, and the agricultural proletariat, mainly sugar cane workers, into the populist program. In order to receive the support of the agricultural proletariat, the PPD initiated a series of labor laws that protected workers against the abuses of employers and accidents in the workplace. These reforms were to complement the application of the New Deal's FLSA of 1938, which included minimum wages and maximum hour rules for the sugar and home needlework industries. To benefit sugar cane workers and the agricultural peasantry, the PPD created state institutions like the Land Authority (1941), which limited private landholding to 500 acres, controlled sugar cane production, and gave workers access to land. Middle-class supporters received employment in the colonial state's bureaucracy. Once in power, the populist leaders understood that to remain in control of the colonial state, they had to apply new labor and social standards to improve the dismal conditions of the working class and the rural peasantry. The populist leaders supported these laws at a time when employers continued to challenge them in the courts.

The populist program was gender and class neutral in theory. This political project was supposed to benefit all Puerto Ricans regardless of class and gender. However, these populist reforms were based on the myth of the male breadwinner. By designating men as breadwinners, the colonial state maintained male control over female labor, largely confining women to household chores and child care while minimizing male contributions to the household.[30] In this context, the state, in essence, institutionalized this myth in the household, the workplace, and in state relations.[31] My contention is that the category of male breadwinner—which considered that if a man and a woman lived together, the man was the head of the household—that was included in some federal programs established in Puerto Rico during the 1930s laid the basis for the New Deal–based populist reforms of the PPD.[32] Since the leadership of the PPD administered New Deal programs during the 1930s, many of the reforms put in motion during the 1940s followed a similar definition of the male breadwinner.[33]

The use of this classification went hand in hand with the benefits of agrarian reform and early industrialization. Once the agrarian reforms were in place, the main beneficiaries were the rural peasants, sugar workers, and sugar cane growers, categories dominated by Puerto Rican men. Since the PPD wanted a solution to the problem of male unemployment, a majority of the industrial jobs available to the working class during 1940–45 were in the sugar industry or sponsored by the federal government. The Works Progress Administration (WPA) and the War Emergency Program (WEP) employed working-class males in the construction sector. During World War II, the construction of roads, military bases for the armed forces, hospitals, schools, and other buildings related to the reforms of the colonial state led to the employment of many working-class males.[34] All of these programs during World War II showed the commitment of both the metropolitan and colonial states to remedying male unemployment.

Working-class female employment was not one of the state's priorities. Even if the manufacture and home needlework sectors employed almost 20 percent of the working population by 1940, the PPD continued to emphasize the social role of women as mothers and wives, not as workers.[35] The PPD portrayed women as the real victims of the big corporations. A 1940 article in *El Batey,* the official newspaper of the PPD, articulated the women-as-victims approach:

> The man goes out every day to work or to look for work. He suffers from hunger and pain, however, he is not all day long seeing the empty burner. He is not all day watching the naked or poorly dressed children. The man is not all day long hearing the cry of the children, who ask for food when they are hungry, and there is nothing to eat. The Puerto Rican man suffers misery but the Puerto Rican female experiences misery every day.[36]

The logic behind this statement was that Puerto Rican women should run the household because their husbands had to work. *El Batey* neither made reference to the origins of women's oppression nor mentioned the mechanisms to overcome their exploitation in the labor force or the household. Clearly, the PPD looked for the support of working-class women as helpers of the populist movement, not as active participants.[37]

The PPD encouraged women to become the moral leaders of their families in order to prevent men from selling their votes. Vote selling was a major problem in Puerto Rico. The PPD took hold of this issue as one of its more important priorities. A 1939 article from *El Batey,* entitled "Women from the Rural Areas Should Read This Article," explained that working-class women, as mothers, daughters, or girlfriends, should encourage their male counterparts not to sell their votes.

> That is why it is your duty to remind the men every day that they have to end this situation of vote selling in an orderly and peaceful way but with men's dignity. The mothers have to tell their sons not to sell their votes. . . . Daughters need to tell their fathers that they have to act as men not like sheep ready for the slaughter. . . . Girlfriends should tell their companions that they do not love men who sell the future of their children.[38]

The PPD encouraged masculinity or machismo to prevent men from selling their votes. Women were just the messengers of the PPD's discourse. Indirectly, the PPD told women that the cause of their misery was the selling of votes by men. By encouraging Puerto Rican masculinity, the PPD was successful in mobilizing male voters. However, even if the populist discourse emphasized working-class women's secondary position in Puerto Rican society, it recognized the importance of women's work and their role in the production and reproduction of the labor force.

The Industrial Supervision Service: Precursor to the Women's Bureau, 1942–45

During the 1941–42 fiscal year the Department of Labor reorganized the WCB. A separation of women's work and children's work led to the creation of two separate entities, the Child Bureau (CB) and the Industrial Supervision Service (ISS). The Department of Labor divided the ISS in five different sections: Men's Work (MWS), Women's Work (WWS), Industrial Homework (IHS), the Hygiene and Safety Section (HSS), and Labor Statistics (LS).[39] The ISS received 40 percent ($167,180.00) of the annual budget assigned to the Department of Labor, a significant part of the budget if compared with the allocations given to the WCB. There was also a significant change in the number of workers employed by the ISS. Instead of fifteen, the ISS had 125 employees, a chief, and an assistant who coordinated investigations and corrected violations of labor laws.

This reorganization led to a stronger enforcement of labor laws in the agricultural sector, particularly in the cultivation and industrial aspects of the sugar cane industry. In 1941–42, the ISS investigated 1,093 industries and 3,882 commercial establishments in which 67.2 percent (23,438) of the employees were men.[40] Again, we notice the greater emphasis placed by the colonial state in improving the living and working conditions of working-class males, especially those employed in the sugar cane sector. However, if gender differences led to the discrimination of working-class women, a closer analysis of the ISS investigations will show that the agency gave preference to female factory workers to the detriment of home needleworkers.

The WWS did not combine efforts with the IHS. Out of 1,042 establishments investigated by the WWS, 49.1 percent were industrial. WWS reports showed that the needlework industry employed less than 4,000 female factory workers in the 1941–42 fiscal year. In contrast, there were almost 40,000 home needleworkers.[41] The possible impact of improving working conditions in home needlework was very limited even after the number of investigations rose from 641 in 1937–38 to 1,541 in 1941–42.[42] These investigations covered only 1.2 percent of the women employed by the home needlework industry and 26.05 percent of the women who worked in the needlework factories. Clearly, the investigators of the ISS were biased.

The ISS began in the 1942–43 fiscal years to give attention to the establishments that employed women. The ISS emphasized the tobacco stripping sector, not the needlework industry or the home needlework industry.[43] The nature of the investigation was whether employers observed working standards. There is no clear indication of an ISS preference for tobacco stripping, however; probably the halt in needlework production gave the ISS the opportunity to investigate other industrial establishments. The number of home needleworkers substantially declined from 40,941 female workers to only 19,701, a difference of 48.1 percent, during the months of June and August 1942. Permits issued to subcontractors declined from 833 (1940–41 fiscal year) to 162 (1942–43 fiscal year).[44] In 1942, Puerto Ricans experienced a crisis related to high rates of unemployment, rising prices of basic foodstuffs, and a decrease in commercial shipping. The unemployment crisis turned the attention of the ISS to agricultural plantations. These investigations increased from 305 plantations and 19,020 workers in the 1941–42 fiscal year to 1,894 plantations and 78,396 workers in the 1942–43 fiscal year.[45]

The WWS played an important role in the metropolitan Children Bureau's (CB) investigation of working women and child care. WWS interviewers tried to investigate the access working-class women had to child care. It was the WWS that called for the creation of nurseries in the most industrialized cities of Puerto Rico. The federal CB's report took for granted that child care was only a problem for urban factory workers, although almost 91 percent of the women employed in manufacture worked for the home needlework industry, according to the ISS reports.[46]

A reorganization of the ISS in 1943–44 maintained the WWS, the MWS, and the IHS. One difference was the creation of the position of area director, who oversaw the actions of twenty-eight district supervisors.[47] The reorganization intended a more efficient approach to the enforcement of labor laws. Most of the district offices devoted their time to the settlement of complaints. However, there were only nine complaints in the IHS in 1943–44. This figure contrasted with 112 violations found in the 1941–42 fiscal year. In 1943–44, the ISS began to issue permits for home needleworkers. From the 43,198 homeworkers reported by employers, almost 20 percent (8,527 homeworkers) received their permits from the ISS. A high quantity of homeworkers requested permits in an industry that normally had difficulty determining the actual number of workers involved in the productive process.[48] Even with these numbers, my findings show that almost 9 percent of these workers sought permits from the government, a percentage that was very high for the industry.[49]

The needlework industry began to recuperate in 1943 due to an increase in the shipments of raw materials for production. The value of needlework output rose from $5,875 million in 1941 to $21,004 million by 1945, and its share of the total export value rose from 6.73 percent in 1941 to 18.08 percent in 1945.[50] The improvements in the needlework industry were part of an artificial boom created by World War II. Concerning employment, the home needlework industry represented more than 44 percent of all women employed in manufacture (100,693) in 1940, and it increased the employment of homeworkers 16 percent from 44,371 to 51,871 in 1950.[51] Two-thirds of the increase in manufacturing employment between 1940 and 1950 came from the home needlework industry.[52]

Women's increasing participation in the labor force compelled the colonial state to address some problems of working-class women. Although women have always worked in Puerto Rican society, in 1940 home needlework was the biggest employer of women on the Island. Employment in the home needlework industry rose from 40,000 in 1941–42 to 60,000 in the 1945–46 fiscal year.[53] Home needlework employment was an important source of income for many working-class families, particularly if we consider the involvement of other family members in the production process.[54] In order to address this increase in the numbers of home needleworkers and women workers throughout Puerto Rico, Manuel A. Pérez, Commissioner of Labor, decided to reorganize the ISS in 1945.

The Women's Bureau, 1945–52

The Puerto Rican DL created the Women's Bureau (WB) in 1945.[55] The DL immediately transferred the IHS and the WWS from the ISS to the WB. The DL organized the WB into two divisions: the Industrial Homework Section and the Women's Work Section. The majority of the officials appointed by the colonial state to the WB were women. Their appointments as social workers of the WB showed that these middle-class advances took place within the limits of service roles traditionally associated with women's work.

Manuel A. Pérez appointed Ofelia Rivera to the position of supervisor of the Women's Bureau, and María T. Quiñones as the chief of the WWS. There is limited information available about both women. However, we know that social workers from the United States' Department of Labor and the metropolitan WB trained both of them in the United States. The training emphasized observing and studying matters concerning the administration of female labor laws and workers' education techniques. Rivera and Quiñones were part of the middle class and had similar ideas regarding the role of working-class women in the family, the labor force, and Puerto Rican society. Both of them continuously published articles in the *Revista del Trabajo,* in which they repeated the discourse of the state.

Quiñones and Rivera were in charge of a complex web of supervisors, area directors, social workers, and working-class women. In contrast to previous state institutions, the WB had to coordinate its actions with the ISS and the CB. Between the WB, ISS, and CB, each institution appointed six area directors, who then reported directly to each institution. These area directors evaluated the actions of eighteen supervisors: six child labor supervisors, six women's work supervisors, and six industrial homework supervisors. The WB had twenty-eight district supervisors who responded to these six area directors, and evaluated, reported on, and helped social workers in the investigations made at the town level.

The responsibilities of social workers included investigating and visiting homes and factories. Social workers also investigated complaints and evaluated

Table 9.1

The Number of Home Workers Reported by Employers, and Investigations by Sector, Women's Bureau, Fiscal Years 1946–1952

Fiscal year	Homeworkers reported	Investigations home needlework	Investigations factory work
1946–1947	72,938	1,210	7,122
1947–1948	60,934	1,664	12,769
1948–1949	52,000	2,072	14,377
1949–1950	57,000	1,125	3,905
1950–1951	54,000	1,176	2,474
1951–1952	43,000	1,016	3,440
Totals	339,872	8,263	44,087

Source: Annual Reports of the Commissioner of Labor, Department of Labor, Reports of the Commissioner of Labor, 1945–1952.

Notes: The reports of the 1950–1951 fiscal years did not provide any information on the number of workers reported by employers. Figures on home needleworkers for the 1950–1951 and 1951–1952 fiscal years are from Dietz, *Economic History,* 226.

the health standards of homes and factories. If a home needleworker requested a permit to use her house for home needlework, it was the social worker who approved or denied the permit. Social workers prepared lectures and disclosed labor laws and decrees in weekly and monthly meetings held in rural communities and factories. Some of these meetings addressed issues like workers' responsibilities, legal rights, family planning, and other topics. The number of social workers employed by the WB was very limited due to the demand for social workers' services.[56] Nonetheless, the work achieved by these social workers at the local level reflected the success of the WB in the education of female workers.

Table 9.1 shows a decrease in the number of homeworkers employed in the home needlework industry between 1946 and 1952. Employment in the home needlework industry reached its highest number in 1946–47 when the industry employed 72,938 homeworkers. Beginning in 1949–50 employment in home needlework experienced a sharp decline. However, it was not until the 1950s that factory manufacturing surpassed home needlework as the primary employer of working-class women.[57]

The purpose of the WB was to enforce laws protecting women as workers. Therefore, one of the responsibilities of the WB was to investigate employers and the conditions under which women worked in factories and at home. Since the home needlework industry employed most of the female working class, the WB should have given home needlework priority over other sectors of the economy. This was not the case. Table 9.1 shows that the number of investigations made by the WB for factory work exceeded by 35,824 the number of investigations of home needlework. At no time were home needlework investigations higher than those of factory work, even when the former employed more female workers. There is also another interesting trend in the investigations of factory workers. Investigations in the factory sector began to decline from 14,377 in 1948–49 to only 3,440 in the 1951–52 fiscal year. The years 1951–52 coincided with the arrival of the first light manufacturing corporations benefiting from Operation Bootstrap's tax incentive structure.

A combination of factors, such as the limited success of state-owned enterprises and changes in the international economy, was responsible for the decline of home needlework. Nonetheless, it was the modernization discourse of the colonial state and the PPD that led the WB to treat home needlework as a thing of the past. Soon after 1945 the international economy went through a process of reorganization. This led to a reorientation of the plans of industrialization on the Island. By exchanging state-owned enterprises for foreign capital, middle-class economic planners started to move against those sectors of the economy they considered backward. By trying to eliminate home needlework, the WB became an important agent of change for the colonial state. The only problem the WB encountered was the large number of Puerto Ricans who earn a wage from this industry. Manuel A. Pérez mentioned that the primary target in the reorganization of the ISS which led to the creation of the WB was the restriction of the home needlework industry:

> Although it would be desirable to suppress homework, this cannot be accomplished in view of the fact that homework probably represents the only source of income of numerous women who cannot attend working places. The policy of the Department is, therefore, to continue regulating homework in a restrictive way in order to ensure homeworkers at least some of the benefits enjoyed by women working in shops and factories.[58]

Home needleworkers were not protected by some of the laws protecting factory workers. Law 73 (of 21 June 1919, reformed in 1930 and amended again in 1942) protected women and children from dangerous occupations, but since home needleworkers did not participate in factories this law did not applied to them. If a home needleworker became pregnant she would not receive maternity benefits nor a resting period of four weeks prior to and after giving birth as stated in law 3 (of 13 March 1942). Home needleworkers did not benefit from law 45 (modified in 1937), which established maximum hours rules for female workers. In the case of home needleworkers, household work extended beyond the eight-hour-per-day limit established by this law. Home needleworkers were excluded from law 84 (of 12 May 1943), which stipulated that any employee hired for an indeterminate time could not be fired without sufficient reason. Throughout the 1940s the PPD revised much of the legislation, making several amendments. It is clear that the middle sector had the intention of improving the working conditions of the labor force, and wanted to protect workers from employer abuses; however, many of these laws protected factory and agricultural workers who were in their majority Puerto Rican men.

During the 1940s, the PPD enacted only one law aimed at protecting home needleworkers. Law 163 (of 15 May 1939, revised in 1943) aimed at protecting home needleworkers from work in unhealthy and dangerous conditions, and it regulated their wages and prevented their exploitation.[59] It also gave the Department of Labor complete control over the home needlework industry. From 1943 until the reorganization of the WB in 1950–51, the Department of Labor supervised and regulated home needlework, determined which articles home needleworkers could produce in their homes, which laws protecting home needleworkers applied to the industry, and the rules that employers, contractors, and subcontractors had to follow in the establishment of home needlework industries.[60] In other words, the colonial state had the means of eliminating home needlework by asserting controls over its creation, production, and development.

Law 163 had the purpose of regulating home needlework rather than protecting home needleworkers as many of the investigations of the WB favored factory work. In deeming homes dangerous and unhealthy for work, the social workers were using criteria that would deem the homes unacceptable for living purposes. One purpose of the establishment of rural communities during the 1940s was to make labor more accessible to capital.[61] It should be no surprise that many of the individuals who resided in rural communities were former home needleworkers whose living and working conditions had been qualified as unhealthy and dangerous. In some cases, then, the resettlement polices of the PPD uprooted families from kin and familial relations, thus forcing other women who worked in factories and other industrial establishments to return to their homes in order to take care of their children. This shows that even if the end result led to improving living conditions, some of the relocations were not voluntary, as popularly portrayed by the PPD.

In terms of salaries, the home needlework industry did not fare any better. The FLSA established a target rate of 25 cents an hour as a set goal for all industries, and in 1940, this was made the minimum wage, rising to 75 cents in 1950. Home needleworkers, however, continued to receive 15 cents an hour until 1949.[62] By comparison, needlework factory workers received between 12.5 and 40 cents an hour. Female workers in the tobacco stripping sector earned 25 cents per hour; others, employed as laundry operatives and janitors in hospitals, received 18 cents an hour, while waitresses, bartenders, cooks, and janitors in hotels, restaurants, cafeterias, and soda fountain establishments earned 30 cents an hour.[63] Since the WB limited the number of investigations to only 8,263 in a six-year span—in an industry that employed almost 56,645 workers on average at the time—hoping for improvements in wages for home needleworkers was unrealistic.

Table 9.2

Violations of Labor Laws, the Number of Violations Corrected by the Women's Bureau, and the Monies Recovered from Wage Claims and Labor Law Violations Reported to the Women's Bureau, Fiscal Years 1945–1952

Year	Violations homework	Violations factory work	Corrections	Monies recovered (in dollars)
1945–1946	—	1,528	992	19,586.67
1946–1947	—	1,312	1,221	28,702.86
1947–1948	—	1,822	1,430	48,168.50
1948–1949	4,061	5,247	5,063	46,600.11
1949–1950	3,083	966	874	43,816.87
1950–1951	3,397	1,857	1,834	45,604.67
1951–1952	3,023	1,370	1,342	44,087.11
Total	13,564	14,102	12,756	276,566.79

Source: Annual Reports of the Commissioner of Labor, Department of Labor, Reports of the Commissioner of Labor, 1945–1952.

Notes: The *Annual Reports* of fiscal years 1946 to 1948 did not include any information regarding the number of violations committed in the home needlework sector. Figures for the corrections of labor law violations only reflect factory work.

One year later, the commissioner of the Department of Labor expressed the need for stricter regulation of the needlework industry. Manuel A. Pérez used a similar narrative to explain the colonial state plans for the home needlework industry.

> Since industrial homework cannot be suppressed at present, however desirable it would be to shift the industrial work from home to shops without seriously affecting our economy, the policy of the Department to continue its regulation in order to insure homeworkers some of the benefits enjoyed by women factory workers, has been followed.[64]

The plans of the colonial state and the PPD were to move home needleworkers into factory jobs before the establishment of Operation Bootstrap. Modernization meant the elimination of home needlework. The preference was industrial production. As soon as Puerto Rican women moved from home needlework employment to factory jobs, the PPD could continue its plans for industrialization. However, by the end of World War II, the colonial state shifted away from one of its primary war years goals, which was to decrease male unemployment. After the war, the goal became the creation of a trained labor force for the industrialization plans.

Table 9.2 shows the role of the WB in finding violations of labor laws, correcting them, and recovering monies due to violations. There were disparities in the number of labor law violations found in factory and home needlework.

Table 9.3

Number of Certificates Issued to Homeworkers, Visits Made by Social Workers, and Homeworkers Reported by Contractors and Subcontractors to the Women's Bureau, Fiscal Years 1945–1952

Year	Certificates	Homeworkers reported	Visits
1945–1946	8,456	59,709	—
1946–1947	10,232	72,938	9,530
1947–1948	22,580	60,934	6,369
1948–1949	18,596	52,000	7,298
1949–1950	21,510	57,000	6,106
1950–1951	28,600	54,000	7,622
1951–1952	18,282	43,000	8,112
Total	128,256	399,581	45,037

Source: Annual Reports of the Commissioner of Labor, Department of Labor, Reports of the Commissioner of Labor, 1945–1952.

Notes: The *Annual Reports* of the 1945–1946 fiscal year did not provide information for contractors and subcontractors, but the report included a total of the permits.

Even when there is no information for the 1945–48 fiscal years, the number of violations found by the WB in the home needlework industry was proportionately higher than those found in factory work.[65] Clearly, even with the creation of the WB and the establishment of labor legislation to protect workers, employers continued to violate labor laws. However, in contrast to the WCB, the WB was successful in correcting almost 91 percent of the violations made by employers. Proof of the WB's commitment to working-class women was the recovery of $276,566.79 for violations.

Table 9.3 shows that some home needleworkers applied for employment certificates. In 1945–46 and 1946–47, only 14.1 percent and 14.0 percent, respectively, of homeworkers had WB certificates. However, from the 1947–48 fiscal year on, there is an increase in the number of homeworkers with certificates. With the arrival of light manufacturing corporations to the island, the number of certificates issued to homeworkers declined 36.0 percent from 28,600 in the fiscal year 1950–51 to 18,282 in fiscal year 1951–52.

By issuing certificates, the WB determined the legality of home needlework. The WB required employers to ask for these certificates. At no time except for the 1950–51 fiscal year did the numbers of home needleworkers who received certificates rise above 40 percent. The rest of the home needleworkers resisted registration attempts by the WB. Employers who used subcontractors did not require their employees to follow the laws established by the WB. Even with the PPD's socioeconomic reforms, working-class families still needed extra income to survive. It is no coincidence, then, that home needleworkers did not register, preferring to work without the certificates.

In contrast to the high percentages of certificates issued and of homeworkers reported by employers, the number of visits made to homes did not increase. Only when the industry began to decline in the 1950s did the percentage of visits rise to 18.8 percent. This figure hit its lowest in the 1947–48 fiscal year, when only 10.4 percent of homeworkers received a visit from the social workers.

The WB determined that the decrease in the number of homeworkers was a direct result of their stronger enforcement of the home needlework industry. Homeworkers went to the factories. The decrease was also apparent in the 64.4 percent fall in the number of permits granted to subcontractors, from 755 in 1946–47 to 488 in the 1947–48 fiscal year. This decrease was a direct consequence of the movement of working-class women to other professions like domestic service, commercial, clerical, and kindred sectors. Puerto Rican women started moving to other sectors of the economy. If we analyze the distribution of female employment in 1950, we can see that domestic work was the second largest occupation for women with 22.4 percent in 1950, followed by clerical and kindred workers with 9.5 percent, and sales workers with 2.8 percent.[66]

Modernization, Gender, and the Women's Bureau

The PPD launched a modernization program with the intention of improving living standards for the poor by developing Puerto Rico's economy. During this process colonial authorities incorporated a modernization ideology into their populist discourse. This combination of ideologies led to greater emphasis on working-class sacrifices. By doing this, the PPD targeted those sectors of the economy that offered greater prospects for economic development and regulated those it considered backward.[67] However, modernization had a gendered perspective. Many of the colonial reforms created by the PPD benefited several sectors of the male population. In this context, the colonial state emphasized the need to maintain Puerto Rico's family structure by keeping working-class women in the household, just when the PPD moved to regulate, control, and eliminate home needlework. In so doing, state institutions like the WB began an active campaign against home needlework, telling Puerto Rican women how to act as women and as workers.

The irony of this situation was that the PPD relied on the sugar sector as being central to their industrialization plans while industries like the home needlework fell into the backward category. No other sector of Puerto Rico's economy, besides home needlework, tobacco stripping, and coffee production, represented the past as did the sugar cane industry. Throughout the first three decades of the twentieth century, the sugar cane sector dominated colonial politics. By influencing local authorities, co-opting labor leaders, and maintaining detrimental working conditions, sugar became a synonym for the past that many Puerto Ricans wanted to forget.

Agrarian reform united the idea of modernization with the concept of male breadwinner. By combining notions of modernization and gender, the PPD directed agrarian reform policies to benefit *colonos,* individual and proportional profit farmers, and small plot recipients. All of these groups consisted mostly of males who had access to land. Nonetheless, modernization and patriarchal values prevented the PPD from completely eliminating the sugar industry. At the economic level, sugar cane employment continued to be an essential component of Puerto Rico's economy. More importantly, it was the primary employer of working-class men. Its complete elimination hindered the PPD's priority of eliminating male unemployment. At the political level, prior to the 1944 election the PPD received a majority in both houses of the Legislature. The sugar absentee corporations were the obstacle in the PPD's attempt to gain control over administrative structures of the colonial state. This required winning the elections for which the PPD needed the support of sugar cane workers.

Once in control of administrative positions in the colonial state, the PPD moved to eliminate home needlework. In this process, the social workers of the WB were essential participants in the process of modernization. This group of women shared similar middle-class values about work, family integration, and the proper role of women in Puerto Rican society. Their appointment to WB's field and administrative positions also corresponded to PPD's notions of women's place within the colonial state. Since the leadership of the PPD considered social work a traditional profession for women (in which middle- and upper-class women could cherish their maternal instincts), many of its leaders thought that these appointments in the colonial state would not be a threat to male authority. However, the notion that women's problems did not transcend the private sphere, and that only women could address the problems of working-class women without interfering with the sanctity of the home, reflected a limited view of women's economic problems during the 1940s.

Social workers began to present industrialization as the cure for all of the evils created by the sugar economy and the home needlework industry. The WB started a campaign, as early as 1945, against the home needlework industry. María T. Quiñones, chief of the WWS, articulated the WB views in a 1945 *Revista del Trabajo* article:

> The needlework industry was the first [industry] to give ample reception to women, and it exploited them UNMERCIFULLY during its first years. This industry which developed at [Puerto Rican] women's expense left as [its] social contributions exhausting and miserable conditions for the workers.[68]

Other articles reflected similar strategies, attempting to make workers recognize their exploiters. However, in contrast to some of the mechanisms used by the PPD (1938) to empower sugar cane workers, these strategies are not used with home needleworkers until 1945. Contrary to sugar cane workers, home needleworkers were not encouraged to rebel, strike, or to use their vote against their exploiters, they were just reminded of their socioeconomic conditions, and the advantages offered by factory employment.

What becomes extremely interesting in the case of Puerto Rico was the reorientation of the industrialization program, better known as Operation Bootstrap, to light manufacturing. Since capital forced the PPD to reorganize their plans for industrialization, the colonial state continuously tried to move home needleworkers from home to factory production.

The intersection of capitalist and patriarchal values was essential to this process of labor formation. After the creation of the WB, social workers started to remind working-class women of their responsibilities as workers and mothers. Rafaela Camacho de Ganoa wrote an article in the *Revista del Trabajo* critical of unruly women:

> We are not concerned by the case of those women who work without any reason to do so for the mere fact that they feel independent, and earn extra money for superfluous expenses because those [women] by only staying in their homes, and excepting their responsibilities imposed by marriage, resolve the problem without any sacrifice, and at the same time, perform all of their duties.[69]

As workers, Puerto Rican women should not organize a strike against the state or an employer because acting in this manner made women behave like men. In other cases, if they worked without a license approved by the WB—as did home needleworkers—they were considered to be rejecting the proper role of Puerto Rican women. As mothers, they had to continue their responsibilities to their children. As wives, women had to sacrifice their role as workers for the benefit of Puerto Rico.

The Women's Bureau, Gender Politics, and the State

The Women's Bureau became the primary agent of change for the colonial state. In this process, the regulation and elimination of the home needlework industry played an important role in the process of early industrialization in Puerto Rico. These routines of bureaucratic administration were examples of everyday state forms and practices that instituted patterns of gender as they politically organized gender subjectivities. The colonial state invoked, appealed, interpellated, regulated men and women not as concrete historical subjects, but as gender categories defined and constructed within particular discourses and practices of ruling.[70] It constructed women as objects of rule, reproducing or restructuring normative gender meanings and subordinate social and political identities in the same process. State policies reflected the state's interests of modernization and its gendered transformations of sterilization, family planning, familial responsibilities, sexual behavior, and character traits.

The social workers of the WB followed the modernization ideology instituted by the colonial state. That is, the state suggested that the control of working-class women's reproduction was imperative for their plans of industrialization. Social workers sought to eliminate some of the obstacles for industrialization like over-population and poverty. In turn, social workers taught their working-class sisters how to deal with these problems. The WB started a family planning strategy created to educate working-class women. In turn, many sectors of society including the Catholic Church were outraged by the state's attempts to control population.[71] Julia Carmen Marchand Paz, a social worker, suggested the idea of family planning in an article in the *Revista del Trabajo*. The author argued that:

> If we [women] are willing to give everything for our children—effort, health, illusion and our own life—would not it be reasonable for us to have [give birth to] those pieces of our hearts [children] when we feel prepared to have them, when we are in good health, when our economic resources are sufficient and our homes well established? You should know that if God is so merciful, would God have wanted you to bear more children than the ones you can attend, maintain and teach to become a useful citizen of Puerto Rico. When you are ready in terms of economic support and medical attention then, you should wish for another.[72]

Through this regulation of female sexuality, colonial authorities established a system of social regulation. In so doing, the WB continued to legitimate the idea that working-class women should follow a specific pattern of conduct that limited their role to that of mothers. In this context, women should stay at home taking care of children while their husbands went to work. However, the WB began an active campaign against working-class women who broke with the PPD's image of true womanhood.

This campaign directed toward the regulation of sexual behavior and character traits led to a further restriction of the working class. Julia Carmen Marchand wrote the following in an article that appeared in the *Revista del Trabajo:*

> The creation of the Women's Bureau responds to working woman's eagerness to remain faithful to her femininity. Her responsibilities as employees do not exempt her from the most high and mandatory function like her maternity.[73]

The social workers of the WB emphasized the importance of femininity as an inherent characteristic of working-class women. Moreover, the colonial state created the WB to regulate female behavior and to keep working-class women feminine. That is, the colonial state used the WB to remind women of their roles as mothers. Working-class women employed in the labor force should remember that their primary role in Puerto Rican society—motherhood—superseded their rights and responsibilities as workers. In other words, the detrimental socioeconomic situation of the working class was a direct consequence of women's participation in the labor force.

Women in rural areas became the bearers of true Puerto Rican womanhood. The PPD exalted rural home needleworkers as exemplary of Puerto Rican womanhood because they had kept themselves outside of the influence of the wave of masculinization that affected the urban female labor force.[74] Rural women, like their male counterparts, were the focus of an intense campaign directed toward gaining their support for the 1940 and 1944 elections. The PPD was successful in this campaign. The PPD tried to push this discourse of true womanhood and moral character traits to other sectors of the female working class. One target was the urban female working class.

The colonial state promoted the interests of American capital with the creation of Operation Bootstrap. This process undermined the association of manhood with gainful employment. From 1947 until 1970, Operation Bootstrap would create the image of the Puerto Rican worker as a female operative. Furthermore, Puerto Rico went through economic changes that led to a decrease in male labor force participation.[75]

During the 1940s, most of the reforms enacted by the PPD had the intention of improving the dismal conditions of working-class males and the unemployed. Since many of these reforms were directed toward the sugar cane sector, the sector of the economy that employed most the male labor force, the state clearly mediated between patriarchy and capitalism. At this time, working-class women began to participate in greater numbers in the economy. Male unemployment pushed working-class families to need another wage for the survival of the family. However, the PPD had to deal with a new situation not experienced by other governments on the Island: working-class women had the right to vote in the elections.

The colonial state considered the home needlework industry as a symbol of the past. In their attempts to modernize the Island, state institutions like the Women's Bureau were responsible for achieving the objectives and programs of modernization. The restriction of the home needlework industry was a primary objective in the plans of the PPD for industrialization. We have seen that not only were sectors of the metropolitan state interested in industrialization as the only solution to Puerto Rico's problems but so were the members of the colonial government, like the commissioner of the Labor Department, who mentioned that the movement of home needleworkers into the labor force was one of the goals of the Women's Bureau. The increasing number of visits and the decline in the number of investigations clearly exemplify the movement as part of the process of industrialization. By the end of the 1950s, the development of light manufacturing corporations dealt a final blow to the home needlework industry. An industry that employed the highest number of women during the 1930s and 1940s dropped to employing only 3.8 percent of working women in 1960.[76]

Modernization and gender played an important role in home needlework regulation. It seemed contradictory that the colonial state tried to keep working-class women outside the labor force to remedy male unemployment, but at the same time tried to regulate and eliminate the home needlework industry, probably the only industry that guaranteed the maintenance of women within the household. However, there was no contradiction. From a patriarchal perspective, Puerto Rican women had been forced to neglect—in the view of the middle sector and its working-class converts—their roles as wives and mothers because of their involvement in the economy. Since the populist reforms improved working conditions of employed males and gave some jobs or land to those who were unemployed, Puerto Rican women had no need to continue working for the home needlework industry even if home needlework was the only source of income for the family. Once capital forced a reorientation of industrialization, the PPD then moved to eliminate home needlework and forced home needleworkers into the mainstream labor force. This movement of the female labor force, however, had to follow a process controlled by the colonial state.

A reorganization plan by newly elected governor Luis Muñoz Marín united the WB and the CB in 1950. The Labor Department organized the new Women and Children's Bureau in three sections: the Women's Section, the Industrial Homework Section, and the Child Section. A justification for this reorganization was that both bureaus had developed an effective system of investigations in the past.[77] However, these investigations protected factories, not home needlework, even when the numbers of homeworkers surpassed those of the workers employed in the factories. The prospects of an export-led industrialization program like Operation Bootstrap signaled the changes in state labor policies and the WB. Manufacturers needed the skilled labor of working-class women who had throughout the years worked in the home needlework industry. It is within this context that we can see the relationship between American capital, the state, and the restrictions applied to the home needlework industry in Puerto Rico.

State reforms related to gender modernized and updated existing patterns of gender inequality, which preserved male supremacy while providing capital greater access to female labor.[78] The number of labor law violations committed during the 1940s showed that even with some supervision of corporations, the violations of labor laws continued with impunity. The elimination of the Women's Bureau in the 1950–51 fiscal year was another consequence of industrialization. No longer would a state institution supervise, investigate, and prosecute American and local capital. Puerto Rico offered something other than cheap labor and political stability. The Island gave American capital a non-interventionist colonial state.

Notes

1. State policies were a reflection of competing discourses that were legitimated by the populist program of the PPD. Since the colonial state needed resources and powers produced elsewhere to legitimize its actions, the PPD articulated the importance of family

unity, male employment, and industrialization as necessary requirements for improving living and working conditions on the Island. In this process, the state intervened to promote changes in the social relations of production and reproduction, and vice-versa. See Joan W. Scott, *Gender and the Politics of History* (New York: Columbia University Press, 1988), 28–50; Michel Foucalt, *The History of Sexuality*, vol. 1: *An Introduction* (New York: Vintage Books, 1980), 92; and Sonia E. Álvarez, *Engendering Democracy in Brazil: Women's Movements in Transition Politics* (Princeton: Princeton University Press, 1990), 19–36.

2. Some of these studies analyze the importance of women's labor force participation, especially in the home needlework industry. María del Carmen Baerga, *Género y trabajo: la industria de la aguja en Puerto Rico y el Caribe Hispánico* (San Juan: Editorial de la Universidad de Puerto Rico, 1993). Other studies trace the changes brought by Operation Bootstrap—Puerto Rico's export-led industrialization program—to the patterns of women's employment, and to working-class household dynamics. See Luz del Alba Acevedo, "Industrialization and Employment: Changes in the Patterns of Women's Work in Puerto Rico, 1947–1982," *World Development* 18, no. 2 (1990): 231–55; Helen Safa, "Female Employment in the Puerto Rican Working Class," in Helen Safa and June Nash, eds., *Women and Change in Latin America* (New York: Bergin and Garvey, 1985), 83–104. Carmen Pérez Herranz, "The Impact of a Development Program on Working Women in the Garment Industry: A Study of Women and Production in Puerto Rico" (Ph.D. diss., Rutgers University, 1990); and Palmira Ríos González, "Women and Industrialization in Puerto Rico: Gender Division of Labor and the Demand for Female Labor Force in the Manufacturing Sector, 1950–1980" (Ph.D. diss., Yale University, 1990).

3. Linzi Manicom, "Ruling Relations: Rethinking State and Gender in South African History," *Journal of African History* 33 (1992): 455–56.

4. Lydia Milagros González García analyzes the role of the Puerto Rican Department of Education in collaborating with American needlework corporations in the establishment of the Philadelphia needlework curriculum as the basis for needlework training in Puerto Rico during the first two decades of the twentieth century. Lydia Milagros González García, *Una puntada en el tiempo: La industria de la aguja en Puerto Rico (1900–1929)* (San Juan: CEREP and CIPAF, 1990).

5. Yamila Azize Vargas, "The Emergence of Feminism in Puerto Rico, 1870–1930," in Vicki L. Ruiz and Ellen Carol DuBois, eds., *Unequal Sisters: A Multicultural Reader in U.S. Women's History* (New York: Routledge, 1994), 261.

6. Blanca Silvestrini, "Women as Workers: The Experience of the Puerto Rican Woman in the 1930s," in Edna Acosta-Belen, ed., *The Puerto Rican Woman: Perspectives on Culture, History and Society* (New York: Praeger, 1986), 66.

7. The involvement of subcontractors in the production process devaluated home needleworkers' earnings, for not only did subcontractors earn a commission from the contractors, but they also kept a part of workers' wages. Blanca Silvestrini and María Dolores Luque de Sánchez, *Historia de Puerto Rico: Trayectoria de un pueblo*. (Madrid: Editorial Cultural Hispanoamericana, 1989), 444.

8. Silvestrini, "Women as Workers," 67.

9. During the 1930s, it was common practice for owners to call the police or armed thugs in order to eliminate strikes in Puerto Rico. In this case, police officials justified their actions by arguing that women were violent and disorderly. However, this did not justify police repression leaving two dead and seventy wounded. Ibid., 67.

10. In 1919, the colonial Legislature approved minimum wages of $4.00 per week for women eighteen years and younger, and $6.00 per week for women eighteen years and older. James L. Dietz, *Economic History of Puerto Rico: Institutional Change and Capitalist Development* (Princeton: Princeton University Press, 1986), 195.

11. Silvestrini and Luque de Sánchez, *Historia de Puerto Rico,* 483.

12. Department of Labor, Bureau of Women and Children in Industry, *Annual Report of the Commissioner of Labor* (San Juan, Puerto Rico, 1937–38), 45.

13. Information regarding the investigations from 1933 to 1936 is almost nonexistent. One reason for the limited information on the activities of the WCB and the small number of investigations for this period is limited resources. Only seven employees were assigned to the WCB. The Department of Labor appointed a director and assistant and five investigators. This information appears in the Organizational Chart of the Department of Labor 1937–38 *Annual Report,* which has no page number.

14. Ibid., 45–46.

15. In 1935 the NIRA was declared unconstitutional, and with it the labor standard provisions died. It was not until June 25, 1938, that this legislation passed as the Fair Labor Standards Act. Dietz, *Economic History*, 175–76, n. 103.

16. In this letter Lupercio Colberg explained that the socioeconomic situation of Puerto Rico was different from that of the United States. Colberg lobbied metropolitan authorities for special treatment for Puerto Rico's manufacturers. Thomas Mathews, *La política puertorriqueña y el Nuevo Trato* (San Juan: Editorial Universitaria, 1970), 128–29.

17. What made Morris Storyk's appointment as director of the NIRA interesting was that he owned a needlework shop in the town of San Juan. Clearly, we can see the appointment of NIRA's director as part of the Coalition's influence in fixing problems for shop and factory owners. Department of Labor, Bureau of Women and Children in Industry, *Annual Report of the Commissioner of Labor* (San Juan, Puerto Rico, 1933–34), 57.

18. Other sectors in the United States supported the elimination of the home needlework industry. Rose Schneiderman, president of the National Trade Union League, agreed with this decision. Schneiderman argued that homeworkers should receive similar wages and conditions to those of factory workers. However, she maintained that the elimination of homework would eventually benefit workers and employers. Eileen Boris, "Needlewomen under the New Deal in Puerto Rico, 1920–1945," in Altagracia Ortiz, ed., *Puerto Rican Women and Work: Bridges in Transnational Labor* (Philadelphia: Temple University Press, 1996), 44–47.

19. Mathews, *La política puertorriqueña,* 128–29.

20. The NIRA codes applied in Puerto Rico did not really change the wage system for the home needleworkers, especially if employers paid by piece and not by a fixed salary. Silvestrini and Luque de Sánchez, *Historia de Puerto Rico,* 484; and Dietz, *Economic History,* 175–76.

21. The Fair Labor Standards Act was a legislation created at the national level in the United States, and applied to Puerto Rico. This legislation was initially applied under the National Industrial Recovery Act of 1933. The FLSA provisions affected all workers engaged in or producing goods for interstate commerce. It set a minimum wage of 25 cents per hour for 1938 and 30 cents for 1939. Dietz, *Economic History,* 226.

22. Department of Labor, Bureau of Women and Children in Industry, *Annual Report of the Commissioner of Labor* (San Juan, Puerto Rico, 1938–39), 34.

23. By applying the FLSA to several industries on the Island, the metropolitan government had the primary purpose of increasing salaries for workers. Many employers stopped production and reduced the number of employed workers as an excuse to circumvent the FLSA. These schemes forced the metropolitan administration to temporarily delay the application of the FLSA. Department of Labor, Bureau of Women and Children in Industry, Annual Report of the Commissioner of Labor (San Juan, Puerto Rico, 1939–40), 36.

24. This code set a forty-four-hour workweek, and a minimum salary of $2.00 for

home needleworkers, and from $3 to $5 a week for workers in factories and workshops, depending upon whether labor was done by hand or by machine. This was in fact a restatement of existing policy. However, this loophole allowed hardship industries to set home needleworkers' hourly wages at 15 cents. Dietz, *Economic History,* 225–26.

25. This argument commenting on the crisis in the needlework industry appeared constantly in the annual reports of the DL from 1938 until 1942. Department of Labor, *Annual Report,* 1938–39, 33–34.

26. Since Puerto Rico relied on U.S. vessels to bring materials for needlework production, and the numbers of ships that transported imports to the Island decreased during the war years, we could argue that the elimination of subcontractors was a consequence of the absence of production materials. Factory owners had to pay extreme attention to quality control and the distribution of materials. By doing so, needlework factories maximized the use of minimal resources. Dietz, *Economic History,* 225.

27. Department of Labor, Industrial Supervision Service, *Annual Report of the Commissioner of Labor* (San Juan, Puerto Rico, 1940–41), 25.

28. Silvestrini, "Women as Workers," 66–67.

29. The subject of populism during the 1940s in Puerto Rico generated a great many studies. Yet even among scholars who study the populist movement, the analysis of women's participation is still absent. Ángel Quintero Rivera, "La base social de la transformación ideológica del Partido Popular Democrático en la década del 40," in Gerardo Navas, ed., *Cambio y desarollo en Puerto Rico: la transformación ideológica del Partido Popular Democrático* (San Juan: Editorial de la Universidad de Puerto Rico, 1980), 35–119. Emilio González Díaz, "Class Struggle and Politics in Puerto Rico During the Decade of the 40's: The Rise of the PPD," *Two Thirds* 2: 1 (1979): 46–58; Juan José Baldrich, "Class and State: The Origins of Populism in Puerto Rico 1934–1952" (Ph.D. diss., Yale University, 1981); and Emilio Pantojas, "Puerto Rican Populism Revisited: The PPD During the Decade of the 1940s," *Journal of Latin American Studies* 21 (1990): 521–58. However, the only exception to those who study populism is Mary Frances Gallart, "Mujeres, aguja y política en el siglo 20 en Puerto Rico: Obdulia Velázquez de Lorenzo, alcaldesa de Guayama, 1952–1956" (Ph.D. diss., Universidad de Puerto Rico, 1992).

30. Although the concept of male breadwinner has been identified in the process of industrialization in Cuba, the Dominican Republic, and Puerto Rico, we still need a study that can pinpoint exactly when this criterion started as part of state policies in Puerto Rico. Helen Safa, *The Myth of the Male Breadwinner: Women and Industrialization in the Caribbean* (Boulder, CO: Westview Press, 1995), 37–58.

31. Ibid., 39.

32. In other Latin American countries the use of head-of-household criteria excluded women from relief programs. Carmen Diana Deere argues that in Peru only one member of the household was officially designated the beneficiary of relief programs. Carmen Diana Deere, "Rural Women and Agrarian Reform in Peru, Chile and Cuba," in Nash and Safa, eds., *Women and Change in Latin America,* 190.

33. The Plan Chardón—which was the basis of some reforms established by the PPD during the 1940s—used the head-of-household criteria to remedy male unemployment. Dietz, *Economic History,* 153.

34. Even if the federal construction sector employed a minority of the male population, 3.1 percent of the labor force in 1940 and 4.5 percent in 1950, it showed the commitment of both the metropolitan and colonial state to remedy male unemployment. Enrique Lugo Silva, *The Tugwell Administration in Puerto Rico, 1941–1946* (México, D.F.: Editorial Cultura, 1955), 104–5.

35. The cult of feminine spiritual superiority—known as *marianismo*—argues that

women are morally superior to men. The PPD challenges women to become the spiritual and moral leaders of their homes by preventing husbands from selling votes. Evelyn P. Stevens, "Marianismo: The Other Face of Machismo," in Ann Pescatello, ed., *Female and Male in Latin America* (Pittsburgh: University of Pittsburgh Press, 1973), 91; and Elsa M. Chaney, *Supermadre: La mujer dentro de la política en América Latina* (México, D.F.: Fondo de Cultura Económica, 1992), 55–86.

36. *El Batey* (Puerto Rico), no. 2, January 1940.

37. During the 1930s and 1940s populism became a dominant ideology in some Latin American countries (Brazil, Mexico, Argentina, for example). Populist movements saw women as auxiliaries rather than active participants. See Sonia E. Álvarez, "Theoretical and Comparative Perspectives on Women's Movements and the State," in Álvarez, *Engendering Democracy*, 21–22.

38. *El Batey* (Puerto Rico), no. 2, April 1939.

39. Department of Labor, Industrial Supervision Service, *Annual Report of the Commissioner of Labor* (San Juan, Puerto Rico, 1941–42), 14.

40. Ibid., 14–15.

41. Ibid., 15–16.

42. Ibid., 18–19.

43. Department of Labor, Industrial Supervision Service, *Annual Report of the Commissioner of Labor* (San Juan, Puerto Rico, 1942–43), 14.

44. Ibid., 15.

45. Ibid., 14.

46. Women in Puerto Rican society were expected to take care of their children while performing homework for the needlework industry. Luisa Hernández Angueira, "El trabajo femenino a domicilio y la industria de la aguja en Puerto Rico, 1914–1940," in Baerga, *Género y trabajo*, 91. The fact that the Women's Work Section began investigations into this matter tell us that social workers were making comprehensive efforts toward improving the living and working conditions of working mothers. Ibid., 32–33.

47. Department of Labor, Industrial Supervision Service, *Annual Report of the Commissioner of Labor* (San Juan, Puerto Rico, 1943–44), 20.

48. Scholars like Lydia Milagros González and James L. Dietz calculated that the home needlework industry employed almost 100,000 workers if we take into account the assistance of helpers and other family members, and because there was substantial undercounting. Lydia Milagros González, "La industria de la aguja de Puerto Rico y sus orígenes en los Estados Unidos," in Baerga, *Género y trabajo,* 74; Dietz, *Economic History,* 224, n. 111.

49. Department of Labor, *Annual Report, 1943–44,* 21.

50. Dietz, *Economic History,* 225

51. Ibid., 224.

52. Ibid., 224.

53. The increase was also a consequence of several factors. Stricter controls by the U.S. government led to increases in wages and stronger enforcement of labor laws on the mainland, forcing some industries to send more materials to Puerto Rico. The accessibility of Puerto Rico to the American market and the exceptional maritime facilities for the transportation of products and materials from and to the Island gave needlework factories another incentive. After 1945 the needlework industry did not encounter the same problems with the transportation of materials and finished goods. Department of Labor, Women's Bureau, *Annual Report of the Commissioner of Labor* (San Juan, Puerto Rico, 1945–46), 27.

54. See note 48.

55. Department of Labor, *Annual Report, 1945–46, 27.*

56. By 1940 social and welfare workers accounted for only 2.0 percent (158) of female employment by occupation, and 3.9 percent (503) in 1950. The limited number of social workers reflected the disparity between this group and the 60,000 homeworkers who requested their assistance. Acevedo, "Industrialization and Employment", 243.

57. Dietz, *Economic History,* 226.

58. Department of Labor, *Annual Report, 1945–46,* 27.

59. Departamento del Trabajo, Negociado de la Mujer, *Leyes y organismos para la protección de la mujer en la industria* (San Juan, Puerto Rico, 1944), 13.

60. Ibid., 14.

61. Dietz, *Economic History,* 201.

62. Ibid., 226.

63. *Revista del Trabajo* (Puerto Rico) 4, no. 78 (October 15, 1945), 3.

64. Department of Labor, Women's Bureau, *Annual Report of the Commissioner of Labor* (San Juan, Puerto Rico, 1946–47), 22.

65. Department of Labor, Women's Bureau, *Annual Reports of the Commissioner of Labor* (San Juan, Puerto Rico, 1945–52).

66. Acevedo, "Industrialization and Employment," 241.

67. The middle sector became a modernizing elite by effectively creating the basis for industrialization. In doing this, they were successful in controlling the colonial state with its populist reforms. Hamza Alavi, "State and Class under Peripheral Capitalism," in Theodor Shanin and Hamza Alavi, eds., *Introduction to the Sociology of Developing Societies* (New York: Monthly Review Press, 1982), 294, 299–300. However, this idea was not exclusive of the Puerto Rican middle sector. Since the beginnings of the 1940s some members of the Roosevelt administration believed that the only possibility for the improvement of the Puerto Rican masses was the industrialization of the Island. Colonial administrators acting as intermediaries of the North American bourgeoisie would determine which sectors of the Puerto Rican economy could guarantee economic development and its prospects for the future. Robert H. Taft to Donald M. Nelson, March 12, 1943. Economic Development Corporation, Puerto Rican Development Corporation, *Annual Report of the Puerto Rican Development Corporation* (San Juan, Puerto Rico, 1943).

68. *Revista del Trabajo* (Puerto Rico) 3, no. 69 (May 31, 1945), 12. Capital letters in original.

69. *Revista del Trabajo* (Puerto Rico), 5, no. 75 (August 31, 1945), 4.

70. Manicom, *Ruling Relations,* 456.

71. Harriet P. Presser, *Sterilization and Fertility Decline in Puerto Rico* (California: Institute of International Studies, 1973); Bonnie Mass, "Puerto Rico: A Case Study of Population Control," *Latin American Perspectives* 4, no. 15 (Fall 1977): 66–81; and Annette Ramírez de Arellano and Conrad Seipp, *Colonialism, Catholicism and Contraception* (Chapel Hill: University of North Carolina Press, 1983).

72. *Revista del Trabajo* (Puerto Rico) 5, no. 99 (August 31, 1946), 7.

73. The articles in *El Batey,* the newspaper of the PPD, from 1939 to 1942 reflected an intense attack on the sugar sector and the encouragement that sugar cane workers should fight for their rights. However, for home needleworkers, it is in 1945 that the *Revista del Trabajo* begins with a similar campaign. *Revista del Trabajo* (Puerto Rico) 5, no. 75 (October 15, 1945), 3.

74. Ibid., 3–4.

75. Acevedo, "Industrialization and Employment," 234.

76. Silvestrini and Luque de Sánchez, *Historia de Puerto Rico,* 525.

77. Department of Labor, Women and Children's Bureau, *Annual Report of the Commissioner of Labor* (San Juan, Puerto Rico, 1950–51), 32.

78. Álvarez, "Theoretical and Comparative Perspectives," 30.

10

Labor Migrants or Submissive Wives: Competing Narratives of Puerto Rican Women in the Post–World War II Era

Carmen Teresa Whalen

Sitting in the Norris Square Senior Citizens' Center in North Philadelphia, Doña Epifanía reminisced about growing up in Coamo, Puerto Rico, and about migrating to Philadelphia. Born in 1919, she was raised with eleven siblings on a farm of eighty-nine *cuerdas*.[1] She recalled, "We lived from the crops and the animals. . . . We harvested a lot. . . . The only thing we sold were the *gandules* [pigeon peas]. . . . My mother worked a lot in the kitchen." She and her mother also took in home sewing. In 1954, as a single parent in search of a "better life," she decided to migrate to the Philadelphia area when a man she knew told her "that there were beans to cook." She cooked for fourteen Puerto Rican agricultural laborers for two years. When she moved to Philadelphia, she stayed with a friend who took her to the garment factory where she worked. Doña Epifanía was hired that day and stayed with the company for seventeen years, until the company moved to Florida. Doña Epifanía then retired.[2]

Doña Epifanía considered herself a "worker." She included herself in the "we" that farmed and provided for the family, adding, "I am the one that helped my father the most." Reflecting on her life, she noted, "I've spent my life working since I was six years old," and remarked, "I don't complain because I was a worker." Doña Epifanía's definition of "work" included a broad range of reproductive and productive labor.[3] Like Doña Epifanía, other migrant women used a broad definition of "work" to validate their many and diverse tasks. They contributed to their household economies in Puerto Rico and in Philadelphia, and did so in a variety of ways. The narratives of Puerto Rican women migrants to Philadelphia suggest the need for a revised definition of labor migration. Puerto Rican women, I argue, were labor migrants in the post–World War II era; they were displaced from Puerto Rico's rural economies, they were recruited as a source of cheap labor, and they migrated in search of work. To consider Puerto Rican women as labor migrants requires attention to sexual divisions of labor in sending and receiving societies and a definition of "labor" that encompasses subsistence labor within the household, paid employment within or beyond the household, informal economic activities, and community work whether paid or unpaid.[4]

Yet Puerto Rican women's narratives and my interpretation of them are just one of the discourses on Puerto Rican women in the post–World War II era. Competing narratives emerged as policy makers in Puerto Rico and in the continental United States constructed their own gendered narratives. Puerto Rican women were at the nexus of policy makers' plans for the island's economic development, which entailed industrialization and the reduction of the population. While policy makers focused on women's reproductive roles, they also portrayed them as a source of cheap labor. In the continental United States, policy makers and social service agencies interpreted the experiences of Puerto Rican women through the emerging culture of poverty paradigm. This was a national discourse that retained the focus on women's reproduction and "overpopulation" while rendering Puerto Rican women's work—their subsistence labor, paid employment, and community work—invisible. This essay examines the ways in which an emphasis on women's reproductive and/or productive roles and definitions of "work" shaped these competing narratives of Puerto Rican women.

Memories of Migration

Puerto Rican women described their migrations from Puerto Rico to Philadelphia in economic terms, emphasizing the impact of changing economic conditions in their local communities and the threats to their rural household economies. In Philadelphia they struggled to recreate their household economies.[5] Although the contexts and the tasks changed with migration, they emphasized the continuity in caring for their families. Domestic responsibilities were theirs, and, at the same time, paid employment within or outside the household was a very real and constant possibility as well as an economic necessity. Contributing to their households encompassed their reproductive and productive tasks, and, at least in retrospect, they validated the work they did in raising their children. These women balanced "productive" and "reproductive" labor in ways that challenge the scholarly distinction between them and that foster a redefinition of labor migration.

Doña Carmen emphasized the economic motivations in explaining her and her husband's decision to leave San Lorenzo for Philadelphia in 1947:

This period of '47 was pretty slow, there wasn't work. There were schools, there was a life, you see, in town, but there wasn't enough for everyone to have a better life. So, what we did was plan for the family, like us, we planned to go to the United States.

Her husband, Don Quintín, drove the town's ambulance. She had worked in a library, in a school, and in Humacao's district court. Then, as she recalled, "I started working for myself." She ran a small thrift shop and sold produce, and cooked at home, catering to the town's wealthier residents and providing lunches for the women who worked at the nearby tobacco factory. She enjoyed this work, but rationing during the war had hurt her business. In 1946, Don Quintín came to the Philadelphia area with a labor contract for seasonal farm work. Doña Carmen followed within the year, selling all of their possessions and bringing their four children with her.[6]

Yet Doña Carmen and other Puerto Rican women did not just follow their husbands. Many came with the intention of finding paid employment in Philadelphia. Doña Carmen went looking for work the day after she arrived. Referring to two friends, she recalled, "I went with them at sunrise to look for work. . . . We came to a garment factory and they needed two people but not three and I told him give it to them and I left. But the 'boss' said that you needed these little scissors and nobody had them, and I went searching for them." Although she never found the scissors, she did find a job—packing shoes at the J. Edward Shoe Company, where she worked for seven years. Married women like Doña Carmen, female heads of household like Doña Epifanía, and single women migrated to Philadelphia in search of jobs. In the postwar era, the city's economy provided jobs for Puerto Rican women in the secondary sector, especially in the garment and food processing industries. By 1950, 33 percent of Puerto Rican women were in the labor force, compared to 34 percent of women citywide.[7]

Doña Margarita emphasized the work she did to take care of her eight children and described the impact of migration on this work. In 1954, she left Santurce and joined her husband, Don Marcelino, in Philadelphia. They already had four children when her husband came to the States with a labor contract for seasonal agricultural work because "the children were already growing and everything was getting more expensive." He left the farm, found an apartment in Philadelphia, and sent for Doña Margarita and the children. The family moved several times between Philadelphia and Santurce. Initially, she recounted that she did not work until after the youngest child was born, but as she continued her narrative this became more complex.[8]

Doña Margarita considered her domestic duties "work." She remarked of her life in Santurce, "But at home I had more than enough work because there was the house, the obligations of the house, getting those that were already going to school ready, washing, going to the public spigot to get on line. It wasn't like everyone had their own plumbing. . . . Then you had to wash diapers, there were no pampers. . . . Nothing by machine, nothing, nothing of convenience or anything, all of this was by hand." She stressed her dedication in caring for her children, "With my children, I raised them myself—none of this someone giving you a hand." In Philadelphia, everyday tasks became easier, while financial hardships created new challenges. She recalled, "You know, when I arrived here, well, everything was different. . . . There I had to wash everything with a washboard, carry all that water. . . . There I had to cook with wood, and then the stove we had—when we were a little better off—was one of those stoves where you put that tank of gas that you had to buy, natural gas." In Philadelphia, she had indoor plumbing and a modern gas stove, and she added, "The milkmen came and left the milk outside; yes, and in the morning, you got up and got your milk, the newspaper and the bread." When they could not afford rice and beans, however, she learned to make a cornmeal mash for her children.

For Doña Margarita, working outside the home was a very real possibility but was complicated by her extensive domestic responsibilities. She had started working as a live-in domestic when she was 12 years old, after her mother died. A few years later, she had her first child and went to live with Don Marcelino. "At least I got a good husband along the way because he never let me work during this period, you see. And I went to work after I had already had the last baby, because it was too much," she reflected, referring to combining paid employment with domestic responsibilities. Her husband died when he was 47 years old and she was 40. She explained, "The baby was already born, and then after that was when I could, you know, look for work. I began then to work." This period of having children, however, appeared as a brief and incomplete hiatus in her work life.

Doña Margarita found paid employment in Santurce and Philadelphia. In Santurce, she contributed to the family's income with paid work within the household. She explained, "I didn't work outside but, yes, there were people who told me 'iron these clothes for me.' . . . So they brought me the clothes and at home, I earned a few dollars, too." In Philadelphia, she and her husband worked on farms for several summers. She recalled, "The worst of my jobs was when my children were growing, here, when we first got here with my husband. So, during the summer we took them to the farms to pick fruits, blueberries. . . . We took them during the summer, to not leave them alone." Several years later, she decided to try working outside the home. She worked for about three months at Whitman's, packing chocolates. She explained, "It occurred to me to try working, but my husband didn't want me to . . . because I had to come from the factory and deal with the house too. It was a lot. . . . It was too much for me, the struggle with the children."

Instead, she contributed to her household through informal economic activities. She helped her comadre (grandmother) and neighbor, who ran a day care and a guest house out of her home. Her oldest children were in school and she took her younger children with her. She described the routine, "After I finished my things in the house, I went to my comadre's house to help her with the children, to feed and bathe them. . . . So then on Fridays when they [the parents] paid her, she always gave me something." Once the children were picked up, she and her comadre began cooking for the men who rented rooms. Again, "So when they paid her, she always gave me a few dollars, and all the food that was left over." She took the food home for her family's dinner. Hence, while her children were younger, Doña Margarita contributed to the household economy by caring for her children and her household, and by working with her comadre and bringing home food and some money.

While balancing paid employment and domestic responsibilities, which were clearly hers, remained difficult, she became confident of her skills and her worth as a worker. When she and her family returned to Santurce in the early 1960s, she worked at an elastics factory, starting on the 3 to 11 P.M. shift. She recalled, "My husband worked during the day and I went at night, but when he arrived I had left the children bathed and . . . all of the food made and everything. . . . We almost didn't see each other in this period because when I arrived, he had already left." She continued, "Yes, I learned it and they made me, I became, supervisor of the night shift but I had to leave this shift because it was very, very difficult for me, very difficult. It was 11 to 7 in the morning. Then after, I came home to deal with the children and it was very little that I could sleep." She decided to relinquish her position as a supervisor and return to the day shift. She explained, "They were the ones that needed me . . . and they changed me without any protest because they knew that I had not asked them for this shift; it was them that asked me to do the favor." After her husband died, Doña Margarita continued at the elastics factory. When she returned to Philadelphia, she found work cleaning people's houses and then working in a box factory.

In addition to paid employment and domestic responsibilities, Puerto Rican women in Philadelphia included "community work" in their definitions of work and minimized the distinctions between paid and unpaid community work. After several years at the shoe factory, Doña Carmen began a long career in human services. Rather than emphasizing the change in jobs, she stressed the continuity in helping the community. She stressed her efforts "to help Hispanics, with housing, with family, with school, with problems." She translated for people at the hospitals, welfare offices, and in the courts. She taught them the English words they needed to buy items at the store. Doña Carmen had been attending the 5th Street Methodist Church, and keeping the guest register as a volunteer. While she was on vacation from the shoe factory, the pastor hired her to work in the church's community center. She recalled, "He hired me as a social worker . . . and that's how I began."[9] For more than ten years, she organized after-school activities for children, Christmas parties, and classes, while also helping people with food and clothing. Later, she worked for the city and continued her studies at Temple University. In the early 1970s, she became the director of the Norris Square Senior Citizens' Center, where she worked for more than twenty years. In her advocacy work for Puerto Ricans, whether paid or unpaid, Doña Carmen saw continuity. In 1992, she reminisced, "I've been a fighter since the first days—for my Puerto Rico. . . . I'm still fighting."[10]

Similarly, Doña María, who was born in Philadelphia in 1930, blurred the distinctions between her unpaid and paid work for the community. When I asked her how she came to work for the Board of Education, she emphasized her earlier involvement with community-based school associations and told me the story of a young boy who came to the doctor's office where she was the receptionist. He had been placed in a bilingual Spanish class even though he did not speak Spanish. Doña María concluded her story, "So I said, 'Don't worry about it, I'll take care of that for you.' So even when I wasn't working, I was working and explaining to them the schools." Here, Doña María implied that even though her paid job was as a receptionist, her real work was helping this young person mediate the school system. As she described her job with the Board of Education, she emphasized its community dimensions. She recalled, "I started the program with four other ladies and myself. . . . The most important part was communication with the parents, going to their houses and giving them information in Spanish. . . . I got to know people in my block, you know, it wasn't like the whole area was strangers." Doña María merged paid and unpaid community work in her narrative and in her life as she continued doing both.[11]

Doña María added community work to the already challenging demands of paid employment and domestic responsibilities.[12] Before she married, she had worked in a dry cleaners and in an umbrella factory. After she was married, she worked at a baking factory, decorating and packing cakes, and she had five children, one of whom died. Her mother or her aunt took care of the children while she was at work. As for the rest of her household duties, she recalled, referring to her husband, "In a way everything was convenient because I was able to get back before he came back and . . . do all the cooking and this and that, and it was done so he didn't have to worry about it. It didn't interfere with the children or with our relationship as long as everything was in place." Clearly, domestic responsibilities remained hers. In addition, as a merchant marine, her husband was away from home often, and they divorced when their youngest daughter was about five years old. As she took on more community work, she did not view this work as a conflict with her responsibilities to her children. Instead, she explained, "All of the things I did together with my kids. I enjoyed doing it together, also, with my kids so that they were able to see things and understand." She took her children, and often their friends, to community events, such as the Puerto Rican Day Parade, which she helped to organize.

Puerto Rican women's narratives reveal the complexities of women's work and provide the basis for a redefinition of labor migration.[13] Women described the impact of economic changes and their search for *mejor ambiente*, or "a better life." Recreating their household economies in Philadelphia meant some combination of caring for their children in a very different environment, finding paid employment, participating in informal economic activities, and fostering the well-being of the Puerto Rican community. They viewed paid employment as part of their responsibilities in contributing to the maintenance of their households; and although most found it challenging to balance household and paid work, they did not express this as a conflict in roles. Instead, paid employment was a possibility, and the nature and rhythm of paid employment were shaped by their other responsibilities to their households. This was an era when jobs for Puerto Rican women were available, even as the types of jobs were limited and the wages low. For many, the balancing of reproductive and productive work resulted in the *double day*. Women remained responsible for domestic duties even as they secured paid employment. Women and their husbands sometimes worked different shifts so that the children were cared for by one of them. Yet, some left the children bathed and the dinner cooked, like Doña Margarita, or came home from work to take care of the domestic duties, like Doña María. In some instances, men shared in domestic tasks. It was often the eldest daughters, however, that helped their mothers with the domestic work of the household. In addition, these women emphasized the continuities in contributing to their households, even as migration changed the contexts of those contributions. Here, their narratives challenge persisting notions that work is something that migrating women discover in the host society. In their narratives, Puerto Rican women used a definition of work that extended beyond paid employment outside the home to include work within the household, paid and unpaid, and community work, paid and unpaid.

Narratives of Puerto Rican Women in Puerto Rico

In Puerto Rico, policy makers' narratives of Puerto Rican women encompassed reproductive and productive roles, but only in limited ways. Instead of the decline of rural household economies, policy makers attributed Puerto Rico's economic woes to "overpopulation" and focused on women in their efforts to reduce the population. Policy makers did not, however, acknowledge women's other reproductive and productive contributions to their households. As policy makers pursued industrialization by invitation, they marketed women as a source of cheap labor. Yet they circumscribed their definition of their work to traditional areas of women's work and to women as supplementary wage earners. These limited notions of women's reproductive and productive roles and the resultant contradictions emerged most clearly in policy makers' program to send women to the continental United States as contracted domestics.

As Puerto Rico's rural economies declined, policy makers blamed "overpopulation" and women's reproduction. A 1944 study circulated by the Puerto Rico Planning Board suggested a consensus on overpopulation and emphasized the role of "mothers." According to the study's authors, "that the basic problem of Puerto Rico is the maladjustment between resources and population is clearly the conclusion of most serious students." They predicted that "the pressure of population on resources, which is already great, will become intolerably greater." By way of solutions, the authors called for "a conscious policy of emigration and birth control." Sensitive to legal restrictions, the authors noted that, "the teaching of contraceptive methods in Puerto Rico has been restricted to mothers who require freedom from pregnancy or spaced pregnancies for their physical health." They continued, "Post-partum sterilization is practiced to a certain extent on a voluntary basis to protect the mother whose health would be endangered by further pregnancies." They suggested, nonetheless, the potentials of expanding both contraception and sterilization. They called for "a continued expansion of the present work" in contraceptive education and considered it "a very small sum to pay annually for the stabilization of Puerto Rico's population." In regard to sterilization, they hinted only that "more could have been performed if facilities had permitted."[14] More sterilizations were subsequently performed. By 1965, one-third of Puerto Rican women between the ages of 20 and 49 had been sterilized, "a rate significantly higher than that of any other country."[15]

As policy makers promoted industrialization, Puerto Rican women emerged as a source of cheap labor. In addition to a complete tax holiday for U.S. corporations in Puerto Rico, the other major attraction of Puerto Rico was low wages for workers, especially women.[16] The minimum wage provision of the Fair Labor Standards Act was not applied in Puerto Rico. Instead, minimum wages in Puerto Rico were determined on an industry-by-industry basis by special committees appointed by the secretary of labor. Recognizing the importance of wage differentials in attracting U.S. industries to Puerto Rico, the ruling political party, the Partido Popular Democrático, opposed the application of the minimum wage in Puerto Rico. In U.S. congressional hearings in 1949, Teodoro Moscoso, the president of the Puerto Rico Industrial Development Company, argued against applying the minimum wage and for "the beauty of this flexible arrangement." Moscoso insisted that low wages, which were approximately 60 percent of those in the United States, and tax incentives did not constitute an unfair recruitment of U.S. companies. In addition, he asserted Puerto Ricans' willingness to work in the least desirable jobs:

> There are certain industries in the United States, Mr. Congressman, which are not looked upon as very desirable. . . . If you go to the United States, to New York, to almost any hotel, you will find that the bus boy or the fellow who scrubs the floor . . . is a Puerto Rican. Well, in Puerto Rico proper, we believe that a lot of jobs, from which people shy away in the States might eventually come down here.

Hence, he argued, wages were low and workers were willing.[17]

Policy makers encouraged labor-intensive, export-oriented industries, like the garment and textile industries, to come to Puerto Rico. Moscoso explained,

"Well, our interest in textiles started pretty much at the beginning of our program . . . we started to look around for a wide-awake firm that could take this mill and operate it for us." He connected the relocation of industry with low wages: "they [New England] are losing the type of industry which people just don't like to work in. A lot of people in New England just don't like to work in a textile mill, because now they can earn much better wages in more skilled operations." He suggested that if these firms did not come to Puerto Rico, many would go to the southern states where wages were lower and labor was unorganized.[18] Similarly, a 1949 pamphlet entitled "Puerto Rico's Potential as a Site for Textile, Apparel and Other Industries" asserted Puerto Rico's benefits, including an abundance of workers, high unemployment and underemployment, "orderly and tranquil" labor relations, and "very few strikes." Emphasizing the availability of women workers, it noted, "Workers in the needlework industry, both men and women, but mostly the latter, are many and are noted for their dexterity and their industry." Labor laws had "recently been liberalized to permit night work for women in textile industries." Perhaps most important, wages in the needlework industry were only 26 percent of those in the United States. The pamphlet concluded, "In virtually all lines and stages of textile and apparel manufacturing the current wage structure of Puerto Rico offers the possibility of substantial advantages to the entrepreneur."[19]

These industries relied on the cheap labor of Puerto Rican women in their homes and in the new factories. By the 1949 congressional hearings, employees of the new U.S. plants numbered 3,793 in shops and 3,440 home workers. Moscoso noted, "The Executive Council of Puerto Rico has adopted a policy that they don't want to stimulate home work," but concluded, "frankly, my personal point of view is that sometimes I get desperate and I wish that even if it were home workers, we wish we had them. Sometimes we just won't be able to avoid all of the evils of industrialization."[20] Even as the home needlework industry declined, new industries continued to employ women. In 1950, the Puerto Rico Industrial Development Company was divided in two, as the Company remained a semi-autonomous public corporation making loans and renting buildings, and the Economic Development Administration or Fomento became the agency responsible for promoting industrialization. By 1952, the apparel and food processing industries provided the majority of new manufacturing jobs. By 1963, Fomento plants employed 70,000 workers, and 60 percent of the new jobs were filled by women. As sociologist Palmira Ríos contends, women's work was "the key to the survival of these highly competitive industries in the new global economy."[21]

Despite policies that increased women's employment, policy makers continued to define women as supplemental earners and to reinforce existing sexual divisions of labor. As the home needlework industry declined, policy makers were loath to consider the displaced women as unemployed. In a 1957 speech, Secretary of Labor Fernando Sierra Berdecia identified 53,000 of the 108,000 people who had joined those "not in the labor force" between 1950 and 1956 as "housewives." Yet, some of Sierra's "housewives" were probably unemployed women, as employment in the home needlework industry had decreased by 29,000 in the same period.[22] Similarly, David Ross, a former employee of the Industrial Development Company, attributed the decreasing labor force first to migration, then to "the voluntary withdrawal from the labor force of unemployed home needle workers for whom no alternative employment opportunities existed." Ross, perhaps unaware of the contradiction, did not explain how women's withdrawal from the labor force could be considered "voluntary" when no other "employment opportunities existed"[23] As Ríos argues, Fomento supported traditional gender divisions of labor.[24] Acknowledging that the beneficiaries of industrialization had been "the major cities, their surrounding metropolitan areas, and city women," Fomento concluded. "It is in the country where additional jobs for men are most needed," and called for more dispersed industrialization, especially heavy industries, that would employ men in rural areas.[25]

Policy makers' contract labor program for domestics highlighted their concerns with overpopulation and the gender-based nature of their contract labor programs. Policy makers were willing to consider women as workers only in areas traditionally defined as "women's work." In 1947, policy makers turned to contract labor as a solution to "overpopulation," and again they focused on women. Their first postwar program was a contract labor program for young, unmarried women to work as domestics in the continental United States. A 1947 Emigration Advisory Committee meeting concluded that "immediate energies should be concentrated on plans for a program for training domestic workers . . . and for helping them get established in the States."[26] This was state-sponsored migration, as the government of Puerto Rico assumed responsibility for recruiting, screening, and training workers and for the labor contract. Labor contracts were signed by the employer and the employee, and were approved by the commissioner of labor of Puerto Rico. The New York State Employment Service arranged the placements for Puerto Rican domestics.

Policy makers' focus on young women revealed their goal of reducing the population. They were optimistic about the demographic effects, but hesitant to proclaim them publicly. Donald J. O'Connor, chief economist of the Office of Puerto Rico, cautioned, "What need not be made clear, except in executive sessions of the legislative committees, is the demographic effect of female emigration." He estimated that 300 jobs on the mainland per week for the next decade or so would halve the projected population figures.[27] For a mere one hundred dollars, he calculated, "one young woman and five unborn children can be transported to the States." The cost to the insular government compared favorably to the costs of education, relief, and health care should this "brood" remain on the island. The program for "young unmarried women" would compensate for the fact that they have "fewer opportunities to save enough for a trip to the mainland, and to work their own way than do boys." O'Connor concluded optimistically, "If Ireland could depopulate itself by emigration, Puerto Rico can."[28]

Planners foresaw additional benefits to the emigration of women, based on traditional gender roles. Women would spark informal networks, send money home, foster dispersion, and reduce the social tensions associated with settlement. O'Connor explained, "It is also obvious that girls, with their typically strong family loyalties will send for their kin" or at least "provide advance-guards which would make easy the entrance of late-comers." A "girl" would "send the amount of her loan, and more, back to her kin for family emergencies and for family travel."[29] In addition, domestics were to be invisible migrants. The first group of thirty trained "girls" were sent to Scarsdale, New York, which was chosen as "a small community with civic agencies that have promised to cooperate in helping the Puerto Rican girls adjust to life in a new country."[30] Although small communities were preferred, O'Connor assumed that even "our relatively wealthy Northeastern cities . . . could each take a hundred trained girls every month and be quite unconscious of their presence as a group in the city for a long time."[31]

Planners emphasized the compatibility of the program with women's roles, merging women's productive and reproductive roles. The training covered household techniques, English, and personal hygiene. Domestic training kept women's limited options open, so that "They need not look forward to a lifetime of domestic service. The capable ones who display initiative will find opportunities in the field of hotel and other institutional housekeeping. . . . And there is always the possibility of marriage on the continent."[32] O'Connor suggested that training prepare the "girls" for domestic work in the States or in Puerto Rico and "should serve them well as mothers and wives." Hence, training should also cover how to "appreciate and use community opportunities for getting acquainted, getting along, getting ahead and getting married."[33] The possibility that domestics would marry in the States increased the potentials for depopulation, for dispersion, and for an "invisible" and problem-free migration.

Although it contracted women as laborers, the program for domestics was based on traditional notions of gender roles and sexual divisions of labor. As a result, labor contracts stipulated working conditions and appropriate behavior for the domestics. The terms and conditions were an improvement over those offered by private recruitment agents, but still fell below those prevailing in urban areas in the States. The one-year labor contracts provided a minimum of $25.00 per week with an increase of $2.50 every three months and a minimum salary of $35.00 per week if employment continued at the end of the contract year. Hours were specified as a maximum of ten hours per day and forty-eight hours per week, with additional hours on call not to exceed three nights per week nor four hours per night. Yet the contract allowed work in excess of these hours provided that it was compensated at double the hourly wage. Puerto Rican women were again marketed as a source of cheap and willing labor. The employees, in turn, agreed to do the work to the employers' specifications, "to maintain a neat and appropriate personal appearance," and "to maintain the decorum of the household, especially with respect to her own guests and her deportment in public."[34]

Despite ambitious goals, the program was short-lived. O'Connor had hoped that "A program pitched toward an *eventual* teaching load of ten thousand girls (and women) per year would not be over-ambitious, inasmuch as the population is expanding so rapidly."[35] The initial proposal called for eight training centers throughout the island, each of which would train sixty "girls" during three-month terms.[36] In February 1948, the first group of twenty-one trained "girls," 18 to 35 years old, were placed in households in Scarsdale, New York. But in October 1949, Petra América Pagán de Colón, director of Puerto Rico's Migration Division, declared the program a "success" and "suspended." The numbers of placements were not high enough for Puerto Rico's policy makers. Pagán de Colón wrote to the Employment and Migration Office in New York. Since "the New York Employment Office could not help us in the placement of large groups of girls," Pagán de Colón explained, "this Program has been suspended and the funds are being used in the training of workers for the hotel industry."[37] Puerto Rico's policy makers had found other "appropriate" work for women in Puerto Rico's expanding tourism industry and had instituted another gender-based contract labor program for men to work as seasonal agricultural laborers on farms in the States.

Policy makers' narratives of Puerto Rican women stressed their roles in "overpopulation" and marketed them as cheap labor. Instead of addressing the decline of rural household economies that included the labor of women, policy makers considered the employment of men more important than that of women. With both the contract labor program for domestics and employment in Fomento firms, Puerto Rican women were cast as appropriate only for jobs traditionally defined as women's work and were still perceived as supplementary wage earners. Even as women's employment in industry increased, policy makers continued to focus on women's roles in reducing Puerto Rico's population. Ross hoped that manufacturing jobs for women would do "more to promote the cause of birth control than all the free clinics that have been operated since the 1930s."[38] As historians Annette B. Ramírez de Arellano and Conrad Seipp suggest, Fomento and the Family Planning Association "enlisted the industrialists' cooperation in checking population growth by stressing the conflict between reproduction and production." Health clinics were established at plants employing women.[39]

Narratives of Puerto Rican Women in the Continental United States

As Puerto Rican women arrived in the continental United States, policy makers and social service workers constructed a "culture of poverty" narrative to interpret their experiences. The culture of poverty was a national discourse, with important local and gendered dimensions, that attributed Puerto Ricans' perceived problems to their culture. Anthropologist Oscar Lewis considered "poverty and its associated traits as a culture . . . with its own structure and rationale, as a way of life which is passed down from generation to generation along family lines." Lewis severed the culture of poverty from the conditions of poverty so that it came to be seen as self-perpetuating and equated with the "national culture" of Puerto Rico. Migrating Puerto Ricans carried this culture of poverty with them; "many of the problems of Puerto Ricans in New York have their origin in the slums of Puerto Rico." For Lewis, the culture of poverty was characterized by little integration with the larger society, little organization in the ethnic community, families that verbally emphasized unity but rarely achieved it, and individuals with a high tolerance for pathologies.[40] The culture of poverty's emphasis on culture, family, and generations implied that women, traditionally held responsible for these domains, were to blame for the "problems" affecting their families and their communities.

The culture of poverty deemed the Puerto Rican family "defective" in comparison to both European peasant families and perceived U.S. norms. For Nathan Glazer and Daniel Patrick Moynihan, poverty was often mitigated by "the existence of a network of culture, religion, art, custom that gives strength and grace and meaning to a life of hardship; and . . . the existence of a strong family system that again enhances life." This was not the case for Puerto Rico, they concluded: "In both these aspects Puerto Rico was sadly defective." In short, Puerto Ricans lacked a "network of culture" and "a strong family system," and as a result, they lacked "the basis for an improvement in life."[41]

Within this narrative, women were portrayed as failures in their reproductive roles. They were "submissive wives" who had too many children, and inadequate mothers. In 1950, C. Wright Mills, Clarence Senior, and Rose Kohn Goldsen summarized the role of the Puerto Rican woman: "The woman is supposed to be submissive, and her submissiveness is guaranteed by a network of manners and politenesses which confines her major sphere of activities to the home, circumscribes her social contacts, and places her under constant surveillance." They contrasted this to their perception of the U.S. norm: "Compared with the continental American family types, however, the despotic father-husband relationship is the dominant island pattern."[42] Similarly, Joseph Fitzpatrick maintained, "in contrast to the characteristics of cooperation and companionship of American families, the woman in Puerto Rico has a subordinate role . . . the wife's role is culturally defined and ordinarily maintained as subordinate to the authority of the husband."[43]

Like their counterparts in Puerto Rico, U.S. policy makers continued to focus on reproduction and attributed Puerto Ricans' "problems" to the fact that they had too many children. U.S. policy makers, however, linked the "population problem" to the other assumed "problem" of Puerto Ricans—lack of a work ethic and welfare dependency. Here, women's roles as workers were ignored, as a basic tenet of the culture of poverty was the lack of a work ethic and the desire for welfare dependency. Glazer and Moynihan defined the "population problem" as a cultural tendency to have too many children, a tendency that migrated with Puerto Ricans to New York City. They wrote, "But old attitudes exist alongside new ones, old-style families alongside new ones, and meanwhile there is a very heavy Puerto Rican birth rate in the city." Hence, "the population problem has been transferred rather than transformed." For Glazer and Moynihan, many of the community's "problems" stemmed from this high birth rate, which fostered poor mothering and dependency. Asking "what kind of care the children get from these mothers," they answered that the main "problem" was "overprotection." Linking overpopulation and dependency, they concluded, "The special misfortune that consigns so many Puerto Ricans to the relief rolls is their large number of children." This became a "circle of dependency," and from this perspective, "The culture of public welfare . . . is as relevant for the future of Puerto Ricans in the city as the culture of Puerto Rico."[44] The high rates of sterilization for Puerto Rican women continued in New York City.[45]

In Philadelphia, policy makers and social service workers drew on the national discourse and shared many of its assumptions. The local discourse mirrored the national discourse in its focus on "problems," the cultural roots of those problems, the lack of a work ethic, and the lack of community organizations. The clearest articulation of Puerto Ricans' lack of a work ethic and its cultural determinants appeared in a 1958 survey by the Friends' Neighborhood Guild. As was often the case, these views were expressed by those most involved with and most interested in assisting Puerto Ricans.[46] The study asserted:

> The Puerto Ricans just do not want to work in many cases. . . . The excuses they invent as to why they didn't need that particular job all cover up the underlying fact that they are very lazy and would prefer to think of ways to collect relief money for not doing anything than look for jobs. . . . It all has to do with the greatest factor of all we must cope with in dealing with the Puerto Rican, the Latin mentality and the Latin tradition which is against work and which sees fit to have the women of the lower class bring in the pay while the man sits home.

Here, Puerto Ricans were portrayed as "lazy" and wanting "to collect relief money." The root of the problem was cultural, located in "the Latin mentality and the Latin tradition" and not in factors such as the economic structure of Philadelphia or employment opportunities. The survey, nonetheless, urged the Guild to "take part in helping them." At the same time, the survey expressed concern with Puerto Ricans' dependency; "let it [the Guild] be known as a place that one does not just come to when one needs a handout. . . . The Guild should tell those with whom it deals that they can do it all themselves and that they should want to, furthermore. Otherwise, we are just breeding a generation of outstretched hands."[47]

Puerto Rican women were again portrayed as "submissive wives" and deficient mothers. Of Latin men, the Guild's survey explained, "If he works during the day, his wife is to stay home where she belongs and not go running around. He is basically very jealous and arbitrary and any Latin woman knows better than to cross him."[48] Like the national discourse, observations on Puerto Rican women were often couched as comparisons to assumed U.S. norms. The Commission on Human Relations emphasized the impact of migration: "The Puerto Rican woman, subservient to the male of the island finds the United States offering a different and vastly improved role in society." The States offered "a multitude of social contacts and diversions outside the home."[49] Puerto Rican women, as "submissive wives," were not considered very good mothers. The Health and Welfare Council complained of a Puerto Rican and African American neighborhood that "school nurses see great neglect on the part of most parents in caring for their children's health problems." Although poverty was mentioned as a contributing factor, the study emphasized instead that "Health superstitions and folkways still prevail with many residents." In short, the study offered a cultural explanation and "neglect."[50] Similarly, the Guild's survey expressed frustration in recruiting Puerto Rican children for summer camp, "I ran into the Latin traditions again as a stopping block . . . no mother is willing to take the responsibility of saying that her child can go to camp for fear that something might happen to him and then she could expect the firing squad from her husband. The father is still the boss."[51] Here, the "submissive wife" and the Puerto Rican mother failed to "take responsibility" for her own children.

In Philadelphia, contradictions emerged as social service workers acknowledged women's high labor force participation but portrayed them as "submissive wives" who worked. Social service workers suggested that Puerto Rican women worked precisely because they were "submissive wives" and because of their husbands' other "culture of poverty" traits. Yet they also portrayed women's employment as a threat to men's masculinity and to the Puerto Rican family, which was already considered "defective." The Guild's survey emphasized the "cultural" roots of women's employment:

> [T]here is a tendency because of old Latin traditions to let the wife work among the lower classes while the husband watches television, which he rarely understands, but he likes the noise and pictures! . . . In one house I actually found three very healthy men in their mid-twenties sitting around while the wife of one and her cousin worked in a factory.[52]

Social service workers assumed that women's employment was something new and one of the "benefits" for women in the States. Stressing the impact of migration, the Commission on Human Relations noted, "the Puerto Rican woman finds . . . it easy to get a job, the pay is far better than on the island and the new wage-earning ability raises her status in the family to the point where she is equal, and sometimes superior, to the male." This employment and women's new ideas about "freedom" caused concern and the Commission cautioned that "they may affect the husband's role as undisputed head of the family. And if the wives are employed outside the household, the husbands find that their authority over their wives is seriously threatened."[53] Similarly, the Nationalities Services Center concluded, "the fact that a woman might have an easier time to earn higher pay than her husband is a threat to the family constellation."[54]

When Petra Pagán de Colón, as director of Puerto Rico's Migration Division, attended a meeting of a social service agency in Philadelphia, she challenged social service workers' stereotypes and highlighted the differing narratives in Puerto Rico and the States. In their meeting notes, the Nationalities Services Committee commented with some surprise, "Mainlanders have often misconceptions about family constellation in Puerto Rico. It was brought out that women are not completely subordinate to their husbands, but in meetings it was observed that they make as much of a contribution as do their husbands." There was another revelation, "It was also found that those workers who had the closest contacts with the Puerto Rican migrants, even though in the beginning they felt them strange and to be so very different, they eventually gained the most positive attitudes about them. They discovered that Puerto Ricans had a long tradition of hard, diligent labor."[55]

Social service workers were also concerned by their perceptions that Puerto Ricans lacked community, a defining characteristic of the culture of poverty. The Guild's survey reflected this view, as well as the assumption that community leaders had to be men: "The crux of the problem lies not in the lack of material, or at least on men with an underlying potential to be the focal point of the neighborhood, but rather in another of the factors that make up the Latin mentality—a complete lack of any social responsibility." Again, the perceived problem, a lack of community, was portrayed as having cultural roots, "the Latin mentality." The Guild used a narrow definition of community, equating community with organizations: "There is no real sense of community spirit and unity as there may be with other nationality groups where you find clubs and all sorts of organizations." The survey conceded, however, "There may not be any community unity among the Puerto Ricans, but there is definitely a warmth within the neighborhood itself and those who like it, really like it." The survey concluded by revealing both the limitations of their narrow definition of community and the invisibility of women's community work: "in the process of becoming Americanized, suggestions are always welcome and the way is made easier just by wanting to help. There are groups doing just that at the moment. One is a group of Puerto Rican women who . . . work their heads off just going around within the community instructing the Puerto Rican women on the ways of making life easier for themselves in the United States."[56]

In the national discourse, Puerto Rican women's work—their paid employment, their unpaid subsistence labor within their households, and their community work—was rendered invisible by the culture of poverty concept. Instead of being seen as economically displaced and migrating in search of work, Puerto Ricans won the dubious distinction of being among the first to be cast as migrating in search of welfare benefits. Glazer and Moynihan, for example, delineated the causes of Puerto Rican migration: "One must not underestimate another set of material advantages: the schools, hospitals, and welfare services."[57] From this perspective, Puerto Ricans could not be labor migrants because they lacked a work ethic and desired welfare dependency. The obstacles that confronted Puerto Ricans stemmed not from a new urban environment, a tight job market, or discrimination, but rather from their own cultural deficiencies. Puerto Ricans were "lazy" and dependent and lacked "any sense of social responsibility." In Philadelphia, the portrayal of Puerto Rican women as "submissive wives" coexisted in a contradictory fashion with an awareness of their roles as workers. Here, Puerto Rican women straddled the abyss between the "feminine mystique" for white, middle-class women and the characterization as "black matriarchs" for African American women.[58]

Conclusions

Although some scholars question oral histories' "subjectivity," this subjectivity can reshape existing interpretations.[59] Puerto Rican women wove their reproductive and productive roles into a single narrative of contributing to and maintaining their households in Puerto Rico and in Philadelphia. It was, they reminisced, a lot of work and at times a difficult balance. Yet, at least in retrospect, these women did not experience it as a conflict in roles. Migration changed the context within which they did this work, but it was not a novelty to balance the reality or possibilities of paid employment with the other responsibilities of home. Their narratives challenge the still resilient portrayal of immigrant women discovering "work" in the host society. In their broad definitions of contributing to their households and of work, these women's narratives break down scholarly binaries that do not adequately reflect lived experience and foster a redefinition of labor migration.

In treating oral histories as just one of several competing narratives, this essay suggests the importance of examining the "subjectivity" of policy makers and of supposedly "objective" sources, such as government and social service agency documents. In both Puerto Rico and the States, policy makers constructed narratives of Puerto Rican women. These state narratives were no less "subjective" than oral history memories. In Puerto Rico, the state's narrative of Puerto Rican women was consistent with prevailing assumptions and with policy goals aimed at reducing Puerto Rico's population and attracting U.S. industries to Puerto Rico. In the States, where racialist constructions merged with gender constructions, Puerto Rican women were viewed through the lens of the culture of poverty paradigm. Narratives continued to emphasize women's responsibility for "overpopulation," but now ignored Puerto Rican women's work in all of its dimensions, avoiding their contributions to their households and their communities and their roles as cheap labor for U.S. industries. Policy makers' "subjectivity," their embedded assumptions, shaped policy initiatives and the provision of social services. Migration provides a window to two different, yet connected, contexts, and these competing narratives of Puerto Rican women suggest the complexity of gender constructions in the postwar era.

Notes

Earlier versions of this essay were presented as " 'I Don't Complain Because I Am a Worker': Puerto Rican Women and Memories of Migration," Oral History Association Annual Meeting, Philadelphia, 10–13 October 1996; and at Project 2000, Institute for Research on Women, Rutgers University, New Brunswick, NJ, 9 April 1997. The author thanks the conference and seminar participants and the editors of this anthology for their helpful comments.

1. A *cuerda* is 0.97 of an acre.

2. Epifanía Velázquez, interview by author, 16 December 1991, Norris Square Senior Citizens' Center, Philadelphia. Translated by author.

3. For a discussion of these terms, see Lourdes Beneria and Gita Sen, "Accumulation, Reproduction, and Women's Role in Economic Development: Boserup Revisited," in *Women's Work: Development and the Division of Labor by Gender,* ed. Eleanor Leacock and Helen I. Safa (New York: Bergin and Garvey, 1986), 141–57.

4. Broader definitions of work are prevalent in the literature on women and development, and are making their way into immigration studies. On women and development, see Leacock and Safa, eds., *Women's Work*; Christine E. Bose and Edna Acosta-Belén, eds., *Women in the Latin American Development Process* (Philadelphia: Temple University Press, 1995); and Helen Safa, *The Myth of the Male Breadwinner: Women and Industrialization in the Caribbean* (Boulder, CO: Westview Press, 1995). On Puerto Rican women and migration, see Rina Benmayor and others, "Stories to Live By: Continuity and Change in Three Generations of Puerto Rican Women," *Oral History Review* 16 (Fall 1988): 1–46; Elizabeth Crespo, "Puerto Rican Women: Migration and Changes in Gender Roles," *Migration and Identity,* vol. 3, *International Yearbook of Oral History and Life Stories,* ed. Rina Benmayor and Andor Skotnes (Oxford: Oxford University Press, 1994), 137–50; and Maura I. Toro-Morn, "Gender, Class, Family, and Migration: Puerto Rican Women in Chicago," *Gender and Society* 9 (December 1995): 712–26. The literature on Puerto Rican women and work is extensive. For examples, see Altagracia Ortiz, ed., *Puerto Rican Women and Work: Bridges in Transnational Labor* (Philadelphia: Temple University Press, 1996); and Edna Acosta-Belén, ed., *The Puerto Rican Woman: Perspectives on Culture, History, and Society,* 2d ed. (New York: Praeger, 1986).

5. For the larger context of Puerto Rican migration to Philadelphia, including a discussion of the causes of emigration, see Carmen Teresa Whalen, "Puerto Rican Migration to Philadelphia, Pennsylvania, 1945–1970: A Historical Perspective on a Migrant Group" (Ph.D. diss., Rutgers, The State University of New Jersey, 1994).

6. Carmen Aponte, interview by author, 7 and 12 December 1991, Norris Square Senior Citizens' Center, Philadelphia. Translated by author.

7. U.S. Department of Commerce, Bureau of the Census, *U.S. Census of Population, 1950;* and U.S. Department of Commerce, Bureau of the Census, as cited in Appendix C in Philadelphia Commission on Human Relations, *Puerto Ricans in Philadelphia: A Study of Their Demographic Characteristics, Problems, and Attitudes* (April 1954; reprint, New York City: Arno Press, 1975). See Whalen, "Puerto Rican Migration to Philadelphia," Chapter 5.

8. Margarita Benítez, interview by author, 11 and 18 August 1996, Philadelphia. Translated by author.

9. Carmen Aponte interview.

10. Carmen Aponte interview (this quote originally in English).

11. María Quiñones, interview by author, 8 and 15, August 1996, Philadelphia. Original in English.

12. On the importance of women's roles in the Puerto Rican community and expanding definitions of "community," see Virginia Sánchez Korrol, *From Colonia to Community: The History of Puerto Ricans in New York City* (Berkeley: University of California Press, 1994). On the importance of kin work, see Marisa Alicea, " 'A Chambered Nautilus': The Contradictory Nature of Puerto Rican Women's Role in the Social Construction of a Transnational Community," Puerto Rican Studies Association Second Conference, 26–29 September 1996, San Juan, Puerto Rico.

13. For a similar argument regarding Latina women's perspectives and experiences reshaping the definition of "politics," see Carol Hardy-Fanta, *Latina Politics, Latino Politics: Gender, Culture, and Political Participation in Boston* (Philadelphia: Temple University Press, 1993).

14. Puerto Rico Planning, Urbanizing, and Zoning Board, "The Population Problem in Puerto Rico" by Frederic P. Bartlett and Brandon Howell (Santurce, Puerto Rico, August 1944), 3, 4, 17, 19, 20. For a critique of the emphasis on "overpopulation" instead of employment levels, see Centro de Estudios Puertorriqueños, *Labor Migration under Capitalism: The Puerto Rican Experience* (New York: Monthly Review Press, 1979).

15. Annette B. Ramírez de Arellano and Conrad Seipp, *Colonialism, Catholicism, and Contraception: A History of Birth Control in Puerto Rico* (Chapel Hill: University of North Carolina Press, 1983), 143.

16. For an overview of Puerto Rico's economic development, see James Dietz, *Economic History of Puerto Rico: Institutional Change and Capitalist Development* (Princeton: Princeton University Press, 1986).

17. U.S. House of Representatives, Congressional Hearings, *Investigation of Minimum Wages and Education in Puerto Rico and the Virgin Islands* (1949), 3, 23.

18. Congressional Hearings, *Investigation of Minimum Wages,* 13, 14.

19. Office of Puerto Rico, "Puerto Rico's Potential as a Site for Textile, Apparel and Other Industries," by Donald J. O'Conner (Washington, DC: 1949), 17, 20.

20. Congressional Hearings, *Investigation of Minimum Wages,* 6, 8–9.

21. Palmira N. Ríos, "Export-Oriented Industrialization and the Demand for Female Labor: Puerto Rican Women in the Manufacturing Sector, 1953–1980," in *Colonial Dilemma: Critical Perspectives on Contemporary Puerto Rico,* ed. Edwin Meléndez and Edgardo Meléndez (Boston: South End Press, 1993), 95.

22. Fernando Sierra Berdecia, "Puerto Rican Agriculture and Manpower," address to Second Farm Placement Conference, 7 and 8 January 1958, San Juan, Puerto Rico.

23. David Ross, *The Long Uphill Path: A Historical Study of Puerto Rico's Program of Economic Development* (San Juan: Editorial Edil, 1969), 157.

24. Ríos, "Export-Oriented Industrialization," 97–101.

25. Puerto Rico, Economic Development Administration (Fomento), "Social Directions in Industrial Development" (January 3, 1957), 1, 8.

26. Daisy Reck to Rex Lee, Division of Territories and Island Possessions, 22 July 1947, Record Group 126, File 9–8–116, Population, Emigration, General, National Archives, Washington, D.C. (hereafter cited as NA 126). For an overview of contract labor programs in Puerto Rico, see Edwin Maldonado, "Contract Labor and the Origins of Puerto Rican Communities in the United States," *International Migration Review* 13 (Spring 1979): 103–21.

27. Donald J. O'Connor, Office of Puerto Rico, to Teodoro Moscoso, Puerto Rico Industrial Development Corporation, 6 June 1947, NA 126.

28. Donald J. O'Connor, Memorandum to Manuel Pérez, Commissioner of Labor, "More on Job Procurement on the Mainland," 13 May 1947, NA 126.

29. O'Connor, "More on Job Procurement on the Mainland," 13 May 1947.

30. "Puerto Rican Girls to Get Jobs Here: Scarsdale to Take First Group Trained on Island for Service as Domestics," New York Times, 30 January 1948, clipping, NA 126.

31. Donald J. O'Connor to Maríano Villaronga, Commissioner of Education, 1 April 1947, NA 126.

32. Memorandum "Suggestions for an Experiment in Placement of Household Workers," 9 June 1947, NA 126.

33. O'Connor to Villaronga, 1 April 1947.

34. "Employment Contract: Puerto Rican Women as Live-In Houseworkers," Department of Labor, Tarea 63–37, Serie 6, Box labeled Borradores Contratos, Archivo General de Puerto Rico, San Juan, Puerto Rico. The Puerto Rico Department of Labor documents are an unorganized collection divided into two "tareas," 63–37 and 61–55 (hereafter cited as Archivo 63–37 or Archivo 61–55).

35. O'Connor to Villaronga, 1 April 1947.

36. Minutes of Emigration Advisory Committee, 18 August 1947, NA 126.

37. Petra América Pagán de Colón to Estella Draper, 3 October 1949, Correspondencia de la Directora, 1949–1950, Box 167, Archivo 61–55.

38. Ross, The Long Uphill Path, 163.

39. Ramírez de Arellano and Seipp, Colonialism, Catholicism, and Contraception, 138.

40. Oscar Lewis, La Vida: A Puerto Rican Family in the Culture of Poverty (New York: Random House, 1965), xliii, xxviii, lii, xi; and Oscar Lewis, "The Culture of Poverty," in Contemporary Cultures and Societies of Latin America, ed. Dwight B. Heath (New York: Random House, 1973), 469–79.

41. Nathan Glazer and Daniel Patrick Moynihan, Beyond the Melting Pot: The Negroes, Fuerto Ricans, Jews, Italians, and Irish of New York City (Cambridge, MA: MIT Press, 1963), 87–88.

42. C. Wright Mills, Clarence Senior, and Rose Kohn Goldsen, The Puerto Rican Journey (New York: Harper and Row, 1950; reprint 1967), 8–9.

43. Joseph Fitzpatrick, Puerto Rican Americans: The Meaning of Migration to the Mainland (Englewood Cliffs, NJ: Prentice-Hall, 1971), 80.

44. Glazer and Moynihan, Beyond the Melting Pot, 99, 98, 123, 125, 118, 120, 122.

45. Iris López, "Agency and Constraint: Sterilization and Reproductive Freedom Among Puerto Rican Women in New York City," Urban Anthropology, nos. 3–4 (1993): 299–323.

46. Friends' Neighborhood Guild, "A Confidential Survey of the Puerto Rican in the Guild Neighborhood" (September 1958), Friends' Neighborhood Guild Record Group, Urban Archives, Temple University, Philadelphia, PA. The Friends' Neighborhood Guild was one of the first organizations to assist Puerto Rican migrants in Philadelphia, and much of their work contradicts the negative views portrayed in the survey. The Guild made the survey "confidential" and noted on the first page, "It is the type of survey which can be helpful to us in planning program [sic] but could be much misunderstood and harmful to the Puerto Rican people if given wider circulation." I use the survey here because it reveals underlying views and assumptions that were widespread at the time. For other activities by the Friends' Neighborhood Guild, see Whalen, "Puerto Rican Migration," 399–410.

47. Friends' Neighborhood Guild, "A Confidential Survey," 2, 11.

48. Ibid., 5–6.

49. Philadelphia, Commission on Human Relations, Puerto Ricans in Philadelphia, by Raymond Metauten (June 1959), 20.

50. Philadelphia, District Health and Welfare Council, Inc., *Community Assessment East of Ninth Street* (January 1960), 60, 13.

51. Friends' Neighborhood Guild, "A Confidential Survey," 10.

52. Ibid., 7.

53. Commission on Human Relations, *Puerto Ricans in Philadelphia*, 20–1.

54. Notes on Annual Meeting, Committee on Puerto Rican Affairs, Health and Welfare Council—Family Division, 8 April 1958, Nationalities Services Center Record Group, Urban Archives, Temple University, Philadelphia, PA.

55. Ibid.

56. Friends' Neighborhood Guild, "A Confidential Survey," 4, 6, 11.

57. Glazer and Moynihan, *Beyond the Melting Pot*, 97.

58. On revisiting the "feminine mystique," see Joanne Meyerowitz, ed., *Not June Cleaver: Women and Gender in Postwar America, 1945–1960* (Philadelphia: Temple University Press, 1994); and on the "black matriarch," see Leith Mullings, "Images, Ideology, and Women of Color," in *Women of Color in U.S. Society,* ed. Maxine Baca Zinn and Bonnie Thornton Dill (Philadelphia: Temple University Press, 1994), 265–90.

59. On oral history and subjectivity, see Virginia Yans-McLaughlin, "Metaphors of Self in History: Subjectivity, Oral Narrative, and Immigration Studies," in *Immigration Reconsidered: History, Sociology, and Politics,* ed. Virginia Yans-McLaughlin (New York: Oxford University Press, 1990), 254–90; and Mary Chamberlain, "Gender and Memory: Oral History and Women's History," in *Engendering History: Caribbean Women in Historical Perspective,* ed. Verene Shepherd, Bridget Brereton, and Barbara Bailey (New York: St. Martin's Press, 1995), 94–110.

11

Political Empowerment of Puerto Rican Women, 1952–1956

Mary Frances Gallart

From Female Impersonations to Empowerment

During the summer of 1952, a group of Puerto Rican women in the town of Guayama arrived at political empowerment.[1] The choice of Obdulia Velázquez de Lorenzo as the mayoral candidate for Guayama, and her subsequent triumph in the November elections, was the result of the concerted actions by a group of women deeply involved in the town's political and economic development. These accomplishments were very important for the development of the town and also, in the long run, for the promise of a primary act that allowed more democratic ways of government in Puerto Rico.

Any woman who stands out in a masculine world is considered exceptional and unique. To engage in party politics, either as a supporter or by actually running for office, requires even more strength and determination in women, since it is still considered part of the public sphere.[2] Therefore, Obdulia Velázquez de Lorenzo's election as mayor of Guayama in 1952 is an exceptional event. However, if we look at Velázquez in the context of her socioeconomic and political group, we can see how her actions, though exceptional, are not isolated. Velázquez responded to and was part of a group of women from Guayama who worked actively in both politics and labor.

The political actions taken by many women like Velázquez have been obscured by the actions of male historical figures. Thus, rediscovering women's actions from a feminist perspective is necessary. According to Carolyn Heilbrun, in her book *Writing a Woman's Life,* women have not defined their own selves. The patterns of behavior that men have established, and women's own internalization of those patterns, have been an obstacle to this self-definition. The situation has led to female impersonations, meaning female actions according to patterns established by men, rather than actions following the principles of femininity.[3] These principles are described by Karen Offen as responding to three important criteria: the recognition of the value of the interpretation that women made of their own lives without the need to define themselves with masculine patterns; consciousness of the injustices to women due to the dominance of men; and the commitment to eliminate such injustices.[4] The research method proposed by Heilbrun pretends to reconstruct the history of common women so as to project the understanding of the great majority of women, who have not distinguished themselves with heroic acts, but whose acts are very significant.

The field literature describes conditions that can be used as models to research women's history. If the traditional biographies of women have only glorified men's figures or described the submission of the women, these are not real descriptions. It is important to describe the realities of women away from the patriarchal control and the interiorization around that control. Historian Blanca Silvestrini has suggested a definition of history as "a dialogue in which both historians and historical subjects would participate, creating a new paradigm for history."[5] To create this new model, we must research women's history from their own perspective so that we may acknowledge their value and become empowered, both. The task of empowering women can only be performed by conducting interviews and acquiring women's testimonies, both from their private and the public spheres, making it possible to reconstruct a history that is closer to the historic events themselves.

This essay will explore the actions of Velázquez and her group of women followers within the framework of their feminine perspective. These women obtained empowerment and moved away from the idea that they were able to attain political power only because of the good will of the men. Besides being good party followers and having proposed the best conciliatory candidate, Velázquez and her supporters obtained political power through hard work in the economic and political arena.

Toward Visibility of Puerto Rican Women in Politics

Patriarchal patterns that have prevailed in Puerto Rican historiography are but one of the obstacles to women's political empowerment. The literature created by the founders of the Popular Democratic Party perpetuates the notion that few women participated in the political process. Somehow this literature gives the impression that women ceased to engage in activities after the labor struggles ended and women's suffrage was obtained.[6] Women actually continued to struggle for political space, but they did so from nonhierarchical and less visible positions.

The lack of knowledge about women's activities should not surprise anyone. An intense personality cult around the Popular Democratic Party's founder, Luís Muñoz Marín, is evidenced in the books and speeches of the party's founder, the literature produced by his biographers, as well as the Commonwealth's educational and explanatory writings.[7] It is as though the party and the man were one and the same. More recently, a new historiography has generated an interpretation of the founding and development of the Popular Democratic Party that takes both economic and social causes into account.[8] Nevertheless, this new historiography fails to acknowledge the contributions of women. The historians give the impression that women were not part of the Popular Democratic Party, although 67,000 women were registered to vote out of a total of 169,626 registered voters in 1948.[9]

The aforementioned literature could lead us to think that all the antecedent activity took place within the political structures created by men, for men, completely disregarding the achievements of women. During the first decades of the twentieth century, women struggled from their positions as workers and suffragists to improve their socioeconomic conditions and gain their own space for political activism. Later, during the 1930s and 1940s, the struggle was transformed to help Popular Democratic Party's cause in less obvious but equally as important roles as before. Many failed to recognize these new forms of action and thought that women no longer participated in the political arena, as if women had retreated after having fought for decades for their political rights. For both politicians and social researchers, women's new participatory styles made them invisible.

The founders of the Popular Democratic Party did take advantage of these less obvious and more subtle ways of engaging in politics developed by women from their private spheres. Although invisible for many politicians, and even for many historians, women's participation in Puerto Rican politics continued, with very important manifestations throughout the Popular Democratic Party's formation and development.

All the elements of visibility and invisibility for women in Puerto Rican politics during the twentieth century can be found in the life history of Obdulia Velázquez de Lorenzo. While popular history describes Doña Obdulia, as everybody knew her, as a humble but educated person without apparent revenues, the documents point in a different direction. A first source to begin reconstructing her life story is her unedited biography, written by Paulino Rodríguez Bernier.[10]

Rodríguez Bernier's biography begins by quoting the origins of Obdulia's parents Juan Velázquez Claudio and Ana Domínguez Rodríguez: "Spanish origin ... Catholics, honest people, and this condition—always working against their interests—brought spoils to their estate and did not help them advance more than moderate means."[11] Obdulia's many and varied life experiences prepared her with leadership skills necessary to be a powerful political leader. Her biographer reports that Obdulia was born in September 1898, and that her parents were very conscious of her education. Together with her two sisters, Ángelita and

Gumersinda, she was sent to the only school in the area of Quebrada Arriba, near the town of Patillas. Under the supervision of the teachers Félix Arias and Pedro Gely, the sisters were able to learn how to read and write. They also learned the "labors proper of the women such as to wedge, weave, sew, and cook besides praying."[12]

Obdulia's childhood and adolescent years were marked by the presence of a missionary:

> Elenita de Jesús, Our Mother Redeemer, as she said she was called, organized a propaganda in favor of the Catholic Apostolic and Roman Religion, uniting an important group of persons for eight years or more of the Barrio Espino of San Lorenzo and Barrio Real of Patillas.[13]

Elenita, considered a saint by her followers, convinced Obdulia's family and many other families to follow her to the area that later came to be known as La Santa Montaña (the holy mountain), located between Patillas and San Lorenzo. During the next ten years, between 1899 and 1909, Elenita had a positive impact on the lives of countryside residents and is still today considered a saint. Although almost a century has passed, the devotion to the preacher Elenita is still very much alive and each week hundreds of Catholics visit the Holy Mountain to ask for her favors.

Paulino Rodríguez Bernier was also influenced by the preacher, since in 1935 he wrote a short novel entitled *Elena, la misionera (leyenda patillense)* (Elena the missionary, legend of Patillas).[14] Rodríguez Bernier recreated the communities' faith in Elenita and in her power to convince her followers to attend the Catholic Church and receive the sacraments.

> The coming of Our Mother, as they called her, was an important act; a blessing for all the mountainous region for all the inhabitants of the forest. The most ferocious converted into lambs, those in concubinage got married, the homes where there were disagreements were converted into heavens.[15]

The author explains that the missionary accomplished her role with the help of other women and a great number of girls:

> The house of Elena had other girls, girls that were chosen of the area to educate and teach them religion. They lived with the gifts that from all areas brought the thousands of followers: gifts in metallic, fabrics, shoes, etc. Everything was used by the goddess to give to the most needy peoples.[16]

The network of women, guided by the Catholic Church's postulates and directed by a woman's perspective, influenced the early childhood of Obdulia and the other girls. Later on, they became women with life philosophies in which their deeds were recognized as important in the development of an ideology.

Obdulia, for example, preached her religion in the countryside between Patillas and San Lorenzo. Besides mastering oratory practices to spread their beliefs, this group of women and girls taught others, from the standpoint of nonhierarchical roles, with their example of a life dedicated to religion. In Obdulia's case, the preaching techniques she learned from the religious leaders were very effective later on when she started pronouncing political messages as Popular Democratic Party leader. Of that eloquence, her niece Sara Velázquez is a witness, stating that Doña Obdulia "went to the countryside and the towns speaking in the tribunes together with Luis Muñoz Marín. When she stood up in a tribune she had that special gift of any good speaker."[17] The special gift also could have been the result of training during her childhood years with the missionary Elenita. Paulino Rodríguez writes that "all the girls that accompanied the missionary had received an internal transformation and that the fresh air of the mountains had formed them into beautiful creatures."[18] Later on she used the same strategies in her political mission.

As an adolescent, Obdulia continued studying in the capital city for two years, after which she went to Quebrada Abajo to marry. According to Rodríguez Bernier, "There was inequality between them, she was eighteen and he was sixty-three. Nicolás Lorenzi [sic] was the name of the husband, ex-commandant of the XI Battalion of the Spanish Army during the Spanish-American War."[19]

The uneven matrimony apparently was happy and able to acquire fortune. The Register of Appraisement and Contributions does not show properties belonging to Obdulia's parents or her husband, but in the fiscal year 1920–21 there is a property belonging to Velázquez Domínguez, Obdulia.[20] For the next fifteen years the properties and their value continue to grow until, in the year 1935, the value slightly decreases. Finally in the year 1940, there is no sign of properties belonging to Obdulia Velázquez Domínguez.[21]

The above information matches the description of Obdulia's biographer, who stated that hurricane San Felipe ruined the crops and even though her husband had a loan from the Federal Bank, they could not solve their economic problems. Doña Obdulia said that when her husband died in 1934, the farms were sold and she could only keep thirty-six acres and a house in Guayama.[22] The prosperous stage of Doña Obdulia's life was unknown in Guayama, where she came to live as a poor widow. This is important because it demonstrates that Obdulia had the education and experience to be able to absorb the axioms of the Popular Democratic Party's message and transmit them with ease to the people.

Having experienced the missionary's and the landowner's world, Doña Obdulia engaged in a new role as she moved to Guayama. She became actively engaged in the town's labor and political movements. Between 1950 and 1951, Velázquez founded and presided over the Unión de Damas de Oficios Domésticos (Ladies' Homeworkers Union). This group of women, which was organized in different towns of Puerto Rico as an answer to the harsh working conditions of the seamstresses who labored mainly from their houses, was very successful in

Guayama.[23] The Ladies' Union of Guayama reached 5,000 members and helped the workers obtain better equipment and salaries. The minutes for the month of May 1950 describe the following agreements:

1. discussion of the uniform they were to wear;
2. division of the activities in committees in which each member will render equal work, no matter what committee they belong to, and the visit to Puente de Jobos to create a subcommittee;
3. recruitment of Mr. Enrique Anglade, president of Pro Industries, to help them and to write a letter to the governor of Puerto Rico, Luis Muñoz Marín, informing [about the union];
4. obtain technical advice from Anglade to obtain land to construct a building:
   a. by donation of Mrs. Monserrate Bruno, or
   b. collection in beneficent dances
   c. asking the Absent Sons and Daughters that instead of donating a milk station, to donate a building for the union
   d. invite Doña Inés [the wife of the governor] to come to Guayama.[24]

The above agreements show the leadership of Doña Obdulia and her group of women. On the one hand, they realized the need to be recognized as a union of women and wanted to have their members wear uniforms. The distribution of work in subcommittees points to the ample vision of the union's leadership. The search for technical advice from industrial leaders demonstrates that they had clear objectives and knew where to look for help. Enrique Anglade was an important leader of the Popular Democratic Party involved in the industrial development of the town and, as we will see, would have a close relationship with Doña Obdulia and her group of women.

The enthusiasm generated by the Ladies' Union led the mayor and other members of the Pro Industries Movement, to pledge to help them. At the May 20th meeting, the mayor called the union "the principal column" and promised the following:

1. a sewing machine that will be sent from La Fortaleza [the governor's house] to the Barrio Corazón so that the women could use it during the working days;
2. the recruitment of Doña Inés [the governor's wife] to take care of—before any other town—Guayama's labor problems;
3. informed that he showed Gatti's pearl factory and the Vocational School to an American visitor that wanted to establish a factory in Guayama, so that he could decide.[25]

With these promises the mayor was supporting the ideas of the group of working women and showed his intentions to help them achieve their goals. But all this enthusiasm met indifference on the part of other socioeconomical groups in Guayama. The town's upper class had little interest in supporting the Ladies'

Union and the mayor faced resistance in finding financial support to follow up on his promises. Mr. Enrique Cruz informed the union of "the indifference that society has demonstrated to the petition for the Pro Industries' collection of $25,000 and assured that from then on they will collect the money from the poor society with sacrifice."[26]

After the above-mentioned setback, Doña Obdulia moved quickly and asked the worker Leocadio Tirado Campos to say a few words to her group. He asked her female supporters to swear fidelity to the group and to force justice upon the people that slandered them.[27] The worker's words confirmed the tensions between different socioeconomic groups and the determination of the working class to continue fighting for better working conditions.

After a summer of continuous work, the Union tested its force during an October meeting. Even though most of the women were working from their homes, they hoped to find a job in the factories or workshops. When the time came to hire seamstresses for the new factories proposed for Guayama, the Ladies' Union was left out, since "the Americans prefer men instead of women and younger girls instead of older more experienced women."[28] As a response to the critical situation, the women reacted immediately, sending a telegram to Governor Luis Muñoz Marín with the following text: "In the name of the 5,000 persons we ask for an interview to deal with the unemployment of Guayama, signed by Obdulia Velázquez, Vicente Palés 95."[29]

A committee was rapidly named for the meeting with the governor, composed of Doña Obdulia and other eight women. The meeting was very important for them since many Union members had been displaced before when workshops closed in the previous decade, and their hopes of obtaining a better-paying job in a factory had been shattered. The results of the conference with the governor, if it took place, were not discussed in the future meetings of the Ladies' Union's book. Apparently the women did not achieve their goal to be considered for work in the factories. As a last resort, members suggested sending a telegram to Doña Inés, wife of the governor, so that she would intervene with her husband on behalf of the Union, but again there is no evidence of any positive results. By February of 1951, Doña Obdulia informed the Union of the need to make changes in the board of directors, implying that she would not consider the presidency again. It was a short meeting and no indications were given about the future of the Union. Based on the past failures and the president's final advice in terms of the organizational and financial problems, the future looked grim.

Although the minutes from this workers' union do not mention the Popular Democratic Party's postulates, their political affiliation is evident. The presence of Mayor Félix Álvarez Bonés, as well as vocational school social worker Marcos A. Ledeé, at the meetings denotes political ties. The help provided by these public officials to the Ladies' Union translated into votes for the party they represented. Considering that in the 1950s Guayama's population was 32,807, the 5,000 members of the Ladies' Union represented a considerable number, and thus was taken into consideration as a political group that was important to court.[30]

Upon reviewing Velázquez's participation in both organizations, we can easily recognize the close relationship between the Ladies' Union and the Popular Democratic Party. Velázquez founded and then held the presidency of the Guayama Ladies Homeworkers' Union while at the same time having direct political participation as member of the Municipal Assembly. She was elected in 1948, and held office until 1952, when her peers appointed her mayor. Since it was not common in Puerto Rico to have many women as members of the municipal assemblies, the women's leadership in Guayama seemed to be strong since three women were elected to the Assembly in 1948. Once Velázquez became a member of the Assembly for the 1948–52 period, her political participation became inscribed in our traditional history. Her participation in the town's development was evident in the Municipal Assembly's minutes, especially in topics pertaining to working women's issues. However, if we consider her participation as an Assembly member only, we lose sight of the other 5,000 women workers who struggled jointly for their socioeconomic improvement within the rank-and-file of the Popular Democratic Party.

Puerto Rican women played an active role in the economic and political development of Puerto Rico during the first half of the twentieth century, but many historians and others have yet to recognize this, partly due to lack of documentation and partly due to the way in which participation is conceptualized. For example, neither the Guayama municipal archives nor the daily press contain any documentation about the Ladies' Homeworkers Union. Had it not been for documents saved in private collections, such as the Union's minutes book, these women's work would never have been acknowledged. Velázquez would have been known in Guayama's history as the only instance in which a woman became mayor, and then only because men decided it.

The Role of Women in the Popular Democratic Party

At the outset of the Popular Democratic Party's electoral victory in 1940, women were considered important. They were encouraged to vote in order to increase general participation at the voting booths every four years. Women were also asked to work in the propaganda distributions and collection projects. Considering that women were first allowed to vote in the elections of 1932, the fact that in the 1940s there were three women elected as mayor for the Popular Democratic Party shows the level of their interest and active participation. The women mayors were Esperanza Y. de Quiñones (1944–63) in the town of Guánica, Felisa Rincón de Gautier (1946–68) in San Juan, and Blanca Colberg (1949–64) in Cabo Rojo.[31]

Perhaps the most important source for reconstructing women's role, assigned by the party, was the so-called Puerto Rican peasant's mail, *El Batey*. This monthly newspaper, distributed free of charge with a volume of 100,000 copies, was printed from March of 1939 to that same month in 1968. During those uninterrupted twenty-nine years, *El Batey* was delivered all around the island through the efforts of many silent women leaders. The monthly articles helped create an ideology that captured the minds and hearts of the PPD faithful.[32]

Besides the usual discourse for both men and women to vote for the party, the newsletter also used more subtle practices in urging women to obtain the votes of men. For example, an article printed in April of 1939 stated the following: "The women of the countryside are the ones who see closely the hunger and suffering of Puerto Rico. . . . If the women force the men to feel shame if he sells himself the economic justice will come. . . ."[33]

The above quote spoke to the women in terms of their suffering due to the poor economic conditions and the social injustices, which their children suffered most. They were made to feel responsible for securing the well-being of their children by eliminating the selling of their votes and those of their husbands. There were many women who responded, as is seen in the following answer of a peasant women in the countryside of the town of Naranjito.

> I wish to be cut by a ray of lightning if I allow my husband to sell my vote one more time! I always thought that for him to bring a bigger bag of groceries and a little bit more of clothes the day of the elections was good for us. But now that you have explained that because of that, the rest of the time I am dealing with an empty pot and with children that do not have anything to eat and with a fire that many times cannot be lighted and with the situation that there are no medicines and no doctors, after I know that, I wish to be cut by a ray of lighting if I allow my husband to sell his vote and if I do not teach my children so that when they grow they know that you do not do that.[34]

This mechanism of ideological penetration gave women, even if they were not participating actively, a sense of belonging and the security that their role in spreading the popular ideology was as important as the active leadership. The importance of the women's roles was again stressed in the following article:

> *El Batey* thinks that women should be more interested to register and vote more than the men, so that the unjust situation for the people of Puerto Rico improves. . . . The husband goes every day to work or to look for work. He suffers and is hungry but is not looking at the poor stove of the house, and is not hearing the cry of the children when they ask for more food and there is none. The man suffers misery but is not always seeing it. The women that gave birth to their children in pain, are the ones that should fight for a happier future for their children.[35]

It is obvious that women were targeted as both direct and indirect contributors to the party. Making them conscious about their suffering due to the abuses of the political parties encouraged them to vote for the Popular Democratic Party and influence their husband's decisions. It is interesting to remember that during the women's suffrage campaign one of the most important impediments to allowing illiterate women to vote was the belief that they would be influenced by their husbands. This idea, apparently, changed drastically. Now, the party not only believed women were capable of choosing their political party but that they were important in influencing the decisions of their husbands, fathers, and children.

An interview with Celia Vicente de Borrero shows a perfect example of the active role of women in the Popular Democratic Party.[36] Although today she is known in town as the wife of the past mayor, Víctor Borrero, her political participation shows a leader formed even before her husband. Vicente said that she worked on the political committee, distributing the electoral cards and serving in the voting tables. Besides her active participation at the party level, she also collaborated with the Home for Children's program directed by Inés Mendoza de Muñoz Marín, wife of the governor of Puerto Rico. The program began in 1942, organized by Florence Arnold Tugwell, the wife of then-governor Rexford Guy Tugwell, and was known as the milk station's program for "that glass of milk with which the stations began."[37]

During the following decades, milk stations developed to form a complete program of nourishment and entertainment:

> So that the 30,000 children of pre-school age that in Puerto Rico receive gratuitously the benefit of a healthy daily breakfast in the 505 stations that operate on the Island, can benefit also from the love and company that help their emotional development together with their physical development.[38]

To guarantee the emotional development of the children, the program designated a group of godmothers, who needed to be women with a "sense of esteem for children and prestige or influence in the community, time to dedicate to the milk stations, leadership qualities, and preferably [residence] in the community where the stations are located or near them."[39]

These godmothers were a good example of how women participated and were able to produce results in benefit of the poor children of Puerto Rico and also for the political party. The godmothers' role was not only to attend to the emotional and physical development of the children but also to foster stability in the community, according to the Popular Democratic Party's postulates. For Celia Vicente de Borrero, her function as a godmother was very important because she became familiar with Guayama's countryside. As a good political leader it was important to know and to be known by the people. Her work in the milk stations of the twelve *barrios* that comprise the town of Guayama allowed her to be a good resource for distributing *El Batey*.

A Conciliatory Candidate

Guayama did not have a woman mayor during the forties, but in the next decade Obdulia Velázquez de Lorenzo became its first and only women mayor. For many, she was a conciliatory candidate who came to solve a tense situation between two Popular Democratic Party groups. In reality, she was a powerful leader who was able to utilize, as a politician, all her religious and labor experiences.

The forties began in Guayama with the election of the first Popular Democratic Party mayor, Félix Álvarez Bonés, who remained in office until his resignation in 1952. The fact that he was reelected for two consecutive terms shows that the Popular Democratic Party had consolidated political power in Guayama. However, Álvarez Bonés's resignation opened the doors for future contenders who, in turn, were unable to reach an agreement and, thus, split the party into two factions. One of the groups was led by Abraham Nieves, a Popular Democratic Party political leader and prosperous businessman residing in Guayama.[40] This faction was apparently in disagreement with Álvarez Bonés's administration. Víctor Borrero, former mayor of Guayama and active Popular Democratic Party leader, affirmed that Álvarez Bonés' resignation was due to "political and administrative problems with Abraham Nieves."[41] Although the former mayor did not want to be more explicit about the actual problems between the factions, it was certain that whoever was mayor needed to have the blessing of the leader of the municipal committee of the Popular Democratic Party.

Acting mayor Rizal Pagán and several leaders were in disagreement with the Popular Democratic Party municipal committee's recommendation, probably because they resisted their undue intervention. Borrero and others objected to the nomination of a figurehead candidate controlled by Abraham Nieves's group. According to Borrero, this disagreement led Rizal Pagán and his group of Assembly members to persuade Obdulia Velázquez de Lorenzo to fill the vacant office of town mayor. Doña Obdulia entered the political scenario as the perfect candidate to solve the Popular Democratic Party's internal rifts. Borrero's male parameters picture her as a very religious woman, always true to the party's postulates, who could thus help the party in the internal reconciliation process. In his mind no one would dare challenge her. Velázquez thus was considered a passive person simply because traditional male parameters had been used to measure her participation. But Borrero's statement clashes against the course of women's participation in Puerto Rican politics. In the face of a solidly male leadership, it is difficult to imagine that Velázquez was chosen to be the mayor merely because she was a good woman. Likewise, it would be impossible to believe that she would accept the nomination to the office of mayor merely for the sake of conciliation. She was a very active woman, both in politics and the labor movement, as I have indicated earlier. While leaders such as Borrero saw her playing a conciliatory role, she had actually been a political activist and her self-image was that of a woman truly immersed in the world of politics.

The designation of Obdulia Velázquez to be Guayama's mayor, although considered by many as a conciliatory act, was clouded by political upheaval. This is evident even in her first message immediately after her appointment:

> When I accepted the appointment as mayor of Guayama, I did it against my own will since I never, even though I was a founding member of the Popular Democratic Party, had ambitions in respect to political positions. But given the crisis . . . in our party in Guayama, I decided to accept the nomination, because in doing so, not only did I think that as a conciliatory candidate I will ease the conflict but also I could serve my town of Guayama as I have always tried since I entered the political life.[42]

The above declarations show the way in which Velázquez saw her role in the Popular Democratic Party. She considered herself a leader, but even though she was a founding member of the party, she never had aspirations to become the mayor. Velázquez argued that she accepted the position because she really thought she could reconcile the groups again. As the following words indicate, her conciliatory role was very different from that of the former mayor of Guayama, Víctor Borrero:

> The political crisis in the municipality of Guayama obeyed the ambitions of a group of men who wanted to impose a candidate against the will and wishes of all the social classes of Guayama's municipality, and that candidate has not had a majority in the local committee composed of thirty-eight members, since fourteen members voted in his favor and fourteen against him. The only interest that I have is to serve my town and my party. If I accepted the charge it is because I am convinced that I have the endorsement of that town that has offered me its cooperation.[43]

Not only was Doña Obdulia convinced of her ability to unify the political groups in Guayama, she was also sure she had the endorsement of the people. These are declarations of a accomplished politician who was sure of herself and of the support of her people, and who dared to face up to the wishes of the men who controlled the Popular Democratic Party.

Empowerment of Guayama's Women

Even with the support of the majority of the people of Guayama, the Popular Democratic Party's top leadership annulled Doña Obdulia's appointment as mayor. The Municipal Committee issued a *quo warranto* order in the District Court of Justice of Guayama.[44] The judicial order allowed the courts to decide the validity of her appointment. In regards to this challenge, Velázquez de Lorenzo stated:

The position that I occupy is at the disposition of my party and I only wait for the coming of our maximum leader, so that he can definitively say the last word. Also, I never asked or moved the political machinery for my appointment. It was asked of me to accept a position that I never ambitioned, and if I accepted I did it for the reason I have already mentioned.[45]

The above are words of a person who has dedicated her life to politics and knows that within her party structure, at that moment, the decisions of Governor Luis Muñoz Marín were more important than the wishes of the local leaders. Nevertheless, her firm decision to continue as mayor of Guayama makes evident both her strong character and the fact that she was not ready to resign because of the desire of the local leaders.

The revision of the case number CD-52–186 of *El pueblo de Puerto Rico, ex rel Esmeraldo González Porrata v. Obdulia Velázquez viuda de Lorenzo*, shows the series of incongruities that came about with Velázquez's appointment as mayor.[46] Doña Obdulia's lawyer, Celestino Domínguez Rubio, defended her, stressing three special conditions of the case. First, he tried to annul deputy Aurelio Torres Braschi's participation in the complaint, stating that he could not carry the *quo warranto* order since he was only representing the Attorney General. Second, he tried to prevent the administration from taking the stand since, he said, it was not compulsory. Finally, he questioned the vote, arguing that since only eleven members in the Municipal Assembly were present at the time, the half-plus-one condition should not be considered, and the six-to-three vote for Doña Obdulia's appointment should prevail.

District Judge Ángel M. Umpierre did not considered the lawyer's statements and ruled that Doña Obdulia was occupying Guayama's mayor position illegally. Since the judge had ruled she was occupying her office unlawfully, Velázquez was ordered to surrender her position, because she was not elected by the necessary half-plus-one number of votes.[47] After the court's decision, Obdulia Velázquez was deprived of the position and the candidate of the Municipal Committee, Vicente Figueroa, was appointed mayor. Nothing could be done at that moment to reinstate Doña Obdulia as mayor of Guayama. But the November elections were just five months away and the people of Guayama did not want to have Figueroa as the party candidate, or as the mayor for the next four years.

Toward the Primary Act

A month after Velázquez's removal, the debate continued as the top leadership refused to give in to the people's demand for a primary election. These demands became stronger every day, as evidenced by the following news item in *El Imparcial*:

More than six thousand people took to the streets in the city, carrying banners demanding primary elections. Candidates Enrique J. Anglade for the House of

Representatives, and Obdulia Velázquez for the Mayor's office, were continuously cheered.[48]

The concentration of Guayama residents in favor of a primary came in response to the frustrated meetings in which party leaders, such as Ponce's mayor Andrés Grillasca, failed to convince Velázquez to withdraw her petition to hold primary elections in Guayama.

Primaries were held in Puerto Rico only when absolutely necessary due to irreconcilable differences between local party leaders. Given the quick consolidation of the Popular Democratic Party under a single leader, primaries were not a priority for its leaders, who believed these were divisive processes. When we look at the printed news media for the 1940s, the only mention of primaries found is one in Río Piedras by the end of 1944.[49] Leaders were demanding that both sides participate in marking the registered voters' lists, to prevent the political future of Popular Democratic Party representatives from being decided by members of other political parties. This was the formula recommended by a primary commission, created to decide these cases. The decision about the marking process shows the control already held by the Popular Democratic Party over political legislation so soon after its creation.

For years, many party members considered the enactment of a primary law to be a priority, even though this would work against the party's absolute control. A great number of articles, particularly editorials, discussed the need to enhance the development of a democratic process. An editorial in *El Mundo,* on October 13, 1951, criticized the delay in implementing the law and pointed out that "primaries represent the true electoral process."[50] The editor argued that an electoral process without primaries deprived voters of choosing their favorite candidates and endowed the maximum leader with the power to choose such candidates:

> An ordinary voter learns who the candidates are just a few days before the elections, having no direct intervention in their selection process. A board within the party makes the choice, which seems to be the only direct representative of the people, but for the most part those board members apparently represent only the political boss who appointed them.[51]

Other advantages discussed, adding to the importance of implementing a primary process, were the following: making sure that the candidates' qualities were known; making sure there was ample discussion of the campaign programs; and affording the candidates greater independence of opinion. In short, although the primary law did not exist, several groups were calling out for its enactment, with little success in the short run. We should keep in mind that a few days after these manifestations, on July 25, 1952, Puerto Rico inaugurated its Commonwealth status. The new political structure pledged, precisely, a more democratic government, thus the enactment of a primary law became imminent.

A front-page article in *El Mundo* on July 19, 1952, announced that Muñoz

Marín was asking the legislature for a primary law. The news article explained that the governor had suggested a primary bill that followed the Uruguayan model, rather than the United States model. The latter provided for primaries on different dates from the election dates, which was seen as an unnecessary additional expense to the government. Furthermore, the article went on to explain that holding primaries on different dates from the general elections would be annoying to voters.[52] These explanations about voters' annoyance sounded like excuses to avoid the approval of a primary law before the elections, for fear of dividing the Popular Democratic Party. Voters were already annoyed, as evidenced by one of the columns published in *El Imparcial*. The paper stated that "groups of Popular Democratic Party leaders in over a dozen towns throughout the Island have risen to voice their demands that party officials authorize primary elections."[53]

At the center of the debate to approve a Primary Act, the people of Guayama continued their efforts to obtain a primary to decide between Doña Obdulia Velázquez and Vicente Figueroa. When all official avenues had been exhausted, women entered the picture as a last recourse: going to the governor's residence and asking Inés Mendoza de Muñoz Marín to speak with her husband on their behalf. According to Borrero, a group of more or less fifty women—plus one man by the name of Mencho Morales—was organized and, having made no prior appointment, asked to see Doña Inés. Six of these women, as recalled by former mayor Borrero, represented the full range of social groups assembled under the Popular Democratic Party. Úrsula Menéndez, Paula Tirado, Elena Ortiz, and Obdulia Velázquez de Lorenzo belonged to the laboring class, whereas María Vaquer and América Anglade were professionals. Everything seems to suggest that both groups of women found a vehicle, within the Popular Democratic Party, for their political struggles. Although this is not a study of social class coalitions in Guayama, we can easily see how a common desire for greater political access blurred class differences. At that time, the primary in Guayama was more important for these Popular Democratic Party women than their class differences.

The outcome of the Fortaleza meeting was a resounding success. Former mayor Víctor Borrero tells the story of a long day of waiting, and of women getting ready to spend the night on the street, next to one of the main gates, without yet having been received by the First Lady. Finally Doña Inés came out, met with them, and then got her husband to meet them in his work pajamas. Upon listening to the women's arguments, Borrero reports that Muñoz Marín said: "We will have a primary, and we will have it next Sunday."[54] Borrero's statement echoes his perception about how the final decision on whether or not to hold primary elections rested solely on Luis Muñoz Marín's shoulders. Although this is partly true, it is also true that the governor recognized the women's leadership in Guayama and that they would continue insisting until achieving their goals.

A look at the daily press documents the enormous efforts made by Popular Democratic Party leaders to reach a consensus without having to go to a primary. The strategies followed ranged from the intervention of senators and mayors to the public's contempt for the principal party leaders. *El Imparcial* published an article about a meeting held on August 14, 1952, in Guayama, at which the two opposing factions in Guayama were present: the group that wanted Obdulia Velázquez de Lorenzo for mayor and Enrique Anglade for House Representative, and the group that favored Vicente Figueroa for mayor and Abraham Nieves for House representative. The conciliators were Senator Agustín Burgos and Ponce mayor Andrés Grillasca. Reports state that these two proposed Obdulia Velázquez de Lorenzo for the House, and Vicente Figueroa for mayor, which did not suit either one of the factions.[55]

The proposition followed the suggestion of the Municipal Committee and the high-ranking leaders of the Popular Democratic Party, who wished Vicente Figueroa for mayor of Guayama during the next four years. Nevertheless, Doña Obdulia and Enrique Anglade had the support of the people. The newspaper reported that hundreds of persons waited in front of the building where conciliators Burgos and Grillasca met. When no positive solution was achieved, the followers of Doña Obdulia announced that they would participate in a demonstration, comprising more than 8,000 persons, to solve the situation by means of open meeting.[56] The massive town participation reflects the importance of the local leaders within the party's structure, leaders who were able to mobilize into action large groups and did not permit that the high-ranking leaders dictate a candidate they did not want.

After the failed attempts to force a conciliation, it seemed that the high-ranking leadership of the party was desperate and even used strong words to force the agreement without primaries. A letter sent by Ramón Rivera Mercado, a party leader from the neighboring town of Salinas, to Luis Muñoz Marín states that the senator from Guayama's district, Ildefonso Solá Morales, who also acted as the general secretary of the party, had insulted him. Rivera Mercado said that besides refusing to visit the town, Solá Morales declared that "if we have to lose one thousand votes in Guayama or two thousand in Salinas, this will not affect us."[57] The general secretary was disturbed since in less than eleven days they had to nominate the mayoral candidates for next November's election and the situation in Guayama was still not resolved.

After all the described attempts to prevent the primary, Luis Muñoz Marín finally gave in and allowed it. The petition, mentioned before, of the women from Guayama at the gates of La Fortaleza apparently was a decisive event in the debate, even though it was not considered important news by any of the newspapers. Remembering the events of that Sunday, September 7, Celia Vicente de Borrero explained that after a strong campaign, the primary took place under a tremendous rainfall, very rare in the dry town of Guayama. She explained that it was a very difficult day, full of discussions and fights in which women participated.[58] Of this stressful day, *El Imparcial* reported that the mayor of Guayama and three other leaders were arrested for disturbing the peace. The events were described by policeman Juan A. Martínez, who reported that

All of a sudden it began raining, and the people tried to enter the electoral college, and Mayor Figueroa tried to prevent them from doing so . . . beginning a discussion with the mayor which ended in a fight, González Porrata intervening for the mayor.[59]

The primary's results were covered by *El Mundo,* together with the celebration of Doña Obdulia and Enrique Anglade.

In the ten town's electoral colleges and the nine of the countryside, 4,779 persons voted. Of those 3,678 voted in favor of Doña Obdulia Velázquez and Anglade, 866 voted in favor of Flor Colón for mayor and 335 voted in favor of the nomination of Vicente Figueroa.[60]

As discussed before, Doña Obdulia had developed a strong following among the working class, by means of her work as president of the Ladies' Union. This leadership position permitted her to be elected as member of the Municipal Assembly and to accept the nomination for mayor. Once her nomination was annulled, Doña Obdulia and her group of female supporters recognized the critical moment and fought until they obtained and won the primary. They had lost a battle but won the war.

After the primary, the rivalries between the two political factions in Guayama were appeased; only several of the losers resigned from the party's Municipal Committee and the winners celebrated their victory. Among the losers, José María Ángeles, who presided over the Municipal Committee, resigned, and in the same manner,

The vice-presidents Vicente Figueroa and Abraham Nieves, the secretary Alfredo Delgado and the treasurer Juanita Rosseau, after the triumph of the Popular candidates that they did not favor, have considered it wise to resign from the Committee so that the winning group can designate the committee they believe is better for the success of their work.[61]

Likewise, for Popular Democratic Party members, the Urugayan-style primary project, to be held on the same date as the general elections, did not meet with the approval of leaders from other parties. The Statehood Party president, Miguel A. García Méndez, expressed his energetic opposition to the Uruguayan-style primaries, arguing that they were intended to solve the Popular Democratic Party's internal problems and, therefore, should be held internally by the party. He also said he disagreed with the project because primary votes on an electoral ballot would give the Popular Democratic Party twice the number of votes for their candidates in the final count.[62]

The complaint by the minority party and the immediacy of election day apparently served to appease the people as far as the Uruguayan-style primaries were concerned. On August 13, *El Imparcial* published a news item containing statements by Speaker of the House Ernesto Ramos Antonini on the defeat of the measure. Ramos Antonini explained that the vote consolidation project proposed by the Uruguayan-style primaries program would be contrary to the recently approved Constitution of Puerto Rico.[63] Nevertheless, the Uruguayan project did appeal to some politicians. A news item on July 22, 1952, reported that incumbent Arcadio Estrada and his opponent, Representative Agustín A. Vélez, would be happy to wait until November for a primary that would decide which one of them became the next mayor of San Sebastián.[64]

The controversy over the primaries apparently started to affect the Popular Democratic Party's unity, and there were those who tried to give the impression that nothing was wrong. In an article of July 17, 1952, in *El Mundo,* Emilio Castro Rodríguez, then president of the Lares Municipal Committee, affirmed that the Popular Democratic Party was not divided because of candidacies. However, documentation exists about a controversy in that same town, where Ramón Mario Ramírez was chosen for the mayoral race, and Luis Santaliz Capestany to run for the House, by means of "an intimate meeting, since this was not a public assembly."[65] This small, intimate meeting does not reflect division, as Castro Rodríguez stated so well, but it definitely does not reflect a full exercise of democracy, either.

In contrast with San Sebastián, there seem to have been no promises made in Guayama to hold a primary at the same time as general elections were being held, so as to appease the rivalries between opposing Popular Democratic Party candidates. Again, "La Voz del Lector" published a letter from Juan Rodríguez asking that primary elections be held not only for mayor and House representative offices, but for district senators as well. This resident in the Guayama senatorial district was protesting because the senators for his town were from Cayey and Caguas, although Guayama was the head of the district.[66] Evidently the tension in Guayama during those months would not subside until a primary was held.

Just as in Guayama and San Sebastián, primary elections were also promised in Utuado in 1952, by special party regulations.[67] It meant nothing other than Governor Luis Muñoz Marín's direct acquiescence in the face of such groups' insistence and his refusal to give in to the party's political machinery. We should note that during August 1952, while there was still a conflict between the two factions in Guayama, the Popular Democratic Party published its Social and Economic Program, approved in an assembly held at the Sixto Escobar Stadium in San Juan, on August 24, 1952. After many years of avoiding a primary law, the document makes a commitment to the people of Puerto Rico, as described in the fourth paragraph:

> We affirm our total commitment to democratic practices, for the political power of the people to be enforced in accordance with the people's will, as provided for by our Constitution. The electoral process, as a natural develop-

ment within a dynamic democracy, must be perfected by the political parties' own regulations, these being the legitimate instruments whereby the people's wishes are expressed. The consultation made by the parties of their members must be done in a clear and precise manner, so the men who undertake the responsibility of exercising authority by the people's mandate can truly be their legitimate representatives. In order to enhance and perfect the electoral process, the Popular Democratic Party, true to its history and the principles that gave it substance and being, shall establish a more adequate method to consult its voters by means of a primaries law.[68]

With this promise to enact a primary law very soon, a new stage in Puerto Rico's political development began. Primaries were granted more and more often as time went by, while the daily press exercised greater pressure to have a primary law approved, as promised by the Popular Democratic Party. Statements made to the press by Senate leader Samuel A. Quiñones also illustrate the interest at that time in getting a bill of law approved to implement the primaries process. Quiñones affirmed that "in due course, the Puerto Rico Senate shall act to establish a primaries law, in order to eliminate any possibility of having candidates elected by influences outside the true sentiments of the people."[69] With these statements, Quiñones reiterated the desire to create a primary law. However, he added that for the upcoming elections that year, 1952, it would be impossible for the Legislature to approve that law. The reasons he wielded were lack of time to study the bills submitted, and the questions raised concerning the constitutionality of certain requirements.

Although the primary law was not approved for the 1952 elections, it did become a political campaign promise until its enactment in 1956. After the Guayama primary, each time a controversy arose between two Popular Democratic Party factions, the leaders would advocate a primary election. This new approach in democratic development was achieved, to a great extent, thanks to the group of women in Guayama and their leader, Obdulia Velázquez de Lorenzo. These women's struggle using nontraditional methods brought about a change in attitudes and the promise of a primary law for Puerto Rico.

With a new outlook for primary elections in the summer of 1952, the different factions within the Popular Democratic Party remained at ease. However, the promise of legislation to grant the law became a matter of deep concern for the voters who saw 1956 fast approaching without any legislation in sight. Francisco Prado Picart, from Juana Díaz, put it in these words, in the "Voz del Lector" section of *El Mundo:*

The primaries law would be an efficient remedy, available to the people, to correct in time whatever excess, conceit, and incompetence may be found in those public officials who . . . never ceasing to make promises and ask for the people's votes, then turn their backs on them and take actions with their own personal interests in mind.[70]

According to Prado Picart, the primary law would solve a number of problems concerning abuse of power in the municipalities as well as in the whole political system. He insisted that the appointed electoral assemblies made their nominations in undemocratic fashion, given that the election obeyed "the will of a handful of citizens, or the whim and fancy of some political chieftain."[71] Interestingly, although a primary law was being contemplated for mayoral and other municipal races, the top Popular Democratic Party leadership thought that applying it in House and Senate races would be difficult. Ildefonso Solá Morales is quoted in *El Mundo,* on February 12, 1955, as saying: "The Commonwealth Constitution provides a date and manner in which an electoral division is to be revised, and until such time as the organization created under the Constitution makes such a revision, it would be difficult to enforce a primaries law on our current districts."[72]

Given that the controversy revolved mainly around differences with the municipalities, as was explained earlier in the case of Guayama, the only commitment made by the Popular Democratic Party's top leadership was to approve that primary law. The above quote from the Popular Democratic Party secretary general, upon proposing a primary law, advocated the most simple and least engaging solution for the party's machinery. The idea was to solve local differences without violence to the party's internal controls, which did respond to the Popular Democratic Party top leadership. Likewise, five days later and in the same newspaper, Solá Morales stressed that "the political parties reserve the right to set their own requirements in choosing their candidates."[73] This statement highlights, once more, the party's control over all primary processes. Finally, the secretary general concluded by saying that "regardless of the outcome of this measure, the Popular Democratic Party will always hold primaries wherever they may be needed."[74]

Muñoz Marín also insisted on the imminence of a primary law. In one of his statements to *El Imparcial,* and referring to the primaries, he points out: "This is a task that must inevitably be tackled, but with great caution, with the most delicate of balances between social reality and public interest factors involved in whatever decisions are made on this matter."[75]

Even with all those promises, there was a certain pessimism in the air as to the prospects of a primary law for the 1956 elections. An editorial column in *El Mundo,* on April 25, 1955, contained just this sort of a pessimistic message, three years having gone by since the law had been promised and with no concrete results in sight. The editors felt the measure was far from becoming a reality, because of the Legislature's refusal to consider it during that year's regular session. The editors concluded by saying that "unless the proposition is merely an excuse not to act on a matter of interest to the people, it seems logical and convenient to reach a decision on the measure during this legislative session."[76]

Pessimism could also be observed in two editorials published by *El Imparcial* in 1953 and 1954. The first one pointed out that, although a primary law was imminent, other auxiliary mechanisms for this law should be considered in order to exercise democracy at its fullest. It also argues that in addition to a primary legislation there should be a voter's registry and a set of regulations for party affiliations.[77] What the editor was calling for, with these precautionary measures, was a truly democratic primary process that is not controlled by the party leaders. The second editorial criticized the idea of avoiding the enactment of a law for fear of creating divisions within a party and, thus, giving a political advantage to the adversaries. Two examples are offered, in which internal division was brought about by a failure to hold primary elections, and yet these votes did not favor any adversaries. In both Caguas (1948) and Salinas (1952) after an impasse, dissidents opted for the creation of a new party rather than join any adversary.[78]

Although everyone was calling for a primary law, it was a challenge for both the majority as well as for the minority parties to pass the law. Many thought this legislation should, again, be postponed for the next four-year period. However, on March 17, 1956, the Senate approved the Primary Act project: "The measure was approved at 11:40 in the evening with 26 votes in favor and none against."[79] The fact that the law was approved by a unanimous vote shows how all sectors in the country understood the need to start establishing a truly democratic system, and that no party wanted to be the one failing to keep a promise made to the people.

The Statehood and Independence parties opposed certain provisions of the law, such as the one that "prohibited any candidates defeated in a given party's primary election from running for office as a candidate for any other party."[80] However, when this provision was eliminated all parties agreed to vote in favor of the measure, though not without first heeding Solá Morales's warning:

> Since this ban would not exist in the law as written, measures should be taken, and rules set up to prevent *"arribistas"* from piggybacking during an electoral process, these being just the sort of people "we had in mind when we thought about protecting the voters."[81]

This primary struggle evidences a series of changes in the composition of the Popular Democratic Party, and the power struggles among new sectors. Thanks to the controversy surrounding the figure of Obdulia Velázquez de Lorenzo, the promised primary law was obtained in 1956. The Guayama primary not only allowed for the exercise of better democracy, but also served to start breaking the molds of a single party, with a single leader, which had been created when the Popular Democratic Party was born.

Conclusion

The recounting of Obdulia Velázquez's life story describes the economical and political empowerment of a group of women from Guayama, Puerto Rico. Under the leadership of Doña Obdulia, the women developed a course of action to help themselves as part of the work force of the town. They created the Ladies' Union to secure better working conditions as seamstresses working from their houses. Their actions as workers were linked with their political participation in the Popular Democratic Party. Although the party recognized very few women in leadership positions, they were very important in the transmittal of the popular ideal, in the private sphere. The women were the ones the party called upon to prevent the selling of the votes to the opponents and to ensure they and their kin voted for the Popular Democratic Party.

The women of Guayama were able to practice their political leadership when a division between two groups occurred in the party. Because of their use of non-hierarchical leadership styles, Obdulia and the group of women were able to serve as a conciliatory group. Yet, the definition of conciliation candidate did not mean the same for the men as for the women leaders of the Popular Democratic Party. While the men considered Doña Obdulia's nomination for mayor as the best option because she was a good and religious woman whom nobody would dare oppose, the female supporters of Velázquez believed that she knew exactly how to rally the people of Guayama, even against the strong PPD's municipal committee.

Doña Obdulia and her group of female followers were able to obtain a primary for Guayama, even against the belief among the Popular Democratic Party's leadership that primaries divided the party. Not only were the women from Guayama able to obtain the promise of the primary through nonhierarchical ways, but they won by an immense majority. The triumph permitted Doña Obdulia to be the candidate for the next November elections, when she was proclaimed the first and only woman mayor of Guayama.

Since women define their world in a different way from men, Doña Obdulia defined her role as administrator of Guayama different from the men before her. What was important for her, such as the youth and children's programs, was insignificant for the men who described her later as an administrator with few accomplishments. Only if we evaluate her work from a woman's perspective can we find her value as a woman mayor. Although not discussed in this essay, her role as mayor of Guayama was defined by important programs connected to women's interests such as the Municipal Library and the Brass Band. Later on, her male successor eliminated these programs because he thought it was more important to dedicate himself to looking for new industries for Guayama.

The results of the primary of the summer of 1952, besides allowing a woman to become the mayor of Guayama, cleared the way for the enactment of the Primary Act in Puerto Rico, passed in 1956. Instead of dividing political parties, the primary law has encouraged a more democratic form of government.

Notes

1. I define empowerment not as the acquisition of political power by means of force, as it has been commonly described, but as a process of acquiring more participation in the

decisions and the political structures of which women have the right to be a part. See Ann Bookman and Sandra Morgen, "Rethinking Women and Politics: An Introductory Essay," in *Women and the Politics of Empowerment* (Philadelphia: Temple University Press, 1988).

2. See Michelle Zimbalist Rosaldo and Louise Lamphere, eds., *Woman, Culture and Society* (Stanford: Stanford University Press, 1974), 8. Rosaldo argues that the emphasis on the maternal roles played by women creates an asymmetric opposition between domestic and public roles. In their private roles women generally have access to the sort of authority, prestige, and cultural value that are attributed to men in the public sphere. Even when women have acquired such power, it is perceived as illegitimate. This power is shaped and limited by women's association with other women in the private world.

3. Carolyn Heilbrun, *Writing a Woman's Life* (New York: Ballantine Books, 1988), 126.

4. Karen Offen, "Defining Feminism: A Comparative Historical Approach" *Signs* (Autumn 1988): 151–52.

5. Blanca Silvestrini, *Women and Resistance: Herstory in Contemporary Caribbean History* (Kingston: Fifth Elsa Goveia Memorial Lecture, University of West Indies at Mona, 1989), 14.

6. See Yamila Azize Vargas, *La mujer en la lucha* (Río Piedras: Editorial Cultural, 1985); Isabel Picó Vidal, "Women and the Puerto Rican Politics Before Enfranchisement," *Homines* 4 (1987): 405–20; Norma Valle Ferrer, *Luisa Capetillo: Historia de una mujer proscrita* (Río Piedras: Editorial Cultural, 1990); María Libertad Gómez, "Experiencias de una mujer graduada en la legislatura," and Ana Roqué de Duprey, "Mensajes," *Revista de la Asociación de Mujeres Graduadas de la Universidad de Puerto Rico,* Río Piedras. UPR 4j, no. 2 (January 1942).

7. The "Estado Libre Asociado" has historically been translated as Commonwealth. See the biographical works of Carmelo Rosario Natal, *La juventud de Luis Muñoz Marín, vida y pensamiento: 1898–1932* (Río Piedras: Editorial Edil, 1989); Lieban Córdova, *Luis Muñoz Marín y sus campañas políticas* (Río Piedras: Editorial Universidad de Puerto Rico, 1985); Robert W. Anderson, *Party Politics* (Stanford: Stanford University Press, 1965); Antonio Fernós Isern, "From Colony to Commonwealth," *Annals of the American Academy of Political and Social Studies* (January 1953): 21; and José Trías Monge, *Historia constitucional de Puerto Rico* (Río Piedras: Editorial Universitaria, 1981), vol. 2, 252.

8. Ángel Quintero Rivera, *La base social de la transformación ideológica del Partido Popular Democrático en la década de 1940–1950* (San Juan: Centro de Estudios de la Realidad Puertorriqueña, 1975); Emilio Pantojas García, "Estrategias de desarrollo y contradicciones ideológicas en Puerto Rico: 1940–1978," *Revista de Ciencias Sociales* 21, nos. 1–2 (March–June 1979): 92; Juan José Baldrich, "Class and State of the Origins of Populism in Puerto Rico, 1934–1952" (Ph.D. diss., Yale University, 1981), 144; Gerardo Navas Dávila, "Surgimiento y transformación del Partido Popular Democrático," in *Cambio y desarrollo en Puerto Rico: la transformación ideológica del Partido Popular Democrático* (Río Piedras: Editorial de la Universidad de Puerto Rico, 1985); Jorge Rodríguez Beruff, *El papel protagónico de Puerto Rico en el contexto de la nueva política de Reagan hacia el Caribe* (San Juan: Cuadernos CEREP, 5, 1983), 8.

9. See Isabel Picó Vidal, "Women and the Puerto Rican Politics," 419, Table 13.

10. This document written by Paulino Rodríguez Bernier, titled *Doña Obdulia Velázquez, su vida y sus hechos* (1957), was kept among Doña Obdulia's belongings, and lent to the author by Obdulia's niece Sara Velázquez, during an interview in April 22, 1992. Even though the book—twenty-eight pages long—is not properly a diary, it can be considered as such since it was written after a series of interviews that Rodríguez Bernier conducted with Doña Obdulia.

11. Rodríguez Bernier, *Doña Obdulia*, 3. Unless otherwise noted, this and all subsequent translations were done by the author.

12. Ibid., 15.

13. See Jaime Reyes, *La santa montaña de San Lorenzo Puerto Rico y el misterio de Elenita de Jesús (1899–1909)* (Mexico: n.p., 1992), 15.

14. See Paulino Rodríguez Bernier, *Cataratas de ensueño, Don Pepino y Elena la misionera* (Cayey: Imprenta Morales, 1939).

15. Ibid., 86.

16. Ibid., 88.

17. Interview with Sara Velázquez, April 22, 1992.

18. Rodríguez Bernier, *Doña Obdulia*, 18.

19. Ibid., 19.

20. The register number 1757 lists 24 acres in Quebrada Arriba with a value of $590 and a house with a value of $30, for a total of $620 and paying $3.72 in contributions. Archivo General de Puerto Rico (hereafter quoted as AGPR), Registro de Tasaciones y Contribuciones, Patillas, 1920.

21. In the year 1942, Obdulia paid $30.43 in contribution for 7,437 acres for a value of $2,805 and two houses and machinery valued at $775, for a total of $3,580. A year later the properties continued growing to 10,576 acres and one more house for a total of $5,760 and paying $54.72 in contributions. AGPR, Registro de Tasaciones y Contribuciones, Patillas, 1925 and 1935. See also, AGRP, Registro de Tasaciones y Contribuciones, Patillas, 1940.

22. Rodríguez Bernier, *Doña Obdulia*, 21.

23. See *Libro de Actas de la Unión de Damas de Oficios Domésticos, 1950–1951.*

24. Ibid., 4–5.

25. Ibid., 7–8.

26. Ibid., 9.

27. Ibid., 10.

28. Ibid., 14.

29. Ibid.

30. See Adolfo Porrata-Doria, *Guayama, sus hombres y sus instituciones* (Barcelona: Jorge Casas, 1972), 84. These 5,000 persons represented by the Ladies' Union included the 2,300 workers employed by Love Industry and 2,700 other workshop employees or at-home contractors.

31. *El Mundo,* November 7, 1952, 12.

32. Luis Muñoz Marín talked about *El Batey* in the following way: "The campaign was of education. The meetings were lessons. *El Batey* was the text. The elections were the test. The people passed brilliantly," in *Historia del Partido Popular Democrático* (San Juan : Editorial *El Batey,* 1984), 100.

33. *El Batey,* sec. IX, April 1939, 4. The copies of *El Batey* were obtained at the Fundación Luis Muñoz Marín (hereafter quoted as LMM).

34. *El Batey,* sec. IX, August 1939, 4.

35. *El Batey,* sec. IX, January 1940, 4.

36. Interview with Celia Vicente de Borrero, February 8, 1992.

37. *El Mundo,* July 16, 1952, 17.

38. Ibid.

39. Ibid.

40. In an interview with Abraham Nieves, on June 8, 1992, I confirmed that he was present at the first meeting organized in Guayama to create the first Popular Democratic Party committee, and that he was elected secretary. He reported that he has participated in Guayama's PPD Municipal Committee since that time. He is still a member of several

PPD boards island-wide. Nieves was among Luis Muñoz Marín's personal friends, and sought his help whenever he needed tickets to travel to New York to make business purchases during World War II. He is a founding member of the Luis Muñoz Marín Foundation and is very proud of the personal letters he still keeps, both from Muñoz Marín and from his wife, Inés.

41. Interview with Víctor Borrero, February 8, 1992.

42. *El Mundo,* May 14, 1952, 7.

43. Ibid.

44. The *quo warranto* is an act by which the Commonwealth of Puerto Rico issues an order to retain an appointment of franchise possessed by a person or corporation. See Civil Code, 1993, art. 640; Const., art. IX, sec. 4, ef. July 25, 1952, in *Leyes de Puerto Rico Anotadas* (Oxford: Equity, 1968), 720. Regarding the court's ruling see, *El Mundo,* May 14, 1952, 7.

45. *El Mundo,* May 14, 1952, 7.

46. See Archivo Central de Tribunales, Administración de Tribunales, San Juan. *Libros de sentencias trimestrales,* Guayama, #40, 9, and case CD-52–186, Guayama.

47. *El Mundo,* June 10, 1952, 16; and *El Imparcial,* June 11, 1952, 4.

48. *El Imparcial,* July 16, 1952, 4.

49. *El Mundo,* December 16, 1944, 17. There was a discrepancy between these two groups of PPD affiliates, who could not come to an agreement on whether to accept voters from an open list or from a marked list. A marked list *(lista punteada)* was one in which voters were identified as party members, based on a verified census.

50. *El Mundo,* October 13, 1951, 6.

51. Ibid.

52. *El Mundo,* July 19, 1952, 1.

53. *El Imparcial,* July 24, 1952, 17.

54. Interview with Víctor Borrero, February 8, 1992.

55. *El Imparcial,* August 16, 1952, 5.

56. Ibid.

57. *El Imparcial,* September 4, 1952, 6.

58. Interview with Celia Vicente de Borrero, February 8, 1952.

59. *El Imparcial,* September 9, 1952, 5.

60. Ibid., 4.

61. *El Imparcial,* September 11, 1952, 6.

62. *El Imparcial,* July 21, 1952, 4.

63. *El Imparcial,* August 13, 1952, 2.

64. *El Imparcial,* July 22, 1952, 17.

65. *El Mundo,* July 17, 1952, 12.

66. *El Mundo,* July 23, 1952, 6. Ildefonso Solá Morales received 60,890 votes and Lionel Fernández Méndez received 60,932. They were both elected senators for the seventh senatorial district and neither one of them lived in the town of Guayama, though this town was the seat for that district.

67. *El Mundo,* March 31, 1952, 1.

68. Popular Democratic Party, *Programa Económico y Social, Status Político,* San Juan, 1952.

69. *El Mundo,* August 14, 1952, 13.

70. *El Mundo,* November 30, 1954, 6.

71. Ibid.

72. *El Mundo,* February 12, 1955, 1, 22.

73. *El Mundo,* February 17, 1955, 5.

74. Ibid.

75. *El Imparcial,* March 16, 1953, 21.
76. *El Mundo,* April 25, 1955, 6.
77. *El Imparcial,* March 17, 1953, 17.
78. *El Imparcial,* November 26, 1954, 17.
79. *El Mundo,* May 19, 1955, 23.
80. Ibid.
81. Ibid.

Index

253

About the Editors and Contributors

Juan José Baldrich is a professor of sociology at the University of Puerto Rico in Río Piedras. He is the author of *Sembraron la no siembra: Los cosecheros de tabaco puertorriqueños frente a las corporaciones tabacaleras, 1920–1934* (1988) and articles about democracy in Jamaica and the social and economic history of tobacco growing and manufacture in Cuba and Puerto Rico.

María de Fátima Barceló-Miller is an associate professor of history at the Universidad del Sagrado Corazón in Santurce, Puerto Rico. She is the author of *Política ultramarina y gobierno municipal: Isabel, 1873–1887* (1984) and *La lucha por el sufragio femenino en Puerto Rico, 1896–1935* (1997).

Linda C. Delgado is director of the Latino/a Student Cultural Center at Northeastern University and a Ph.D. candidate at the Graduate Center of the City University of New York. Her dissertation is titled: "Puerto Ricans in New York City, 1914–1974: A Contextualization of the Jesús Colón Papers."

José Flores Ramos is a librarian at the School of Architecture at the University of Puerto Rico in Río Piedras and also a Ph.D. candidate at the University of Puerto Rico in Río Piedras. His master's thesis was titled, "Eugenesia, higiene pública y alcanfor para las pasiones: La Prostitución en San Juan, 1876–1919."

Mary Frances Gallart is an assistant professor in the Department of Humanities at the University of Puerto Rico in Río Piedras. She is revising her dissertation, "Mujeres, aguja y política: Obdulia Velázquez de Lorenzo, Alcaldesa de Guayama (1952–1956)," for publication.

Gladys M. Jiménez-Muñoz is an assistant professor at the School of Education and Human Development at the State University of New York at Binghamton. She is the author of many articles regarding issues of gender, sexuality, race, and politics in twentieth-century Puerto Rico and a dissertation on the Puerto Rican women's suffrage movement.

Félix V. Matos Rodríguez is an assistant professor of history at Northeastern University. He is currently revising a book, tentatively titled, *"Mujeres de la Capital": Women and Urban Life in Nineteenth-Century, San Juan, Puerto Rico (1820–1868),* for publication.

Félix O. Muñiz-Mas is a Ph.D. candidate in history at the State University of New York at Albany. His dissertation focuses on the role of gender in the political and economic development of Puerto Rico in the 1930s and 1940s.

Altagracia Ortiz is a professor of history and Puerto Rican Studies at the John Jay College (CUNY). She is the author of *Eighteenth-Century Reforms in the Caribbean: Miguel de Muesas, Governor of Puerto Rico, 1769–76* (1983), and editor of *Puerto Rican Women and Work: Bridges in Transnational Labor* (1996).

Carmen Teresa Whalen is an assistant professor of Puerto Rican and Hispanic Caribbean studies and history at Rutgers University. She is currently writing a book on Puerto Rican migration to Philadelphia in the post–World War II era.